European Union and its Neighbours in a Globalized World

The series publishes monographs and edited volumes in the field of European and international law and policy. A special focus is put on the European neighbourhood policy, current problems in European and international law and policy as well as the role of the European Union as a global actor. The series supports the publishing and distribution of research results of cross-border research consortia. Besides renowned scientists the series is also open for publication projects of young academics. The series emphasizes the interplay of the European Union and its neighbouring countries as well as the important role of the European Union as a key player in the international context of law, economics and politics.

Jasminka Pecotić Kaufman • Gentjan Skara
Alexandr Svetlicinii
Editors

Competition Law and Policy in the Western Balkans

Springer

Editors
Jasminka Pecotić Kaufman
Faculty of Economics and Business
Department of Business Law
University of Zagreb
Zagreb, Croatia

Robert Schuman Centre for Advanced Studies
European University Institute
Florence, Italy

Gentjan Skara
Department of Law
Epoka University
Tirana, Albania

Alexandr Svetlicinii
Faculty of Law
University of Macau
Macao SAR, China

ISSN 2524-8928 ISSN 2524-8936 (electronic)
European Union and its Neighbours in a Globalized World
ISBN 978-3-031-93755-2 ISBN 978-3-031-93756-9 (eBook)
https://doi.org/10.1007/978-3-031-93756-9

This Springer imprint is published by the registered company Springer Nature Switzerland AG
The registered company address is: Gewerbestrasse 11, 6330 Cham, Switzerland

About the Book

This book analyses the development of competition law systems in the Western Balkans (WB) countries—Albania, Bosnia and Herzegovina, Kosovo, Montenegro, North Macedonia, and Serbia—over the past three decades. The primary focus is on examining the impact of aligning these legal systems with EU competition law. The book adopts a bottom-up approach to explore national competition law systems, addressing the particular challenges faced by individual jurisdictions that arise from the specificities of their legal traditions. In addition to detailed national reports on each jurisdiction, the final comparative chapter offers a horizontal examination of the WB's competition law systems. In this pioneering study, we collect and analyse empirical data for WB jurisdictions from 2012 to 2022, encompassing both institutional and enforcement data. This approach provides unique and original insights into the development of competition law systems in these countries.

Contents

Editors and Contributors

About the Editors

Jasminka Pecotić Kaufman is a Full Tenured Professor of Law at the University of Zagreb, Faculty of Economics and Business, Department of Business Law and a Part-Time Professor at the Robert Schuman Centre for Advanced Studies, European University Institute (EUI). Her research focuses on the challenges of enforcing competition rules in European post-socialist countries. Prof. Pecotić Kaufman's scholarly work has been published in the Journal of Antitrust Enforcement, the World Competition Law and Economics Review, the Review of Central and East European Law, and the Yearbook of Antitrust and Regulatory Studies. She has been a Jean Monnet Fellow and a Fernand Braudel Senior Fellow at the EUI, as well as a Non-Resident Senior Research Fellow at the Institute for Consumer Antitrust Studies at Loyola University Chicago. She is a member of the Editorial Board of the Yearbook of Antitrust and Regulatory Studies (YARS), a member of the International Advisory Board of the Institute for Consumer Antitrust Studies, and a non-governmental Advisor (NGA) to the International Competition Network. Prof. Pecotić Kaufman serves on the ASCOLA Board and co-chairs its Southeast Europe chapter. She is the President of the Croatian Competition Law and Policy Association (HDPPTN) and the founder of the Šoljan Competition Law and Policy Conference series.

Gentjan Skara is a Lecturer in EU Law and Competition Law at the Department of Law, Epoka University College, Albania. Genti holds an LLB from the University of Tirana (Albania), an MA in European Studies from Epoka University (Albania), and an LLM in "South East European Law and European Integration" from the University of Graz. In 2020, Genti received a PhD from the University of Ferrara in "EU Law and National Legal Systems". A revised version of his thesis was published by Springer Nature as a monography titled "Europeanisation of Private Enforcement of Competition Law: The Case of Albania" in 2022. Additionally, Genti has been a visiting researcher at the Institute of Corporate and International Commercial Law,

University of Graz (Austria), the Department of International Law, University of Ljubljana (Slovenia) and European Institute for Global Studies, University of Basel (Switzerland) and RECAS Fellow. From October 2012 until July 31, 2023, Genti was a full-time member of the Department of Law at "Bedër" University College, teaching International and EU law courses. As of 1 August 2023, Genti is a full-time lecturer of EU Law and competition law courses at Epoka University. Besides academic engagement, Genti is a National Legal expert for the "Internal Market and Competition" of EU acquis near the Ministry of European and Foreign Affairs, Republic of Albania and has provided its expertise to different organizations. His research interests relate to EU Law, competition law, the harmonization of laws, and the relations between law and technology.

Alexandr Svetlicinii is an Associate Professor at the University of Macau, Faculty of Law, where he also serves as Programme Coordinator of the Master of International Business Law in English Language. Prior to joining the University of Macau, Dr. Svetlicinii was a senior researcher at the Jean Monnet Chair of European Law at the Tallinn Law School, Tallinn University of Technology, in Estonia. Prof. Svetlicinii's work in the field of competition law has appeared in Common Market Law Review, European Law Review, Journal of Antitrust Enforcement, World Competition Law and Economics Review, Journal of European Competition Law & Practice, European Competition Law Review, Yearbook of Antitrust and Regulatory Studies, Market and Competition Law Review, among other journals. In addition to his academic work, Dr. Svetlicinii served as Co-Director of ASCOLA (Academic Society for Competition Law) South-East Europe Chapter, the Non-Governmental Advisor (NGA) to the International Competition Network (ICN) (working group Mergers). He has recently published the monograph Chinese State-Owned Enterprises and EU Merger Control (Routledge, 2021).

Contributors

Bojana Hajdini Department of Law, Epoka University, Tirana, Albania

Kanita Imamović-Čizmić University of Sarajevo, School of Law, Sarajevo, Bosnia and Herzegovina

Nebojša Jovović Agency for Protection of Competition, Podgorica, Montenegro

Pranvera Këllezi Kellezi Legal, Geneva, Switzerland

Goran Koevski Faculty of Law "Iustinianus Primus", University "Ss. Cyril and Methodius", Skopje, North Macedonia

Vuk Leković Gecić Law Firm, Belgrade, Serbia

Dijana Marković-Bajalović Union University, School of Law, Belgrade, Serbia

Veljko Milutinović Faculty of Business Studies and Law, Union Nikola Tesla University, Belgrade, Serbia

Avdylkader Mucaj Pristina, Kosovo

Jasminka Pecotić Kaufman Faculty of Economics and Business, Department of Business Law, University of Zagreb, Zagreb, Croatia
Robert Schuman Centre for Advanced Studies, European University Institute, Florence, Italy

Gentjan Skara Department of Law, Epoka University, Tirana, Albania

Darko Spasevki Faculty of Law "Iustinianus Primus", University "Ss. Cyril and Methodius", Skopje, North Macedonia

Alexandr Svetlicinii Faculty of Law, University of Macau, Macao SAR, China

Borka Tushevska Gavrilovikj Faculty of Law, Goce Delcev University, Stip, North Macedonia

Introduction

Jasminka Pecotić Kaufman, Gentjan Skara, and Alexandr Svetlicinii

This book examines the development of competition law systems in the Western Balkans (WB) countries—Albania, Bosnia and Herzegovina, Kosovo,[1] Montenegro, North Macedonia, and Serbia—over the past three decades. The analysis centres on the impact of aligning these legal systems with European Union (EU) competition law. In addition to detailed national reports for each jurisdiction, the final comparative chapter provides a comprehensive overview of the region's competition law landscape. Our pioneering study compiles and analyses empirical data from 2012 to 2022 for the WB jurisdictions, covering both institutional and enforcement aspects. This approach offers unique and original insights into how competition law systems have evolved in these countries.

At the 1998 European Council in Vienna, the EU introduced the term 'Western Balkans' and subseqently initiated the Stabilization and Association Process

[1] Some authors of this chapter considered it important to include the following statement: "This designation is without prejudice to positions on status, and is in line with UNSCR 1244 and the ICJ Opinion on the Kosovo declaration of independence".

J. Pecotić Kaufman
Faculty of Economics and Business, Department of Business Law, University of Zagreb, Zagreb, Croatia

Robert Schuman Centre for Advanced Studies, European University Institute, Florence, Italy
e-mail: jpecotic@net.efzg.hr

G. Skara (✉)
Department of Law, Epoka University, Tirana, Albania
e-mail: gskara@epoka.edu.al

A. Svetlicinii
Faculty of Law, University of Macau, Macao SAR, China
e-mail: alexandrs@um.edu.mo

J. Pecotić Kaufman et al. (eds.), *Competition Law and Policy in the Western Balkans*, European Union and its Neighbours in a Globalized World 22,
https://doi.org/10.1007/978-3-031-93756-9_1

Table 1 WB countries and EU integration

WB country	Signature of SAA	Entry into force of SAA	Application for membership submitted	Candidate status granted	Accession negotiations opened
Albania	12 June 2006	1 April 2009	24 April 2009	27 June 2014	25 March 2020
Bosnia and Herzegovina	16 June 2008	1 June 2015	15 February 2016	15 December 2022	21 March 2024
Kosovo	25 July 2014	1 April 2016	15 December 2022	(potential candidate)	–
Montenegro	15 October 2007	1 May 2010	15 December 2008	17 December 2010	29 June 2012
North Macedonia	9 April 2001	1 April 2004	22 March 2004	16 December 2005	25 March 2020
Serbia	29 April 2008	1 September 2013	22 December 2009	1 March 2012	21 January 2014

Source: Data compiled by the authors based on information from the European Neighbourhood Policy and Enlargement Negotiations (DG NEAR).

(SAP)—its policy framework for WB region,[2] aimed at supporting democratization, economic development, and regional cooperation.[3] Rather than being a geographical or historical term, the concept of 'Western Balkans' is a "political, geopolitical and technical term" that was created to denote Southeast European countries which were not EU Member States at the time (with Bulgaria (2007), Croatia (2013), Romania (2007), and Slovenia (2004) having subsequently joined the EU).[4]

The WB countries are on a long and challenging path toward EU membership. Compared to Central and Eastern European states that joined the EU in 2004 (Czechia, Hungary, Poland, Slovakia, and Slovenia), 2007 (Bulgaria and Romania) and 2013 (Croatia), the pre-accession process for the Western Balkans has been notably longer. For instance, while it took Poland and Croatia twelve to thirteen years to join the EU after signing their association agreements, most WB countries have already passed the fifteen-year mark since signing their Stabilisation and Association Agreement (SAAs), with the end of accession negotiations still uncertain (see Table 1).

The WB's EU journey was charted at the Thessaloniki Summit in 2003, where the EU reiterated "its unequivocal support to the European perspective of the Western Balkan countries".[5] However, over more than two decades later, these countries continue to struggle to meet all accession criteria.[6] Challenges such as contested statehood (Kosovo), name dispute (North Macedonia), and persistent difficulties in advancing rule of law reforms, combating organized crime, and corruption have slowed progress.[7]

[2]European Council (1998).

[3]Grabar-Kitarović (2007); Phinnemore (2003).

[4]Lika (2023).

[5]Commission (2003).

[6]Vukasović (2024); Malaj and Polo (2023).

[7]Dzankic 2023, pp. 213–214.

Political integration into the EU has been slow, and the WB countries find themselves at different stages of their European integration journey.[8] The length of the accession process does not guarantee success. For example, North Macedonia signed its SAA in 2001, but accession negotiations only began in 2022. Bosnia and Herzegovina obtained candidate status in 2022. Meanwhile, Montenegro, and Serbia are leading the group in terms of progress. All WB countries except Kosovo have been granted candidate status; Kosovo remains a potential candidate due to its contested statehood, with several EU Member States not recognizing its independence proclaimed in 2008. Accession negotiations have opened for most WB countries, except Bosnia and Herzegovina and Kosovo.

The introduction of modern competition laws in the WB, set against the backdrop of EU enlargement, was mandated by the SAAs concluded between the EU and the respective WB jurisdictions.[9] Under the SAA's approximation clause, WB countries have gradually harmonized national laws, including in the area of competition policy, with the EU *acquis*. The SAA also required the establishment of independent competition authorities and the application of EU competition law standards as interpretative instruments for cross-border cases.[10] Additionally, the European Commission's soft laws in the area of competition law have been transposed by WB competition authorities through notices and guidelines to further enhance harmonization.[11]

While legislative alignment has generally been achieved, WB jurisdictions continue to face enforcement and institutional challenges, including:

a. deficiencies in the institutional capacity of national competition authorities;
b. insufficient enforcement efforts;
c. modest fining policies;
d. limited experience of national judges in applying competition rules; and
e. underdeveloped competition culture.[12]

To address these challenges, this volume provides a systematic analysis of competition law and policy across all WB jurisdictions, offering country reports and setting out the trajectories of their development. The book assesses the current state of harmonization with the EU competition acquis and explores institutional capacity, enforcement records, and prominent cases.

Each country report follows a common methodological matrix, covering the following topics:

a. historical development of competition law systems;
b. application of EU law by national competition authorities and courts;

[8] Uvalić (2023); Milenković (2022).

[9] Leka and Jusufi (2024).

[10] Svetlicinii (2023).

[11] Bernatt et al. (2018); Malinauskaite (2019).

[12] Pecotić Kaufman and Šimić Banović (2021).

c. institutional and normative frameworks;
d. national specificities;
e. enforcement and fines;
f. judicial review;
g. private enforcement; and
h. current trends and challenges.

This comprehensive approach distinguishes our study from previous, more limited examinations of competition policy in the region.[13]

Written by experts from legal practice, academia, and competition authorities, this book provides a critical assessment and policy guidance for governments and national competition authorities (NCAs) to accelerate the harmonization of national competition law systems with the EU *acquis*. The book offers an authoritative and rigorous overview of competition law and policy in the region, making this scholarship accessible to a broader audience both within and beyond the Western Balkans.

The book is divided into seven chapters: six country reports and one comparative chapter. Chap. 2 "Albania" is written by Bojana Hajdini, Senior Lecturer at Epoka University in Tirana, Pranvera Kellezi, an attorney at law in Geneva, and a member of the Swiss Competition Commission, and Gentjan Skara, Head of Law Department at Epoka University. Chap. 3 "Bosnia-Herzegovina" is written by Dijana Marković-Bajalović, Tenured Professor at Union University Law School in Belgrade, and Kanita Imamović-Čizmić, Full Professor of Law at the University of Sarajevo. Chap. 4 "Kosovo" is authored by Avdylkader Mucaj, independent researcher. Chap. 5 "Montenegro" is written by Nebojša Jovović, Director at the Montenegrin competition authority. Chap. 6 "North Macedonia" is written by a group of scholars including Goran Koevski, Professor at the Faculty of Law Iustinianus Primus, Ss. Cyril and Methodius University in Skopje, Borka Tushevska Gavrilovikj, Full Professor at the Faculty of Law at University Goce Delcev in Stip, and Darko Spasevski, Professor at the Faculty of Law Iustinianus Primus, Ss. Cyril and Methodius University in Skopje. Chap. 7 "Serbia" was contributed by Veljko Milutinović, Associate Professor at Faculty of Business Studies and Law, Union Nikola Tesla University, Belgrade, and Vuk Leković, a practicing lawyer at Gecić Law firm in Belgrade. The final comparative chapter is written by the book editors: Jasminka Pecotić Kaufman, Professor of Law at the Faculty of Economics and Business, University of Zagreb, and Part-Time Professor at the Robert Schuman Centre for Advanced Studies, European University Institute; Gentjan Skara, Lecturer in EU Law and Competition Law at Epoka University in Tirana; and Alexandr Svetlicinii, Associate Professor of Global Legal Studies at the University of Macau.

Our core methodology is rooted in traditional legal doctrine. Authors examine national competition legislation, jurisprudence of the national courts, and decisions of the NCAs, supplemented by relevant national antitrust legal doctrine, where

[13] Penev and Marušić (2013); Begović and Popović (2018).

available and relevant. The historical method is employed to trace the evolution of competition law and policy, enforcement practices, and legislative changes due to EU integration. The final chapter adopts a comparative research method, complemented by empirical analysis, to examine the WB jurisdictions, following the structure of the country reports.

This book provides original insights into the functioning of WB competition law systems over the past three decades. Despite challenges in data collection, the accumulated evidence forms a solid foundation for further research into the development of national competition law systems in the context of EU integration. We are deeply grateful to the national rapporteurs for their invaluable contributions and dedicated work throughout this project. We also wish to thank the anonymous reviewers for their constructive comments and suggestions. Professor Pecotić Kaufman extends profound gratitude for the research leave provided by the Faculty of Economics and Business, University of Zagreb, and for the invaluable support of a Jean Monnet Fellowship and a Fernand Braudel Senior Fellowship at the European University Institute, during the tenure of which this book was completed.

References

Begović B, Popović VD (eds) (2018) Competition authorities in South Eastern Europe: building institutions in emerging markets. EBRD and Springer

Bernatt M, Botta M, Svetlicinii A (2018) The right of defence in the decentralized system of EU competition law enforcement: a call for harmonization from Central and Eastern Europe. World Competition Law Econ Rev 41(3):309

Commission (2003) EU-Western Balkans Summit Thessaloniki. Available at: https://ec.europa.eu/commission/presscorner/detail/en/PRES_03_163. Accessed 3 Jan 2025

Dzankic J (2023) Perceptions and misperceptions of EU conditionality in the Western Balkans: a case of a capability-expectations gap? In: Uvalic M (ed) Integrating the Western Balkans into the EU: overcoming mutual misperceptions (Palgrave Macmillan), at 213–214.

European Council (1998) Vienna European Council: presidency conclusions. 11–12 December 1998. Available at: https://www.europarl.europa.eu/summits/wie1_en.htm. Accessed 28 January 2025

Grabar-Kitarović K (2007) The stabilization and association process: The EU's soft power at its best. Eur Foreign Aff Rev 12(2):121

Leka D, Jusufi G (2024) The stabilization and association agreements in the Western Balkans as a tool for trade promotion and regional reconciliation. Corp Law Gov Rev 6(1):38

Lika L (2023) The meaning of the Western Balkans concept for the EU: genuine inclusion or polite exclusion?/. Southeast Eur Black Sea Stud 24(1):63

Malaj D, Polo E (2023) An evidence-based analysis of the EU's hampered transformative power in the Western Balkans. J Lib Int Affairs 9(3):215

Malinauskaite J (2019) Harmonisation of EU competition law enforcement. Springer

Milenković M (2022) Trajectories of differentiated EU integration for the Western Balkans. In: Leruth B, Ganzle S, Trondal J (eds) The Routledge handbook of differentiation in the European Union. Routledge

Pecotić Kaufman J, Šimić Banović R (2021) The role of (in)formal governance and culture in a national competition system: a case of post-socialist economy. World Competition Law Econ Rev 44(1):81

Penev S, Marušić A (eds) (2013) Competition policy in Western Balkan countries. Westminster Foundation for Democracy, Western Balkans Parliamentary network of committees for economy, finance and budget Institute of Economic Sciences, Belgrade
Phinnemore D (2003) The stabilization and association process: A framework for European Union's Integration? In: Elbasani A (ed) European integration and transformation in the Western Balkans: Europeanization or business as usual? Routledge
Svetlicinii A (2023) The elephant in the room turns twenty: the effect on trade and the enforcement of the EU Competition Law by the National Competition Authorities. J Eur Competition Law Pract 14(8):483
Uvalić M (ed) (2023) Integrating the Western Balkans into the EU – overcoming mutual misperceptions. Springer
Vukasović D (2024) The uncertainty of waiting: the liminality of the Western Balkans in the process of EU enlargement. J Contemp Eur Stud 33:232. https://doi.org/10.1080/14782804.2024.2365314

Jasminka Pecotić Kaufman is a Full Tenured Professor of Law at the University of Zagreb, Faculty of Economics and Business, Department of Business Law and a Part-Time Professor at the Robert Schuman Centre for Advanced Studies, European University Institute (EUI). Her research focuses on the challenges of enforcing competition rules in European post-socialist countries. Prof. Pecotić Kaufman's scholarly work has been published in the Journal of Antitrust Enforcement, the World Competition Law and Economics Review, the Review of Central and East European Law, and the Yearbook of Antitrust and Regulatory Studies. She has been a Jean Monnet Fellow and a Fernand Braudel Senior Fellow at the EUI, as well as a Non-Resident Senior Research Fellow at the Institute for Consumer Antitrust Studies at Loyola University Chicago. She is a member of the Editorial Board of the Yearbook of Antitrust and Regulatory Studies (YARS), a member of the International Advisory Board of the Institute for Consumer Antitrust Studies, and a non-governmental Advisor (NGA) to the International Competition Network. Prof. Pecotić Kaufman serves on the ASCOLA Board and co-chairs its Southeast Europe chapter. She is the President of the Croatian Competition Law and Policy Association (HDPPTN) and the founder of the Šoljan Competition Law and Policy Conference series.

Gentjan Skara is a Lecturer in EU Law and Competition Law at the Department of Law, Epoka University , Albania. Genti holds an LLB from the University of Tirana (Albania), an MA in European Studies from Epoka University (Albania) and an LLM in "South East European Law and European Integration" from the University of Graz. In 2020, Genti received a PhD from the University of Ferrara in "EU Law and National Legal Systems". A revised version of his thesis was published by Springer Nature as a monography titled "Europeanisation of Private Enforcement of Competition Law: The Case of Albania" in 2022. Additionally, Genti has been a visiting researcher at the Institute of Corporate and International Commercial Law, University of Graz (Austria), the Department of International Law, University of Ljubljana (Slovenia) and European Institute for Global Studies, University of Basel (Switzerland) and RECAS Fellow. From October 2012 until July 31, 2023, Genti was a full-time member of the Department of Law at "Bedër" University College, teaching International and EU law courses. As of 1 August 2023, Genti is a full-time lecturer of EU Law and competition law courses at Epoka University. Besides academic engagement, Genti is a National Legal expert for the "Internal Market and Competition" of EU acquis near the Ministry of European and Foreign Affairs, Republic of Albania and has provided its expertise to different organizations. His research interests relate to EU Law, competition law, the harmonization of laws, and the relations between law and technology.

Alexandr Svetlicinii is an Associate Professor at the University of Macau, Faculty of Law, where he also serves as Programme Coordinator of the Master of International Business Law in English Language. Prior to joining the University of Macau, Dr. Svetlicinii was a senior researcher at the

Jean Monnet Chair of European Law at the Tallinn Law School, Tallinn University of Technology, in Estonia. Prof. Svetlicinii's work in the field of competition law has appeared in Common Market Law Review, European Law Review, Journal of Antitrust Enforcement, World Competition Law and Economics Review, Journal of European Competition Law & Practice, European Competition Law Review, Yearbook of Antitrust and Regulatory Studies, Market and Competition Law Review, among other journals. In addition to his academic work, Dr. Svetlicinii served as Co-Director of ASCOLA (Academic Society for Competition Law) South-East Europe Chapter, the Non-Governmental Advisor (NGA) to the International Competition Network (ICN) (working group Mergers). He has recently published the monograph Chinese State-Owned Enterprises and EU Merger Control (Routledge, 2021).

Competition Law and Policy in Albania

Gentjan Skara, Pranvera Këllezi, and Bojana Hajdini

1 Introduction

In the early stages of transitioning from a centrally planned to a free market economy, like other post-communist countries, Albania aimed at opening the markets, privatising state-owned enterprises and maintain macroeconomic stability.[1] As the adoption of Constitutional Provisions (1991) paved the way for the transition to a free market and the opening up to foreign investment,[2] Albania experienced high commodity prices due to scarcity and a shrinking economy inherited from the communist regime. Concentration was very high in many markets and there were continuing efforts to privatise state monopolies and attract foreign investment. The collapse of domestic agricultural production in the last years of the socialist economy and the dismantling of cooperatives in agriculture forced the government to open the market to imports, which led to the emergence of import cartels. Albania undertook several reforms, including liberalising prices, balancing the budget deficit, setting up

[1] Goranson and Volkai (2003).

[2] Law 7491/1991 on Major Constitution Provision [1991] OJ Special edition, Arts 10–12.

G. Skara (✉)
Department of Law, Epoka University, Tirana, Albania
e-mail: gskara@epoka.edu.al

P. Këllezi
Kellezi Legal, Geneva, Switzerland
e-mail: pranvera.kellezi@kellezi-legal.ch

B. Hajdini
Department of Law, Epoka University, Tirana, Albania
e-mail: bhajdini@epoka.edu.al

J. Pecotić Kaufman et al. (eds.), *Competition Law and Policy in the Western Balkans*, European Union and its Neighbours in a Globalized World 22,
https://doi.org/10.1007/978-3-031-93756-9_2

a new banking system, privatising the economy and liberalising trade, with assistance from the International Monetary Fund (IMF) and the World Bank (WB).[3]

Establishing and developing competition law and policy in a transition economy has been a challenging task. Anti-competitive practices continuously jeopardized the establishment of a free and competitive market.[4] The first competition law in Albania was introduced in 1995 and provided the basis for a competition policy.[5] The Competition Act (1995) included antitrust, unfair competition and consumer protection provisions. It also contained numerous sectoral exemptions, ranging from banking to forestry.

While the competition legislation was in force, a significant portion of its provisions remained unapplied.[6] Government resorted to the threat of regulation whenever high demand—or likely cartels—caused prices of consumer goods to soar. The quasi-absent enforcement of the Competition Act (1995), coupled with prevailing economic conditions and the dependence of political parties on funding from a few companies, made civil society and the political establishment aware of the need for rules to ensure competition in the market.[7] This created a favourable environment for the adoption of strong competition rules in the early 2000s. Work on a new law within the Ministry of Economic Affairs began around 2002 with the support from *Deutsche Gesellschaft fur Technische Zusammenarbeit* (GIZ).[8] Albania, at that time, was in the early phase of discussions with the European Union (EU). The prospect of negotiating an SAA[9] with the EU gave a boost to the cause of competition protection.[10]

The new Act on Protection of Competition 9121/2003 (hereafter "Competition Act") entered into force in December 2003.[11] The Competition Act made specific reference to the market economy guaranteed by Article 11 of the Constitution and was based on the EC Treaty and EC competition rules [Arts 81 and 82], with which it was fully compatible. The Competition Act established an independent institution

[3] Pashko (1993); Muço (1996).

[4] Kazani (2015), p. 87.

[5] Law 8044/1995 On Competition [1995] OJ 27.

[6] Skara (2021), p. 326; UNCTAD (2015), p. 13.

[7] Civil society and media increasingly referred to competition rules and pointed out the links between the owners of big undertakings and politicians as a threat to democracy. In 2004, the implementation of competition law entered as a political objective in the programmes of political parties.

[8] GIZ, formerly GTZ, functions as the German government's development aid agency and initiated its operations in Albania as early as 1988.

[9] Stabilisation and Association Agreement between the European Communities and their Member States, of the one part, and the Republic of Albania, of the other part - Protocols – Declarations [2009] OJ L 107/166 (hereafter SAA with Albania).

[10] Official negotiations started in March 2003, the SAA was signed in 2006, and entered into force in 2009.

[11] Law 9121/2003 For Competition Protection [2003] OJ 71 (hereafter Competition Act unless stated otherwise).

for the enforcement of competition rules—the Competition Authority (*Autoriteti i Konkurrencës*). Since 2003, the Competition Act has been amended twice. The last amendment occurred in 2010 as an obligation to further the harmonisation with the EU competition *acquis*.

This chapter provides a comprehensive analysis of the development of competition law and policy in Albania. It describes how Albanian competition law and policy have evolved and analyses to what extent Albanian competition law follows the EU competition *acquis*. Furthermore, the chapter discusses the role of the Albanian Competition Authority (hereafter ACA) responsible for the enforcement of competition rules (public enforcement) and outlines the main deficiencies and obstacles to why private enforcement remains underdeveloped. The chapter concludes with the main trends and current challenges that the ACA faces in enforcing competition rules.

The chapter is structured as follows. Section 2 provides a historical outline of competition law and policy in Albania, followed by a brief description of the relationship between the EU and Albanian legal systems, including competition law (Sect. 3). Section 4 analyses the institutional and normative foundations of competition law in Albania. Section 5 outlines national specifics that differ from the EU competition *acquis* or that have been erased/amended in the process of harmonization with the EU *acquis*. Section 6 discusses the selected cases where the ACA has referred to the EU competition rules. Section 7 provides statistical data on enforcement and sanctioning extracted from the ACA's annual reports. Sections 8 and 9 describe Albania's judicial review and private enforcement of competition law. Section 10 summarizes current trends and future challenges for enforcement of competition law in Albania.

2 Historical Development of the Competition Law in Albania

During the transition to a free market, like other post-communist countries, the main objective for Albania was to open the market, privatise state-owned enterprises and maintain macroeconomic stability.[12] In 1992 and 1993, the first series of commercial laws were adopted. In 1994, the new Civil Code was adopted. It contained only two provisions, respectively Articles 638 and 639, on unfair competition in the area of intellectual property rights.[13]

The Competition Act, adopted in 1995, was based on a so-called "step-by-step approach" aimed at introducing basic rules for the protection of competition.[14] The

[12] Goranson and Volkai (2003).

[13] Law 7850/1994, On the Civil Code of the Republic of Albania [1994] OJ 11 (Albanian Civil Code).

[14] Competition Act (1995).

level of sanctions was low; conversely, the risk of non-implementation was high. Directorate for Economic Competition (*Drejtoria e Konkurrencës Ekonomike)*, subordinated under the Ministry of Economic Affairs and responsible for the enforcement of the law, was understaffed and lacked the resources to build up a practice or act as a deterrent to companies engaging in anti-competitive practices.[15] The Ministry of Economic Affairs was responsible for both competition policy and the supervision of the privatisation of state assets, creating an inherent conflict of interest within the Ministry. In the early 2000s, a consensus took shape within the Ministry that a new law on competition should be enforced by a specialised agency that would be independent from the government.

During the 1990s, foreign investment, and hence new market entry, remained low, making it very difficult to challenge strong position of state-owned or newly privatised monopolies. These difficulties stemmed from factors such as the country's small domestic market size, low purchasing power, and the tumultuous political landscape within Albania and the war-torn Balkan region. The Competition Act (1995) included a de-concentration provision requiring the government to break up public companies with a dominant position before privatising them. However, this went largely unenforced, mainly because there was little incentive to break up monopolies before privatisation but also because divestitures were difficult to manage and risky in some activities, such as banking. State-owned companies with a strong market position were able to generate more revenue from privatisation, which reduced the incentive to lower their market share through divestment. The government needed to attract foreign investors who would pay a premium for the target's strong market position. Furthermore, during this period, businesses struggled to access capital. The financial system could not provide sufficient capital, and an informal market developed, leading to the pyramid schemes and their collapse in 1997. This exacerbated the problem of access to capital, further worsening the issue of capital accessibility. From a cultural standpoint, Albanian entrepreneurs tend to rely less on debt and show a preference for partnerships while approaching risk-taking with caution. This cultural inclination has further impeded the growth prospects of companies.

In 1998, after several years of negotiations and discussions, the new Constitution of the Republic of Albania was adopted by referendum. Article 11 of the Constitution defined Albania's economic system as a market economy and guaranteed freedom of economic activity. The lack of enforcement of the Competition Act (1995) and the general economic conditions created a favourable environment for the adoption of stronger competition rules in the early 2000s. Albania, at that time, was in the early phase of discussions with the EU. The need for competition rules was intrinsic, while the EU accession negotiations acted as an extrinsic force to support internal advocates of stronger competition rules.

[15] Competition Act (1995), Art 57.

The prospect of negotiating an SAA in 2003 with the EU gave a boost to the cause of competition protection.[16] A few years later, by signing the SAA in 2006, Albania would commit itself to ensuring that its existing and future legislation in the field of competition and state aid is progressively made compatible with the EU *acquis* and to establish an independent authority entrusted with the necessary investigative and enforcement powers.[17] When the draft act was prepared in 2002, it was decided to take a maximalist approach and to introduce the full legislative arsenal of investigative powers and sanctions including searches of premises and persons. This was no easy task for a Parliament that, given the country's long history of dictatorship, was very wary of the abuse of state power. The vagueness of the competition rules was challenging for a country now committed to the rule of law. At the request of the Ministry of Justice, efforts were made to create more explicit rules on agreements and abusive behaviour in order to increase legal certainty for companies. The Ministry of Justice realized the risk of introducing broad discretionary powers in the definition of restrictions on competition (infringements), together with broad investigative and sanctioning powers for the new authority. This was reflected in drafting further examples of abusive behaviour and detailed rules for agreements. These specific provisions have been eventually removed, and the provisions on agreements and abuse of dominance become a copy of Articles 101 and 102 TFEU.

The new Competition Act entered into force in December 2003 and aims to protect "free and effective competition".[18] Free competition refers to the freedom of market participants to offer or purchase goods and services without restriction. It is based on the principle of market economy as provided in the Albanian Constitution. The protection of effective competition is the benchmark for maximising social welfare. Thus, competition law has become a fundamental legal basis for the functioning and safeguarding of the market economy.

The Competition Act was based on the EC Treaty and EC competition rules. At the time of the preparation and adoption of the law, Regulations 1/2003 and 139/2004[19] were in consultation procedure. The Competition Act was based on these draft regulations introducing, for instance, commitments procedure and power to require behavioural and structural remedies,[20] before the entry into force of the respective EU regulations. The Ministry of Economic Affairs wanted to introduce an individual exemption procedure for anti-competitive agreements to allow the new authority to gain experience and to provide legal certainty for companies. The Competition Act still contains a notification requirement to obtain individual exemption, while the 2010 amendment empowered the ACA to adopt block exemption

[16] Official negotiations started in March 2003, the SSA was signed in 2006, and entered into force in 2009.

[17] SAA with Albania, Arts 70 and 71.

[18] For an overview see Këllezi (2005, 2009).

[19] Council Regulation (EC) No 139/2004 of 20 January 2004 on the control of concentrations between undertakings (the EC Merger Regulation) [2004] OJ L24/1.

[20] Competition Act, Article 45.

regulations.[21] The individual exemption procedure has not been widely used by companies, raising questions about its usefulness in a system based on block exemptions[22] and the legal uncertainty that it may create about the validity of unnotified agreements.

The Competition Act is based on the three pillars of competition law: (i) anti-competitive agreements; (ii) abuse of dominant position, and (iii) merger control. It provided for the establishment of an independent competition authority. Furthermore, the Competition Act contains detailed rules on administrative and civil procedures and rules for the imposition of fines.

The Competition Act has been amended twice. The first amendment in 2006 changed the criteria for being elected as a member of the ACA and the reasons for releasing members of the ACA. Article 20(c) of the Competition Act stipulated that the candidate for the ACA membership must be recognised in the field of economic or legal sciences or for management skills and professionalism in different economic sectors. The 2006 Competition Act amendment changed this criterion, requiring that a suitable candidate for a member of the ACA should have at least five years of academic experience or hold a doctoral degree in law or economics with a research interest in civil law or administrative law. Also, the 2006 Competition Act amendment changed the reasons for releasing the ACA members. Instead of the absence for more than three months for an unjustified reason, the 2006 Amendment decreased the absence to not more than one month for an unjustified reason, with the release to be decided by the decision of a majority in the Parliament.

In 2010, the 2003 Competition Act was revised to redraft several provisions without significantly changing their scope.[23] The 2010 amendment, firstly, improved the scope of the competition law in line with the EU competition law. The 2003 Competition Act was applicable only for undertakings that directly or indirectly have or may have an influence in the market or for undertakings operating outside Albanian territory but whose effects influenced market competition in Albania's territory. In line with Article 106 TFEU, the 2010 amendment extended its scope of application to: (i) public undertakings and undertakings granted by the State with special or exclusive rights to perform certain economic activities; and (ii) undertakings entrusted with the operation of services of general economic interests or having the character of a revenue-producing monopoly as far as competition law enforcement does not obstruct the fulfilment of tasks.[24]

Second, the 2010 amendment clarified the definition of agreement and dominant position. According to the 2010 amendment, an agreement is "the agreements and/or concerted practices of two or more undertakings, and the decisions or the recommendations of associations of undertakings, regardless their form, written or not, or

[21] Competition Act, Article 6.

[22] Competition Act, Article 48.

[23] Law 10 317/2010 For some additions and changes in the law no 9121 date 28. 07. 2003 for Competition Protection [2010] OJ 135.

[24] 2010 Amendment of Competition Act, Art 1.

binding force".[25] Whereas dominant position was defined as "a position of economic strength enjoyed by one or more undertakings which enables them to prevent effective competition on the market by giving them the power to behave, with regard to demand or supply, independently of other market participants such as competitors, customers or consumers".[26] As can be seen, both definitions are in line with the EU competition *acquis*.

Third, the 2010 amendment introduced provisions on the *de minimis* rule for the agreements of minor impact on competition, individual and block exemptions.[27] The fulfilment of the conditions for individual exemptions are fully in line with Article 101(3) TFEU. Whereas agreements that do not significantly restrict competition on the market may be exempted from the prohibition if the aggregate share of all the undertakings that are parties to the agreement does not exceed: (i) 10% of the respective market where the participants are actual or potential competitors and (ii) 15% of the respective market where the participants are not actual or potential competitors.

Fourth, the 2010 amendment transposed literally Article 102 TFEU and repealed the third paragraph of Article 9, which allowed the abusing undertaking to prove that its practice was committed for objective reasons of a legal or economic nature and it has not committed an infringement. Meanwhile, in the area of merger control, a new test for merger appraisal in line with the EU law development in the area of merger control was introduced.[28]

3 Relationship of Albanian Competition Act with the EU Law

The Constitution of Albania, adopted in 1998 and last amended in 2022, does not specifically address the status of EU law in the Albanian legal system.[29] Article 116 of the Constitution of Albania, considered as the provision which defines the sources of law, mentions ratified international agreements without referring to the EU law. The applicability of EU law is regulated under a general clause of ratified international agreements and norms issued by international organisations. According to Article 122(2) of the Constitution of Albania, the Stabilisation and Association Agreement with Albania is considered an international agreement after it has been published in the Official Journal and has priority over the domestic legal norms. Furthermore, Article 122(3) emphasises the supremacy of norms issued by the

[25] 2010 Amendment of Competition Act, Art 2.

[26] 2010 Amendment of Competition Act, Art 2.

[27] 2010 Amendment of Competition Act, Arts 4–6.

[28] 2010 Amendment of Competition Act, Art 8.

[29] Law 8417/1998 The Constitution of the Republic of Albania [1998] OJ 28 as last amended by Law 16/2022 (The Constitution of Albania).

international organisation [the EU] in the case of conflict with domestic law "when the direct application of the norms issued by the organisation is expressly contemplated in the agreement ratified by the Republic of Albania for participation therein."

The SAA between the EU, Member States and Albania was signed in 2006 and entered into force in April 2009,[30] six years after the entry into force of the Competition Act. Meanwhile, parallel to the process of ratification of the SAA by the EU Member States, the EU and Albania concluded an Interim Agreement, which entered into force in December 2006, intending to implement trade components, including provisions related to competition rules (Articles 37 and 38 of the Interim Agreement, respectively).[31] SAA provided for the gradual approximation of domestic legislation with the EU *acquis*.[32]

SAA, Title VI "Approximation of Laws, Law Enforcement and Competition Rules" adopts a two-part approach. On the one hand, the SAA requires Albania to harmonise national legislation with that of the EU. According to Article 70 (1) of the SAA, both parties "recognise the importance of the approximation of Albania's existing legislation to that of the Community and for its effective implementation" and "Albania shall endeavour to ensure that its existing laws and future legislation shall be gradually made compatible with the Community *acquis*." The SAA sets a priority of certain areas to be approximated. The approximation process shall be done over a transitional period of a maximum 10 years, divided into two stages.[33] The first stage, starting on the SAA's signing date, focuses on the internal market *acquis*, including competition law. The second stage shall focus on the remaining part of the *acquis*.

On the other hand, it had become standard to include in the association agreements provisions on competition policy, including the state aid rules. SAA Article 71 links competition rules with the functioning of the Agreement itself: to enhance a candidate country's overall economic well-being and political stability. The primary role of Article 71 is to contribute to Albania's pre-accession adoption of the EU *acquis*. Accordingly, "the following shall be incompatible in so far as they may affect trade between the Community and Albania:

(i) all agreements between undertakings, decisions by associations of undertakings and concerted practices between undertakings which have as their object or effect the prevention, restriction or distortion of competition;
(ii) abuse by one or more undertakings of a dominant position in the territories of the Community or of Albania as a whole or in a substantial part thereof;
(iii) any State aid which distorts or threatens to distort competition by favouring certain undertakings or certain products.[34]

[30] SAA with Albania, Art 1(2).

[31] Interim Agreement on Trade and trade-related matters between the European Community, of the one part, and the Republic of Albania, of the other part [2006] OJ L 239.

[32] SAA with Albania, Art 1(2).

[33] SAA with Albania, Art 6.

[34] SAA with Albania, Art 71 (1).

Moreover, SAA Article 71(2) explicitly states that any practices contrary to Article 71 shall be assessed "on the basis of criteria arising from the application of EU competition law", in particular from Articles 101, 102, 106 and 107 TFEU and the "interpretative instruments" adopted by the EU institutions. According to Cremona, interpretative instruments include the Court of Justice of the European Union judgement, the Commission's decision in competition cases and various soft law measures, namely, the Commission's Guidelines and Notices.[35] While the Albanian Competition Act remains silent on the assessment of national provisions in light of EU competition law, based on the general harmonisation clause (Article 70 of the SAA) and Article 71 of the SAA, the ACA has an obligation to rely on EU competition *acquis,* concerning agreements affecting trade between the EU and Albania.[36]

Following the direct applicability of the SAA provisions on fundamental freedoms into the Albanian domestic legal system, national courts are faced with judicial harmonisation.[37] According to Albi, judicial harmonisation means that "the national courts should apply the interpretation of the European Court of Justice and take account of the EU legislation when applying the provisions of domestic laws or the provisions of Europe Agreements".[38] Experience from CEE countries and other Western Balkan jurisdictions show a "Euro Friendly" approach toward application of EU Law by national courts even before accession or case practice assessing restrictive agreements in the light of EU law or the Commission's soft laws.[39]

The Albanian courts have also followed the "Euro-Friendly" approach.[40] Since the entry into force of the SAA (April 2009), Albanian courts have emphasised in their decisions the importance of the approximation process and have assessed domestic legislation in the light of EU law. In several decisions, the Constitution Court of Albania has applied EU law as a persuasive source of law to support the court's decision.[41] In these decisions, the Constitutional Court of Albania or the High Court of Albania did not clarify why they relied on EU law and the place it has in the Albanian legal system.

For the first time, in the judgment of 2 July 2020 and judgment of 8 July 2020, the Civil College of the High Court of Albania clarified the obligation to approximate domestic law in compliance with the EU *acquis* stemming from Article 70 of the SAA with Albania. In the Court's view, Article 70 of the SAA with Albania establishes the positive obligation for the legislature to consider the EU law as a

[35] Cremona (2003), pp. 269–271.

[36] Cremona (2003), pp. 269–271; Skara and Hajdini (2021), pp. 237–243.

[37] Albi (2005), p. 52.

[38] Albi (2005), pp. 52–53.

[39] Albi (2007), p. 39; Kühn (2005a), p. 55; Kühn (2005b), p. 563; Meškić and Samardžić (2014), pp. 69–70; Lang and Mataija (2014), pp. 95–96; Georgievski et al. (2014), p. 122; Vukadinović et al. (2014), p. 150; Pecotić Kaufman and Malnar (2016), pp. 346–348.

[40] Skara and Hajdini (2021).

[41] Judgment of 24 July 2009, Albanian Constitutional Court, V-24/09, [2009] OJ 119.

basic standard during the law-making process. Secondly, Article 70 SAA with Albania "imposes an obligation on judicial bodies, in the course of their daily work of resolving disputes, to the extent possible, to apply and interpret the law in the spirit of Community law."[42]

Also, the Constitutional Court of Albania (hereafter Constitutional Court) has assessed the constitutionality of domestic law in light of Articles 70 and 71 of the SAA. In 2013, the Constitutional Court was asked to declare unconstitutionally two Council of Ministers' decisions, which created a concession contract for fuel marking and monitoring services in Albania. The concession contract was signed for a period of 10 years, giving exclusive rights to the concessionaire. The claimant argued *inter alia* that the concession contract established a dominant position and is in breach of the SAA. In its reasoning, the Constitutional Court noted that:

> under the Stabilisation and Association Agreement, practises contrary to Article 71 (competition and other economic provisions) are assessed based on criteria arising from the application of the competition rules applicable in the Community, in particular Articles 81, 82, 86 and 87 of the Treaty establishing the European Community, and interpretative instruments used by Community institutions.[43]

In this context, the Constitutional Court referred to the Court of Justice of the European Union case law when a certain activity was given by the public authority to a company with exclusive rights.[44] While the Constitutional Court assessed these two Council of Ministers' decisions in light of EU competition law, it did not explain its recourse to the SAA provisions, namely whether the EU law was a source of law directly applicable as a result of the SAA or whether it was only an interpretation aid that inspired the judges when applying domestic rules, similar to comparative assessment of other legal orders, and the overall impact of SAA and EU rules on the Albanian legal system.

---

[42] Judgment of 2 July 2020, the Civil Chamber of the High Court, N 213, [2020], para 16.1; Judgment of 8 July 2020, the Civil Chamber of the High Court, N 213, [2020], para 15.1.

[43] Judgment of 21 March 2014, Albanian Constitutional Court, V-14/14, [2014] OJ 50, para 31.

[44] Judgment of 18 March 1997, *Cali v. Servizi ecologici porto di Genova SpA,* C-343/95, ECLI:EU:C:1997:160, paras 16–23; Judgment of 19 January 1994, *SAT Fluggesellschaft mbH v Eurocontrol,* C-364/92, ECLI:EU:C:1994:7, para 30; Judgment of 19 May 1993, *Paul CORBEAU,* C-320/91, ECLI:EU:C:1993:198, para 14.

4 Institutional and Normative Framework of Competition Authority in Albania

4.1 Albanian Competition Authority: Structure, Organisation and Competences

As the Competition Act entered into force, an independent competition authority was established to protect free and effective competition in the market.[45] The European Commission considers Albanian Competition Authority (ACA) as an operationally independent authority within the sense of Article 71 SAA, and gives the following assessment in its 2023 report:

> Regarding the institutional framework, the Albanian Competition Authority is responsible for implementing the Law on the protection of competition. It is an operationally independent authority reporting to parliament. It can adopt implementing legislation, impose fines and remedies, prohibit mergers or authorise them, with or without conditions. Parties may appeal against the ACA's decisions before the courts.[46]

The ACA is a public entity which comprises of two bodies: (i) the Commission and (ii) the Secretariat. The Commission is a collegiate body composed of five members. It consists of a chairperson elected by the Parliament. The other four members of the Competition Commission are elected by the majority of the votes of all members of the Parliament. In contrast, the deputy chairperson is elected by the Competition Commission members at the Commission's first meeting.[47] To ensure the independence of the Competition Commission, Article 21(3) regulates how the Competition Commission members are nominated. Accordingly, one member is nominated by the President of the Republic of Albania, the remaining four members are nominated by the Council of Ministers and by the Parliament of Albania. Respectively, the Council of Ministers proposes two members and the Parliament proposes two members. Members' term in office is limited to five years, renewable for two consecutive terms. To be elected as a Competition Commissioner, the following conditions have to be fulfilled: (i) Albanian citizenship; (ii) not less than 15 years of work experience; (iii) at least five years in academia or to have a title or scientific degree in economics or law, with a specialisation in civil or administrative Law; and (iv) not dismissed from employment or civil service as a result of disciplinary measures.[48] While the intention was to ensure that members had the necessary expertise in law or economics, in a small country where access to academic positions and titles tends to be restricted, this unnecessarily limits the circle of individuals who can be considered for these positions.

---

[45] Competition Act, Arts 2 and Art 18.

[46] Commission (2023), p. 86.

[47] Competition Act, Art 21 (1).

[48] Competition Act, Art 20.

Article 24 of the Competition Act outlines the main duties and competencies of the Competition Commission, which are as follows. The Competition Commission sets out the national competition policy, which aims to preserve the competition process and promote effective competition in the market. It also adopts regulations and guidelines for the implementation of competition law. In this context, the Competition Commission has adopted regulation on the functions of the ACA and other notices or guidelines. The latter have been adopted in line with the European Commission's Notices and Guidelines, as the ACA attempted to increase the level of approximation of domestic law with EU competition *acquis*.[49] Most Notices or Guidelines were translated literally into Albanian language, with minor changes. The Competition Commission supervises the work of the Secretariat in the application of the competition law provisions. It adopts decisions on the basis of the Competition Act, respectively: (i) establish infringements under the competition law; (ii) impose sanctions; (iii) impose interim measures; (iv) approve commitments of the undertakings; (v) impose the appropriate behavioural and/or structural remedies to restore competition and (vi) assess concentrations.

The Competition Commission represents the ACA in Albania and abroad. The Competition Act empowers the ACA to cooperate with foreign institutions and international organisations dealing with competition policy. In this context, the ACA signed bilateral and multilateral agreements or memoranda of understanding. The purpose of these instruments is to promote and strengthen cooperation between the parties in the area of competition law by: (i) exchanging of non-confidential information on legislative developments and cases; (ii) organising study visits and experts training; (iii) attending conferences, workshops, seminars or other activity organised by parties; (iv) online meeting or consultation on issues of mutual interests; (v) exchanging of non-confidential documents, studies, annual reports, journals; and (vi) participating jointly in research with academic institutions or other organisations.[50]

The Competition Commission is a collegiate body. Decisions are taken with the vote of the simple majority of the members present.[51] The decisions are valid when at least four members are present at the meeting, from which one should be either the Chairman or the Deputy Chairman.[52] Article 23 stipulates the conflict of interest as the only justification for not participating in the Commission meetings. In the case of a tie vote, the Chairman or Deputy Chairman cast the decisive vote. Abstentions are not permitted.[53]

[49] Skara (2022), pp. 251–253.

[50] As an example, see Memorandum of Partnership in the field of Competition Policy between the Albanian Competition Authority and the Hellenic Competition Commission (2021).

[51] Competition Act, Art 26 (2).

[52] Competition Act, Art 26 (1).

[53] Competition Act, Art 26 (2).

The Competition Commission, as a decision-making body, is supported by the Secretariat.[54] The Secretariat has the following responsibilities for the supervision of the application of competition law. It monitors and analyses the conditions on the market for the development of free and effective competition.[55] The Secretariat carries out the administrative investigations of ongoing cases based on the Code of Administrative Procedures, Competition Act and other legislation in force.[56] It compiles and submits investigation reports based on which the Competition Commission takes decisions.[57] The Secretariat oversees the implementation of the decisions taken by the Commission.[58]

Unlike the Competition Commission members who are elected by the Parliament, the employees of the Secretariat are appointed based on civil service recruitment procedures.[59] The Secretariat is headed by the Secretary-General, who is appointed by the Commission.[60] The Secretary-General is in charge of the day-to-day work of the Secretariat. More specifically, the Secretary-General is responsible for: (i) applying the competition rules in dealing with competition cases; (ii) preparing and submitting the final report of the preliminary or in-depth investigation to the Competition Commission; (iii) coordinating the work of the Secretariat Departments; (iv) preparing the annual report of the Authority; (v) co-operating with other institutions in Albania and abroad to resolve the cases; and (vi) signing Secretariat written correspondence.[61]

The structure of the Secretariat contains five directorates following the main pillars of competition law.[62] The Production Markets Surveillance Directorate focuses on the manufacturing markets and other markets such as energy, gas and fuels, construction, forests, extracting and mineral industries, agriculture/farming, livestock, fishing, chemical goods, manufacturing, as well as any other productive activity.[63] The Non-Production/Service Markets Surveillance Directorate oversees and investigates service markets and other non-productive activities such as electronic communications, technology information and media, financial market, health, tourism, transportation, as well as other services.[64] The Directorate for Market Analysis and Methodologies carries out the assessment of the conditions of markets

[54] Competition Act, Art 27 (3).

[55] Competition Act, Art 28 (a).

[56] Competition Act, Art 28 (b).

[57] Competition Act, Art 28 (c).

[58] Competition Act, Art 28 (d).

[59] Competition Act, Art 27 (2).

[60] Competition Act, Art 27 (1).

[61] Competition Act, Art 29.

[62] Decision of Parliament 27/2021 for some changes in the Decision of the Parliament 43/17 for the Approval of the Structure and Organization of the Competition Authority [2021] OJ 39.

[63] ACA Decision No 563 of 25 October 2018 on the approval of Regulation for Organization and Functioning of Competition Authority [2018] Official Bulletin 14, Art 20.

[64] Ibid, Art 21.

and conducts economic analysis in cases of concentrations, general studies, monitoring and market inspection.[65] The Directorate for Legal, Integration and Judicial Affairs is responsible for implementing the priorities related to the negotiation process as the ACA is the leader and coordinator of Chapter 8 "Competition Policy".[66] Also, this directorate assesses the compliance of the acts and bylaws with the Albanian competition law and is entrusted with the approximation of competition legislation with the EU competition *acquis*.[67] The Directorate for Human Resources, Budget, and Communication is responsible for organising and creating working conditions through the effective and efficient management of financial resources and human resources. This directorate is also responsible for public relations of the ACA.

4.2 Main Substantive and Procedural Norms

4.2.1 Prohibited Agreements

Unlike the Competition Act (1995), which included provisions on unfair competition and consumer protection,[68] the Competition Act covers only: (i) prohibited agreements; (ii) abuse of the dominant position; and (iii) control of concentrations. Article 4 of the Competition Act regulates prohibited agreements and is modelled after Article 101 TFEU. Competition Act does not contain a legal definition of the notion of a cartel and it is treated similarly to other types of anti-competitive agreements. Article 4 prohibits all agreements that have as their object or effect the prevention, restriction, or distortion of competition. The particular forms of prohibited agreements are those which:

a) directly or indirectly fix purchase or selling prices, or any other trading conditions;
b) limit or control production, markets, technical development, or investment;
c) share markets or sources of supply;
d) apply dissimilar conditions to equivalent transactions with other trading parties, thereby placing them at a competitive disadvantage;
e) make the conclusion of contracts subject to acceptance by the other parties of supplementary obligations which, by their nature or according to commercial usage, have no connection with the subject of such contracts.

Similarly to Article 101(2) TFEU, the prohibited agreements under Article 4 (1) of the Competition Act, which are not exempted under individual exemption (Article 5), block exemptions (Art 6) and do not fall under *de minimis* agreements (Article 7) are null and void.[69] Article 7 states that insignificant agreements may be exempted

[65] Ibid, Art 22.
[66] Ibid, Art 24.
[67] Ibid, Art 23.
[68] cf Competition Act (1995), Art 27–42.
[69] Competition Act, Art 4 (2).

from the prohibition if the combined market share of the parties does not exceed 10% of the market for horizontal agreements and 15% for non-horizontal agreements. The wording suggests an exclusion from the scope of Article 4, but the use of the word "may", suggests a certain degree of discretion from the ACA. The Albanian Competition Authority Regulation on *de minimis* agreements explains the criteria and clarifies that *de minimis* exemption does not apply to price fixing.[70]

Similar to Article 101(3) TFEU, the Competition Act provides for the possibility of individual exemption of agreements or block exemption of certain categories of agreements, decisions, and concerted practices. The conditions for individual exemption are similar to those stipulated in Article 101 (3) TFEU. Accordingly, the agreement shall not be prohibited if they contribute to:

> improving the production or distribution of goods and/or services or to promoting technical or technological or economic progress, while allowing customers or consumers a fair share of the resulting benefit, and which do not: i) impose on the participating undertakings restrictions which are not indispensable to the attainment of these objectives; and ii) significantly restrict competition in respect of the products or services which are subject of those agreements.[71]

Additionally, Article 6 provides for the possibility of block exemption for certain categories of agreements. The conditions to be met in order to benefit from the block exemption are regulated in the Regulation on the block exemption of categories of vertical agreements and concerted practices,[72] which transposes the Commission Regulation 330/2010.[73] Moreover, as the EU competition *acquis* is dynamic, the newly adopted Commission Regulation 2022/720 on the application of Article 101(3) of the TFEU to categories of vertical agreements and concerted practices remains to be transposed.[74]

4.2.2 Abuse of Dominant Position

Provisions concerning abuse of dominant position are largely in line with the Article 102 TFEU. Article 9 of Competition Act prohibits any abuse by one or more undertakings of a dominant position.[75] Dominant position is defined as "a position

---

[70] ACA Decision No 121 of 10 September 2009 on de minimis agreements [2009] Official Bulletin 5.

[71] Competition Act, Art 5.

[72] ACA Decision No 234 of 19 August 2012 on the approval of the Regulation on the block exemption of categories of vertical agreements and concerted practices [2012] Official Bulletin 8.

[73] Commission Regulation 330/2010 of 20 April 2010 on the application of Article 101(3) of the Treaty on the Functioning of the European Union to categories of vertical agreements and concerted practices [2010] OJ L102/1.

[74] Commission Regulation (EU) 2022/720 of 10 May 2022 on the application of Article 101(3) of the Treaty on the Functioning of the European Union to categories of vertical agreements and concerted practices (Text with EEA relevance) [2022] OJ L 134/4.

[75] Competition Act, Art 9 (1).

of economic strength enjoyed by one or more undertakings which enables them to prevent effective competition on the market by giving them the power to behave, with regard to demand or supply, independently of other market participants such as competitors, customers or consumers”.[76] As can be seen, the Competition Act does not include a legal presumption of dominance based on certain market share. Instead, Article 8 of the Competition Act provides the criteria for appraisal of dominant position. To determine whether certain undertakings enjoy a dominant position, the following factors should be considered:

i) the relevant market shares of the investigated undertakings and those of the other competitors;
ii) barriers to entry into the relevant market;
iii) the potential competition;
iv) the economic and financial power of the undertakings;
v) the economic dependence on suppliers and purchasers;
vi) the countervailing power of buyers/customers;
vii) the development of the undertaking’s distribution network and access to the sources of supply of products;
viii) the undertaking’s links with other undertakings; and other characteristics of the relevant market, such as the homogeneity of the products, the transparency of the market, the undertaking cost and size symmetries and the stability of demand or free production capacities.[77]

In the same vein as Article 102 TFEU, Article 9 (2) envisages the prohibition of any abuse by one or more undertakings of a dominant position in the markets, particularly consisting in:

a) directly or indirectly imposing unfair purchase or selling prices or other unfair trading conditions;
b) limiting production, markets or technical development;
c) applying dissimilar conditions to equivalent transactions with other trading parties, thereby placing them at a competitive disadvantage;
d) making the conclusion of contracts subject to acceptance by the other parties of supplementary obligations which, by their nature or according to commercial usage, have no connection with the subject of such contracts.

4.2.3 Merger Control

The Competition Act is applicable to all undertakings operating in the territory of the Republic of Albania, as well as to undertakings that operate abroad, when it is demonstrated that the consequences of these activities affect competition in the territory of Albania. In the case of mergers, the Competition Act does not stipulate specific rules regarding the extraterritorial mergers (foreign mergers). Thus, general merger control rules are applicable as well to foreign mergers, if the threshold stipulated in Article 12 (1) Competition Act is met.[78]

---

[76] Competition Act, Art 3 (5).

[77] Competition Act, Art 8.

[78] Competition Act, Arts 10–17 and 53–64.

Similar to the EU Merger Regulation, a concentration of undertakings arises when a change of control results from:

a) the merger of two or more independent undertakings or parts of undertakings;
b) the acquisition, by one or more natural persons already controlling at least one undertaking or by one or more undertakings, whether by purchase of securities or assets, by contract or any other legal means, of direct or indirect control of the whole or parts of one or more other undertakings;
c) direct or indirect control of one or more undertakings or parts therein.[79]

The concentrations should be notified to the ACA for authorization before completion if, in the financial year preceding:

a) the aggregate worldwide turnover of all the participating undertakings exceeds ALL 7 billion, and the individual turnover in Albania of at least one of the participating undertakings exceeds ALL 200 million; or:
b) the aggregate turnover in Albania of all the participating undertakings exceeds ALL 400 million, and the individual turnover of at least one of the participating undertakings on the domestic market is over ALL 200 million.[80]

According to Article 13, the Competition Commission can prohibit a concentration that significantly restricts competition in the market, particularly as a result of the creation of a dominant position. In assessing concentrations, the Competition Commission may consider the economic efficiencies resulting from the concentration.[81]

4.3 Procedural Provisions

4.3.1 Procedural Provisions for Restrictive Agreements and Abuses of Dominant Position

Regarding restrictive agreements and abuses of dominant position, the ACA may conduct a general inquiry in any sector of the economy. The inquiry may be initiated on its own initiative or following a request by the Parliament or other regulators if there are concerns that the competition is being restricted or the market is distorted.[82]

The ACA Secretariat initiates a preliminary investigation, with the approval of the Competition Commission, both *ex officio* or following a complaint submitted by third parties related to the prevention, restriction or distortion of competition.[83] The purpose of preliminary investigation is to enquire whether there are sufficient grounds and evidence to support the opening of an in-depth investigation. During

[79] Competition Act, Art 10 (1).

[80] Competition Act, Art 12 (1).

[81] Competition Act, Art 13 (2).

[82] Competition Act, Art 41 (1).

[83] Competition Act, Art 42 (1). At the 20th anniversary of the Competition Act conference held on 23–24 November 2023, Skenderi (2023) stated that 281 complaints were filed for the period 2017–2022.

this stage, the ACA has a procedural obligation to inform the parties of the initiation of proceedings. The parties under investigation do not have the right to access the case files.[84] At the same time, the ACA maintains the name of the complainant confidential.[85] The Competition Act does not regulate time limits for the preliminary investigation. In the absence of such regulation, the Secretariat shall conduct the investigation pursuant to the Code of Administrative Procedures.[86] Therefore, referring to the general rule in Article 91 of the Code of Administrative Procedure, the duration of the preliminary investigation should not exceed three months.

If the preliminary investigation shows that there are indications of anti-competition infringements, the Competition Commission decides to start an in-depth procedure and specify the procedural investigation steps to be taken by the Secretariat.[87] The Competition Commission's decisions are published in the Official Bulletin, where it states the purpose of the investigation, the parties concerned and invites interested third parties to take part in the investigation. Unlike the preliminary investigation, which refers to the general rules of the Code of Administrative Procedure, Article 43 (2) of the Competition Act provides the duration of an in-depth investigation, which is six months from the moment of opening of the in-depth inquiry. In case of an in-depth investigation, the Competition Commission can extend its duration.[88]

According to the procedural rules stipulated in the Competition Law Act, the parties have the following procedural rights: (i) right to be informed about the proceedings; (ii) right to access the case file after the preliminary report has been issued; (iii) right to submit observations and objections; (iv) right to be heard before the final decision is taken;[89] (v) right of confidential treatment; and (vi) privilege against self-incrimination. In addition to the procedural rights, parties to the infringement proceedings have the following obligations: (i) obligation to cooperate with the competition authority; (ii) obligation to provide correct, complete or non-misleading information; and (iii) obligation not to oppose the ACA's inspections.

4.3.2 Procedural Provisions for Concentrations

As the notification for a merger is filed in compliance with the Guidelines on the notification in merger cases,[90] the ACA shall notify the undertaking about the receipt

[84] Competition Act, Art 42 (2).

[85] Competition Act, Art 42 (3).

[86] Competition Act, Art 27 (3).

[87] Competition Act, Art 43 (1).

[88] Competition Act, Art 43 (3).

[89] Competition Act, Art 39.

[90] Competition Act, Art 53; ACA Decision No 82 of 23 June 2008 on the approval of the Guidelines on the notification in merger cases and respective annexes I and II attached [2008] Official Bulletin 3.

of the notification and shall communicate whether the notification is complete. If the notification is incomplete, the ACA shall ask the undertakings to complete the notification within a time limit[91] or request additional information.[92] Once the notification is completed, it is published on the ACA's Official Website and the Official Bulletin.

The ACA conducts preliminary and in-depth assessments of notified concentrations. In the preliminary procedure, the ACA assesses whether the concentration has any indications of significant restriction of competition in the market.[93] If the concentration does not have any indications of significant restriction, the Competition Commission authorises the concentration within two months from the date of the notification. Otherwise, if the Competition Commission finds that concentration shows any indications of significant restriction of competition, it shall authorise the concentration with conditions or it may open an in-depth assessment.[94]

Once the in-depth procedure is open, the Competition Commission has to decide within three months of the date of initiation of the in-depth assessment whether to prohibit the concentration.[95] If the undertakings propose commitments for eliminating the significant restriction of competition not later than two months from the date of initiating the in-depth procedure, the Competition Commission has two months to decide whether to prohibit the concentration or to authorise it with the proposed commitments.[96] In the case that the Commission's decision has not been communicated within the deadlines set, the concentration is considered authorised and may be put into effect unless the deadline has been extended by the Commission by request or with the consent of the notifying party.[97]

4.4 *Investigative and Sanctioning Powers*

4.4.1 Investigative Powers

The ACA Secretariat is responsible for conducting investigations and inspections pursuant to the Competition Commission's decisions.[98] Upon the Secretariat's request, the Competition Commission authorises the ACA Secretariat inspectors to conduct inspections. During the inspection, the ACA inspectors must present the authorisation to the undertakings under inspection. The authorisation must contain

[91] Competition Act, Art 54.
[92] Competition Act, Art 55.
[93] Competition Act, Art 56 (1).
[94] Competition Act, Art 56 (1).
[95] Competition Act, Art 57 (1).
[96] Competition Act, Art 57 (2).
[97] Competition Act, Art 57 (3).
[98] Competition Act, Art 35 (1).

the object and the purpose of the inspection.[99] If the inspection is prevented by undertaking under the investigation, the ACA Secretariat may require the assistance of the police.[100] For the period 2017–2022, a total of 253 dawn raids have been conducted.[101] The number of dawn raids has increased from 2017 to 2022. Respectively, the ACA conducted 16 dawn raids in 2017; 20 dawn raids in 2018; 12 dawn raids in 2019; 38 dawn raids in 2020; 58 dawn raids in 2021 and 109 dawn raids in 2022.[102]

The ACA has the power to request information from third parties, undertakings or associations of undertakings.[103] If an undertaking or natural person does not provide the requested information within the deadline requested by the ACA Secretariat or provides incomplete information, the Competition Commission may request it by a decision. Both the Secretariat's request and the Competition Commission's decision must state the legal basis, purpose of request or decision, the deadline within which information must be provided and the fines in case of not complying with the request or decision.[104]

The Secretariat investigators and other persons authorised by the Competition Commission may carry out inspections on business premises without court warrant. According to Article 36, inspection on business premises may take different forms such as: (i) entering into the premises, transportation vehicles and on the territory of the undertakings during working hours; (ii) examining the books and other business records both in a written or electronic form; (iii) taking or providing, copies, or extracts from the books or records; and (iv) sealing any premises for inspection or seizing books or business records for not more than 72 hours, if it is necessary for the investigation. The ACA may seize original documents for not more than 72 hours. The District Court where the seizure takes place, upon a request from ACA, may extend the time limit from not more than 72 hours to not more than six months.[105] The ACA inspectors and other persons authorised by the Competition Commission may ask any representative or staff of the undertaking under inspection for further explanations on the subject matter for facts and documents related to the object and the purpose of the inspection.[106]

The ACA Secretariat may carry out inspections on non-business premises. By a court decision of the District Court, which has jurisdiction over the place of the inspection, the ACA investigators have the power to enter: (i) the apartment/house of administrators, managers, directors, and other staff members; (ii) the residences and headquarters of natural and legal persons who are responsible for commercial,

[99] Competition Act, Art 35 (2).
[100] Competition Act, Art 35 (3).
[101] Skenderi (2023).
[102] Skenderi (2023).
[103] Competition Act, Art 33 (1).
[104] Competition Act, Art 33 (3).
[105] Competition Act, Art 38.
[106] Competition Act, Art 36 (d).

accounting, administrative, fiscal, or financial management. In these cases, the ACA has to inspect non-business premises from 7:00 to 18:00. The ACA, pursuant to a District Court decision, may inspect other premises, equivalent to the apartment/ house if there is reason to believe that on such premises are books or other professional documents that are deemed necessary to prove the infringement of Articles 4 and 9 of the Competition Act.

4.4.2 Sanctioning Powers

Part VI of the Competition Act provides sanctions for infringements of substantive and procedural competition rules, which are of an administrative nature. Concerning the substantive infringement, the Competition Act allows sanctions on: (i) undertakings or associations of undertakings that have committed substantive infringements (Art 74) and (ii) individuals who have committed or contributed to these infringements (Art 78). Based on Article 74 of the Competition Act, the Competition Commission may impose on undertakings or associations of undertakings sanctions not exceeding 10% of their aggregate annual turnover[107] in the previous financial year if the undertakings or associations of undertakings:

a. infringe Article 4 "prohibited agreements between undertakings" or Article 9 "abuse of a dominant position";
b. fail to comply with the the Commission's decision on interim measures;
c. fail to comply with the conditions and obligations established by the ACA decisions ordering to cease an infringement (Art 45);
d. implement a concentration that results in competition restrictions, contradiction with the obligation to notify or the obligation to suspend the concentration until it has been authorised;
e. implement a concentration that is prohibited by the Commission or do not take the necessary measures to restore the competition.

Based on Article 78 of the Competition Act, an individual may be fined not more than ALL 5,000,000, if he/she has been involved intentionally or negligently for substantive or procedural infringement. Since its establishment, the ACA has imposed one individual fine with an amount ALL 30,000.[108]

In addition to substantial infringements, the Competition Act provides sanctions for procedural infringements. According to Article 73 of the Competition Act, the Commission may impose procedural fines up to 1% of the infringer's aggregate annual turnover on an undertaking or an association of undertakings for a procedural infringement, particularly by:

---

[107] The Competition Act does not explicitly specify whether "aggregate annual turnover" refers to national or worldwide turnover.

[108] ACA Decision No 67 of 24 December 2007 for individual fines against Mr. Kajo Hallka [2008] Official Bulletin 2.

a) providing incorrect, incomplete or misleading information in response to a decision or request for information or not providing the information within the deadline specified in the decision or request for information;
b) providing incorrect, incomplete or misleading information or additional data in the notification of an agreement or a concentration;
c) producing the required books or other business records in incomplete form during an inspection in business premises or refusing to submit them;
d) refuse to answer any questions on facts concerning the inspection in business premises, providing inaccurate, incomplete or fraudulent answers, obstructing the inspections, or refusing to answer any questions on facts;
e) breaking a seal put on by the officials during an on-the-spot inspection; and
f) not notifying a concentration that is subject to merger control.

Besides imposing a fine, Article 76 of the Competition Act provides for periodic penalty payments intended to compel offenders to fulfil particular obligations or to comply with the ACA's decisions ordering either termination of the violation or imposing measures to restore competition. Since its establishment until end of 2022, the ACA has not imposed a periodic fine. It should be noted that the Albanian competition law allows the ACA to apply both periodic penalty payments and procedural fines with regard to the same infringements.

The ACA may impose on undertakings periodic penalty payments for each working day of delay until the termination of the unlawful behaviour. The amount of the fine shall not exceed 5% of their average daily turnover of the preceding financial year. The amount of the fine is calculated from the date the decision was taken. The periodic payment is imposed to induce the offenders to commit any of the following actions:

a) to cease a substantive antitrust infringement in accordance with the decision by which it has been established;
b) to comply with a decision ordering interim measures;
c) to comply with a commitment made binding by a commitment decision;
d) to supply complete and correct information in accordance with the decision or request for information;
e) to submit to on-the-spot inspections in business premises;
f) to take the necessary measures for restoring competition.

In fixing the amount of the fine, the ACA takes into consideration both the gravity and the duration of the infringement.[109] The amount of the fine shall not exceed 1% of the aggregate turnover of the preceding financial year for the non-substantive infringement (Art 73). For the substantive infringement (Art 74), the amount shall not exceed 10% of the aggregate turnover of the preceding financial year of each of the active member undertakings in the market concerned in the infringement of the

[109] Competition Act, Art 74 (1).

Table 1 The ACA's Annual Budget for the period 2012–2022

Year	The ACA's Annual Budget (in ALL)	The ACA's Annual Budget (in EUR)[a]
2012	60,134,000	432,497.41
2013	60,688,000	432,826.35
2014	63,402,206	452,932.07
2015	63,890,000	457,548.71
2016	63,800,000	464,451.14
2017	66,752,000	497,761.69
2018	80,655,400	632,157.85
2019	77,960,000	633,976.10
2020	75,700,000	611,674.64
2021	73,273,520	598,374.52
2022	74,624,400	627,419.25

Source: Authors' own calculation based on Albanian Competition Authority Annual Reports 2012–2022

[a] Calculation based on average exchange rate for the relevant year

association of undertaking.[110] In the case that it is possible to calculate or estimate objectively the illegal profits of undertakings acquired by infringing the Competition Act, these illegal profits constitute the minimal amount of fine.

In addition to the fines, the ACA, on its own initiative or following a request from the undertakings concerned, may adopt all the necessary interim measures.[111] Interim measures can be taken only in the cases of an urgency due to the risk of serious and irreparable damage to competition on the basis that there might be an infringement of articles 4 and 9 of Competition Act. The decision of interim measures is taken for a specific time and may be renewed when it is necessary.[112]

4.5 *Competition Authority's Budget and Staff*

The ACA is financed by the state budget, approved by the Parliament as a separate section in the State budget law.[113] As can be seen from the Table 1, during the period 2012–2017, the ACA's annual budget approved by Parliament was increased from ALL 60 million to almost ALL 67 million. The largest approved budget was in 2018 with an amount of ALL 80 million. From 2019 until 2022, despite an increase in staff numbers, the ACA's budget has been reduced. This decrease may be due to the ACA's next year's budget reflecting previous year's expenditures.

[110] Competition Act, Art 74 (2).

[111] Competition Act, Art 44 (1).

[112] Competition Act, Art 44 (2).

[113] Competition Act, Art 31.

Table 2 Albanian Competition Authority staff, including Competition Commission members for the period 2012–2022

Year	Total staff
2012	35
2013	35
2014	36
2015	37
2016	37
2017	39
2018	43
2019	46
2020	46
2021	46
2022	46

Source: Authors' own calculation based on ACA's Annual Reports 2012–2022

As regards human resources capacity, the ACA has increased the number of staff from 35 in 2012 to 46 in 2022 (see Table 2). The structure of the ACA is decided by Decision 27/2021 of the Albanian Parliament. It includes Competition Commission members (the Chairman and 4 Commissioners), officials composed of economists, lawyers, information technology experts and support staff.[114]

5 National Specifics that Differ from the EU Competition *Acquis*

Albania, as a candidate for EU membership, has an obligation to harmonise its domestic legislation with the EU *acquis* and ensure its proper implementation. As noted in Sect. 3, the Albanian Competition Act was drafted with the assistance of *GIZ* and modelled in line with the EU competition provisions, the draft Regulations 1/2003 and 139/2004 and a number of Commission's notices and guidelines. Moreover, in 2010, the Competition Act was amended aiming to advance further the approximation with the EU competition law.[115] Overall, the Albanian competition legislative framework is broadly in line with the EU *acquis*.[116]

While the 2010 Amendment increased the harmonisation level, it introduced the individual exemptions for the anti-competitive agreements. According to Article 5 of the Competition Act, individual exemption may be allowed if the agreement contributes to the improvement of the production or distribution of goods and/or services or to promoting technological or economic progress while allowing customers or consumers a fair share of the resulting benefit. In addition, these

[114] Albanian Parliament Decision 27/2021.

[115] Skara (2021), p. 245.

[116] Commission (2023), p. 86.

agreements should not impose any restriction on undertakings or significantly restrict competition in respect of the products or services.

Individual exemptions of the restrictive agreement are granted by the Competition Council upon request of the undertakings. Individual exemptions are limited in time and may be given with conditions and obligations to be fulfilled by the undertakings.[117] Competition Act allows the extension of the individual exemption if the conditions in Article 5 are met. The extension is granted only to participating undertakings that have provided individually their consent to the ACA for exemption three months before the expiry of the exemption.[118]

6 Application of National and EU Competition Rules by the Albanian Competition Authority

Since its establishment, from 1 March 2004 until 2022, the ACA has taken 470 substantive decisions.[119] The authors have identified dozens of cases where the ACA relies on the EU competition rules, the case law of the Court of Justice of the European Union, European Commission's decisions in competition cases and various soft laws such as Commission Guidelines and Notices to interpret domestic legislation. The remaining part of this section discusses the main decisions where parties or the ACA have referred to the EU primary or secondary law or the European Commission's soft law.

6.1 Anticompetitive Agreements

On 12 November 2012, the undertaking Alba Trans submitted a complaint to the ACA arguing that the National Association of Intercity Transportation, composed of three undertakings, traded in unfair conditions by not recognising the tickets of Alba Trans for the passenger transport services in the city of Tirana. Pursuant to this complaint, the ACA decided to determine whether there is a restrictive agreement between three undertakings in the market of monthly tickets for passenger transport services in the city of Tirana.[120]

---

[117] Competition Act, Art 50(2).

[118] Competition Act, Art 50(4).

[119] Data are compiled based on the Albanian Competition Authority Annual Report from 2005 to 2022.

[120] ACA Decision No 290 of 23 July 2013 on imposing a fine on undertakings "Ferlut" Sh.a., "Tirana Lines" Sh.p.k., "Alba Trans" Sh.p.k., "Tirana Urban Trans" Sh.a. and "Parku i Transportit Urban të Udhëtarëve" Sh.p.k. for restricting the competition in the market for the sale of the general and student monthly tickets in the city road transport service in the city of Tirana [2013] Official Bulletin 9.

During the proceedings, one of the undertakings, respectively Ferlut, relied on the CJEU jurisprudence concerning the behaviour of the undertakings in the market of the trading of general subscriptions. In its claim, Ferlut Sh.p.k. argued that the issuance of a high number of tickets by Tirana Municipality is why three undertakings refused to sell tickets for November 2012. Moreover, Ferlut Sh.p.k. brought the *Suiker Unie and Others v Commission* argument where the market was restricted due to government intervention to justify such behaviour.[121]

Furthermore, the ACA examined whether the undertakings restricted competition by object. The ACA referred to the EU Guidelines on the applicability of Article 101 TFEU to horizontal cooperation agreements.[122] According to the Commission's Guidelines, for an agreement to have restrictive effects on competition, it "must have, or be likely to have, an appreciable adverse impact on at least one of the parameters of competition on the market, such as price, output, product quality, product variety or innovation".[123] In the present case, the agreement has restricted the trade of 50% of the quantity of students' tickets for 2007 and 50% of the amount of students' tickets for the period 2008–2012. The ACA concluded that this agreement falls under the restrictive agreements, as a result of which the decision-making independence of the parties has been reduced.[124]

6.2 Abuse of Dominant Position

One of the first and most important cases concerned the mobile telecommunications market. The ACA investigated whether two mobile carriers operating in the Albanian telecommunications markets—AMC and Vodafone Albania—abused the dominant position. The ACA found that these two companies, in 2004–2005, abused their collective dominant position by charging retail prices higher than the prices of the same product in similar market conditions and significantly higher than the costs incurred by the two operators. In the end, the ACA imposed a fine of around 2% of the 2005 annual turnover of AMC and Vodafone Albania, around USD 4.5 million.[125]

In its decision, the ACA has relied heavily on CJEU cases, Commission decisions and Commission's soft law to: (i) define the relevant product market; (ii) assess the

---

[121] Judgment of 16 December 1975, *Coöperatieve Vereniging "Suiker Unie" UA and others v Commission of the European Communities*, Joined cases 40-48/73, 50/73, 54-56/73, 111/73, 113/73 and 114/73, ECLI:EU:C:1975:174.

[122] Guidelines on the applicability of Article 101 of the Treaty on the Functioning of the European Union to horizontal co-operation agreements [2011] C 11/01.

[123] ibid, para 27.

[124] ibid, para 27.

[125] ACA Decision No 59 of 09 November 2007 on the Abuse of Dominant Position in the Mobile Telecommunication Market by Albanian Mobile Communication Sh.a. and Vodafone Albania Sh.a. [2008] Official Bulletin 2.

dominant position; and (iii) assess the abuse of the dominant position. In defining the relevant product market, the ACA referred to the Commission guidelines on market analysis for electronic communications networks and services[126] and the Commission's merger decision.[127] The ACA concluded that mobile and fixed telephony services constitute separate markets.[128]

In assessing the dominant position, the ACA argued that the definition of the dominant position given under the Competition Act should follow the logic of Article 102 TFEU. Whereas, for the existence of a dominant position by two companies, the ACA referred to the *Hoffmann-La Roche* case, where the CJEU noted that:

> 39. The existence of a dominant position may derive from several factors which, taken separately, are not necessarily determinative, but among these factors, a highly important one is the existence of very large market shares.
>
> [...]
>
> 41. An undertaking which has a very large market share and holds it for some time, by means of the volume of production and the scale of the supply which it stands for - without those having much smaller market shares being able to meet rapidly the demand from those who would like to break away from the undertaking which has the largest market share - is by virtue of that share in a position of strength which makes it an unavoidable trading partner and which, already because of this secures for it, at the very least during relatively long periods, that freedom of action which is the special feature of a dominant position.[129]

Furthermore, the ACA cited the *AKZO* case, where the CJEU found that a market share of 50% is evidence of the existence of a dominant position.[130]

In assessing the abuse of dominant position by imposing unfair or excessive prices, the ACA referred to several CJEU's cases such as *General Motors*, *United Brands* and *SACEM*.[131] The ACA applied the test developed in *British Leyland v Commission* to determine whether the companies abused their dominant position.[132] Pursuant to the CJEU's case law, the ACA concluded that the presence of one

[126] Commission guidelines on market analysis and the assessment of significant market power under the Community regulatory framework for electronic communications networks and services [2002] OJ C 165/6.

[127] Commission Decision of 20 September 2001, *Pirelli/Edizione/Olivetti/Telecom Italia,* Case COMP/M.2574, para 33.

[128] ACA Decision No 59 of 09 November 2007, para 19.

[129] Judgement of 13 February 1979, *Hoffmann-La Roche v Commission,* C-85/76, ECLI:EU:C:1979:36.

[130] Judgement of 3 July 1991, *AKZO Chemie BV v Commission of the European Communities,* C-62/86, ECLI:EU:C:1991:286, para 60.

[131] Judgement of 13 November 1975, *General Motors v Commission,* C-26/75, ECLI:EU:C:1975:150, para 12; *United Brands v Commission,* C-27/76, para 250; Judgement of 13 July 1989, *Lucazeau and Others v SACEM and Others,* Joined cases C-110/88, C- 241/88 and C-242/88, ECLI:EU:C:1989:326.

[132] Judgement of 11 November 1986, *British Leyland v Commission*, C-226/84, ECLI:EU:C:1986:421.

criterion is sufficient to prove the existence of the abuse of the dominant position.[133] In this decision, the ACA did not explain why it referred to EU Law, but it clearly considered the EU case law for interpreting the Albanian competition provisions.

In another case, the ACA had to determine whether the Albanian Football Federation abused the dominant position.[134] In 2018, the ACA opened an investigation into the Albanian Football Federation concerning its economic activities.[135] To determine whether the Albanian Football Federation abused its dominant position, the ACA considered the CJEU cases and Commission's decisions[136] and decided that competition rules are applicable to sports only in so far as it constitutes an economic activity.[137]

Moreover, the ACA assessed the sale of media rights by referring to the Commission decisions[138] concerning joint selling of media rights to German Bundesliga,[139] FA Premier League[140] and joint selling of commercial rights of the UEFA Champions League.[141] In these decisions, the Commission found that joint selling of the media rights constitutes a restriction of competition contrary to Article 101(1) TFEU, as it hinders competition between clubs in the sense of marketing their rights individually.[142] In light of the CJEU and Commission's cases and evidence presented by the Secretariat, the Competition Commission found that the Albanian Football Federation has abused its dominant position. The Competition Commission ordered the sports association to reduce the scope and duration of the joint sale of the television rights for no more than three years, where the rights are separated and sold to different operators.[143]

---

[133] ACA Decision No 59 of 9 November 2007, para 64.

[134] ACA Decision No 693 of 14 May 2020 on the determination of the abuse of the dominant position of the Albanian Football Federation concerning the economic activity that develops and granting of conditions and obligations [2020] Official Bulletin 16.

[135] ACA Decision No 564 of 25 October 2018 on the opening of the preliminary investigation procedure against the Albanian Football Federation concerning the economic activity that develops [2018] Official Bulletin 14.

[136] Judgement of 18 July 2006, *Meca-Medina and Majcen v Commission,* C-519/04 P, ECLI:EU:C:2006:492; Commission Decision of 19 January 2005, *Joint selling of the media rights to the German Bundesliga*, COMP/C-2/37.214, OJ L 134/46; Commission Decision of 02 April 2003, *Newscorp / Telepiù,* COMP/M. 2876 Newscorp/Telepiù.

[137] ACA Decision No 693 of 14 May 2020, paras 29–30.

[138] ibid, paras 48–52.

[139] Commission Decision of 19 January 2005, *Joint selling of the media rights to the German Bundesliga*, COMP/C-2/37.214, OJ L 134/46.

[140] Commission Decision of 22 March 2006, *Joint selling of the media rights to the FA Premier League,* COMP/C- 2/38.173, OJ C 7.

[141] Commission Decision of 23 July 2003, *Joint selling of the commercial rights of the UEFA Champions League,* COMP/C.2/37.398, OJ L 291/25.

[142] ACA Decision No 693 of 14 May 2020, para 51.

[143] ibid.

6.3 Concentrations

Almost a third of all ACA's decisions are in the field of merger control. Concerning applying EU competition rules in merger cases, the ACA has referred to the Commission's decisions to define the relevant product market. In around 70 concentration cases that have not raised competition concerns, the ACA concluded that "referring to Commission practice on similar cases, the question of market definition will be left open".[144] While ACA acknowledges "Commission practice on similar cases" to define the product market dimension, ACA did not cite any specific decisions by the Commission or explain why it should consider Commission's practice. On the other hand, there are only a few cases in the field of merger control where the ACA has cited or referred to the EU competition *acquis*.

One of the most prominent cases is the acquisition of ABCom by Vodafone Albania.[145] In this case, the ACA relied on the Commission's decision to assess the differences between mobile and fixed Internet access services.[146] Vodafone Albania acquired control over ABCom, a company providing Internet services. In analysing the product market definition, the ACA referred to the *Orange/Jazztel* case, where the Commission argued that fixed and mobile broadband services are not substitutable for a number of reasons, such as: (i) different uses (mobile broadband permits mobility but also access to mobile applications); (ii) different capacity and pricing models (mobile broadband, unlike fixed broadband, is almost always capped at a certain amount of data transferred and is also invoiced per amount of data traffic) (iii) and different speeds (only 4G/LTE mobile technology can provide comparable speeds to fixed broadband).[147]

Furthermore, the ACA relied on the Commission's decisions to define relevant product markets for mobile and fixed call termination in the wholesale market.[148] Based on the Commission's decisions, the ACA concluded that each mobile or fixed network constitutes a separate market for termination because there is no substitute

---

[144] As examples see: ACA Decision No 681 of 5 March 2020 on the authorization of the concentration realised through the acquisition of control of the company RBM Assicurazione Salute S.p.A from the company Intesa Sanpaolo Vita S.p.A. [2020] Official Bulletin 16; ACA Decision No 705 of 10 September 2020 on the authorization of the concentration realised through the acquisition of control of the company Euroconsult Rental Division S.p.A by the company Intesa Sanpaolo S.p.A. [2020] Official Bulletin 16.

[145] ACA Decision No 676 of 7 February 2020 on the authorization with conditions and obligations of the concentration realised through the acquisition of control of ABCom Sh.p.k. by Vodafone Albania Sh.a. [2020] Official Bulletin 16.

[146] Commission Decision of 19 May 2015, *ORANGE / JAZZTEL*, Case M.7421, paras 50–53.

[147] ibid, para 50.

[148] Commission Decision of 01 March 2010, *T-Mobile/ Orange*, COMP/M.5650, para 37; Commission Decision of 03 August 2012, *Vodafone/ Cable & Wireless*, COMP/M.6584, para 23; Commission Decision of 20 September 2013, *Vodafone/ Kabel Deutschland*, COMP/M.6990, para 117; Commission Decision of 03 August 2016, *Vodafone/ Liberty Global/ Dutch JV*, COMP/M.7978, para 210.

for call termination on each individual network. Finally, in assessing the effects of this conglomerate merger on competition, the ACA considered the Guidelines on the assessment of non-horizontal mergers[149] and the Commission decisions. As foreseen in the Guidelines on the assessment of non-horizontal mergers, conglomerate mergers do not cause any competition problems. Very often, conglomerate mergers are seen as a way to increase efficiency in the market. The ACA cited several cases decided by the Commission where, by joining a strong fixed offer with a strong mobile offer, the conglomerate merger could somewhat speed up the uptake of fixed-mobile bundles[150] and increase the competition regarding fixed-mobile bundles.[151]

7 Enforcement and Sanctioning Statistics for the Period 2012–2022

Since its establishment on March 1, 2004, the ACA has concluded inquiries in many sectors of the economy, such as: energy, telecommunications, banking, insurance, public procurement and concessions, transport, fuels, pharmaceutics, food, hospitals, and education.[152] A considerable number of decisions concerning anti-competitive practices or abuse of the dominant position have been identified and detected.

Considering these statistics, it can be argued that the ACA has played an important role in safeguarding free and effective competition in Albania. The ACA is also committed to continuing to strengthen the enforcement of competition rules.[153] As shown in Table 3, the ACA resources have been primarily expended on authorising economic concentrations rather than on antitrust enforcement. It is not clear whether the block exemption regulations for agreements adopted by the ACA are sufficiently clear for the companies or whether the undertakings are reluctant to apply for an individual exemption. For the period 2012–2022, the ACA has taken

[149] Guidelines on the assessment of non-horizontal mergers under the Council Regulation on the control of concentrations between undertakings [2008] OJ C 265/6.

[150] Commission Decision of 09 August 2018, *T-Mobile Austria/ UPC Austria*; COMP/M.8808; Commission Decision of 03 August 2016, *Vodafone/ Liberty Global/ Dutch JV*, COMP/M.7978; Commission Decision of 19 May 2015, ORANGE / JAZZTEL, COMP/M.7421; Commission Decision of 02 July 2014, *Vodafone/ ONO*; COMP/M.7231; Commission Decision of 20 September 2013, *Vodafone/ Kabel Deutschland*; COMP/M.6990; Commission Decision of 03 August 2012, *Vodafone/ Cable & Wireless*, COMP/M.6584; Commission Decision of 08 October 2018, *Tele2/ Com Hem Holding*, COMP/M.8842.

[151] Commission Decision of 04 February 2016, *Liberty Global/ BASE Belgium*, COMP/M.7637, para 364; Commission Decision of 03 August 2016, *Vodafone/ Liberty Global/ Dutch JV*, COMP/ M.7978, para 627.

[152] ACA (2006, 2007, 2008, 2009, 2010, 2011, 2014, 2015, 2016, 2017, 2018, 2019, 2020a, 2021). For the sectors investigated in 2022, see ACA (2022), p. 21.

[153] Commission (2022), pp. 79–80; Commission (2021), pp. 78–79.

Table 3 The total number of ACA substantive decisions for the period 2012–2022

Year	2012	2013	2014	2015	2016	2017	2018	2019	2020	2021	2022	Total
Concentrations	9	13	8	11	12	16	30	24	19	31	46	219
Abuse of Dominant position	2	0	3	3	5	9	14	11	7	16	7	77
Restrictive Agreement	2	1	7	6	7	2	8	4	7	28	18	90
Exempted Agreement	1	1	1	1	4	0	1	0	0	1	2	12
Interim Measure	0	1	0	1	0	2	2	2	3	0	0	11
Commitment decisions	0	0	0	0	0	0	0	0	1	0	0	1
Total												410

Source: Data compiled by authors based on the Albanian Competition Authority Annual Report for the period 2012–2022

410 substantive decisions on concentrations, abuses of dominant position, restrictive agreements, exempted agreements, interim measures, and commitments.[154]

Out of 410 substantive decisions by the ACA for the period 2012–2022, 219 decisions relate to authorising concentrations, 90 decisions relate to restrictive agreements, and 77 decisions relate to abuse of dominant position. At the beginning of its operation, the ACA prosecuted several so-called naive cartels, where undertakings, due to a lack of legal culture, were involved in an illegal price-fixing or market-sharing cartel and publicly announced their coordinated price increases.[155] Recently, the ACA has been very active in prosecuting cartels operating in different sectors such as pharmaceuticals, bid rigging in public procurement, the transport sector and the insurance sector.

Table 4 shows the number of approved concentrations for the period 2012–2022. For this period, 218 mergers have been approved in phase one and 1 in phase two.[156] Furthermore, as can be seen from Table 4, the number of extraterritorial concentrations has increased, whereas concentrations affecting the Albanian market were decreasing.

A more serious issue relates to the amount of the fine or the collection of the fine. Since 2012, the ACA has imposed around EUR 3.83 million of fines on companies found in breach of the competition law, both concerning fines for substantive and procedural infringement of competition law in Albania. While this amount is considerable considering the size of both the Albanian economy and of the undertakings concerned, the amount of fine per year or collection of the fine is very low because the ACA decisions are appealed and until the end of the process the fine cannot be collected. For instance, between 2013–2015, the ACA took four decisions imposing a total fine of ALL 6 109 561.[157] As noted by the 2016 EC Progress Report, "most of the fines imposed by the authority in the past have not yet been collected".[158]

---

[154] Conditions and Obligation results from failure to comply with the conditions and obligations established by the Authority's decisions ordering: an infringement to end (Art 45); individual exemptions (Art 50/2); preliminary ruling (Art 56); in-depth procedures (Art 57); and temporary clearance.

[155] ACA Decision No 56 of 24 September 2007 on the abolishment of the agreements in the concrete production market in Tirana Region [2007] Official Bulletin 1; ACA Decision No 184 of 07 May 2011 on the opening of the preliminary investigation in the market of the production and sale of bread in Vlora City [2012] Official Bulletin 7; ACA Decision No 146 of 17 June 2010 on the closing of the preliminary investigation in the market of the production and sale of bread in Korca City [2011] Official Bulletin 7.

[156] ACA Decision No. 579 of 20 December 2018 for the initiation of the in-depth procedure in the assessment of the transaction between Piraeus Bank, as well as Balfin SHPK and Komercijalna Banka AD Skopje [2018] Official Bulletin 14. For more on this case, see Nazifi (2023), pp. 188–199.

[157] ACA Decision No 265 of 5 February 2013 (merger non-notification); ACA Decision No 318 of 2 June 2014 (failure to provide data on time); ACA Decision No 341 of 27 October 2014 (late merger notification); ACA Decision No 290 of 23 July 2013 (restrictive agreement).

[158] Commission (2016), pp. 40–41.

Table 4 Number of merger decisions for the period 2012–2022

Year	Number of approved extraterritorial concentration in Albania	Number of approved concentrations in Albanian market	Total
2012	5	4	9
2013	3	10	13
2014	4	4	8
2015	6	5	11
2016	2	10	12
2017	10	6	16
2018	17	13	30
2019	16	8	24
2020	15	4	19
2021	27	4	31
2022	41	5	46
Total	**146**	**73**	**219**

Source: Data compiled based on the Albanian Competition Authority Annual Report for the period 2012–2022

Such a low level of fine collection is related mainly to the non-execution of the ACA's decisions and delays in the court proceedings. According to Article 80 of the Competition Act, the fines imposed by the ACA are enforceable and executed in accordance with the Civil Procedure Code. As noted by various ACA Annual Reports, the amounts of fines imposed by the ACA have not been collected for years, mainly due to delays in court proceedings. For this reason, obtaining reliable data is difficult. Nevertheless, the amount of collected fines is very low. For instance, during the first ten years of activity (2004–2014), the ACA imposed around 8 million Euros of fines for the breach of competition rules. But, even after a final ruling by the court confirming the ACA decision was delivered, only 25% of this sum was collected by the judicial executors.[159] Also, only in 2022, the ACA managed to collect some of the fines imposed by the Competition Commission in 2018.[160]

As shown in Table 5, from 2012 until 2022, the ACA has imposed fines in 27 cases, respectively, 11 fines for procedural infringement (under Article 73) and 16 fines for substantive infringement (under Article 74). During this timeframe, no periodic or individual fines were imposed. In 2007, the ACA imposed an individual fine to Mr. Kajo Hallka, chairman of bread undertaking "Apollonia" in Fier.[161]

According to Article 73 of the Competition Act, the Competition Commission may impose fine not exceeding 1% of their aggregate turnover in the preceding financial year for procedural infringement if undertakings or associations of

[159] Nazifi and Broka (2015), p. 137.

[160] Monitor (2023).

[161] ACA Decision No 67 of 24 December 2007 for individual fines against Mr. Kajo Hallka [2008] Official Bulletin 2, 70.

Table 5 Number of fines imposed by the ACA for the period 2012–2022

	Fines for procedural infringement (Art 73)	Fines for substantive infringement (Art 74)	Periodic fines (Art 76)	Individual fines (78)	Total for each year
2012	4	3	0	0	7
2013	1	1	0	0	2
2014	2	1	0	0	3
2015	0	0	0	0	0
2016	0	0	0	0	0
2017	0	0	0	0	0
2018	2	4	0	0	6
2019	0	0	0	0	0
2020	1	2	0	0	3
2021	0	3	0	0	3
2022	1	3	0	0	4
Total	**11**	**16**	**0**	**0**	**27**

Source: Author calculation based on ACA Annual Reports from 2012 to 2022

undertakings: (i) provide incorrect, incomplete or misleading information in response to a Commission request, or do not provide the data within the deadline specified; (ii) provide incorrect, incomplete or misleading information in their notifications; (iii) produce the required books or other business records in incomplete form during inspections or refuse to submit the requested information; (iv) refuse to answer any questions on facts and provide inaccurate, incomplete or fraudulent answers or obstruct the inspections; (v) they break the seal put by the officials of the Authority and (vi) do not notify a concentration within the stipulated deadline. As shown in Table 6, for the period 2012–2022, the ACA has imposed 11 fines for procedural infringements of competition rules, mainly for: (i) the late notification; (ii) non-notification; (iii) obstructing the inspection; (iv) not providing data in the due time and (v) providing incorrect, incomplete or misleading information to the Commission. The total amount of fines imposed by ACA is ALL 8,336,369. The most common reason relates to non-notification or late notification of mergers.

Table 7 shows the total amount of fines imposed by ACA for substantive infringements of competition rules. For the period 2012–2022, the ACA has taken 16 decisions to fine companies for infringement of competition rules.[162] 10 decisions relate to the restrictive agreement; 5 decision are on the abuse of dominant position and one decision is undefined. According to Article 74 Competition Act, the Competition Commission may impose a fine not exceeding 10% of their aggregate turnover in the previous financial year for substantive infringement if the

[162] As will be explained in Sect. 7, judicial review takes too long due to ongoing reform. Moreover, it is impossible to calculate any successful appeals. Therefore, the number of fines does not reflect successful appeals.

Table 6 Fines imposed by ACA for procedural infringement of competition rules (Art 73)[a]

Year	Number of fines	Fines (in ALL)	Fines (in EUR)[b]
2012	4	964,000	6933.10
2013	1	100,000	712.95
2014	2	200,000	1428.60
2015	0	–	–
2016	0	–	–
2017	0	–	–
2018	2	1,471,200	11,529.55
2019	0	–	–
2020	2	5,601,169	45,263.84
2021	0	–	–
2022	0	–	–
Total	11	8,336,369	65,868.04

Source: Data compiled by the authors based on the ACA Annual Report 2012–2022

[a] All values are nominal values

[b] Calculation based on average exchange rate for the relevant year

Table 7 Fines imposed by ACA for substantive infringement of competition rules (Art 74)[a]

Year	Nr of fines per year	Fines (in ALL)	Fines (in EUR)[b]
2012	3	98,211,083	706,535.70
2013	1	6,079,561	43,361.68
2014	0	–	–
2015	0	–	–
2016	0	–	–
2017	0	–	–
2018	4	99,249,903	777,859.61
2019	0	–	–
2020	2	39,052,370	315,546.91
2021	3	6,500,000	53,086.92
2022	3	222,611,048	1,871,729.34
Total	16	471,703,965	3,767,120.16

Source: Data compiled by the authors based on the ACA Annual Report 2012–2022

[a] All values are nominal values

[b] Calculation based on average exchange rate for the relevant year

undertakings or associations of undertakings have: (i) infringed article 4 "restrictive agreement" or article 9 "abuse with dominant position"; (ii) contravened a decision ordering interim measures; (iii) failed to comply with a condition and obligation established by a decision pursuant to article 45, article 50 (2), articles 56, 57, and 60 (2); (iv) put into effect a concentration which results in competition restriction in the market and (v) put into effect a concentration prohibited by the Commission or do not take the necessary measures to restore the competition. The total amount of fines is almost ALL 472 million, or around EUR 3.77 million. The highest fine in terms of annual turnover was imposed in 2017 in the *EKMA* case with 9.99%.[163] Whereas in terms of amount, the largest fine until December 2022 was imposed by Decision No 874 of 25 March 2022 concerning the wholesale of DAP, Nitrate and Urea chemical fertilisers (restrictive agreement) with ALL 192,154,582.

In the Albanian Criminal Code,[164] there is a specific crime related to unfair competition through coercion. In 1995, when the Criminal Code was adopted, unfair competition through coercion was not a criminal act. In 2004, the Albanian Criminal Code was amended and included Article 170/b titled "Unfair Competition through Coercion". According to this provision, exercising competitive actions by means of threats or violence is punishable by imprisonment from one to four years.[165] In 2007, a second paragraph was added to Article 170b addressing only the actions that harm competition aim activities financed wholly or partly by the state or public entities. In this case, the prison sentence is increased by one-third.[166] Article 170b is part of the crimes committed in commercial companies. Its object is to protect free and effective competition in commercial matters against any action that constitutes physical or psychological violence. Therefore, only the case of unfair competition that includes elements of coercion are criminalized and penalized, while any violation of unfair competition remains punishable by the provisions of the Competition Act and is punished administratively by a fine. Despite the existence of a provision in the Criminal Code addressing the punishment of violations of competition law, there is no reported case on the application of Article 170/b of the Criminal Code. As shown in the figure, the sanctioning of competition violations is predominantly conducted through an administrative procedure under the jurisdiction of the ACA.

8 Judicial Review

The Competition Act provides the judicial review of the final decisions of the competition authorities. According to Article 79 of the Competition Act, the ACA's decisions can be appealed only before the Tirana District Court, which has the discretion to review both the establishment of the facts and the application of the law. The concentration of cases before one court was done to facilitate the training of judges and ensure that judges have sufficient expertise to deal with cases over the years. An appeal against the ACA's decision should be filed within 30 days from the date of notification of the decision. The appeal has a suspension effect on the

[163] The fine was appealed and still not a final decision has been taken.

[164] Law 7895/1995 Criminal Code in the Republic of Albania [1995] OJ 2 as last amended by Law 24/2021 [2021] OJ 87.

[165] Law 9275/2004 On Some Additions and Changes in Law No. 7895, Dated 27.1.1995, "Criminal Code of the Republic of Albania", as amended [2004] OJ 69.

[166] Law 9686/2007 On Some Additions and Changes in Law No. 7895, Dated 27.1.1995, "Criminal Code of the Republic of Albania", as amended [2007] OJ 27.

execution of the ACA's decision. The Tirana District Court has the power to: (i) uphold the decision of the ACA; (ii) annul it entirely or partially; and (iii) refer it back to the ACA. More specifically, the Tirana District Court may decide on the legality of the ACA decision wholly or partly, including the amount of the fine. The judgments of the Tirana District Court are subject to appeal before the Court of Appeals, whose judgments are subject to recourse to the High Court of Albania.

In May 2012, the Albanian Parliament adopted Law 49/2012 'on the Administrative Courts and Adjudication of Administrative Disputes'.[167] The Law 49/2012 was an important step in reforming the judicial system, ensuring legal review of administrative decisions by independent courts, increasing transparency and fighting corruption in the civil service. The Law 49/2012 was supposed to enter into force 15 days after publication in the Official Journal. However, its implementation was delayed pending the entry into force of the Law on the High Court.[168] As of November 2013, six administrative courts of the first instance, the Administrative Court of Appeal and the Administrative College of the High Court, were set up.

The adoption of Law 49/2012 affected the public enforcement of competition law. The Tirana District Court was replaced by the Administrative Court in Tirana, which is tasked to review ACA's decisions. The judgements of the Administrative Court of First Instance are subject to appeal before the Administrative Court of Appeals in Tirana,[169] whose judgements are subject of recourse to the High Court of Albania if: (i) there is an error in the application of material or procedural law that has a particular importance for the development of the judicial practice; (ii) the appealed decision is different from the practice of the Administrative College of the High Court or the United Colleges of the High Court;[170] (iii) there are serious violations of procedural norms that bring invalidity of the decision or the trial procedure.[171] The Court acts on the substance of the case, reviewing both the establishment of facts and the application of the law.[172] All antitrust cases pending before the District Court were transferred to the Administrative Court in Tirana, the Administrative Court of Appeals in Tirana, or the Administrative College of the High Court.

---

[167] Law 49/2012 on the Administrative Courts and Adjudication of Administrative Disputes [2012] OJ 53, Art 7. The Law 49/2012 has been amended three times and the last amendment was in 2021 (Law 49/2021). These amendments did not affect the provisions on division of administrative courts or competences.

[168] Commission (2013), p. 7.

[169] Law 49/2012, Art 10 (2).

[170] The High Court in Albania is structured in 3 Colleges, respectively, the Criminal College, Civil College and Administrative College. The latter has the jurisdiction to deal with administrative recourse from the Appeal Court. If there is a need to change the judicial practice of the High Court, upon a request of the Chairman of the High Court of one College, the High Court adjudicates through the United College of High Court. Law 98/2016 The Organisation of the Judicial Power in the Republic of Albania" [2016] OJ 209 as amended, Arts 31–33.

[171] Law 49/2012, Art 58.

[172] Law 49/2012, Art 35.

From 2005, when ACA became functional, until the end of 2022, about 86 ACA's decisions have been appealed at the district court and later to the administrative court of first instance or to the High Court.[173] An exact number of ACA decisions that have found judicial confirmation is difficult to calculate because cases are still in the process of review at one of the levels of the judiciary. For instance, as of 2013, out of 6 important ACA decisions for abuse of dominant position and prohibited agreements, the entire cycle of judicial review has been completed for only one case.[174] In many of the quashed decisions, ACA considered that judges have paid more attention to administrative and procedural law rather than to the substantive aspects of competition law. As observed by Broka and Nazifi, in many of the quashed decisions, the reasoning of the court was not clearly elaborated, neither "why a given practice had not constituted an anti-competitive behaviour, nor what would be the necessary evidence to prove the infringement".[175] In the ACA's view, the court's reasoning was not very clear to argue whether a given practice constituted anti-competitive behaviour or what would be the necessary evidence to prove the infringement.[176] In its 2012 Annual report, the ACA stated that:

> It is vital to the good functioning of the markets – which, in simpler words means increased consumer well-being - that the justice system absorbs and conveys the philosophy of competition protection in the fairest manner possible. Not only is the reasoning of decisions in the light of the protection of public interest a legal obligation under the law, but also, and above all, it is a moral duty since it affects the well-being of the citizens.[177]

Additionally, the ACA decisions are quashed at various court levels due to the lack of evidence to prove the existence of a cartel.[178] For instance, in 2012, the ACA fined eight insurance companies for restricting the market obligatory insurance. The insurance companies appealed the ACA decision to the Administrative Court of First Instance which confirmed the ACA decision. Again, the insurance companies successfully appealed to the Administrative Court of Appeal. In its reasoning, the Administrative Court of Appeal stated that:

> In its decision-making process, the Albanian Competition Authority failed to prove the existence of any agreement or concerted practice that infringes principles of free competition, as listed in Article 4 of Albanian Competition Law. Also, it was not possible to prove that by means of any agreement the companies have set the same prices.[179]

Similarly, the ACA decision to impose a fine on four undertakings for participation in the prohibited agreement was quashed due to insufficient evidence and procedural

[173] Authors calculation based on Albanian Competition Authority Annual Reports from 2005 to 2022. For the period 2014–2022, the authors have identified 56 cases.

[174] ACA (2013), pp. 32–33.

[175] Nazifi and Broka (2015), p. 137.

[176] ibid, p. 137.

[177] ACA (2012), p. 4.

[178] ACA (2020b); Broka (2013).

[179] ACA (2013), pp. 34–35.

issues.[180] In 2010, ACA imposed a fine on four undertakings for participation in the prohibited agreement. Two undertakings appealed the case to the Tirana Judicial District Court, which partly quashed the Competition Commission decision. In its reasoning, the Court argued that evidence presented by the Competition Commission "may create doubts about the possibility of the existence of the agreement but cannot create certainty in the existence of these alleged agreements".[181] Also, the court pointed out several problems with investigation procedures such as: (i) targeting only four undertakings; (ii) a limited time period; and (iii) not requesting relevant information from responsible institutions. Finally, the court stated that the Competition Commission had not respected the criteria stipulated in Article 75 of the Competition Act to calculate the fine.[182] The ACA appealed the decision to the Administrative Court of Appeal, which overturned the decision of the court of first instance of Administrative Court and upheld the Competition Commission decision.[183] Again, two undertakings appealed the decision to the Administrative College of the High Court. The Administrative College of the High Court quashed the decision of the Administrative Court of Appeal and confirmed the decision of the court of first instance of Administrative Court. It argued that the existence of a prohibited agreement in procurements between companies operating in the relevant market to prevent the participation of other subjects was not proven based on the evidence presented by the ACA. Moreover, the Administrative College of the High Court confirmed infringement during the investigation procedure and the way of setting the fine in relation to the alleged violation.[184]

In another case, the Tirana District Court annulled the ACA decision imposing a fine on two undertakings in the wheat import and flour production market.[185] On 22 January 2009, the ACA Secretariat inspected the premises of two undertakings. In the final report of in-depth investigation, the Secretariat concluded that these two undertakings: (i) contain full information on imports for each company; (ii) make joint purchase, but the custom declaration is under the name of one company; (iii) share customs expenses, transportation expenses and other expenses in the amount of 50% to 50%; (iv) keep accurate data on each other's bilateral obligations (receipts and debtor balances), the amount of grain purchased and customs clearance costs;

---

[180] ACA Decision No 154 of 1 October 2010 for the prohibition of the agreement between the companies "Classic" Sh.p.k., "Hyundai Auto Albania" Sh.p.k., "Noti" Sh.p.k. and "Ultra Motors" and imposing fines on them for restricting competition in the new vehicle procurement market [2010] Official Bulletin 6.

[181] Judgment of 17 April 2016, Administrative College of High Court of Albania, N 228 [2016], para 15 (1).

[182] Broka (2012b).

[183] Judgment of 10 December 2012, Court of Appeal of Tirana, N 2906 [2012]; Broka (2012c).

[184] Judgment of 17 April 2016, Administrative College of High Court of Albania, N 228 [2016], paras 21–38.

[185] Decision No 125 of 25 May 2009 imposing a fine on the companies "Atlas" Sh.a. and "Bloja" Sh.a. for restriction of competition in the wheat import market, the production and sale of flour for the production of bread [2009] Official Bulletin 5.

(v) own together 50.24% of the wheat import market, technology and high processing capacities, becoming a powerful factor limiting free and effective competition in the market.[186] Based on this evidence, the Competition Commission concluded that these undertakings have restricted and distorted the competition. Therefore, this agreement is prohibited and a fine is imposed on the two companies.

The ACA decision was appealed to the Tirana District Court. In its reasoning, the Tirana District Court concluded that the restriction and distortion of competition cannot be proved based on the evidence presented by the ACA. According to the court's decision:

> it is true that the two companies are companies with long experience in the field of trading flour and importing wheat and that they occupy a large weight in the trading of these products, as well it is true that only for a small amount of sale invoices, it turned out that the price was so close and in some cases similar, but this can never constitute a prohibited agreement between the parties.[187]

Moreover, the Court went on to argue that the data contained in the files does not match exactly. The Court stated that:

> Albanian Competition Authority's claim cannot be proved that electronic files found in the premises of companies had accurate and detailed information on joint prices, joint customs clearance, joint payment of VAT on import, etc. According to the documents received from the General Directorate of Customs, the content of those documents cannot prove the fact that these companies have cleared the same amount of wheat together or paid the customs duties on behalf of the other.[188]

Regarding the issue of lending quantities of grain between the companies to guarantee the continuous supply of the market, the court stated that "none of the provisions of the Albanian Competition law foresees the prohibition to exchange of products from one company to another with similar or even the same activity in the market".[189]

Whereas on the immediate price increase as a result of the development in the international market, the Court argued that:

> the increase in the prices of cereals in the world market would definitely have an immediate impact on the domestic market, since the plaintiff would have to buy again in the international market already with a higher price than before, quantity of grain thus fulfilling its contractual obligations with foreign suppliers.[190]

---

[186] Decision No 113 of 19 May 2009 on Prohibition of the agreement in the wheat import and flour production market between the companies "Atlas" Sh.a. and "Bloja" Sh.a. [2009] Official Bulletin 5.

[187] Quoted in ACA (2015), p. 42.

[188] ibid, p. 42.

[189] ibid, p. 42.

[190] ibid, p. 42.

In the end, the Tirana District Court annulled the ACA's decision. The Tirana District Court decision was appealed to the Appeal Court and High Court. Both the Appeal Court and the High Court confirmed the Tirana District Court's decision.[191]

Another challenge relates to the 2016 judiciary reform in Albania, which has affected the court proceedings. The dismissal of judges due to the vetting process has increased the backlog and the length of proceedings. Consequently, the ACA decisions are affected by judiciary reform and are still pending in various instances in courts.

Finally, training of lawyers and judges on competition law is very important. Recently, the (EU) competition law courses have been introduced in the curricula of public and law schools. The courses are taught in Albanian or English.[192] On the other hand, the School of Magistrates, which is responsible for preparing judges, provides a course in competition law, which was included in the commercial law module. The course was introduced very early in the curriculum, in 2001–2022. Whereas, in 2004, the competition law course was introduced in the continuous education program of the School of Magistrates. By reviewing the continuous education program of the School of Magistrates on the official website, the last training on competition law was given in May 2017. This training lasted for two days (16–17 May 2017). Recently, in November 2024, the ACA, in collaboration with UNCTAD and EBRD and supported by the School of Magistrates, organised a training module with foreign judges and international experts for Albanian judges.

9 Private Enforcement of Competition Law

Since the adoption of the first Competition Act in 1995, private enforcement of competition law has been possible. The Competition Act (1995) contained a specific provision on the possibility of individuals to seek damages caused by the infringement of competition rules.[193] Furthermore, the Competition Act (1995) stipulated the competent court to deal with the actions for damages. The district courts were empowered to deal with actions for damages. Other substantial and procedural rules of action for damages for infringement of competition rules is regulated by the: (i) the general rules of civil liability stipulated in the Civil Code[194] and (ii) the Code of Civil Procedure.[195]

---

[191] Broka (2012a).

[192] Broka (2022), pp. 99–102; Skara (2023).

[193] Competition Act (1995).

[194] Albanian Civil Code, Articles 608–647.

[195] Law 8116/1996 Code of Civil Procedure of Albanian Republic [1996] OJ 9 as last amended by Law 38/2017.

Currently, Part IV of the Competition Act contains 4 provisions, respectively Arts 65–68, concerning the possibility of private litigation for damages caused by the infringement of competition rules. The Competition Act regulates: (i) the material scope of the right to ask compensation for infringement of competition rules; (ii) standing to claim compensation; and (iii) the competent court. The material scope of the right to ask compensation for infringement of competition rules is foreseen in Article 65 (1) of the Competition Act. This Article reads as follows:

> 1. A person impeded in its activity, by a prohibited agreement as referred in Article 4 of this Law, or by an abusive practice as referred in Article 9 of this Law, may challenge this action in court and request:
>
> a) [...];
> b) reparation or compensation of damages caused by these practices, in accordance with relevant provisions of the Civil Code.

Article 65 (1) of the Competition Act determines that "a person impeded in its activity" shall be entitled to bring an action for damages for infringement of competition law. In line with the CJEU cases, standing to claim compensation shall have every person, be it a natural or legal person.[196] Concerning the possibility of indirect purchasers to claim compensation for an infringement of competition rules, the Albanian competition law remains silent. Also, the Competition Act does not explain the causal link between the unlawful act and damage. In this situation, the general rules of civil liability are applicable.[197] Furthermore, the Competition Act (Art 65) does not impose limitations on parties that can file a damages lawsuit.

The Competition Act stipulates the court's jurisdiction to deal with actions for damages for infringement of competition rules. Article 68 of the Competition Act provides the District Court of Tirana as a competent court to deal with competition rules including the actions for damages. In contrast to the Competition Act (1995), this provision (Art 68 of the Competition Act) avoids problems in choosing the competent court and at the same time, ensures better judicial performance.[198]

Other substantive and procedural rules concerning actions for damages for infringement of competition law are regulated by the provisions of the Civil Code and the Code of Civil Procedure. The limitation period, calculation of compensation, joint and several liability, and quantification of harm are regulated by the general rules of civil liability stipulated in the Civil Code. Disclosure of evidence is regulated by the provisions of the Code of Civil Procedure. Passing-on overcharge are not recognised in the Albanian legal system. Moreover, the Civil Code does not contain

[196] Judgement of 20 September 2001, *Courage Ltd v Bernard Crehan and Bernard Crehan v Courage Ltd and Others*, C-453/99, ECLI:EU:C:2001:465; Judgement of 13 July 2006, *Vincenzo Manfredi v Lloyd Adriatico Assicurazioni SpA and others, joined C-295/04 to C-298/04*, ECLI:EU: C:2006:461.

[197] Semini (2006), pp. 251–256; Skara (2021), p. 328.

[198] Nazifi and Broka (2015), pp. 138–139. Nazifi and Broka (2016).

any provisions on consensual dispute resolution or collective redress. Also, concerning the legal effects of the ACA decisions on subsequent damages, the Competition Act remains silent.

As Albania has an obligation to approximate domestic competition law in line with the EU competition *acquis* and ensure its proper implementation, on 26 June 2019, the ACA adopted a guideline to transpose the EU Damages Directive.[199] The Guideline on Damages reproduces literally the wording and the structure of the EU Damages Directive. It introduced a number of new substantive and procedural rules that were either absent in the Albanian legal system or not in compliance with the EU Damages Directive.

While the adoption of the Guideline on damages is welcomed to further the approximation process, in practice, it has no effect on civil actions for damages. Instead of proposing to amend the Competition Act, the ACA adopted a non-binding act which does not bind courts. If a case on action for damages for infringement of competition rules is submitted to the District Court of Tirana, the national judge will rely on the Competition Act and the general rules on civil liability as established by the Civil Code and the Code of Civil Procedure. Thus, despite the Guideline on damages adoption, still Competition Act, the Civil Code, and the Code of Civil Procedure will apply for action for damages.[200]

The private enforcement of competition rules has been possible since 1995. However, until now, no claim for action for damages has been filed in the Tirana District Court. Main reasons for this state of affairs are primarily the lack of competition culture of undertakings or consumers to claim compensation for infringement of competition rules. The second reason relates to the absence of a specific legal framework and collective redress mechanism in the Albanian legal system.[201] While ACA has found in several cases the abuse of dominant position in different sectors, no claim for damages was brought before the Tirana District Court.

The absence of a collective redress mechanism and lack of legal knowledge constitute an obstacle for injured persons to claim for damages for infringement of competition rules. In this context, the collective redress mechanism has to be introduced in the Albanian legal system.[202] Moreover, the ACA should raise awareness among individuals and businesses for the possibility of private enforcement of competition law as well as the consequences of their failure to react.[203]

[199] Guideline on the damages caused and actions for infringement of the provisions of Law no. 9121, dated 28.07.2003 "On Protection of Competition", as amended [2019] Guideline No 3 (hereafter cited as Guideline on damages).

[200] For more on the impact of EU law on private enforcement of competition rules see: Bogdani and Canco (2021); Skara (2021); Skara (2022), pp. 271–280.

[201] Bogdani and Canco (2021); Skara (2021); Skara (2022), pp. 268–271.

[202] The Albanian legal system does not recognize the collective redress. A draft law has been prepared by EDEN, Qendra për Nisma Ligjore Qytetare and CR Partners and endorsed by 70s other NGO. But still, the draft law has not been discussed in the Parliament. EDEN et al. (2023).

[203] Skara (2021), p. 329.

10 Current Trends and Future Challenges to Enforcing Competition Law

As Albania continues to pursue the EU membership, it needs to ensure that competition law is fully aligned with the EU competition *acquis* and effectively implemented. The 2010 amendment introduced more clarity and harmonised the Competition Act further with the EU competition *acquis*, and ACA has been very active in transposing EU secondary sources and Commission soft laws. In its 2023 progress report, the European Commission considered that "Albania's legislative framework is broadly in line with the EU acquis and the SAA. The Law on the Protection of Competition is largely aligned with Article 101 TFEU (restrictive agreements) and Article 102 TFEU (abuses of dominant position)".[204]

The main challenge for legal harmonization is introducing a competition law that is fully in line with the EU competition *acquis* and addresses the current development of EU competition law. Currently, the ACA has been very active in transposing EU secondary sources and Commission soft laws. However, harmonisation of public and private enforcement tools in line with the EU Damages Directive and ECN+ Directive is far from being completed. The transposition of these directives through a non-binding act of ACA does not have any legal effect. Proper transposition of these directives should increase the level of harmonisation of national competition law with the EU competition *acquis* and ensure effective implementation of competition rules.

The enforcement of the Competition Commission's decisions remains low and most importantly, the collection of fines. As discussed, most of the fines imposed by the ACA in the past have not yet been collected due to court proceedings delay or non-execution of the ACA's decision. Lack of enforcement of the Competition Commission's decisions puts into question the institution's credibility to ensure fair and effective competition.

The ACA has to play a more active role in the enforcement of competition rules. As discussed above, the ECN+ Directive has not been transposed properly. Transposition of the ECN+ Directive would ensure a greater guarantee for the ACA independence, and most importantly, the ACA will be equipped with a sufficient number of qualified staff as well as sufficient financial and technical resources necessary for the effective performance of their duties and the effective application of national competition rules.

The growth of digital platforms has created new challenges for national competition authorities. In this regard, the ACA lacks the necessary human, financial, and technical resources to deal with these kinds of cases. To the authors' best knowledge, the ACA has not taken any decision concerning competition in the digital markets. In two cases, the ACA has emphasised "the growth of online platforms and its impact on competition" but did not explore further how online platforms affect

[204] Commission (2023), p. 86.

competition.[205] In this context, an amendment of the current competition legislation is a first step. Additionally, the ACA staff needs to be equipped with the necessary skills and necessary financial resources to tackle tech companies that distort competition and apply proper competition rules for the digital market.

As Albania is a relatively small economy, it is necessary to raise awareness of competition policy among businesses and consumers. In several cases, undertakings have concluded an agreement between them for price increase and then have publicly announced in the media.[206] Such practice shows a low level of awareness of competition policy. The ACA, as a responsible institution to promote competition, needs to raise awareness of effective implementation of competition law and leniency rules by organising seminars, workshops or conferences with different stakeholders such as academia, students, business, individuals, lawyers or judges. The latter need to have the necessary knowledge and skills to apply correctly competition law provisions.

11 Conclusion

The development of competition law in Albania has been a response to internal needs and demands for safeguarding competition, underlining the country's strong commitment to a market-oriented economy. This determination to promote competitive market dynamics culminated in 2003 with the establishment of the independent competition authority, the ACA, which was granted substantial investigative and sanctioning powers. Inspired by the legal framework of the EU, Albania's path towards competition protection was and remains an internal imperative, enabled and reinforced by the prospect of EU accession.

Recognising competition as a catalyst for economic growth, innovation and equitable market opportunities, domestic stakeholders have strategically used the EU competition *acquis* to promote a culture of competition and ensure its effective enforcement. This harmonious alignment between national aspirations and EU legislation has not only strengthened Albania's commitment to a competitive market, but also underlined its harmonious integration into the wider European

[205] ACA Decision No 723 of 17 November 2020 for the closure, with clauses and obligation, of the in-depth investigation in the bank sector for Raiffeisen Bank, National Bank of Tirana, Credins Bank and Intesa SanPaolo Bank' [2020] Official Bulletin 16, para 57–58; ACA Decision No 779 of 4 March 2021 on monitoring the decision No 723 of 17 November 2020 for the closure, with clauses and obligation, of the in-depth investigation in the bank sector for Raiffeisen Bank, National Bank of Tirana, Credins Bank and Intesa SanPaolo Bank for the period 2019–2020 and giving some recommendation [2021] Official Bulletin 17, paras 6; 12; ACA Decision No 875 of 8 April 2022 on the Authorization of the Concentration realised through the Acquisition of the Mooney Group S.P.A. from the companies Banka 5 S.P.A. and Enel X S.R.L. [2022] Official Bulletin 18.

[206] ACA Decision No 57 of 01 October 2007 on the Abolishment of the Agreement in the Bread Production Market in Fier District [2008] Official Bulletin 2, 12; ACA Decision No 146 of 17 June 2010.

framework. Albania's forward-looking approach to competition law underlines its firm belief in the principles of competition as a cornerstone of economic development and prosperity. In summary, two decades after the adoption of the Competition Act, competition provisions have been, to a large extent, successfully aligned with the principles of the EU competition *acquis*.

Throughout its existence, the ACA has carried out extensive investigations and issued numerous decisions, demonstrating its active role in ensuring a competitive market. At the same time, its sanctioning and investigative powers did not lead to over-enforcement or over-regulation of the market. This is particularly noteworthy for transition economies, as it strikes a delicate balance between incentivising firms to invest and innovate, while avoiding increases in costs and uncertainty. In a broader context, the ACA has overcome major challenges and has become an indispensable institution for both businesses and consumers. Its key role has been recognised by the media and civil society. Given its relatively recent establishment, its commendable performance in the complex context of a transitional economy underlines its achievements. Nevertheless, strengthening institutional capacity and ensuring the availability of adequate financial and technical resources remain top priorities. Raising the quality of enforcement and decision-making to even higher standards and enabling private enforcement are now pressing challenges. In conclusion, the ACA's journey to date is a testament to its successful establishment, functioning and achievements, reflecting its key role in promoting competitive markets and safeguarding the interests of all stakeholders in Albania's evolving economic landscape.

Table of Cases

Albania

Judgement of 24 July 2009, Albanian Constitutional Court, V-24/09, [2009] OJ 119
Judgement of 11 January 2011, High Court, No 22, [2011] OJ Special Edition 125
Judgement of 17 January 2011, High Court, No 1, [2011] OJ 88-e
Judgement of 10 December 2012, Court of Appeal of Tirana, N 2906 [2012]
Judgement of 21 March 2014, Albanian Constitutional Court, V-14/14, [2014] OJ 50
Judgement of 17 April 2016, Administrative College of High Court of Albania, N 228 [2016]
Judgement of 2 July 2020, the Civil Chamber of the High Court, N 213, [2020]
Judgement of 8 July 2020, the Civil Chamber of the High Court, N 213, [2020]

Court of Justice of European Union

Judgement of 13 November 1975, *General Motors v Commission,* C-26/75, ECLI: EU:C:1975:150

Judgement of 16 December 1975, *Coöperatieve Vereniging "Suiker Unie" UA and others v Commission of the European Communities*, Joined cases 40-48/73, 50/73, 54-56/73, 111/73, 113/73 and 114/73, ECLI:EU:C:1975:174

Judgement of 14 February 1978, *United Brands v Commission*, C-27/76, ECLI:EU: C:1978:22

Judgement of 13 February 1979, *Hoffmann-La Roche v Commission*, C-85/76, ECLI:EU:C:1979:36

Judgement of 11 November 1986, *British Leyland v Commission*, C-226/84, ECLI: EU:C:1986:421

Judgement of 13 July 1989, *Lucazeau and Others v SACEM and Others*, Joined cases C-110/88, C- 241/88 and C-242/88, ECLI:EU:C:1989:326

Judgement of 3 July 1991, *AKZO Chemie BV v Commission of the European Communities*, C-62/86, ECLI:EU:C:1991:286

Judgement of 19 May 1993, *Paul CORBEAU*, C-320/91, ECLI:EU:C:1993:198

Judgement of 19 January 1994, *SAT Fluggesellschaft mbH v Eurocontrol*, C-364/92, ECLI:EU:C:1994:7

Judgement of 18 March 1997, *Cali v. Servizi ecologici porto di Genova SpA*, C-343/95, ECLI:EU:C:1997:160

Judgement of 20 September 2001, *Courage Ltd v Bernard Crehan and Bernard Crehan v Courage Ltd and Others*, C-453/99, ECLI:EU:C:2001:465

Judgement of 13 July 2006, *Vincenzo Manfredi v Lloyd Adriatico Assicurazioni SpA and others, joined C-295/04 to C-298/04*, ECLI:EU:C:2006:461

Judgement of 18 July 2006, *Meca-Medina and Majcen v Commission*, C-519/04 P, ECLI:EU:C:2006:492

Croatia

Case P. Z. Auto, the decision of the Constitutional Court of Croatia, 13 Feb 2008, U-III-1410/2007

Commission

Commission Decision of 20 September 2001, *Pirelli/Edizione/Olivetti/Telecom Italia*, Case COMP/M.2574

Commission Decision of 02 April 2003, *Newscorp / Telepiù*, COMP/M. 2876 Newscorp/Telepiù

Commission Decision of 23 July 2003, *Joint selling of the commercial rights of the UEFA Champions League*, COMP/C.2/37.398, OJ L 291/25

Commission Decision of 19 January 2005, *Joint selling of the media rights to the German Bundesliga*, COMP/C-2/37.214, OJ L 134/46

Commission Decision of 4 July 2005, *Lufthansa/Swiss*, COMP/M.3770

Commission Decision of 22 March 2006, *Joint selling of the media rights to the FA Premier League,* COMP/C- 2/38.173, OJ C 7
Commission Decision of 01 March 2010, *T-Mobile/ Orange*, COMP/M.5650
Commission Decision of 03 August 2012, *Vodafone/ Cable & Wireless*, COMP/ M.6584
Commission Decision of 20 September 2013, *Vodafone/ Kabel Deutschland*, COMP/M.6990
Commission Decision of 02 July 2014, *Vodafone/ ONO*, COMP/M.7231
Commission Decision of 19 May 2015, *ORANGE / JAZZTEL*, Case M.7421
Commission Decision of 04 February 2016, *Liberty Global/ BASE Belgium*, COMP/ M.7637
Commission Decision of 03 August 2016, *Vodafone/Liberty Global/Dutch JV*, COMP/M.7978
Commission Decision of 08 October 2018, *Tele2/ Com Hem Holding*, COMP/ M.8842
Commission Decision of 09 August 2018, *T-Mobile Austria/ UPC Austria*; COMP/ M.8808

Table of Legislation

Albania

Law 7491/1991 on Major Constitution Provision [1991] OJ Special edition
Law 7850/1994, On the Civil Code of the Republic of Albania [1994] OJ 11 as last amended by Law 113/2016 [2016] OJ 219
Law 8044/1995 for Competition [1995] OJ 27
Law 8116/1996 Code of Civil Procedure of Albanian Republic [1996] OJ 9 as last amended by Law 38/2017 [2017] OJ 98
Law 8417/1998 The Constitution of the Republic of Albania [1998] OJ 28 as last amended by Law 16/2022 (The Constitution of Albania)
Law 9121/2003 for Competition Protection [2003] OJ 71
Law 9275/2004 On Some Additions and Changes in Law No. 7895, Dated 27.1.1995, "Criminal Code of the Republic Of Albania", as amended [2004] OJ 69
Law 9374/2005 on State Aid [2005] OJ 36
Law 9499/2006 For some changes on the law no 9121 date 28. 07. 2003 for Competition Protection [2006] OJ 37
Law 9686/2007 On Some Additions and Changes in Law No. 7895, Dated 27.1.1995, "Criminal Code of the Republic of Albania", as amended [2007] OJ 27

Law 10 317/2010 For some additions and changes in the law no 9121 date 28. 07. 2003 for Competition Protection [2010] OJ 135
Law 49/2012 on the Administrative Courts and Adjudication of Administrative Disputes [2012] OJ 53
Law 98/2016 The Organisation of the Judicial Power in the Republic of Albania [2016] OJ 209

Bosnia

Competition Act of Bosnia and Herzegovina, Official Gazette of BiH, No. 48/05, 76/07 and 80/09

European Union

Treaty on the Functioning of the European Union (TFEU Consolidated version 2016) [2016] OJ C 202/1
Council Regulation (EC) No 1/2003 of 16 December 2002 on the implementation of the rules on competition laid down in Articles 81 and 82 of the Treaty (Text with EEA relevance) [2003] OJ L 1/1
Council Regulation (EC) No 139/2004 of 20 January 2004 on the control of concentrations between undertakings (the EC Merger Regulation) [2004] OJ L24/1
Commission Regulation (EC) No 773/2004 of 7 April 2004 relating to the conduct of proceedings by the Commission pursuant to Articles 81 and 82 of the EC Treaty [2004] L 123/18
Commission Regulation (EU) No 267/2010 of 24 March 2010 on the application of Article 101(3) of the Treaty on the Functioning of the European Union to certain categories of agreements, decisions and concerted practices in the insurance sector [2010] L 83/1
Commission Regulation 330/2010 of 20 April 2010 on the application of Article 101(3) of the Treaty on the Functioning of the European Union to categories of vertical agreements and concerted practices [2010] OJ L102/1
Commission Regulation (EU) 2022/720 of 10 May 2022 on the application of Article 101(3) of the Treaty on the Functioning of the European Union to categories of vertical agreements and concerted practices (Text with EEA relevance) [2022] OJ L 134/4
Council Directive 96/67/EC of 15 October 1996 on access to the ground handling market at Community airports [1996] L 272/36
Directive 2003/54/EC of the European Parliament and of the Council of 26 June 2003 concerning common rules for the internal market in electricity and repealing Directive 96/92/EC [2003] L 176/37

Directive 2014/104/EU of the European Parliament and of the Council of 26 November 2014 on certain rules governing actions for damages under national law for infringements of the competition law provisions of the Member States and of the European Union (Text with EEA relevance) [2014] OJ L 349/1

Interim Agreement on Trade and trade-related matters between the European Community, of the one part, and the Republic of Albania, of the other part [2006] OJ L 239

Stabilisation and Association Agreement between the European Communities and their Member States, of the one part, and the Republic of Albania, of the other part – Protocols – Declaration [2009] OJ L 107/166

References

ACA (2006) Annual Report 2006 and Main Goals for 2007. ACA. Tirana

ACA (2007) Annual Report 2007 and Main Goals for 2008. ACA. Tirana

ACA (2008) Annual Report 2008 and Main Goals for 2009. ACA. Tirana

ACA (2009) Annual Report 2009 and Main Goals for 2010. ACA. Tirana

ACA (2010) Annual Report 2010 and Main Goals for 2011. ACA. Tirana

ACA (2011) Annual Report 2011 and Main Goals for 2012. ACA. Tirana

ACA (2012) Annual Report 2012 and Main Goals for 2013. ACA. Tirana

ACA (2013) Annual Report 2013 and Main Goals for 2014. ACA. Tirana

ACA (2014) Annual Report 2014 and Main Goals for 2015. ACA. Tirana

ACA (2015) Annual Report 2015 and Main Goals for 2016. ACA. Tirana

ACA (2016) Annual Report 2016 and Main Goals for 2017. ACA. Tirana

ACA (2017) Annual Report 2017 and Main Goals for 2018. ACA. Tirana

ACA (2018) Annual Report 2018 and Main Goals for 2019. ACA. Tirana

ACA (2019) Annual Report 2019 and Main Goals for 2020. ACA. Tirana

ACA (2020a) Annual Report 2020 and Main Goals for 2021. ACA. Tirana

ACA (2020b) The Albanian Administrative Court of First Instance in Tirana ascertains the abuse of the dominant position by the national football federation *(Albanian Football Federation)*, [2020] e-Competitions, Art. N° 98146

ACA (2021) Annual Report 2021 and Main Goals for 2022. ACA. Tirana

ACA (2022) Annual Report 2022 and Main Goals for 2023. ACA. Tirana

ACA Decision No 113 of 19 May 2009 on Prohibition of the agreement in the wheat import and flour production market between the companies "Atlas" Sh.a. and "Bloja" Sh.a. [2009] Official Bulletin 5

ACA Decision No 116 of 29 May 2009 for exemption from the prohibition of the agreement between "Tirana International Airport" Sh.p.k. and "AIR BP Albania" Sh.a. for ensuring the storage and trading of aircraft fuel, as well as the aircraft supply service at the International Airport of Tirana "Nënë Tereza" [2009] Official Bulletin 5

ACA Decision No 121 of 10 September 2009 on de minimis agreements [2009] Official Bulletin 5

ACA Decision No 125 of 25 May 2009 imposing a fine on the companies "Atlas" Sh.a. and "Bloja" Sh.a. for restriction of competition in the wheat import market, the production and sale of flour for the production of bread' [2009] Official Bulletin 5

ACA Decision No 146 of 17 June 2010 on the closing of the preliminary investigation in the market of the production and sale of bread in Korca City [2010] Official Bulletin 6

ACA Decision No 154 of 1 October 2010 for the prohibition of the agreement between the companies "Classic" Sh.p.k., "Hyundai Auto Albania" Sh.p.k., "Noti" Sh.p.k. and "Ultra

Motors" and imposing fines on them for restricting competition in the new vehicle procurement market [2010] Official Bulletin 6
ACA Decision No 184 of 07 May 2011 on the opening of the preliminary investigation in the market of the production and sale of bread in Vlora City [2012] Official Bulletin 7
ACA Decision No 221 of 11 April 2012 on abusing the dominant position of the company "Romano Port" Sh.a. in the market of loading-unloading of liquefied petroleum gas by sea [2012] Official Bulletin 8
ACA Decision No 225 of 28 May 2012 on the exemption from the prohibition of the cooperation agreement between insurance market companies on the exchange of information for the service of the Border Motor Vehicle Policy for responsibilities towards third parties [2012] Official Bulletin 8
ACA Decision No 234 of 19 August 2012 on the approval of the Regulation on the block exemption of categories of vertical agreements and concerted practices [2012] Official Bulletin 8
ACA Decision No 239 of 26 July 2012 on imposing a fine on the company "Media Vizion" for the late notification of the realised concentration [2012] Official Bulletin 8
ACA Decision No 265 of 5 February 2013 On imposing a fine on the company Viloil Sh.a for the non-notification of the concentration realised through the acquisition of control of Viloil Sh.a through the transfer of 70% of the shares of the capital, from the company "City Investment Holding S.A", to the shareholders Mr Apostol Goçi and Mr Albano Aliko" [2013] Official Bulletin 9
ACA Decision No 290 of 23 July 2013 on imposing a fine on undertakings "Ferlut" Sh.a., "Tirana Lines" Sh.p.k., "Alba Trans" Sh.p.k., "Tirana Urban Trans" Sh.a. and "Parku i Transportit Urban të Udhëtarëve" Sh.p.k. for restricting the competition in the market of the sale of the general and student monthly tickets in the city road transport service in the city of Tirana [2013] Official Bulletin 9
ACA Decision No 318 of 2 June 2014 on imposing a fine on the company Heaney Assets Corporation for not providing data within the time limit defined in the Commission's Decision [2014] Official Bulletin 10
ACA Decision No 341 of 27 October 2014 on the imposition of a fine on the company "Pelikan" Sh. p.k. for late notification of the concentration carried out with CMA CGMA Agencies Worldwide for the creation of the independent company CMA CGMA Albania Sh.p.k. [2014] Official Bulletin 10
ACA Decision No 56 of 24 September 2007 on the abolishment of the agreements in the concrete production market in Tirana Region [2007] Official Bulletin 1
ACA Decision No 563 of 25 October 2018 on the approval of Regulation on Organization and Functioning of Competition Authority [2018] Official Bulletin 14
ACA Decision No 564 of 25 October 2018 on the opening of the preliminary investigation procedure against the Albanian Football Federation concerning the economic activity that develops [2018] Official Bulletin 14
ACA Decision No 57 of 01 October 2007 on the Abolishment of the Agreement in the Bread Production Market in Fier District, [2008] Official Bulletin 2
ACA Decision No 59 of 09 November 2007 on the Abuse of Dominant Position in the Mobile Telecommunication Market by Albanian Mobile Communication Sh.a. and Vodafone Albania Sh.a. [2008] Official Bulletin 2
ACA Decision No 67 of 24 December 2007 for individual fines against Mr. Kajo Hallka [2008] Official Bulletin 2
ACA Decision No 676 of 7 February 2020 on the authorisation with conditions and obligations of the concentration realised through the acquisition of control of ABCom Sh.p.k. by Vodafone Albania Sh.a. [2020] Official Bulletin 16
ACA Decision No 681 of 5 March 2020 on the authorisation of the concentration realised through the acquisition of control of the company RBM Assicurazione Salute S.p.A from the company Intesa Sanpaolo Vita S.p.A. [2020] Official Bulletin 16

ACA Decision No 693 of 14 May 2020 on the determination of the abuse of the dominant position of the Albanian Football Federation concerning the economic activity that develops and granting of conditions and obligations [2020] Official Bulletin 16

ACA Decision No 705 of 10 September 2020 on the authorisation of the concentration realised through the acquisition of control of the company Euroconsult Rental Division S.p.A by the company Intesa Sanpaolo S.p.A. [2020] Official Bulletin 16

ACA Decision No 723 of 17 November 2020 for the closure, with clauses and obligation, of the in-depth investigation in the bank sector for Raiffeisen Bank, National Bank of Tirana, Credins Bank and Intesa SanPaolo Bank' [2020] Official Bulletin 20

ACA Decision No 779 of 4 March 2021 on monitoring the decision No 723 of 17 November 2020 for the closure, with clauses and obligation, of the in-depth investigation in the bank sector for Raiffeisen Bank, National Bank of Tirana, Credins Bank and Intesa SanPaolo Bank for the period 2019-2020 and giving some recommendation [2021] Official Bulletin 17

ACA Decision No 82 of 23 June 2008 on the approval of the Guidelines on the notification in merger cases and respective annexes I and II attached [2008] Official Bulletin 3

ACA Decision No 874 of 25 March 2022 on the review of the Report "on the in-depth investigation in the import market and wholesale of DAP, Nitrate and Urea chemical fertilisers, to companies: "ARLI INTERNACIONAL" Sh.p.k., "AGRO BLEND" Sh.p.k., "MBM" Sh.p.k., "ECO-GREEN" Sh.p.k., "LILA" Sh.p.k., "AGRO-MENS" Sh.p.k., "ÇAÇA" Sh.p.k., "IAM" Sh.p.k., "AGROHELP-SA" Sh.p.k. and "BESNIKU" Sh.p.k. [2022] Official Bulletin 18

ACA Decision No 875 of 8 April 2022 on the Authorization of the Concentration realised through the Acquisition of the Mooney Group S.P.A. from the companies Banka 5 S.P.A. and Enel X S.R.L. [2022] Official Bulletin 18

ACA Decision No. 579 of 20 December 2018 for the initiation of the in-depth procedure in the assessment of the transaction between Piraeus Bank, as well as Balfin SHPK and Komercijalna Banka AD Skopje [2018] Official Bulletin 14

Albi A (2005) EU enlargement and the constitutions of Central and Eastern Europe. Cambridge University Press, Cambridge

Albi A (2007) Selected EU judgments by CEE Constitutional Courts: lessons on how (not) to amend constitutions. Croatian Yearb Eur Law Policy 3:39–58

Bogdani MP, Canco M (2021) Private enforcement of competition law: Albanian challenges in the reflection of EU requirement. SEE Law J 1(8):45

Broka P (2012a) The Tirana Court of Appeals upholds the District Court's judgement quashing the NCA decision concerning a concerted practice case in the markets for wheat import and production of flour *(Atlas / Bloja)*, [2012] e-Competitions, Art. N° 49031

Broka P (2012b) The Tirana District Court quashes the decision of the Albanian Competition Authority on bid rigging in the new cars public procurement (*Classic / Noti*), [2012] e-Competitions, Art. N° 50361

Broka P (2012c) The Tirana Court of Appeals confirms NCA decision that fined companies involved in bid rigging in a public procurement case *(Classic/Noti*), [2012], e-Competitions December, Art. N° 51797

Broka P (2013) The Tirana District Court quashes a decision of the Albanian Competition Authority on bid rigging in the security and guarding services public procurement *(Eurogjici)*, [2013] e-Competitions, Art. N° 58576

Broka P (2022) Albania. In: Aksamovic D, Simunovic L (eds) Defining challenges and obstacles to competition law enforcement in South and East European countries. Final Report. Available at https://jmcoe-competition.com.hr/wp-content/uploads/2022/12/Report.pdf. Accessed 16 Feb 2025

Commission guidelines on market analysis and the assessment of significant market power under the Community regulatory framework for electronic communications networks and services [2002] OJ C 165/6

Commission (2013) Albania 2013 Report. Communication. SWD(2013) 414 final

Commission (2016) Albanian 2016 Report. Communication. SWD(2016) 364 final

Commission (2020) Albanian 2020 Report. Communication. SWD(2020) 354 final
Commission (2021) Albanian 2021 Report. Communication. SWD(2021) 289 final
Commission (2022) Albanian 2022 Report. Communication. SWD(2022) 332 final
Commission (2023) Albania 2023 Report. Communication. SWD(2023) 690
Cremona M (2003) State aid control: substance and procedure in the Europe agreements and the stabilisation and association agreements. Eur Law J 9(3):265
Decision of Parliament 27/2021 For some changes in the Decision of the Parliament 43/17 For the Approval of the Structure and Organization of the Competition Authority [2021] OJ 39
EDEN et al (2023) Draft Law on Collective Redress. Available at: https://www.qag-al.org/publikime/padite_kolektive.pdf. Accessed 16 Feb 2025
Georgievski S et al (2014) Application of the law of the European Union in the Republic of Macedonia. In: Koevski G et al (eds) European Union Law Application by the National Courts of the EU Membership Aspirant Countries from South-East Europe. Centre for SEELS, Skopje
Goranson L, Volkai J (2003) Competition Law and Policy in South East Europe. OECD J Compet Law Policy 5(2):7–82
Guideline 'on the damages caused and actions for infringement of the provisions of Law no. 9121, dated 28.07.2003 "On Protection of Competition", as amended' [2019] Guideline No 3
Guidelines on the applicability of Article 101 of the Treaty on the Functioning of the European Union to horizontal co-operation agreements [2011] C 11/01
Guidelines on the assessment of non-horizontal mergers under the Council Regulation on the control of concentrations between undertakings [2008] OJ C 265/6
Guidelines on the method of setting fines imposed pursuant to Article 23(2)(a) of Regulation No 1/2003 [2006] OJ C 210/2
Kazani J (2015) Aspekte Ligjore të së Drejtës së Konkurrencës dhe Konkurrenca në Sistemin Elegtroenergjitik Shqiptar. PhD Thesis, University of Tirana
Këllezi P (2005) Das neue Wettbewerbsgesetz in Albanien. Monatshefte für Osteuropäisches Recht 6:415
Këllezi P (2009) Competition law in Albania. Concurrences N° 2-2009
Kühn Z (2005a) European law in the empires of mechanical Jurisprudence: the judicial application of European law in Central European candidate countries. Croat Yearb Eur Law Policy 1:55–73
Kühn Z (2005b) The application of European law in the new Member States: several (early) predictions. German Law J 6:563
Lang GI, Mataija M (2014) Application of EU law by Croatian Courts and relevant constitutional provisions. In: Koevski G et al (eds) European Union law application by the National Courts of the EU Membership Aspirant countries from South-East Europe. Centre for SEELS, Skopje
Memorandum of Partnership in the field of Competition Policy between the Albanian Competition Authority and the Hellenic Competition Commission (2021). Available at: https://caa.gov.al/wp-content/uploads/2023/05/MOU_ACA_HCC.pdf. Accessed 16 Feb 2025
Meškić Z, Samardžić D (2014) The application of EU law in Bosnia and Herzegovina. In: Koevski G et al (eds) European Union law application by the National Courts of the EU Membership Aspirant Countries from South-East Europe. Centre for SEELS, Skopje
Monitor (2023) Autoriteti i Konkurrencës në 2022 arriti të arkëtonte gjoba për herë të parë pas katër vitesh. Available at: https://www.monitor.al/autoriteti-i-konkurrences-ne-2022-arriti-te-arketonte-gjoba-per-here-te-pare-pas-kater-vitesh/. Accessed 16 Feb 2025
Muço M (1996) Economic transformation in Albania. Int Spect Ital J Int Aff 31(1):65
Nazifi E (2023) Përqëndrimet e Ndërmarrjeve: Kontrolli dhe Vlerësimi i tyre (Undertaking concentrations: their control and assessment). University of Tirana. PhD Thesis
Nazifi E, Broka P (2015) Review of ten years of Albanian competition law developments. Yearb Antitrust Regul Stud 8(11):129
Nazifi E, Broka P (2016) Grounds for private enforcement of Albania competition law. Yearb Antitrust Regul Stud 9(13):61

OECD Global Forum on Competition (2004) Challenges/Obstacles faced by Competition Authorities in Achieving Greater Economic Development through the Promotion of Competition: Contribution from Albania. Paris

Pashko G (1993) Obstacles to economic reform in Albania. Europe-Asia Stud 45(5):907

Pecotić Kaufman J, Malnar V (2016) The interaction between EU regulatory implants and the existing Croatian legal order in competition law. In: Kovač M, Vandenberghe AS (eds) Economic evidence in EU competition law. Intersentia Ltd

Semini MT (2006) E Drejta e Detyrimeve dhe e Kontratave: Pjesa e Përgjithshme. Skanderbeg Books, Tirana

Skara G (2021) The transposition of the antitrust damages directive in Albania as an EU candidate country. J Eur Compet Law Pract 12(4):326

Skara G (2022) Europeanisation of private enforcement of competition law: the case of Albania. Springer

Skara G (2023) International Competition Law. Available: https://eis.epoka.edu.al/curricula/syllabus/18566/1/122. Accessed 16 Feb 2025

Skara G, Hajdini B (2021) Enforcement of the European Union before the Albanian Constitutional Court and the High Court. J Lib Int Aff 7(3):229

Skenderi Dh (2023) Enforcement Record: Dawn Raids 2017-2022. 20th Anniversary of the Law on Competition Protection in Tirana, Albania

UNCTAD (2015) Voluntary peer review of competition law and policy: Albania. UN

Vukadinović DR et al (2014) Application of EU law by Serbian Courts pre-accession issues. In: Koevski G et al (eds) European Union law application by the National Courts of the EU Membership Aspirant countries from South-East Europe. Centre for SEELS, Skopje

Gentjan Skara is a Lecturer in EU Law and Competition Law at the Department of Law, Epoka University, Albania. Genti holds an LLB from the University of Tirana (Albania), an MA in European Studies from Epoka University (Albania) and an LLM in "South East European Law and European Integration" from the University of Graz. In 2020, Genti received a PhD from the University of Ferrara in "EU Law and National Legal Systems". A revised version of his thesis was published by Springer Nature as a monography titled "Europeanisation of Private Enforcement of Competition Law: The Case of Albania" in 2022. Additionally, Genti has been a visiting researcher at the Institute of Corporate and International Commercial Law, University of Graz (Austria), the Department of International Law, University of Ljubljana (Slovenia) and European Institute for Global Studies, University of Basel (Switzerland) and RECAS Fellow. From October 2012 until July 31, 2023, Genti was a full-time member of the Department of Law at "Bedër" University College, teaching International and EU law courses. As of 1 August 2023, Genti is a full-time lecturer of EU Law and competition law courses at Epoka University. Besides academic engagement, Genti is a National Legal expert for the "Internal Market and Competition" of EU acquis near the Ministry of European and Foreign Affairs, Republic of Albania and has provided its expertise to different organizations. His research interests relate to EU Law, competition law, the harmonization of laws, and the relations between law and technology.

Pranvera Këllezi is a Commissioner of the Swiss Federal Competition Commission and a business lawyer based in Geneva with over 20 years of experience advising companies on Swiss and European competition law, commercial law, data protection, corporate governance, and economic regulation. She studied Economics at the University of Tirana, holds a law degree (2000) and a PhD in Competition Law (2007) from the University of Geneva, an LL.M. in European Law from the College of Europe in Bruges (2004), and a Board Director Diploma from IMD, Lausanne. Dr. Këllezi teaches EU Internal Market Law at HE-ARC Neuchâtel and Law and Economics at the University of Neuchâtel. She is presently advising the Albanian government on state aid matters. Previously, she taught competition law at the School of Magistrates in Tirana (2002–2008) and played a key role in developing Albania's competition framework by advising on the drafting of the "Law on Protection of Competition" (2003) and the "Law on State Aid" (2006), as well as providing guidance to the Albanian Competition Authority during its formative years (2006–2009).

Bojana Hajdini is a distinguished academic and legal expert, currently serving as a Lecturer in Criminal and Public Law at the Department of Law, Epoka University. She brings extensive academic and institutional experience, having previously lectured at the Faculty of Law, University of Tirana, as well as at other higher education institutions in Albania. Her professional career includes high level positions in public administration, such as Head of the Legal Opponent Office at the Ministry of Justice, Advisor on Human Rights at the Cabinet of the Prime Minister, and State Advocate. Assoc. Prof. Hajdini has authored and co-authored numerous publications in national and international academic journals. Her main research interests include human rights, public and criminal law, legislative drafting, and the rule of law.

Competition Law and Policy in Bosnia and Herzegovina

Dijana Marković-Bajalović and Kanita Imamović-Čizmić

1 Introduction

Bosnia and Herzegovina (B&H) started developing competition laws in the first decade of the twenty-first century within the framework of the EU Stabilisation and Accession Process. By 2010, it adopted the Competition Act of B&H and a set of bylaws broadly harmonised with the EU competition *acquis* and established a body responsible for enforcing competition law—the Competition Council of B&H—CC (*Konkurencijsko vijeće BiH/Konkurencijski savjet BiH*).[1] The complexity of the state structure of Bosnia and Herzegovina and its political controversies affected the development of competition law and the further harmonisation with EU law. Nevertheless, competition law has established its roots in B&H. The necessity of pursuing an effective competition policy has never been disputed by businesspeople, academics, legal professionals and common citizens. The research on competition law and policy in Bosnia and Herzegovina aims to describe the present competition protection model and to point out its main deficiencies and obstacles to further strengthening the competition policy in B&H.

After this introduction, Sect. 2 provides the historical outline of the B&H statehood and market economy development as the basic prerequisites for creating competition law. Section 3 outlines B&H's relationship with the EU and the consequences for the national competition law system. Section 4 analyses the

[1] The website of the Competition Council is available at https://bihkonk.gov.ba/en/home/.

D. Marković-Bajalović (✉)
Union University, School of Law, Belgrade, Serbia
e-mail: dijana.markovicbajalovic@pravnifakultet.edu.rs

K. Imamović-Čizmić
University of Sarajevo, School of Law, Sarajevo, Bosnia and Herzegovina
e-mail: k.imamovic-cizmic@pfsa.unsa.ba

J. Pecotić Kaufman et al. (eds.), *Competition Law and Policy in the Western Balkans*, European Union and its Neighbours in a Globalized World 22,
https://doi.org/10.1007/978-3-031-93756-9_3

normative and institutional foundations of competition law in B&H by focusing on principal inconsistencies with EU law and deficiencies in institutional structure and procedural setup that prevent effective investigations and decision-making. Section 5 describes national specifics that differ from the EU competition *acquis*. Section 6 analyses the recent landmark cases decided by the Competition Council, followed by the enforcement and sanctioning statistics in Sect. 7. Section 8 analyses the Court of B&H's practice in deciding on the legality of the Competition Council's decisions, followed by a discussion on the regulatory framework of the private enforcement of competition law in Sect. 9. Section 10 outlines the criminal enforcement of competition law. Section 11 enumerates principal challenges for the future.

2 Historical Development of Competition Law in Bosnia and Herzegovina

The end of World War II (WWII) marked the establishment of a socialist Yugoslavia.[2] Postwar Yugoslavia became a federative state, with Bosnia and Herzegovina as one of its constituent republics. Yugoslavia pursued the planned state economy in the first decades after WWII, leaving no room for restrictive business practices. Starting from the 1950s, state intervention in the economy slowly loosened. As of 1953, workers became joint proprietors of companies and enjoyed self-management rights, while companies competed in the Yugoslav internal market. Goods, services and workers circulated freely between the constituent republics. Legislative competencies for regulating the economy resided with the federal state.

The 1963 Constitution of the Socialist Federative Republic of Yugoslavia declared the prohibition of monopolistic alliances as one of its principles.[3] In 1967, the federal legislator passed the Law on Trade in Goods,[4] which prohibited anti-competitive practices. In 1963, the Supreme Economic Court sanctioned an agreement concluded between a producer and a trader, obliging the producer to supply the trader exclusively. The court found this agreement to be a practice aimed at gaining a preferential position in the market.[5]

In 1974, the Yugoslav legislator enacted the Law on Suppressing Unfair Competition and Monopolistic Agreements.[6] The Law defined monopolistic agreements

[2]The full name of the state was the Federative People's Republic of Yugoslavia in the period 1946–1963 and the Socialist Federative Republic of Yugoslavia in the period 1963–1992.

[3]Constitution of the Socialist Federative Republic of Yugoslavia [1963] Basic provisions, para. II.

[4]Law on Trade in Goods [1967] Official Gazette of SFRY, No 1/1967.

[5]Supreme Economic Court, Pkž-23/65, 31.05.1965.

[6]Law on Suppressing Unfair Competition and Monopolistic Agreements [1974] Official Gazette of SFRY, No 24/1974.

as agreements between two or more business organisations[7] on business terms, aiming to restrict or prevent free competition, by which one or more business organisations achieve or may achieve a monopolistic or privileged position in the market in relation to other business organisations or consumers.[8] The Law broadened the definition of monopolistic agreements to include agreements concluded in any form and tacit agreements. The prosecution of tacit agreements depended on the possibility of proving the prohibited result—a monopolistic or privileged position of one or more business organisations.[9] The Law equated abuse of monopolistic or privileged placement in the market with monopolistic agreements regarding their negative consequences and sanctions.[10]

The Law did not distinguish between horizontal and vertical agreements. Exclusive agreements between producers and sellers in wholesale and retail were prohibited. In the 1974 case, the Supreme Economic Court stated that an agreement obliging one party not to sell products of other producers was contrary to good business usage and principles of healthy competition in the trade of goods.[11] Agreements between domestic and foreign companies were excluded from the prohibition.[12] Yugoslav companies could make exclusive agreements to export and import goods and services.[13]

The 1974 Law determined practices that constituted the abuse of monopoly or privileged position in the market—refusal to sell and selling or buying goods and services under conditions and in a manner that represented an abuse of privileges resulting from being the only or prevailing seller or buyer.[14] It is worth noting that this prohibition captured only legal and natural monopolies.[15] The legislator did not recognise the possibility of creating a monopoly (or a privileged market position) by beating up other competitors in healthy competition. Civil courts declared monopolistic agreements null and void.[16] The victims could sue for damages and require the court to prohibit further exploiting the monopolistic position.[17] Violators of the Law had to pay fines for economic offences.[18]

The true effects of the 1974 Law were minor. One reason was that it provided two important exceptions. Firstly, business organisations from the same industry could

[7]The exact term used in the law was "associated labour organisation" (*organizacija udruženog rada*). It represented a form of company that existed in socialist Yugoslavia.

[8]Law on Suppressing Unfair Competition and Monopolistic Agreements (1974), Art 3 (1).

[9]ibid, Art 3 (3).

[10]ibid, Art. 3 (3).

[11]Supreme Economic Court, Pkž-22/64, 14.09.1974.

[12]Law on Suppressing Unfair Competition and Monopolistic Agreements (1974), Art 10.

[13]Biro (1976), pp. 74–75.

[14]Law on Suppressing Unfair Competition and Monopolistic Agreements (1974), Art 11.

[15]ibid, Art 4.

[16]ibid, Art 12.

[17]ibid, Art 13 (3).

[18]ibid, Art 24.

enter into agreements within the Yugoslav Chamber of Commerce on fair behaviour in the internal and foreign markets and on the development of healthy competition.[19] The legal writers explained that competition conditions differed in various economic branches, necessitating agreements between enterprises on healthy competition in the same industry. For example, an agreement to lower prices in internal trade was considered fair. The same deal in foreign trade was contrary to the public interest. Biro gave examples of natural and legal monopolies: a monopoly of a mining company controlling the only mine in a country or local monopolies of companies providing communal services.[20] Secondly, monopolistic agreements based on law or regulation were not prohibited.[21]

The second, much more important reason for minor importance of competition legislation was that in the 1970s and 1980s, Yugoslavia replaced state planning with the so-called "agreed economy." Business organisations were forced by law to divide into smaller structures. Through "self-management agreements," they agreed about production and trade, income distribution, and other economic and social aspects. Within such a framework, the prosecution of anti-competitive agreements became obsolete.

In the second half of the 1980s, before the dissolution of Yugoslavia, the socialist Yugoslav government initiated the economy's transition. Among other legislative actions aiming to set a basis for the shift from socialist toward a market economy, the Yugoslav legislator amended the 1974 Law in 1986 by introducing norms concerning abuse of dominant position and clarifying the status of "self-management agreements".[22] The legislator widened the scope of articles dealing with monopolistic agreements to include "self-management agreements". The constitutionality of one of the amended provisions was disputed before the Constitutional Court. A business association contested the 1986 Amendments declaring recommendations on prices and participation of business associations in setting prices as a category of monopolistic agreements. The Constitutional Court rejected the petition acknowledging the legislator's right to define the scope of monopolistic arrangements.[23] However, the line dividing the prohibition of monopolistic agreements and the permissibility of "self-management arrangements" remained blurred even after the 1986 Amendments.[24]

---

[19] Article 7 of the Law on Suppressing Unfair Competition and Monopolistic Agreements [1974].

[20] Biro (1976), p. 22.

[21] Article 9 para 2 of the Law on Suppressing Unfair Competition and Monopolistic Agreements [1974].

[22] Law Amending and Supplementing the Law on Suppressing Unfair Competition and Monopolistic Agreements [1986], Official Gazette of SFRY, No 72/1986.

[23] Decision of the Constitutional Court of Yugoslavia, 8.06.1988, Official Gazette of SFRY, No 51/1988.

[24] Varadi (1999), p. 237.

On the wave of economic reforms, the Yugoslav legislator adopted the Law on Trade in 1990.[25] The 1990 Law declared the free trade principle and prohibited illegal trade restrictions.[26] It prohibited unfair competition—an act of a trader contrary to business ethics and good business usage that causes or might cause damage to another trader, i.e. a competitor.[27]

Following the dissolution of SFRY, the former Yugoslav republics became independent states. The Assembly of the Republic of Bosnia and Herzegovina declared B&H independence in 1992, following the referendum held on 1 March 1992. The referendum results were not recognised by the B&H citizens of Serbian nationality, who abstained from it. In April 1992, the war in the territory of B&H started, and it ended almost four years later, in 1995, by signing the General Framework Agreement for Peace in Bosnia and Herzegovina on 14 December 1995 (Dayton Agreement).[28] Annex 4 of the Dayton Agreement comprised the Constitution of Bosnia and Herzegovina. The Constitution established two B&H entities: the Federation of B&H (FB&H) and the Republic of Srpska (RS). In the Dayton Agreement's aftermath in 1997, the international arbitration settled the status of the contested Brčko district.[29]

Annex 10 of the Dayton Agreement provided for the institution of the Office of the High Representative (OHR) in Bosnia and Herzegovina to oversee the civilian implementation of the agreement, representing the countries involved in the Dayton Agreement through the Peace Implementation Council (PIC). In 1997, the PIC granted further substantial powers to the OHR to avoid delay and obstruction in implementing the Dayton Agreement. Under so-called Bonn authorities, the OHR can adopt binding decisions when local parties seem unable or unwilling to act and remove from office public officials who violate the Dayton Agreement and legal commitments in general. The OHR used Bonn authorities to create a separate Brčko District in 2000[30] and to adopt several important laws.

The two B&H entities passed trade laws in the second half of the 1990s that defined monopolistic agreements similarly to the ex-Yugoslav Law on Trade from 1990. Under the FB&H and RS Laws on Trade, monopolist agreements represented "the relationship between traders aiming at distortion or prevention of free competition, which brings or might bring one or more traders into an advantageous position in relation to other traders or consumers".[31]

[25] Law on Trade [1990] Official Gazette of SFRY, No 40/1990.

[26] ibid, Art 4.

[27] ibid, Art 50.

[28] General Framework Agreement for Peace in Bosnia and Herzegovina (1995).

[29] Brcko Arbitral Tribunal for Dispute Over the Inter-Entity Boundary in Brcko Area Award (1997).

[30] High Representative's Decision on the Establishment of the Brcko District of Bosnia and Herzegovina (2000).

[31] Article 42 para 2 FBIH Law on Trade [1995], Official Gazette of FBiH, No 2/95, 19/96, 14/97; Article 36 RS Law on Trade [1996], Official Gazette of RS No 16/96, 52/01.

Article I.4 of the B&H Constitution set the ground for the unified internal market in Bosnia and Herzegovina:

> Freedom of movement exists throughout Bosnia and Herzegovina. Bosnia and Herzegovina and entities will not disturb the full freedom of movement of persons, goods, services and capital throughout Bosnia and Herzegovina. No entity will conduct any control on the border between entities.

Article III.1 of the Constitution did not include competition law when enumerating the state legislative competencies. Based on Article III.3 of the Constitution, the legislative competence presumption goes to the Bosnia and Herzegovina entities: "All governmental functions and authorities that are not explicitly entrusted to Bosnia and Herzegovina institutions by this Constitution belong to entities." Strictly construing this provision would mean the competence to enact competition laws belonged to entities.

Despite rigid stipulations in Article III.3, the state legislator considered competition law necessary to create and maintain the internal market in Bosnia and Herzegovina by referring to the theory of implicit state powers and international obligations of B&H.[32] The B&H Parliament adopted the Competition Act in 2001.[33] It was soon realised that the 2001 Act needed to be harmonised with the EU competition *acquis*. The most important deficiencies of the Competition Act 2001 included sharing enforcement powers between the state and entity institutions, the limited regulation of anti-competitive activities, and the complete absence of sanctioning provisions. Besides, the Competition Act 2001 listed the possibility of block exemption of anti-competitive agreements and other categories of market activities from the prohibition, including abuses of dominant position and concentrations. It did not regulate individual exemptions and *de minimis* agreements.[34] In parallel to the 2001 Act, the trade laws of the two B&H entities remained in force.

3 Relationship of Bosnia and Herzegovina Competition Act with the EU Law

The Stabilisation and Association Process (SAP) started in 1999, aiming to integrate Western Balkans (WB) countries including Bosnia and Herzegovina. The SAP is based on four pillars: bilateral Stabilisation and Association Agreements (SAA), autonomous trade measures, financial assistance procured through the Instruments of Pre-Accession (IPA), and regional cooperation. At the Thessaloniki Summit held in 2003, the European Council confirmed the SAP as the EU policy towards the WB countries. In 2008, the EU Member States and Bosnia and Herzegovina concluded

[32] Trifković (2006), p. 68; Hasić (2010), p. 27; Ćatić (2019), p. 292.

[33] Competition Act [2001] Official Gazette of BiH, No 30/01.

[34] Trifković (2006), pp. 70–71.

the SAA.[35] All EU Member States ratified SAA by 2011. Despite ratification, SAA entering into force was delayed due to the failure of B&H to comply with the 2009 decision of the European Court for Human Rights (ECtHR) in the *Sejdić-Finci* case.[36] The EU made compliance with *Sejdić-Finci's* decision an additional condition for the SAA implementation.[37] The SAA entered into force on 1 June 2015,[38] after the presidency of Bosnia and Herzegovina committed to undertaking necessary reforms. The Presidency commitment was reaffirmed by signatures of the representatives of fourteen political parties.

Bosnia and Herzegovina applied to join the EU in February 2016. The European Commission assessed the country's preparedness for EU membership in the 2019 Analytical Report accompanying the Commission's Opinion on the B&H application. In the competition policy area, the Commission called B&H to align its legislative framework with the EU *acquis* further and improve procedural provisions and the decision-making body's election process.[39] In the meantime, the Commission has noted no progress in the competition law enforcement field.[40] Bosnia and Herzegovina took no steps to remove ethnic-based decision-making procedures and vetoes from the Competition Council. Besides, the Commission observed that Bosnia and Herzegovina should further align its implementing legislation on competition and state aid with the EU *acquis*.

---

[35] Stabilisation and Association Agreement between the European Communities and their Member States, of the one part, and Bosnia and Herzegovina, of the other part [2015] OJ L 164.

[36] *Sejdić and Finci v. Bosnia and Herzegovina*, European Court of Human Rights, Judgment of 22 December 2009, Applications Nos. 27796/06 and 34836/06.

[37] The *Sejdić-Finci* case concerned two B&H citizens of Roma and Jewish ethnicity who could not stand for election to the Presidency and the House of People of the Parliamentary Assembly because of their ethnicity. The B&H Constitution provided for a complex multi-level state structure based on power-sharing mechanisms. It identified three "constituent peoples" entitled to share power in each level of government - namely Serbs, Croats, and Bosniaks. The constitutional provisions on three constituent peoples effectively prevent members of ethnic minorities and members of constituent peoples living in areas of the country dominated by two other constituent peoples from standing for election or being appointed as officials in state and lower-level institutions and bodies. ECtHR found that while the urgent need to restore peace at the time of the Dayton Agreement could explain the absence of representatives of other ethnicities at the peace negotiations, the maintenance of this system no longer satisfied the proportionality requirement. The court ordered the country to revise its Constitution by removing the discriminatory provisions. B&H has failed to implement the *Sejdić-Finci* decision for more than a decade after the ECtHR ruling. The disagreement of the ruling political parties on constitutional and electoral reforms is the principal reason for the country's omission to comply with the decision. OHR intervened shortly before the elections held on 2 October 2022 by imposing electoral standards and amending the FB&H Constitution to address functionality issues and the timely formation of FB&H authorities.

[38] Meanwhile, the European Community and B&H implemented the Interim Agreement on trade and trade-related issues. Interim Agreement on trade and trade-related issues between the European Community of the one part, and Bosnia and Herzegovina, of the other part [2008] OJ L 169/3.

[39] Commission (2019), p. 102.

[40] Commission (2022).

In December 2022, the European Council granted candidate status to Bosnia and Herzegovina. Although B&H did not fulfil all required criteria, the EU leaders wanted to facilitate necessary reforms in B&H to accelerate the accession process.[41] The European Council made the country's candidate status conditional upon it taking the recommended steps to strengthen the rule of law, the fight against corruption and organised crime, migration management, and the protection of fundamental rights.

The SAA sets out a general obligation for B&H to harmonise its legislation with EU law and to effectively implement it. Under Article 70(1) SAA, B&H shall endeavour to ensure that its existing laws and future legislation are gradually made compatible with the EU *acquis*. BiH shall ensure that existing and future legislation will be properly implemented and enforced.

The SAA lays down specific provisions on competition in Article 71, covering anti-competitive agreements, abuses of dominant position and state aid. It also includes the obligation to apply competition rules to public undertakings and undertakings with special and exclusive rights. B&H must establish operationally independent authorities to supervise the application of the competition rules. Article 71 para 1 SAA reads as follows:

> The following are incompatible with the proper functioning of this Agreement, insofar as they may affect trade between the Community and Bosnia and Herzegovina:
>
> a) all agreements between undertakings, decisions by associations of undertakings and concerted practices between undertakings which have as their object or effect the prevention, restriction or distortion of competition;
> b) abuse by one or more undertakings of a dominant position in the territories of the Community or of Bosnia and Herzegovina as a whole or in a substantial part thereof;
> c) any State aid which distorts or threatens to distort competition by favouring certain undertakings or certain products.

Anti-competitive practices defined in Article 71(1) SAA must be assessed under the criteria arising from applying the EU competition rules (Articles 101, 102, 106 and 107 TFEU) and interpretative instruments adopted by EU institutions. It is *communis opinio* within B&H's legal scholars' community that Article 71 SAA obliges B&H competition authorities to implement EU case law if an anti-competitive practice affects trade between B&H and EU.[42] The CC can follow EU case law in substantive aspects of competition law enforcement. Competition Act explicitly provides this power of the CC: "The Competition Council, for assessment of a given case, can use the case law of the European Court of Justice and the decisions of the European Commission."[43]

The CC occasionally refers to the EU case law to support its decision-making. For example, in the alleged abuse of dominance case in the retail telecom market,[44] the

[41] Popović (2023).

[42] Morait (2014).

[43] Competition Act [2005], Art 43 (7).

[44] Competition Council, *Telekom BiH v. MTEL, Logosoft, Blicnet, Telrad & Elta Kabel*, UP 04-26-2-014-84/21, 4.04.2022.

CC referred to *United Brands* when discussing the expert witness finding that the defendant charged unfair/excessive prices. The CC rejected the expert witness analysis since it did not use a cost-price ratio test to establish excessive prices, contrary to the methodology that CJEU endorsed in *United Brands*.[45] The powers of the CC to refer to EU case law have yet to raise constitutionality issues. The parties in the proceedings often invoke EU case law. The Court of B&H accepted the reference to EU case law as valid. For example, the Court of B&H referred to *Gencor*,[46] when discussing the issue of admissibility of third parties' submissions in merger control proceedings before the CC.[47]

4 Institutional and Normative Framework of Competition Authority in Bosnia and Herzegovina

The legislative and enforcement mandate regarding competition policy rests entirely with the state institutions of Bosnia and Herzegovina. The B&H Parliament adopted the new Competition Act in 2005[48] to eliminate its predecessor's drawbacks and establish the Competition Council as the sole competition law enforcer throughout B&H. The 2005 Act was amended in 2007[49] and 2009.[50]

4.1 Competition Council

Competition Act defines the Competition Council—CC (*Konkurencijsko vijeće/ Konkurencijski savjet*) as an independent body which should ensure the consistent application of the Act on the entire territory of Bosnia and Herzegovina, having exclusive competence to decide on the existence of prohibited anti-competitive acts.[51] The CC is a legal person with a seat in Sarajevo, the capital city of Bosnia and Herzegovina.

Since the CC is formed at the level of the state of Bosnia and Herzegovina, it is subject to laws that apply to institutions and bodies of Bosnia and Herzegovina. Pursuant to the Law on Ministries and Other Administrative Bodies of Bosnia and

[45] *United Brands v. Commission*, para. 251–252.

[46] *Gencor Ltd v. Commission*, T-102/96.

[47] *Telemach v. Competition Council of B&H*, S1 3 U 038507 21 Uvp, 23.02.2022.

[48] Competition Act [2005] Official Gazette of B&H, No 48/05.

[49] Official Gazette of B&H, No 76/07.

[50] Official Gazette of B&H, No 80/09.

[51] Competition Act [2005], Art 21.

Herzegovina[52] and the Decision on annual work planning and the method of monitoring and reporting in the institutions of Bosnia and Herzegovina,[53] the CC is obliged to adopt an annual work plan. The work plan principally concerns the CC's realisation of obligations *vis-a-vis* the Council of Ministers and other B&H institutions. It enumerates legislation to be drafted and submitted to competent institutions for endorsement, strategic and planning documents and reports to be prepared, activities related to SAA and Competition Act implementation, as well as administrative and professional activities to be performed. The work plan merely specifies the type of activity and the implementation timespan. It does not identify policy objectives and principal economic sectors to be investigated. The annual work plan is made publicly available before its adoption and is open to comments through e-consultations. Each annual work plan must be harmonised with the Medium-Term Work Plan, adopted for three years. The CC submits work reports to the Parliamentary Assembly of B&H. The annual work report is made publicly available before adoption and is open to comments through e-consultations.

The term "Competition Council" denotes, at the same time, the institution itself and its decision-making body. The Competition Council, as a decision-making body, consists of six counsellors. The B&H Council of Ministers appoints three counsellors, one each from among three constituent peoples. The Federation of Bosnia and Herzegovina Government appoints two CC members, while the Republic of Srpska Government appoints one CC member. Competition Act does not require the respective governments to select CC counsellors from amongst the three constituent peoples. However, the FB&H Government has regularly appointed one Bosniak and one Croat, while the RS Government has appointed a Serb. The chairmanship of the Competition Council rotates among the counsellors. The B&H Council of Ministers appoints the Chairman/Chairwoman annually upon the CC's proposal.[54]

The CC's internal structure is fairly simple. The CC Technical Service, consisting of professional staff, is responsible for conducting investigations and other administrative matters[55] and is subordinated to the Competition Council. The Technical Service Head is accountable to the CC Chairman.[56] The CC has two branches in the Federation of Bosnia and Herzegovina (Mostar) and the Republic of Srpska (Banja Luka).[57] Branch offices do not have separate investigating and decision-making powers. Investigating officers sitting in branch offices investigate cases related to

[52] Law on Ministries and Other Administrative Bodies of Bosnia and Herzegovina [2003] Official Gazette of B&H, No 5/03, 42/03, 26/04, 42/04, 45/06, 88/07, 35/09, 59/09, 103/09, 87/12, 6/13, 19/16 and 83/17.

[53] Decision on annual work planning and the method of monitoring and reporting in the institutions of Bosnia and Herzegovina [2014], Official Gazette of B&H, No 94/14.

[54] Competition Act, Art 22(4).

[55] Rulebook on Internal Organisation of the Competition Council of Bosnia and Herzegovina (2020), Art 5.

[56] Competition Act, Art 9 (4).

[57] Competition Act, Art 20 (2).

geographic markets in the vicinity of the branch office. Heads of branch offices report to the CC Chairman.[58]

The CC members participate in decision-making on competition cases. The CC assigns each case to one of its members—a rapporteur,[59] who manages the investigation and prepares a draft decision together with a case handler.[60]

4.2 *Principal Substantive Provisions of the Competition Act*

The Competition Act regulates "prohibited competition activities",[61] that is, agreements having as their object *and* effect preventing, restricting or distorting market competition,[62] abuse of dominant position,[63] and the concentrations of economic entities resulting in a significant distortion of efficient market competition in the entire B&H territory or its significant part.[64]

4.2.1 Sphere of Application

Competition Act applies to all natural and legal persons who, summarily regarded as "economic entities" or undertakings, are directly or indirectly engaged in the production and sale of goods and services, involved in the trade of goods and services and who, with their actions, can prevent, restrict or distort competition in the entire territory of Bosnia and Herzegovina or a significant part of the market.[65] In the past, the CC interpreted this provision widely to comprise acts of state authorities and public bodies, which limited competition in the execution of state powers. The construction derived from the grammatical interpretation of Article (1)(b), specifying the application of the Competition Act to bodies of state administration and local self-government "when directly or indirectly participating in *or influencing* the market". The CC considered that state and local authorities influence the market when they issue legal acts with provisions restricting competition.[66] In recent years,

---

[58] Rulebook on Internal Organisation of the Competition Council of Bosnia and Herzegovina (2020), Art 9 (4).

[59] Competition Act, Art. 9 (4).

[60] Competition Act, Art. 20 (2).

[61] Competition Act, Part II. The title of the Part II is misleading. Instead of prohibiting anti-competitive activities, the Competition Act prohibited competitive activities.

[62] Competition Act, Art 4 (1).

[63] Competition Act, Art 10.

[64] Competition Act, Art 13.

[65] Competition Act, Art 2(1).

[66] For the overview of previous CC case law concerning the application of the Competition Act upon the state and public authorities see Svetlicinii (2013b).

the CC has changed its position by differentiating cases when state bodies participate in commercial transactions (acts *iure gestionis*) from cases involving state and local bodies' imposition of rights and obligations to economic operators through exercising state powers (acts *iure imperii*). The Court of B&H affirmed this view in the case *Polyclinic v. Competition Council of B&H*:

> Acts which are debited to the Ministry of Health of the Sarajevo County and the Agency for Health Insurance of the Sarajevo County do not represent prohibited agreement under Article 4 of the Competition Act, since these are acts concerning the execution of public, legally regulated authorities, outside of the scope of the Competition Act, and not the acts of persons participating in the market.[67]

The Court of B&H referred to several CJEU cases in its decision: *Port of Genoa*,[68] *SAT Fluggesellschaft mbH v. Eurocontrol*,[69] *Wouters*,[70] and *Poucet and Pistre*.[71]

4.2.2 Anti-competitive Agreements

Article 4 of the Competition Act generally replicates Article 101 TFEU. The novelty that the B&H legislator brought was the enumeration of various forms in which prohibited agreements may appear:

> Prohibited are agreements, contracts, certain provisions of the agreement or contract, joint actions, explicit and implicit agreements of economic entities, as well as decisions and other acts of economic entities that have aimed at and resulted in prevention, restriction or distortion of market competition in the relevant market.

When transposing Article 101 TFEU into national law, the B&H legislator made an error that restricted the scope of the prohibition of anti-competitive agreements in Article 4 of the Competition Act. Instead of separating phrases 'aimed at' and 'resulted in' with a conjunction 'or', the legislator inserted a connector 'and'. Consequently, the literal meaning of Article 4 is that only agreements aiming *and* resulting in the prevention, restriction or distortion of competition are forbidden in B&H law.[72] Nevertheless, some legal writers have interpreted that categories of prohibited agreements listed in Article 4 para 1 are prohibited *per se*.[73] Therefore, it is needless to prove the existence of anti-competitive effects when prosecuting these

---

[67] Competition Council, *Polyclinic v. Competition Council of B&H,* S1 3 U 024742 18 U2, 5.04.2018.

[68] C-343/95, ECR 1997 I-01547.

[69] C-364/92, ECR 1994 I-00043.

[70] C-309/99, ECR 2002 I-01577.

[71] Joined cases C-159/91 and C-160/91, 1993 I-00637.

[72] Jerkić (2018).

[73] The categories of *per se* prohibited agreements are identical as those listed in Article 101 TFEU:

a) direct or indirect fixing of selling and purchase prices or any other trade conditions;
b) limiting or controlling production, markets, technical development or investment;
c) sharing of markets or sources of supply;

categories of anti-competitive agreements.[74] In its practice, the CC tacitly confirmed this view. It did not go into an investigation of anti-competitive effects whenever it proved the existence of hard-core restrictions. For example, in the case of *Digital Asset Management d.o.o. Banja Luka v. Raiffeisen Bank BiH d.d.*,[75] the CC found the practice of Raiffeisen Bank BiH illegal to prevent its clients from pursuing crypto-currency trading over accounts opened at Raiffeisen. The CC established this practice as violating Article 4(1)(b) of the Competition Act, which prohibits agreements restricting or controlling production, trade, technical development, or investments. The CC found that the Raiffeisen Bank banning clients from pursuing crypto-currency trade affected market competition and it was contrary to Article 4(1)(b).[76] It did not go further to investigate the effects of the Raiffeisen Bank act on the market.

Competition Act provides for individual and group exemption of anti-competitive agreements. Under Article 5 para 1 of the Competition Act, parties may request the CC to issue an individual exemption of their agreement, provided that it fulfils conditions from Article 4 para 3. A CC decision on individual exemption is merely declaratory since the Competition Act has not established sanctions for parties who fail to request an individual exemption. Suppose the CC initiates an investigation to sanction parties for breaching Article 4 para 1 of the Competition Act. In that case, they still have a chance to prove that their agreement fulfils the conditions for exemption specified in paragraph 3 of the same article.[77] In addition, if the parties submit a request for exemption, but the CC does not decide upon it within a three-month deadline, a legal presumption arises that the agreement is exempted from Article 4 prohibition.[78]

A CC decision to approve the individual exemption would improve the parties' legal certainty.[79] The exemption is valid for up to five years.[80] However, the parties are not shielded absolutely from sanctioning during the exemption period. The CC may invalidate the exemption if it has been based on incomplete and false information, if material conditions and circumstances in the relevant market have significantly changed, or if a party breaches obligations determined in the CC decision.[81]

---

d) application of dissimilar conditions to equivalent transactions with other economic entities, thereby placing them at a competitive disadvantage;

e) conclusion of contracts subject to acceptance by the other parties of additional obligations which, by their nature or according to commercial usage, have no connection with the subject of such contracts.

[74] Trifković (2006), p. 79.

[75] Competition Council, UP 02-26-2-042-55/21, 16.11.2022, p. 2.

[76] ibid, p. 28. The legal character of the prohibited Raiffeisen bank act is not known, since the CC anonymised this information in the public version of its decision.

[77] Competition Act, Art 8 (4).

[78] Competition Act, Art 5 (2) in conjunction with Art 41 (1)(b).

[79] Trifković (2006), p. 82.

[80] Competition Act, Art 6 (2).

[81] Competition Act, Art 5 (3).

Competition Act authorised the CC to adopt block exemptions of categories of agreements.[82] In 2006, the CC adopted the following decisions on block exemptions:

- Decision on block exemption of agreements between economic entities which are active on the same level of production or supply (horizontal agreements), in particular, concerning research, development and specialisation;[83]
- Decision on block exemption of agreements on the transfer of technology, licensing and know-how;[84]
- Decision on block exemption of insurance agreements;[85]
- Decision on block exemption of agreements on distribution and repair of motor vehicles;[86]
- Decision on block exemption of agreements between economic entities which are active on different levels of production or supply (vertical agreements).[87]

The block exemptions were drafted using the EU block exemption regulations in force at that time as a model without explicitly referring to them. The CC has never amended the block exemption decisions, regardless of the European Commission's activity in adopting new block exemption regulations in 2010, 2014, and 2022. In the 2022 Report, the European Commission stressed the need for B&H to harmonise the Competition Act and implementing bylaws in line with the EU *acquis*.[88]

The Competition Act laid down a general exemption for agreements between parties with insignificant market shares (*de minimis* agreements). Market share thresholds defined in the Competition Act are intrinsically identical to those determined by the European Commission.[89] A *de minimis* exemption does not apply to agreements containing hard-core restrictions.[90] The CC adopted a decision specifying hard-core restrictions in 2005,[91] following the black-listed restrictions in the EU block exemption regulation from 1999,[92] which is no longer in force in the EU.[93] In

[82] Competition Act, Art 7.

[83] Official Gazette of B&H, No 15/06.

[84] Official Gazette of B&H, No 15/06.

[85] Official Gazette of B&H, No 15/06.

[86] Official Gazette of B&H, No 16/06.

[87] Official Gazette of B&H, No 18/06.

[88] Commission (2022), p. 77.

[89] Notice on agreements of minor importance which do not appreciably restrict competition under Article 101(1) of the Treaty on the Functioning of the European Union (*De Minimis* Notice), OJ C 291/01.

[90] Competition Act, Art 8 (2).

[91] Decision on agreements with minor value [2005], Official Gazette of B&H, No 86/05.

[92] Commission Regulation (EC) No 2790/1999 of 22 December 1999 on the application of Article 81(3) of the Treaty to categories of vertical agreements and concerted practices [1999] OJ L 336, Art 4.

[93] By comparison, the Commission Regulation from 2022 contains a much more detailed list of hard-core restrictions in vertical agreements. See Article 4 of the Commission Regulation

addition, the 2005 Decision effectively widened the Competition Act *de minimis* exemption scope by determining market share thresholds in case of parallel (network of) agreements with similar effects[94] and a permissible increase of market shares.[95]

4.2.3 Abuse of Dominant Position

Competition Act defines the dominant position in Article 9, generally following the CJEU definition in *United Brands*[96] and *Hoffmann-La Roche*:[97]

> An economic entity has a dominant position on a relevant market of goods and services when, owing to its market power, it can behave in the relevant market considerably independently of its actual and potential competitors, buyers, consumers or suppliers, taking into account the share of that economic entity in the relevant market, shares of its competitors in that market, as well as the legal and other barriers for other economic entities to enter the market.[98]

Due to the inadequate legal drafting, the B&H legislator effectively limited the scope of the CC discretion concerning the choice of criteria for assessing the independence of market behaviour to three elements: market share of allegedly dominant entity, market shares of its competitors and legal and other barriers to market entry.

The German Act against Restraints of Competition has inspired the B&H legislator since the Competition Act has also defined legal presumptions for individual and collective dominance, much like the German legislator did.[99] Competition Act lays down market share thresholds, which constitute a rebuttable legal presumption on the existence of an individual dominant position. An economic entity is presumed to possess a dominant position if its market share exceeds 40%.[100] In addition, two or three economic entities are assumed to be collectively dominant when their joint market share in the relevant market exceeds 60%. In the case of four or five economic entities, a joint market share exceeding 80% suffices to create a presumption of collective dominance.[101] Regrettably, the Competition Act omitted the essential conceptual determinants of the collective dominance definition in the

(EU) 2022/720 of 10 May 2022 on the application of Article 101(3) of the Treaty on the Functioning of the European Union to categories of vertical agreements and concerted practices [2022] OJ L 134.

[94] Decision on agreements with minor value [2005], Art 4.

[95] ibid, Art 5.

[96] Judgment of 14 February 1978, *United Brands v Commission,* C-27/76, ECLI:EU:C:1978:22, para 65.

[97] Judgment of 13 February 1979, *Hoffmann-La Roche v Commission,* C-85/76, ECLI:EU:C:1979:36, para 38.

[98] *United Brands,* para 65; *Hoffmann-La Roche,* para 38.

[99] Act against Restraints of Competition (GWB), Art 18 (4) and (6).

[100] Competition Act, Art 9 (2).

[101] Competition Act, Art 9 (4).

German Act: the non-existence of significant competition between (allegedly) dominant entities and their joint fulfilment of elements required for dominance.[102]

The CC adopted in 2006 the Decision on defining categories of dominant position[103] based on powers laid down in Article 9 para 5 of the Competition Act. The CC extended the Competition Act's dominant position definition in several ways. Firstly, it has added a requirement that a dominant economic entity restricts or prevents effective competition to the principal condition of independent behaviour in the relevant market.[104] Consequently, only economic entities that restrict or prevent competition due to independent market behaviour enjoy a dominant market position. Effectively, the CC has combined market conduct and performance elements when defining market dominance,[105] contrary to the EU case law and many national competition authorities' practices. Secondly, the CC has equalled a dominant position with the non-existence of competition or the existence of insignificant competition[106] by faultily taking over the definition from the German Act against Restraints of Competition.[107] Thirdly, the CC has equated the dominant position with the possession of significant market power. The economic entity's significant market power is determined across a list of criteria, including:

a) Market share – determined based on the sale or buying volume, financial strength, or production capacities;
b) Relevant market structure and economic relationship with competitors;
c) The ability to maintain prices above the competitive level (restrict production and quality);
d) Access to supply sources (raw materials) or distribution channels;
e) The scope of vertical integration in the relevant market;
f) Economic regulators, investment barriers to entry/exit the relevant market for potential economic subjects;
g) Technological advantages, patents, intellectual and industrial property rights and similar rights.[108]

The listed criteria are not exhaustive. The CC may introduce additional factors when assessing market dominance.[109] Some of the listed criteria are difficult to apply in

[102] GWB, Art 18 (5).

[103] Decision on the definition of categories of dominant position [2006] Official Gazette of B&H, No 18/06.

[104] ibid, Art 2(1).

[105] Uzinidis (2016).

[106] Decision on the definition of categories of dominant position [2006], Art 2(2).

[107] Article 18 para 1 of the Act against Restraints of Competition (GWB) reads as follows:

(1) An undertaking is dominant where, as a supplier or purchaser of a certain type of goods or commercial services on the relevant product and geographic market, it

1. has no competitors,
2. is not exposed to any substantial competition, or
3. has a paramount market position in relation to its competitors.

[108] Decision on defining categories of dominant position, Art 3 (2).

[109] Poljić (2014), p. 119.

practice and even confusing, such as "the ability to maintain prices above the competitive level" and "economic regulators, investment barriers to entry/exit the relevant market for potential economic subjects."

Article 10 para 2 of the Competition Act defines the abuse of dominant position by listing the typical anti-competitive practices identically with Article 102 TFEU. Here again, the CC extended the Competition Act scope by enumerating additional categories of abuse in its 2006 Decision:

a) Price discrimination (different prices) of a certain product or service on different relevant geographic markets;
b) Continuous offer and sale to buyers of products and services under unfair (low) prices, which result in deterring buyers from buying similar products or services from competitor providers (so-called "loyalty rebates"—direct rebates or secret rebates);
c) Determining the prices of products or services below the production costs aiming to eliminate competition;
d) Unjustified cancellation or reduction of production or sale of products or services which has negative consequences upon consumers;
e) Production or market restrictions resulting from exclusive agreements (special rebates, discounts, financial advantages);
f) The ability of an economic entity to determine conditions in the relevant market based on its offer or demand, which makes it possible to increase profit unjustifiably;
g) Refusal of access to other economic entities, under reasonable financial compensation, to facilities, equipment, transition network or other infrastructure equipment in the possession or used by a dominant economic entity if other economic entities are not able to act in the same market in which the dominant entity is active without being able to use such equipment or capacities jointly and if the dominant economic entity does not prove that such joint use is not feasible due to operative, technical or other reasons.[110]

The CC aimed to increase legal certainty by specifying abuse of dominance categories in more detail. However, the result reached was far from what was desired. The CC disregarded numerous factors relevant to identifying abuse of dominance in the case of most common abuses, such as price discrimination, predatory pricing, loyalty rebates, exclusive agreements, refusal to supply, etc. By simplifying the definition of these abuse categories, the CC widened its discretion in applying Article 10 of the Competition Act. Moreover, the CC equated a dominant entity's ability to determine market conditions with the abuse in Article 10(f) of the 2006 Decision. It essentially prohibited market dominance as such.

In its decisions, the CC has continuously referred to the Decision on defining categories of dominant position alongside the relevant Competition Act

[110] Decision on the definition of categories of dominant position [2006], Art 9.

provisions.[111] The legality of the Decision has never been disputed before the Constitution Court of B&H despite the controversy over whether the CC went beyond the legal powers entrusted to it by Article 9(5) of the Competition Act.

4.2.4 Concentrations

The Competition Act's substantive provisions on concentrations are broadly in line with the EU Merger Regulation.[112] Article 12 para 1 of the Competition Act identifies three categories of concentrations: (i) mergers; (ii) acquisitions of control or prevailing influence of one or more economic entities over another economic entity or entities or their parts; and (iii) joint ventures acting as a separate entity established on a lasting basis between two or more independent economic entities.

The principal criterion for assessing concentrations is the 'significant distortion of efficient competition,' supplemented by the market dominance criterion. Concentrations of economic entities that result in significant distortion of efficient competition on the entire market of Bosnia and Herzegovina or its considerable part are prohibited, particularly those that create or strengthen dominant market position.[113]

Competition Act imposes an obligation for concentration participants to notify a concentration before its implementation. Depending on what happens first, they must notify a concentration within fifteen days of signing the agreement, the publication of a public offering or acquisition of control. Participants may notify a concentration earlier if they demonstrate their intention to concentrate by means of agreement, memorandum of understanding, letter of intent signed by all parties to the concentration or publication of intent to purchase shares.[114] They must suspend implementing the concentration until the CC issues approval or after they satisfy conditions and measures imposed by a CC decision conditionally approving the concentration.[115]

The threshold for concentration notification is defined cumulatively, based on the aggregate turnover of concentration participants on the world market and the turnover realised in the B&H market. Concentrations of parties who realized total annual turnover on the world market of at least BAM 100 million, and at least two of them realised total annual income in the B&H market of at least BAM 8 million, come under the CC scrutiny. Alternatively, instead of criteria of aggregate turnover in the national market, joint market share criteria apply. Regardless of the turnover in

[111] See, for example, Competition Council, *Telemach v. BiH Telekom*, UP-01-26-2-018-173/17, 6.04.2023.

[112] Council Regulation (EC) No 139/2004 of 20 January 2004 on the control of concentrations between undertakings [2004] OJ L 24.

[113] Competition Act, Art 13.

[114] Competition Act, Art 16 (1) and (2).

[115] Competition Act, Art 18 (4).

the national market, parties to a concentration must notify it if their combined market share in the internal market of B&H exceeds 40%.[116]

When assessing the effects of intended concentration, the CC applies the criteria similar to those listed in Article 2 of the EU Merger Regulation: the structure of the relevant market; the effects of concentration on the other actual or potential competitors; the market position of the concentration participants, their market shares, economic and financial strength; the possibilities and choice available to suppliers and customers; economic, legal and other barriers to market entry; levels of internal and international competitiveness of concentration participants; trends of supply and/or demand of relevant goods and/or services; trends of technical and economic development; the interests of consumers.[117]

4.3 *Proceedings Before the Competition Council, Investigating and Sanctioning Powers*

The CC conducts proceedings of an administrative character. Competition Act lays down special procedural rules, while the Administrative Proceedings Act of B&H (APA)[118] subsidiarily applies based on Article 26 of the Competition Act and Article 3 APA.[119]

The CC starts investigations at the request of a party or *ex officio*. Every legal or natural person may request the CC to start a proceeding if it demonstrates legal or economic interest. Besides, business associations, consumer associations and executive authorities in B&H are authorised to request CC to initiate proceedings against alleged competition law infringers.[120] In line with the Competition Act's explicit provision, the burden of proof lies with the third party in proceedings commenced upon a third-party request.[121] Due to this peculiar provision, the CC plays a twofold role in the proceedings. When the CC starts proceedings *ex officio*, it must prove the Competition Act infringement. At the same time, in cases initiated upon a third party's request, the CC acts as a judge who expects parties to bring evidence to support their claims. Needless to say, most cases are initiated upon third parties' requests. Parties to an anti-competitive agreement bear the burden of proof that their agreement satisfies conditions for exemption under Article 4 para 3 of the Competition Act.

[116] Competition Act, Art 14 (1) (b).

[117] Competition Act, Art 17.

[118] Administrative Proceedings Act of B&H [2002], Official Gazette of B&H, No 29/02, 12/04, 88/07, 93/09, 41/13, 53/16 (APA).

[119] Competition Act, Art 26.

[120] Competition Act, Art 27.

[121] Competition Act, Art 36.

The CC derives its investigating powers from Article 35 of the Competition Act. Parties in proceedings and third parties, upon a request of the CC, must provide the required information in writing or orally and provide access to media storing the requested information and documents. Besides, they must grant access to business premises, immovable and movable property, business records, databases and other documentation. If there is reasonable suspicion that the parties or other persons are in possession of documents or other resources relevant to establishing the facts in the proceedings, the CC may ask a court to issue a warrant for searching apartments or premises of parties and other persons and seizure of items and documents.

The B&H legislators failed to indicate in the Competition Act which court is competent to issue warrants for searching apartments and premises. Laws regulating the organisation of courts in B&H and procedural matters also miss provisions on the court's competence to issue warrants upon a CC request. Due to the legislator's failure to determine which court is responsible for issuing warrants for searching premises, the CC cannot conduct an unannounced inspection (dawn raid). It must first request parties to grant access to their business premises, which eliminates the surprise element when conducting inspections of business premises. For this reason, the CC has never conducted a dawn raid.

The CC can impose interim measures based on *prima facie* established competition infringement, provided that the infringement causes direct damage to an economic entity, economic sector or consumer interests. In a decision on interim measures, the CC may request from parties to terminate an activity, satisfy specific conditions or implement other steps necessary to eliminate harmful anticompetitive acts. The interim measures may last up to three months. The CC can renew them if it finds them necessary and justifiable.[122]

Competition Act provides for guarantees of parties' rights. The CC must hand over an act initiating a proceeding to a defendant and third parties, if there are any, and ask them to respond.[123] Parties have a right to access files upon a written request.[124] The CC must hold a hearing in cases involving parties with conflicting interests. In other cases, the CC will hold a hearing if it finds it useful for solving the subject matter.[125] At the end of an investigation, the CC may inform the parties of the content of a decision it intends to pass. The Competition Act does not obligate the CC to send parties a statement of objections. However, this obligation stems from the general principles of B&H administrative proceeding law. Based on Article 10 APA, an administrative authority must hear parties on all crucial facts and circumstances. The CC does not comply with this duty in its practice.[126]

The CC is not empowered to accept the parties' commitments in cases concerning anti-competitive agreements and abuses of dominant position. This is a significant

[122] Competition Act, Art 40.

[123] Competition Act, Art 33.

[124] Competition Act, Art 37.

[125] Competition Act, Art 39.

[126] Information obtained from the interview with the Law Office Karanović & Nikolić.

deviation of B&H competition law from the EU *acquis*. However, a CC decision finding an infringement may contain recommendations and/or sanctions and other measures for parties.[127] Nothing prevents the parties from proposing the CC commitments they are ready to accept during proceedings, which the CC can subsequently formulate as "recommendations and other measures" in its final decision.

Competition Act Articles 18 and 19 empower the CC to impose remedies in concentration cases. The CC may conditionally approve a concentration by determining measures, conditions, and deadlines for implementation. Competition Act does not limit CC's discretion when choosing appropriate remedies. In particular, the CC is not bound by the parties' proposals regarding the types of commitments.[128] However, the CC must respect the parties and public interest and adhere to the proportionality principle when determining remedies in concentration cases. Under Article 5 APA, an administrative authority must facilitate parties' enactment of their rights by ensuring they do not harm third parties' interests or contradict the public interest. When the administrative authority imposes obligations to parties based on law, it should implement measures determined in regulations that are advantageous for the parties, provided that these measures are suitable to attain the law's goals.[129]

The Competition Act specifies measures the CC can impose if parties implement a concentration contrary to the CC prohibition or without notifying the CC. The CC can order the parties to sell off company shares, prohibit or restrict the execution of voting rights or order a cessation of a joint venture or other concentration forms.[130] It remained unclear whether the CC may order a divestiture of a merger.[131] Article 19 of the Competition Act does not specify this remedy explicitly. However, the phrase "other concentration forms from Article 12" is wide enough to include this type of remedy. The CC has not yet used these powers in its practice. It investigated concentrations implemented without notification and imposed fines on merging parties. In the case of *Klas/Sprind*, the CC prohibited a concentration between two bakery companies, finding that Klas would strengthen its dominant position. It imposed fines upon Klas for submitting false data relevant to determining the market share of merging parties.[132]

The Competition Act entrusted the CC with the power to impose fines and periodic penalty payments. The CC can impose fines for serious breaches of competition law amounting to 10% of the total annual turnover of an undertaking. The CC takes the worldwide turnover of an undertaking as the basis for calculating fines and penalties since the term 'total turnover' implies the turnover realised

[127] Competition Act, Art 43(3).

[128] Kulenović (2016), p. 13.

[129] APA, Art 5 (3).

[130] Competition Act, Art 19.

[131] Competition Act, Art 12 (1)(a).

[132] Competition Council, *Klas/Sprind,* UP 01-06-26-033-65-II/08, 6.04.2009. The full text of the CC decision, in this case, is not available in electronic form. For a short description of the case see CC (2009).

worldwide. The turnover is calculated based on the year preceding the year in which the infringement occurred. Article 48 of the Competition Act enumerates serious infringements of competition law:

i) Conclusion or participation in an agreement distorting, preventing or restricting market competition;
ii) Abuse of dominant position;
iii) Implementing a prohibited concentration;
iv) Implementing a concentration before the CC decides upon it;
v) Failure to comply with the CC decisions taken in antitrust and merger cases.

In case of minor infringements of competition law, the CC can impose a fine not exceeding 1% of the total turnover of an undertaking. Article 49 of the Competition Act defines minor violations: disobeying the CC procedural acts concerning requests for information or providing false or incomplete information; failure of merging parties to notify a concentration within a period specified in Article 16 of the Competition Act; failure to comply with a warrant of a competent court for a search of an apartment or business premises.

Apart from sanctioning legal entities, i.e. companies and other legal persons, the CC can impose a fine upon a responsible natural person ranging between BAM 5000 and 15,000 for minor violations[133] and between BAM 15,000 and 50,000 for serious competition law infringements.[134]

The Competition Act authorised the CC to regulate the method of periodic penalty payments. The CC issued a Decision on the definition of the manner of periodic penalty payments in 2006.[135] The grounds for imposing periodic penalty payments defined by the Decision are similar to those provided in Article 24 of Regulation 1/2003.[136] The Decision has determined circumstances in which the CC can impose periodic penalty payments on undertakings: to put an end to a an anti-competitive agreement; to comply with a CC decision on interim measures; to comply with measures and conditions made binding in abuse of dominant position and concentration cases; to submit complete and true information upon a CC request; to comply with CC procedural orders. The CC can impose periodic penalty payments to parties in the proceedings not exceeding 5% of the average daily turnover in the preceding year.[137]

[133] Competition Act, Art 48 (2).

[134] Competition Act, Art 49 (2).

[135] Decision on the closer definition of the manner of periodic penalty payments [2006] Official Gazette of B&H, No 31/06.

[136] Council Regulation (EC) No 1/2003 of 16 December 2002 on the implementation of the rules on competition laid down in Articles 81 and 82 of the Treaty [2003] OJ L 1/1.

[137] Competition Act, Art 50 (1).

4.4 *Competition Council: Budget and Staff*

The CC is an independent institution financed from the State Budget. B&H is a small open economy[138] whose GDP in 2021 amounted to EUR 19,995 million and GDP per capita EUR 5791.[139] At the same time, the CC is a small state institution in terms of the number of employees and the available budget. The effectiveness of its operation is proportional to the available budget and staff.

According to the CC's Rulebook on Internal Organization, the total envisaged staff is 29, as follows: CC Members—6, Head of Professional Service—1, Expert Advisors for Legal Affairs Related to Competition—3, Expert Advisors for Economic Affairs Related to Competition—3, Expert Advisor for Translation, Senior Expert Associate for Promotion of Market Competition—1, Senior Expert Associate for Legal Affairs—1, Senior Expert Associate for Financial Affairs—1, Senior Expert Associate for Information Technology—1, Expert Associate for Competition Matters—1, Technical Secretary—1, Technical Operator—2, Driver-Courier—1, Head of Mostar Office—1, Expert Advisors for Competition in Mostar—2, Head of Banja Luka Office—1, Expert Advisors for Competition in Banja Luka—2.

Analysis of the data collected from annual work reports, the report on CC's budget execution and the Law on the Budget of B&H Institutions and the Implementation of International Obligations[140] (see Table 1 and also Table 2) indicates that the CC does not operate with sufficient financial resources or human capacities to respond to the challenges of enforcing competition law in Bosnia and Herzegovina. A brief analysis of the budget structure shows that most of the budget is being spent on employee salaries and allowances, and the budget lacks the so-called development dimension that would provide means for continuous improvement and procurement of modern technology as resources necessary for the daily work and training of the CC staff. Furthermore, the temporary financing system often affects the implementation of the CC work program.[141] Therefore, to ensure effective competition law enforcement, more financial resources and a larger CC budget must be allocated, and the organizational structure must be changed to include more employees involved in solving competition cases who will be constantly educated.

---

[138] Imamović-Čizmić et al. (2021), p. 190.

[139] Agency for Statistics of Bosnia and Herzegovina (2023).

[140] Due to the fact that the reports of the Competition Council are not standardized, data has been collected from various sources for specific years within the reference period 2012–2022.

[141] For many years, the B&H Parliament has been delayed in adopting the annual state budget due to political reasons. In such circumstances, B&H state institutions must operate based on so-called temporary financing, meaning that the Council of Ministers adopts quarterly decisions on temporary financing under Article 11 of the Law on Financing the B&H Institutions [2004], Official Gazette of B&H, No 61/2004, 27/2008, 49/2009, 42/2012, 87/2012, 32/2013, 38/2022.

Table 1 The CC budget for the period 2012–2022[a]

Year	Budget (in BAM)	Budget (in EUR)[b]
2012	1,475,000.00	753,167.50
2013	1,383,000.00	707,626.90
2014	1,288,000.00	658,683.20
2015	1,345,000.00	687,708.50
2016	1,350,000.00	690,255.00
2017	1,368,000.00	699,338.40
2018	1,337,000.00	683,654.10
2019	1,353,000.00	691,698.90
2020[c]	1,239,000.00	633,335.70
2021[d]	1,239,000.00	633,335.70
2022[e]	1,382,000.00	706,964.60

Source: Authors' own calculation based on CC Annual Reports for a period 2012–2022; Reports on the budget execution of the CC and the Law on the Budget of the Institutions of Bosnia and Herzegovina and the international obligations of Bosnia and Herzegovina 2012–2022; Report on the work of the BiH Council of Ministers (2012–2022)

[a] Calculation based on average exchange rate for the relevant year

[b] All values are nominal values

[c] CC Budget Execution Report (2021)

[d] The temporary financing of the institutions of Bosnia and Herzegovina occurred in the period from 1 January until 31 December 2021

[e] The temporary financing of the institutions of Bosnia and Herzegovina occurred in the period from 1 January to 30 June 2022. The Law on Budget No 42/22 was adopted in June 2022, according to which the CC was allocated the 2022 budget of BAM 1,382,000.00

Table 2 Total CC staff for the period 2012–2022

Year	Total staff
2012	25
2013	25
2014	26
2015	26
2016	26
2017	26
2018	28
2019	28
2020	28
2021	25
2022	25

Source: Authors' own calculation based on CC Annual Reports for a period 2012–2022; Reports on the budget execution of the CC and the Law on the Budget of the Institutions of Bosnia and Herzegovina and the international obligations of Bosnia and Herzegovina (2012–2022)

5 National Specifics That Differ from the EU Competition Acquis

Concerning substantive provisions, the wording of Article 4 of the Competition Act created a major difference between B&H and EU law. At first glance, Article 4 Competition Act appears to be harmonised with Article 101 TFEU. However, when analysed in detail, significant differences emerge. As noted above, Article 4 stipulates two cumulative conditions for violating the law. For an agreement to be prohibited, it must have the purpose *and* effect of preventing, limiting or distorting market competition in the relevant market. At the same time, Article 101 TFEU sets these conditions alternatively. Secondly, Article 101 TFEU provides for an open list of prohibited business practices, whereas Article 4 does not. Article 4 provides the following:

> Prohibited are agreements, contracts, certain provisions of the agreement or contract, joint actions, explicit and tacit agreements of economic entities, as well as decisions and other acts of economic entities (hereinafter: agreements) that have aimed at *and* resulted in prevention, restriction or distortion of market competition in the relevant market, *which relate to*: ...

The wording "which relate to:" limits the CC's authority to qualify as a violation of any agreement not enumerated in the Competition Act. It means that anti-competitive agreements, regardless of their harmful effect on competition, will not be prohibited unless they fall under the examples listed in Article 4.

Regarding procedural provisions, the EU competition *acquis* does not interfere with Member States' right to choose competition law enforcement model.[142] They are free to designate administrative authorities or courts, or both administrative authorities and courts, as competition law enforcers.[143] Directive 2019/1 specifies the essential requirements for national competition authorities to apply competition rules independently, impartially, effectively and by safeguarding the undertaking's right of defence.[144] The CC's institutional setup and procedural rules prevent it from being an independent, impartial, and effective enforcer of competition rules. The CC constitution and decision-making rules allow it to pursue the interests of B&H constituent peoples and simultaneously prevent efficient decision-making.

Article 24(2) of the Competition Act sets out the rule for the CC's decision-making: "The Competition Council issues decisions by a majority of the present members, provided that at least one member of each constituent people votes for a decision. A member of the Competition Council cannot abstain from voting." The cited rule constitutes a ground for ethnic-based veto rights. It is sufficient that two

[142] See more on the EU competition enforcement model: Marković-Bajalović (2022).

[143] Regulation 1/2003, Art 35.

[144] Directive (EU) 2019/1 of the European Parliament and of the Council of 18 December 2018 to empower the competition authorities of the Member States to be more effective enforcers and to ensure the proper functioning of the internal market [2019] OJ L 11, Arts 3 and 4.

CC members from the same ethnicity are absent from the CC session or vote against a decision to prevent the adoption of any decision or a procedural conclusion.

Another specific feature of the B&H competition regime is the strict procedural deadlines. Under Article 41 of the Competition Act, the CC must issue a final decision before the expiration of the following deadlines:

a) Six months in anti-competitive agreements cases (proceedings conducted under Article 4 Competition Act);
b) Three months when deciding upon a request for an individual exemption from the prohibition of anti-competitive agreements based on Article 5 of the Competition Act;
c) Four months in abuse of dominance cases (proceedings conducted under Article 11 Competition Act);
d) Three months in concentration cases where the CC issued a conclusion to carry out an in-depth investigation (proceedings carried out based on Article 18 paras 6 and 7 Competition Act).[145]

Exceptionally, the CC may extend the deadline for issuing a decision for an additional three months when it is necessary to determine the facts or if it relates to sensitive industries or markets.[146] If the CC does not finalise an investigation and adopt a decision by the above deadlines, a legal presumption arises that a defendant has complied with the law:

a) If the CC does not issue a decision on the individual exemption within three months, it is considered that the subject agreement is exempted from Article 4 para 1 prohibition;[147]
b) In abuse of dominance cases, if the CC does not issue a decision within four months, it shall be deemed that the concluded agreement or practice of the economic entity does not represent the abuse of dominant position;[148]
c) In concentration cases, if the CC does not issue a conclusion to start an investigation within 30 days after receiving a notification or does not issue a decision within three months after initiating the investigation, the concentration shall be deemed compatible with the Competition Act.[149]

The combination of ethnic-based veto and strict procedural deadlines prevented the CC from adopting unpopular decisions in politically sensitive cases. The *Agrokor/ Mercator* concentration represents a striking example of strategic CC decision-making.[150] The case involved a Croatian conglomerate active in food production and retail in the Western Balkans markets and the largest Slovenian retail chain. On

[145] Competition Act, Art 41 (1).
[146] Competition Act, Art 41 (2).
[147] Competition Act, Art 5 (2).
[148] Competition Act, Art 11 (2).
[149] Competition Act, Art 18 (5) and (6).
[150] Competition Council, *Agrokor/Mercator,* UP 05-26-1-014-374-II/13, 10.6.2014.

28 June 2013, the CC received the concentration notification. After extending the deadline for investigation, the CC prepared a draft decision and sent it to the applicants. The applicants proposed remedies, considering the CC assessment that the concentration would create or strengthen the dominant position of *Agrokor* in the retail sector on several geographic markets. The CC had to decide upon the final decision on 13 May 2014. However, the proposed decision was not adopted since the requirements under Article 24 para 2 CA were not fulfilled. Article 24 para 2 CA requires that at least one member of each constituent ethnicity vote for a Council decision as a necessary condition. Since two CC members from the same constituent ethnicity were absent from the CC session, the proposed decision in the *Agroko*r case lacked at least one vote from this ethnicity, which was necessary for the decision to become valid. Consequently, the CC adopted a decision on 10 June 2014 declaring that the concentration was deemed approved based on Article 18(7) CA.[151]

The European Commission openly criticised the ethnic-based veto right in its 2022 Report: "As for the institutional framework, the functioning of the Competition Council is significantly impeded by tight procedural deadlines and ethnic-based decision-making procedures, which require decisions to be supported by at least one representative of each constituent people to have legal effect".[152] B&H still needs to show the political will to amend CA provisions regarding CC composition and the decision-making process.

6 Application of National and EU Competition Rules by the Competition Council and Discussion of the Most Significant Cases

6.1 Anti-competitive Agreement on Crypto-Currency Market

The case of *Digital Asset Management v Raiffeisen Bank* is the first to be linked to the trade in crypto-currencies and has opened up many issues in B&H competition law. One of the key questions was how the concept of prohibited agreements, as regulated by Article 4 of the Competition Act, can be applied in this specific case where no meeting of minds existed between Raiffeisen Bank and Digital Asset Management, opposing parties in the proceedings.[153] The case is also significant

[151] See also: Marković-Bajalović (2020), pp. 45–47.

[152] Commission (2022), p. 77.

[153] The earlier practice of the General Court (the Byer case from 2004) shows that unilateral conduct can fall within the concept of an agreement. However, recent case law sets boundaries to the teleological interpretation of the concept of an agreement under Article 101 TFEU. In ruling on an appeal against the judgment of the General Court, the European Court, however, emphasises that the actions of an undertaking, which are merely the expression of the unilateral policy of one of the contractual parties, cannot fall under this concept, nor the provision of Article 101 TFEU. The

for addressing the intersection of traditional banking services and emerging digital asset markets. The case revolves around Raiffeisen Bank's alleged obstruction of transactions related to digital asset trading, which the CC found to violate competition law. This decision emphasises the role of financial institutions in ensuring fair access to payment services for businesses operating in the digital economy and highlights the growing regulatory challenges in balancing traditional financial regulation with the rise of blockchain and cryptocurrency activities.

On 16 November 2022, the CC rendered a Decision establishing that Raiffeisen Bank[154] operating on the relevant market for the provision of savings account and current account services and payments operations pertaining to these accounts, by applying (…),*[155] made impossible the provision of service of transactions created in the name of trading and intermediation in trading of digital assets using an account opened at Raiffeisen Bank, which constitutes a prohibited agreement in light of Article 4 (1) b) of the Competition Act, and imposed a fine of BAM 250,000.00 for this violation.

Namely, Digital Asset Management d.o.o. Banja Luka (DAM), the main registered activity of which is the intermediation in trade specialised in certain products or groups of other products, filed a request on 27 September 2021 to initiate proceedings against Raiffeisen Bank for violation of the Competition Act, Article 4 (1) (b) and (d). The aforementioned provisions refer to prohibited agreements, specifically agreements that limit or control production, markets, technical development or investment or apply dissimilar conditions to equivalent transactions with other economic entities, thereby placing them at a competitive disadvantage.

The complainant claimed that Raiffeisen Bank limited the market and applied dissimilar conditions to equivalent transactions with other economic entities by rejecting an incoming foreign payment to the account of DAM resulting from linking the supply and demand of cryptocurrencies and realisation of orders from DAM clients by unilaterally terminating the agreement on opening an account for domestic payments based on its internal rules. DAM concluded an agreement with the world's leading cryptocurrency exchange, Payward Ltd., London, operating under the brand Kraken; in view of the above, the unilateral termination of the agreement on opening an account for domestic payments disabled the complainant's intermediation in the trade of digital assets.

DAM lodged a complaint pertaining to the rejection of incoming payment, i.e., to the return of payment, and requested an explanation as to the legal basis—which law or bylaw was applied as a ground for the return of funds. There was no response to the complaint. With the aim of protecting their rights, DAM also addressed the Banking Agency of the Republic of Srpska as the regulator of the banking market of

Competition Council did not consider the case law of the CJEU in its decision, contrary to its standard practice.

[154] Competition Council, *Digital Asset Management d.o.o. Banja Luka v Raiffeisen Bank d.d. Bosna i Hercegovina, Branch Office Banja Luka*, UP 02-26-2-042-55/21, 16.11.2022.

[155] (…)*- The data constitutes a business secret.

the Republic of Srpska and a supervisory authority in terms of the Law on the Prevention of Money Laundering and Financing of Terrorist Activities.[156] However, the regulatory body declared itself incompetent and suggested that the applicant defend its rights before the court in civil proceedings.

Raiffeisen Bank confirmed that DAM opened an account for regular business and that upon concluding the contract, DAM submitted the current extract from the court register, as well as the APIF Notification on the classification of the economic operator by activity. The documents show that DAM is registered to perform economic activity number 46.18—Intermediation in trade specialised in certain products or groups of other products. Raiffeisen Bank stated that it was not evident from the submitted documents that DAM actually trades in cryptocurrencies. It learned about this activity for the first time when the first incoming payment from the Payward Ltd. platform arrived at the DAM account opened with the Bank. Raiffeisen Bank asked DAM to provide the legal basis for the incoming payment, as stipulated by regulations governing the operations of banks in Bosnia and Herzegovina. DAM submitted an Agreement to the Bank, which reflected cryptocurrency trading. The Bank claimed that neither regulations in Bosnia and Herzegovina foresaw cryptocurrency operations, nor could any company be registered for such economic activity. The Bank also pointed out that, given that the Bank's internal procedures did not allow cryptocurrency trading transactions—trading which is not regulated by positive legislation in B&H—the Bank was forced to reject the transaction to the account of DAM, which resulted from cryptocurrency trading; therefore, the incoming payment was rejected, and the funds received on the DAM account were returned. The Bank challenged the competence of the CC to handle issues related to the application of regulations on the prevention of money laundering—as the request to initiate proceedings against the Raiffeisen Bank was mainly based on them. Furthermore, the Bank stated that there was no violation of Article 4 (1) b) of the CA—"limiting or controlling production, markets, technical development or investment", as Raiffeisen was not the only bank operating on the market of Bosnia and Herzegovina, or the Republic of Srpska where DAM was registered.

The CC, bearing in mind the claims by the parties and the opinions of economic experts and the Banking Agency of B&H, established that the economic operator Raiffeisen Bank entered into a prohibited agreement within the meaning of Article 4 (1) (b) of the Competition Act on the relevant market for the provision of savings account and current account services and payments operations pertaining to these transactions by applying (…)*, resulting in termination of the agreement on opening an account for domestic payments with the complainant.[157] The CC did not elaborate

[156] Official Gazette of B&H, No 47/2014 and 67/2016.

[157] The case concerned the agreement between the bank and its customer on opening and maintaining a current account and payment services provision. Banks in BiH typically conclude standard form agreements with their clients. Parties, in this case, did not dispute the existence of an agreement between them. For this reason, the CC did not analyse the notion of agreement in its decision. It can be only presumed that the Raiffeisen Bank terminated the agreement with DAM

on why the bank's termination of a contract with a single customer represented the limitation or control of production, markets, technical development or investment in the sense of Article 4 (1)(b) of the Competition Act. It simply stated that "no legal provision regulates that economic entities should not or ought not to engage in cryptocurrency trade considering the danger of money laundering and financing terrorist activities; therefore, it disabled the Claimant and all economic entities engaged in cryptocurrency trading the access to its relevant product – the provision of services of giro and current account of citizens and civil legal entities and payment transactions." The CC neither stated whether the unilateral termination of a contract by a bank represents a restriction of competition by object nor investigated the effects of the bank's practice on the relevant market. Even though the CC's endeavour to support the development of a new financial service in the market of Bosnia and Herzegovina is worth praising, an in-depth analysis of the relevant market and the effects of the bank's restrictive practice would enlighten the CC approach concerning this type of anticompetitive behaviour.

6.2 *Public TV Broadcasters' Abuse of Dominance Case*

The *OBN* case reflects two important problems in B&H competition law. The first issue concerns the position of public broadcasters in the B&H market, which dominate the TV broadcasting market and related advertising markets. The second issue pertains to the fixed legal deadlines for case resolution, which, together with the conditions outlined in Article 24 of the Competition Act, affect the efficiency of the Competition Council.

On 14 September 2016, the CC issued a Decision stating that pursuant to Article 11(2) of the Competition Act, legal entities Radio-Television of Bosnia and Herzegovina, Radio-Television of the Republic of Srpska and Radio-Television of the Federation of Bosnia and Herzegovina did not abuse their dominant position within the meaning of Article 10(2) (a), (c) and (d) of the Competition Act.[158] The CC concluded the case with a procedural decision provided for in Article 11(2), stipulating that the CC omission to render a decision within the period referred to in Article 41 (four months), creates a legal presumption that an agreement or conduct of a legal entity does not constitute abuse of dominance. The Competition Act does not stipulate the CC's obligation to issue a procedural decision in such cases. However, the CC has established practice to render decisions confirming that a competition infringement has not occurred due to the CC's failure to decide substantively in the case within a prescribed time limit.

---

based on its standard terms. The relevant part of the CC decision was not published due to the Raiffeisen Bank's request to protect some information as a business secret.

[158] Competition Council, *RTV BiH, RTV FBiH, RTRS*, UP 01-26-3-08-167-II/13, 14.09.2016.

OBN d.d. Sarajevo filed an application to initiate proceedings against Radio-Television of Bosnia and Herzegovina, Radio-Television of the Republic of Srpska, and Radio-Television of the Federation of Bosnia and Herzegovina for the establishment of the existence of a prohibited agreement and abuse of dominance. RTV B&H, RTV RS, and RTV FB&H, as public broadcasters, issued a joint Price List for advertising services and sale of advertising space at their TV channels in 2013. Subpoint A of this Price List specified that public broadcasters have a leadership position on the market, and subpoint B posed a condition on advertisers spending a part of their advertising budget on commercial TV channels, must allocate 80% of their budget for advertising on the public broadcasters. As long as a legal entity performed as the public broadcasters requested, it was entitled to a loyalty discount of 50%. OBN noted that loyalty discounts of around 50% were considered disproportionate to usual commercial discounts, thus representing an obstacle to market competition. OBN also stated that the Price List (point III, subpoint B) provided that a legal entity would receive another 10% discount on advertising if they did not use the advertising services of commercial TV broadcasters.

In view of the complexity of the case and the necessary additional analyses to establish the facts and assess the evidence, the CC decided that the time frame for making a final decision was short and adopted a Conclusion, extending the deadline by an additional three months. The CC prepared a draft decision and voted on it. However, the legal conditions stipulated in Article 24(2) of the Competition Act were not met, since the CC members from each constituent people did not vote for a decision. The deadline for issuing a substantive decision expired without the CC deciding on finding competition infringement. Instead, the CC issued a procedural decision, declaring that there was no abuse of the dominant position by the business entities BHRT, RTRS, and FTV.[159]

The CC initiated new proceedings against the same three TV broadcasters and Media Pool d.o.o and issued a decision finding the abuse of the dominant position in the advertising market in 2023.[160] The CC found that the Committee of the Public RTV System in B&H[161] (*Javni RTV sustav BiH*) adopted a decision establishing the price list that the three TV broadcasters applied in their contractual relations with advertising companies. The price list included quantity discounts. The discount percentage differed for companies advertising their products and marketing agencies, manifestly favouring the latter compared to advertisers. The CC found this practice constituted a prohibited agreement. Despite the reference to Competition Act Article 4 on anticompetitive agreements in the explanatory part of the decision, the CC found the practice illegal under Article 10 of the same act, prohibiting the abuse of dominant position, finding that three TV broadcasters enjoy a collective

[159] Decision No. 01-26-3-08-148-II/13 of March 6, 2014.

[160] Competition Council, *RTV BH, RTV FBH, RTRS and Media Pool*, UP-01-26-3-09-47/2023, 30.05.2023.

[161] The Committee is established under Article 7 of the Law on Public RTV System of BiH, Official Gazette of BiH, No 78/2005, 35/2009, 32/2010, 51/2015, 25/2016.

dominant position. The CC considered the quantity rebates as fidelity rebates by referring to *Suiker Unie*.[162] The CC referred to EUCJ cases *Aalborg Portland*[163] and *Dresdner Bank*[164] when stating that practices constituting restrictive agreements are usually secretly applied and that they need to be proved by relying on indirect evidence, which in its entirety establishes proof of competition infringement.[165]

The CC conclusion regarding the collective dominant position of RTV broadcasters was not substantiated with evidence. The CC missed the point considering that the Committee of the Public RTV System in B&H consisted of representatives of public TV broadcasters. The Committee does not have legal powers to issue decisions on advertising prices by public RTV broadcasters.[166] The Committee's decision on the joint Price List represented an outright agreement violating Article 4 of the Competition Act, since RTV broadcasters agreed on advertising prices within the Committee. The Committee's decision on prices was a decision of the association of undertakings within the meaning of Article 101 TFEU.

6.3 Merger Control Case: Procedural Rights of Parties to Concentration

Article 6 of the European Convention on Human Rights (ECHR) protects the fundamental right to a fair trial, entailing also the right to legal protection, i.e. access to the court. The aforementioned article guarantees the right to a fair trial in civil and criminal matters and in certain administrative procedures. Concerning competition law, Article 6 ECHR may be relevant when a party contests a procedure or decision of a competition authority, claiming that there has been a violation of the right to a fair trial.

On 13 April 2011, company Bimal, Brčko, signed a contract with two other companies - B. (with a registered office in the Republic of Srpska) and C. (with a registered office in the Federation of Bosnia and Herzegovina)—to establish a legal entity E. (as a joint venture) for the waste packaging management.[167] Two years after the contract was signed, Bimal and its two contracting parties officially notified the CC about establishing legal entity E, per Article 16 of the CA. Acting in accordance

[162] *Suiker Unie and Others v. Commission*, Joined cases 40 to 48, 50, 54 to 56, 111, 113 and 114-73, C-40/73, 16.12.1975, ECLI:EU:C:1975:174.

[163] Joined Cases C-204/00 P, C-205/00 P, C-211/00 P, C-213/00 P, C-217/00 P and C-219/00 P, 7.01.2004, ECLI:EU:C:2004:6.

[164] *Dresdner Bank AG and Others v. European Commission*, Joined Cases T-44/02 OP, T-54/02 OP, T-56/02 OP, T-60/02 OP and T-61/02 OP, 27.09.2006, ECLI:EU:T:2006:271.

[165] Competition Council, *RTV BiH, RTV FBiH, RTRS and Media Pool*, p. 16.

[166] Law on Public RTV System of BiH [2005] as amended, Art 8 (1).

[167] *Bimal d.d. v. Bosnia and Herzegovina*, Judgment of 31 August 2021, Application No. 27289/17, 31.08.2021.

with the statutory deadlines and considering the competition effects of the concentration in the relevant geographical area of the entire territory of Bosnia and Herzegovina, the CC adopted a Decision on 1 August 2013,[168] finding that the concentration fell under the CA, since it represented a full-function joint venture, and as such, it was subject to the notification obligation. Furthermore, the CC found that the parties did not notify the concentration within the legal time limit of fifteen days and had implemented it before the CC confirmed it was compliant with the CA. The CC imposed separate fines on the three companies. In the case of Bimal, the penalty included a fine of BAM 104,572.00 (0.04% of its annual turnover in 2010) for failure to submit the notification to the CC within the legal time limit and a fine of BAM 329,403.00 (or 0.126% of its annual turnover in 2010) for implementing the concentration before obtaining a CC decision confirming that it was compliant with the CA.

On 5 August 2013, Bimal d.o.o. submitted a proposal for the renewal of the procedure to the CC, claiming that the Council was not correctly informed of its turnover, and after that, all three companies jointly submitted a proposal for the renewal of the procedure to the CC, referring to the previous proposal submitted by Bimal, and expanding the initial proposal to the calculation of fines based on incorrect information about annual turnover and the relevant geographic market definition. The CC issued a decision adopting the request related to the calculation of imposed fines based on the correct amount of turnover. The fines imposed on Bimal were decreased to BAM 57,998.00 (0.04% of its annual turnover in 2010) for failure to submit the notification to the CC within the legal time limit and BAM 182,693.00 (or 0.126% of its annual turnover in 2010) for implementing a concentration before obtaining a CC decision confirming that it was compliant with the CA.

On 29 August 2013, the three companies jointly initiated an administrative dispute against the CC's decision before the Court of Bosnia and Herzegovina. In the lawsuit, they stated that the legal entity they founded did not represent a concentration within the meaning of the CA. Consequently, the notification to the CC about establishing this legal entity was not mandatory. The complaint read that the CC did not adequately define the relevant geographic market and that the imposed fines were unlawful and draconian. The Court of B&H submitted the complaint filed in the administrative dispute to the CC, soliciting its response, and ordered the CC to submit the complete file related to the case in question. The CC followed the court order. The Court of B&H rendered a judgment on 16 November 2015,[169] confirming the decisions of the CC dated 1 August 2013 and 10 October 2013. Bimal neither received the CC's response to the complaint in the administrative dispute nor its subsequent notice submitted to the court. Using the extraordinary legal remedy, on 22 December 2015, the three companies jointly submitted a request to review the judgment of the Court of B&H to the Appellate Division of the Court. Pursuant to the provisions of the B&H Law on Administrative Disputes, the CC

[168] Competition Council, *Bimal d.d.*, 02-26-1-09-14-II/13, 1.08.2013.

[169] Court of BiH, S1 3 U 013779 13 U, 16.11.2015.

submitted its response to the request for review of the judgment of the Court of B&H, stating its position regarding the definition of a geographic market and the alleged unlawfulness of the imposed fines. The Court did not deliver this response to Bimal. On 11 April 2016, the Appellate Panel of the Court of B&H rejected the request to review the judgment of the Court of B&H.[170]

After that, on 17 June 2016, Bimal filed an application with the Constitutional Court of B&H against the judgments passed in the administrative dispute procedure and appealed under Article 6 of the European Convention on Human Rights due to the failure of the Court of B&H to provide them with the CC's response to their complaint in the administrative dispute and their request for review of the judgment of the Court of B&H of 16 November 2015, which violated the principles of equality of parties to the proceedings. The Constitutional Court rejected the application as unfounded.[171] After exhausting all national remedies, Bimal filed the Application before the European Court of Human Rights (ECtHR) in 2017.

The procedure before the ECtHR can be divided into two phases. The first phase involves establishing the applicability of Article 6 of the Convention for the Protection of Human Rights and Fundamental Freedoms (ECHR) in the specific case. The second phase is to decide whether Article 6 ECHR has been violated in the case of Bimal, which implies the merits of the matter. In the context of the applicability of Article 6, the Court established that it was a special procedure for assessing violations of competition law in which the CC as a public body imposes fines for violations of the law, which are not criminal law measures by nature. However, in view of the purpose of the provisions governing the issue of concentration on the B&H market, the competence of the CC arising from the general interest of society and the fact that criminal laws most often protect such interest, the Court considered that Article 6, in its criminal nature, was applicable to the procedure in question. The Court examined the parties' allegations on merits. In this context, it examined whether the procedure was unfair because the Court did not deliver Bimal the CC responses during the judicial review procedure. The B&H government pointed out that the submission of the CC responses was contrary to national law, claiming that the review procedure in an administrative dispute and civil procedure is specific and that regardless of the rights of the parties under Article 6 ECHR, the administrative procedure does not follow identical rules. According to the B&H Government, Bimal's rights were protected by granting it access to the file.

The ECtHR found that in this case,[172] the respect for the right to a fair trial, guaranteed by Article 6 (1) ECHR, required that Court of B&H allow Bimal to read the response submitted by the opposing party and respond to it. However, Bimal did not get this opportunity, and ECHR Article 6 was violated. In view of the ECtHR decision in Bimal case and to harmonise the procedure before the Constitutional Court of B&H with the ECtHR practice under ECHR Article 6(1), the Constitutional

[170] Court of BiH, S1 3 U 013779 15 Uvp, 11.04.2016.

[171] Constitutional Court of Bosnia and Herzegovina, AP-2430/16, 15.09.2016.

[172] *Bimal d.d. v. Bosnia and Herzegovina*, Judgment of 31 August 2021, Application No. 27289/17.

Court of B&H adopted a Conclusion on the delivery of responses to the application to the applicants on 16 December 2021.[173]

7 Enforcement and Sanctioning Statistics for the Period 2012–2022

The CC annual work reports present data on fines and administrative fees collected (see Table 3). Namely, the collected fines and fees (stipulated by the Competition Act) represent revenue to the budget of B&H institutions.[174] It should be emphasised that the annual reports are not methodologically uniform. Besides, they do not contain data on the amount of fines imposed per type of competition law violation. For this reason, it was impossible to present exact data on fines imposed according to the type of competition infringement.

When comparing the range of fines the CC can impose under the Competition Act to the actual fines imposed in the period 2012–2022, it becomes evident that the CC has been implementing a lenient sanctioning policy. Besides, the total fines

Table 3 The total amount of imposed fines and administrative fees[a] (2012–2022)[b]

Year	Total imposed fines (in BAM)	Total imposed fines (in EUR)[c]	Total administrative fees (in BAM)[d]	Total administrative fees (in EUR)[c]
2012	2,421,354.75	1,238,452.92	72,093.92	36,843.87
2013	1,345,595.95	687,568.90	95,650.00	48,915.05
2014	703,673.00	359,791.60	153,650.00	78,519.75
2015	–	–	123,000.00	62,873.90
2016	624,492.93	319,197.90	234,574.24	119,903.12
2017	11,000.00	5,624.30	120,822.00	61,777.28
2018	285,657.83	146,059.80	504,711.00	258,041.00
2019	60,750.00	31,073.50	137,710.00	70,431.90
2020	151,094.00	77,234.40	118,750.00	60,731.90
2021	646,350.00	330,529.50	646,350.00	330,529.50
2022	300,000.00	153,390.00	128,101.00	65,521.60

Source: Authors' own calculation based on CC Annual Reports for the period 2012–2022

[a] All values are nominal values

[b] In the Annual Reports on the Work of the Competition Council, there is no data on the amount of fines imposed for specific types of violations of the Competition Act. The authors submitted an inquiry to the Competition Council to obtain the requested data; however, the CC did not comply with their request

[c] Calculation based on average exchange rate for the relevant year

[d] Administrative fees are paid for procedural actions before the CC in cases such as reviewing the adopted decision, notification of concentration, etc.

[173] Constitutional Court of B&H, SU-02-1056/21.

[174] Competition Act, Art 60.

decreased during the same period. Total fines in 2012 amounted to around EUR 1.238 million, while in 2022, the CC imposed only around EUR 153,390 in fines. In most cases, the CC imposed fines on concentration parties who did not comply with the obligation to notify a concentration before its implementation. Generally, the CC did not have many cases concerning abuse of dominant position and anticompetitive agreements in 2012–2022, which explains the small amount of fines levied.

In 2023, the CC imposed a BAM 200,000 fine on three TV broadcasting companies and a marketing agency, Media Pool, for implementing discriminatory prices and loyalty rebates in the advertising market.[175] Each party was fined equally. The CC did not explain the method used to calculate the fine, and it did not publish data concerning the annual turnover of TV broadcasters and Media Pool. Despite the lack of data, it can be easily presumed that the fine represented only a minor fraction of the infringers' annual turnover. In the case *Digital Asset Management v. Raiffeisen Bank*, which was decided under Article 4 of the Competition Act on prohibited agreements, the CC imposed BAM 250,000.00 on Raiffeisen Bank.[176]

The CC has rarely imposed remedies to re-establish effective competition in the market since the CC is authorised to impose remedies only in the case of prohibited concentrations or non-notified concentrations under Article 19 of the CA (see Table 4).

8 Judicial Review

Proceedings before the CC are administrative procedures. According to Article 43(5) of the Competition Act, the decision of the Competition Council is final. The Competition Act, in Art. 46, stipulates that "the injured party to the proceedings may lodge an administrative dispute before the Court of Bosnia and Herzegovina, within 30 days from the date of receipt or publication of such decision".

8.1 Court of Bosnia and Herzegovina

The Court of B&H is competent to resolve administrative disputes in lawsuits against the CC's decisions. Presently, the Court of B&H has 51 judges.[177] The Court panels comprise three judges each. The cases are allocated to the panels in an automatic case allocation system. The Court of B&H has three divisions: criminal, administrative and appellate (see Fig. 1).

[175] Competition Council, *RTV BiH, RTV FBiH, RTRS, and Media Pool*, UP-01-26-3-09-47/2023, 30.05.2023.

[176] 250,000 BAM.

[177] Court of B&H (2024).

Table 4 Number of decisions of the CC by types of CA violations (2012–2022)

Year	Prohibited agreements	Abuse of a dominant position	Concentrations
2012	10	3	12
2013	6	7	16
2014	13	7	19
2015	7[a]	7	23
2016	5[b]	5	11
2017	5[c]	1	12
2018	5[d]	1	24
2019	–	1[e]	9
2020	4[f]	11	12
2021	6	7[g]	10
2022	2[h]	4	12

Source: Authors' own calculation based on CC Annual Reports for the period 2012–2022

[a] The CC Annual Report 2015 states that in 2015, 43 cases were received, final decisions were made for 31 cases. Of the total number of cases received, 16 related to the area of restrictive agreements and abuse of a dominant position, and 7 final decisions were adopted at the meetings of the CC

[b] The CC (2016) Annual Report 2016 states that in 2016, 34 cases were received, 19 related to prohibited agreements and abuse of a dominant position, and at the sessions the Council of Competition made five final decisions related to prohibited agreements and abuse of a dominant position and one related to determination of individual prohibited agreements

[c] The CC Annual Report 2017 states: "Of the 41 cases received, 14 relate to prohibited agreements and abuse of a dominant position. The Council of Competition adopted 6 final decisions, namely: two decisions suspending the procedures for establishing a prohibited agreement, one decision dismissed the request for establishing prohibited agreement, one decision rejecting the request for establishing a prohibited agreement and one decision rejecting the request for establishing an individual exemption from prohibited agreements. The Council of Competition adopted one decision rejecting the request for establishing abuse of a dominant position."

[d] The CC Annual Report 2018 states: "Out of a total of 49 cases received, 14 refer to prohibited competitive activities, namely: three cases refer to prohibited agreements and 11 to abuse of a dominant position. The Council of Competition made 6 final decisions: one request to establish a prohibited agreement is rejected as unfounded, one request to establish a prohibited agreement was dismissed due to lack of jurisdiction, one request to establish abuse of a dominant position was dismissed as unfounded, one request was dismissed due to lack of jurisdiction, and two proceedings to determine a prohibited agreement were suspended due to withdrawal of the parties."

[e] The 2019 CC Annual Report states: "Out of a total of 31 cases received in the field of competition in 2019, eight cases related to prohibited competitive activities, namely: five cases related to the area of prohibited agreements and three to the abuse of a dominant position. In the mentioned areas, at the meetings of the Council of Competition, one final decision was adopted: one request to determine the abuse of a dominant position due to actual lack of competence was rejected, while the remaining seven cases are pending."

[f] The CC Annual Report 2020 states: "Out of a total of 35 cases received in the field of competition in 2020, 16 cases related to prohibited competitive activities, namely: three cases related to the area of prohibited agreements and 10 to abuse of a dominant position and another three cases related to prohibited agreements and abuse of a dominant position. At the sessions, the Council of Competition adopted 8 final decisions: one request to determine a prohibited agreement was suspended, and three requests to determine abuse of a dominant position were suspended, and one request related to both prohibited competitive activities was suspended. Two requests to determine the abuse of a dominant position were rejected, and one decision was made that confirms the abuse of a dominant position. The remaining eight cases are pending."

(continued)

Table 4 (continued)

[g] The CC Annual Report 2021 states: "Out of a total of 53 cases received in the field of competition in 2021, 27 cases related to prohibited competitive activities, namely: 15 cases related to the area of prohibited agreements and six to abuse of a dominant position and 6 cases related to prohibited agreements and abuse of a dominant position. At the sessions, the Council of Competition adopted 12 final decisions: one request to determine a prohibited agreement, and one request to determine abuse of a dominant position, and three requests on both legal grounds were rejected as unfounded, the existence of a prohibited agreement was established in three cases and the existence of abuse of a dominant position in one case, two requests were dismissed due to a lack of jurisdiction, and in one case it was considered that there was no abuse of a dominant position. The remaining 15 cases are pending."

[h] The CC Annual Report 2022 states: "Out of a total of 31 cases received in the field of competition in 2021, 11 cases related to prohibited competitive activities, namely: seven cases related to the area of prohibited agreements and four to abuse of a dominant position, of which one case was closed on both grounds. At the sessions, the Council of Competition adopted five final decisions: two requests for the determination of prohibited agreements were rejected, one request for the determination of a dominant position was rejected, the existence of abuse of a dominant position was determined in two cases, in one case it was determined that there was no abuse of a dominant position while in in one case the party waived the request. The remaining cases are pending."

The Administrative Division comprises the Department for Administrative Disputes, Litigation/Civil Department, and the Executive Department (Enforcement Procedure Subdivision/Section). The Administrative Department solve administrative disputes. It decides on lawsuits against final administrative acts of the institutions of Bosnia and Herzegovina, including the CC. In all administrative disputes, the Court decides in a panel composed of three judges unless otherwise stipulated by law. The Appellate Division consists of three Sections. Section III rules on appellations upon decisions of the Administrative Division.

Parties can submit an extraordinary legal remedy against the decision of the Administrative Division of the Court of B&H. Law on Administrative Disputes (LAD) provides for the following types of extraordinary legal remedies:[178]

i. Request to reopen the procedure, decided by the Administrative Division of the Court of B&H;
ii. Request for the protection of legality, decided by the Appellate Division of the Court of B&H;
iii. Request to reconsider the court's decision, decided by the Appellate Division of the Court of B&H.

As mentioned earlier, the Competition Act regulates judicial protection against the final decisions of the CC. A defendant party to the proceedings may lodge an administrative dispute before the Court of B&H within 30 days from receipt or publication of such decision.[179] This deadline is significantly shorter than the

[178] This procedure and types of decisions are also valid in the procedure regarding the lawsuit on the decision of the CC.

[179] Competition Act, Art 46.

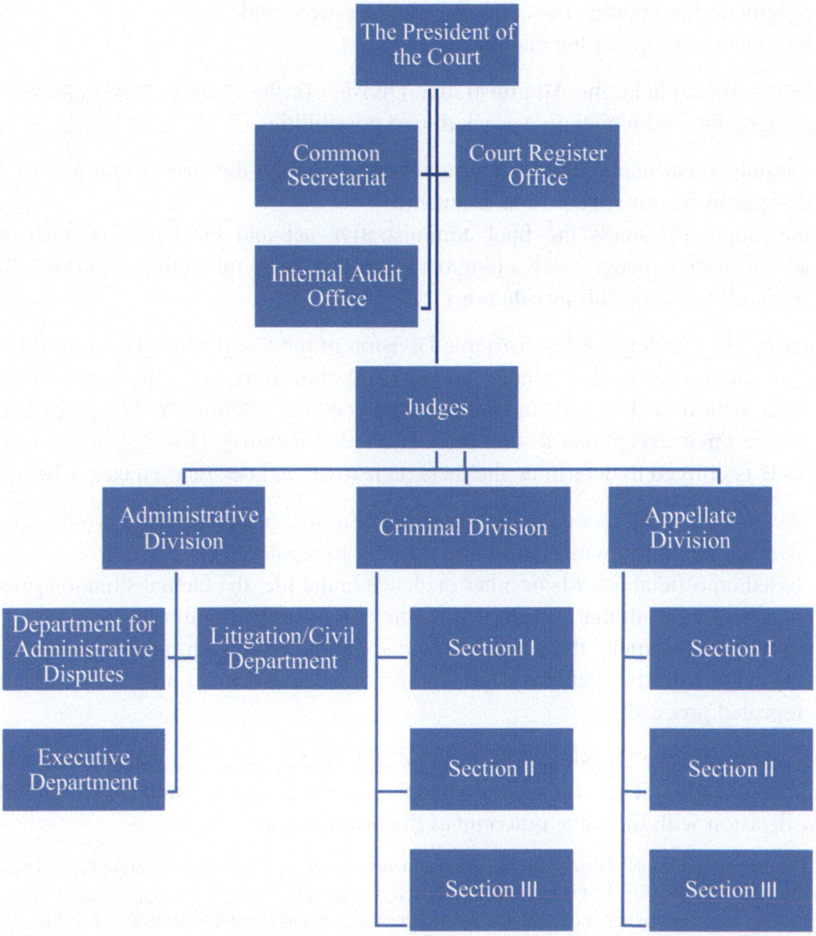

Fig. 1 Organisation chart of the Court of Bosnia and Herzegovina. Source: Court of B&H (2024)

deadline for filing a lawsuit (60 days) provided for in the Law on Administrative Disputes.[180]

The Administrative Division of the Court of B&H can issue two types of decisions: a decision dismissing the lawsuit for the reasons established by LAD and a judgment that resolves the administrative dispute.

Generally, the Administrative Division of the Court of B&H resolves the dispute based on facts established in the administrative procedure and may render two types of judgments as follows:

[180] Law on Administrative Disputes of BiH (LAD), Official Gazette of B&H, No 19/2002, 88/2007, 83/2008 and 74/2010.

i. judgment that upholds the administrative decision; and
ii. judgment that rejects the claim as ill-founded.

If the claim is upheld, the Administrative Division of the Court of B&H annuls the challenged final administrative act with two possibilities:[181]

i. the judgement annuls the final administrative act and the case is returned to the competent institution for re-assessment;
ii. the judgment annuls the final administrative act and the Court resolves the administrative matter. Such a judgment replaces the annulled final administrative act in all respects (full jurisdiction).

Situations in which the Administrative Division of the Court of B&H can decide in full jurisdiction are limited. Under Art. 34 LAD, the Court, as a rule, decides based on facts determined in the first instance proceedings (administrative procedure). There are three exceptions to this rule. The Administrative Division of the Court of B&H is obliged to determine the facts on its own and decide on a case where:[182]

i. the repetition of proceedings before an administrative authority would cause damage to a party which would be difficult to repair;
ii. based on official records or other evidence in the file, the factual situation *prima facie* differs from that determined by the administrative authority
iii. in the same dispute, the Court has already annulled the administrative act, and the administrative authority has not followed the Court's instructions in the repeated proceedings.

The Administrative Division of the Court of B&H explained its position concerning the situation when it had already annulled the administrative act, and the CC issued a new decision with the same outcome as the original one:

> The interpretation of the law by the court always relates to a specific, concrete case. The court can adopt a legal opinion concerning the interpretation of the law applicable to that specific case only when a factual situation is completely and correctly determined. If this is not the case, the court, when annulling an administrative act in applying Article 34 para. 2 of the Law on Administrative Disputes, points out how the law should be interpreted and applied – when all essential facts are determined confidently and within the correctly conducted procedure. Therefore, the position of the court in this situation is always conditional, that is, depending on the factual circumstances determined in the repeated proceedings, and provided that all irregularities to which it was pointed by the judgment are eliminated, the administrative authority can issue an administrative act solving an administrative matter in the same way, whereas not departing from the judgment and the position of the court.[183]

A party that is dissatisfied with the Court's judgment (i.e., the judgment of the Administrative Division of the Court of B&H) can use one of the above-mentioned

[181] Article 37 (2) and 4 LAD.
[182] Article 34 (2) LAD.
[183] Court of B&H, *Polyclinic v. Competition Council of B&H,* S1 3 U 024742 18 U2, 5.04.2018.

Table 5 Total number of judgments of the Court of Bosnia and Herzegovina in cases related to the decisions of the Competition Council for the period 2010–2022

Type	Anti-competitive agreements	Abuses of dominant position	Concentrations	Total
Number of judgments of the Court of B&H, which upheld the lawsuit against the decision of the CC	–[a]	–[a]	–[a]	48
Number of judgments of the Court of B&H rejecting the lawsuit against the decision of the CC	52	56	11	119

Source: Data collected based on the questionnaire sent to the Court of Bosnia and Herzegovina for a period 2012–2022
[a] The Court of B&H did not provide data on the number of judgments per case type

extraordinary legal remedies: a request to reopen the procedure, a request for the protection of legality or a request to reconsider the court's decision. Depending on the type of extraordinary legal remedy used the Appellate Division or the Administrative Division of the Court decide in the second instance.

8.2 *Handling Lawsuits Based on the Decisions of the Competition Council*

For the purposes of this chapter, research was conducted on the number of cases initiated before the Court of B&H based on Article 46 of the Competition Act. Table 5 shows the total number of judgments of the Court of B&H on lawsuits against decisions of the CC for the period 2010–2022, the number of judgments which upheld the lawsuit against the decision of the CC and the number of judgments rejecting the lawsuit against the decision of the CC. The fifth column of the table shows the number of judgments of the Appellate Division of the Court of B&H in proceedings where an extraordinary legal remedy was used and the lawsuit against the Competition Council was rejected (in 84.61% of cases).

It is apparent that the court of B&H upheld a small number of lawsuits against the CC decisions, whereas it rejected a significant number of lawsuits. When analysing the number of judgments per case type, it is evident that the Court decided in a significantly smaller number of concentration cases (see Table 6). In contrast, the number of cases concerning abuse of dominant position and prohibited agreements is almost equal. This is logical, considering that very few CC decisions in concentration cases are disputed by parties.

Notably, the Administrative Division of the Court of B&H has eight judges working on all competition-related cases, which limits efficiency in addition to budgetary restrictions. The judges of the Administrative Division of the Court of B&H resolve other administrative disputes besides competition law cases.

Table 6 Total number of judgments of the Court of B&H per case type

Type	Anti-competitive agreements	Abuses of dominant position	Concentrations	Total
Number of judgments where the Administrative Division of the Court of B&H (1st instance) rejected a lawsuit against a CC decision	35	31	2	68
Number of judgments of the Administrative Division of the Court of B&H (2nd instance) rejecting requests to reopen the procedure (extraordinary legal remedy)	13	12	1	26
Number of judgments of the Appellate Division of the Court of B&H (2nd instance) confirming a judgment of the Administrative Division by which a lawsuit against a CC decision was rejected	12	10	0	22

Source: Data collected based on the questionnaire sent to the Court of Bosnia and Herzegovina for a period 2012–2022

The Court of B&H's practice in applying competition law is not consistent. The Court further complicated the important issue regarding the personal sphere of application of B&H competition law by rendering conflicting decisions.[184] Concerning the application of the Competition Act upon state organs and public authorities, in 2018, the Court made it clear that acts entailing the execution of state powers cannot be sanctioned under the law protecting market competition.[185] It made a reference to several relevant EU cases in its decision to support its view. In 2022, however, the Court stated that organs from all levels of the state power fall under the Competition Act. It went further to say that a rulebook adopted by a state organ which restricts the free entrance of economic operators to the B&H market constitutes a prohibited agreement under Article 4(1) Competition Act.[186] The case concerned a rulebook issued by the Ministry of Health FB&H under the Law on Health Protection,[187] preventing medical institutions in private ownership from conducting sanitary inspections. The Court found that the Ministry did not execute public authorities stipulated by the Law on Health Protection since the Law does not restrict the right to perform sanitary inspections to public health institutions. It considered that the activity of the Ministry was of economic character since the rulebook, with restrictive provisions not founded in the Law of Health Protection, effectively prevented private providers of health services from accessing the market

[184] See also on this point Svetlicinii (2013a).

[185] Court of B&H, *Polyclinic v. Competition Council of BiH,* S1 3 U 024742 18 U 2, 5.04.2018.

[186] Court of B&H, *Federal Ministry of Health v. Competition Council of BiH,* S1 3 U 035154 22 Uvp, 21.04.2022, p. 96.

[187] Official Gazette of FB&H, No 46/2010, 75/2013.

and competing with state health institutions. Although the Court was right to say that the Ministry went beyond the powers entrusted to it by law, it overlooked the fact that the Ministry did not perform any economic activity when it adopted the contested rulebook.

The Court discussed the CC's authority to enforce fines by collecting payments from companies belonging to the same company group but not being directly involved in competition infringement. In 2012, the CC rendered a decision against the Serbian beer company Apatinska pivara a.d concerning the abuse of dominant position.[188] Apatinska pivara was a subsidiary of the Netherlands company Starbev Netherlands BV. The CC decision against Apatinska pivara stipulated a provision authorising the CC, in case the defendant does not pay the fine voluntarily within the specified timeline, to collect the fine from Starbev subsidiaries present in the B&H–Cervesia Zagreb d.o.o. and Zagrebačka pivara d.d. The appellant argued that the CC imposed the fine on Apatinska pivara and not the Starbev group. Therefore, the CC could not collect fines from other companies within the group. However, the Court of B&H confirmed the CC decision based on the Competition Act definition of undertaking, which also covers connected undertakings.[189] It further stated that the Competition Act provisions on extraterritorial application of competition law would only make sense if the CC could collect fines from legal entities from the same company group in the domestic market.[190] The Court failed to distinguish between the substantive notion of undertaking in competition law and the procedural notion of a party in the proceedings. Since Starbev Netherlands and its subsidiaries from Croatia did not participate in the proceedings as parties, the CC could not stipulate in its decision that it would collect fines from locally present subsidiaries of Starbev Netherlands.

9 Private Enforcement of Competition Law

Lawsuits for compensation of damages caused by competition law infringements can be conceptualised based on civil delict, in line with the general provisions of the Law on Obligations.[191] The Competition Act does not stipulate provisions for the filing of lawsuits for compensation for damages caused by competition violations

[188] Competition Council, *Apatinska pivara a.d.*, 02-26-028-145-II/11, 4.09.2012, Official Gazette of B&H, No 6/2013.

[189] Competition Act, Art 2(2).

[190] Court of B&H, *Molson Coors d.o.o. v. Competition Council of BiH*, S1 3 U 011234 14 Uvp, 3.10.2014, Bulletin of the Case Law, No 5/2015, p. 135.

[191] Law on Obligations [1978], Official Gazette of the SFRY, No 29/1978, 39/1985, 45/1989 - decision of the Court of Justice and 57/1989, Official Gazette of the RB&H, No 2/1992, 13/1993 and 13/1994 and Official Gazette of FB&H, No 29/2003 and 42/2011; Law on Obligations, Official Gazette of the SFRY, No. 29/1978, 39/1985, 45/1989 - decision of the Supreme Court of Justice and 57/1989 and Official Gazette of the RS, No. 17/1993, 3/1996, 37/2001, 39/2003 and 74/2004.

and the possibility of imposing civil sanctions or interim measures.[192] However, the Law on Obligations provides for the nullity of a contract breaching Article 4 of the Competition Act. It is worth noting that the civil procedure laws of B&H entities lay down a possibility of bringing collective actions by associations, organs, and other organisations who pursue activities aiming to protect citizens' legally founded rights and interests.[193] However, a special law dealing with protecting specific rights and interests needs to stipulate the powers of associations and other bodies to bring collective action.[194] Since the Competition Act does not provide for the authority for business and consumer associations and other bodies engaged in the protection of rights and interests of these categories to bring civil actions, the B&H civil procedure laws' stipulations remain *nudum ius*.

What remains an option for the parties who have suffered damages is to file an individual action for compensation of damages in civil proceedings where they need to prove the amount of damages and the CC decision is a means of proof of a competition violation. The effects of final administrative acts in civil court proceedings are not explicitly regulated in the B&H civil procedure laws. The laws on civil procedure of the FB&H and RS stipulate that a civil court can decide on the existence of a certain legal right or relationship if another court or competent organ has yet to decide on the same issue (a preliminary legal issue).[195] In case the competent organ (i.e. an administrative authority) later issues a final decision which solves the same legal issue differently, a party in the civil court's proceedings may ask for reopening the case based on Article 255(1)(7) of the Civil Procedure Law of the FB&H and RS. The Court of B&H takes a firm position that it is bound by a final decision of an administrative authority if a party has missed the opportunity to challenge the decision before the administrative court.[196] However, this opinion of the courts is disputed in the part of ex-Yugoslav legal theory, arguing that it jeopardises the independence of courts.[197]

Consequently, a final decision of the CC finding a Competition Act violation constitutes *prima facie* evidence concerning the existence of a competition law infringement. A claimant must prove the causal link between the competition law infringement, the damage caused by the defendant, and the amount of damages. In practice, this evidence is in the possession of the CC and a defendant party. Civil courts in B&H (and that is the case in other ex-Yugoslav jurisdictions) lack the power to request third parties to submit the evidence needed to prove the amount of

[192] Imamović-Čizmić and Grbo (2018), pp. 57–58.

[193] Law on Civil Procedure of the Federation of BiH [2003], Official Gazette of FB&H, No 53/2003, 73/2005, 19/2006 and 98/2015, Art 453a; Law on Civil Procedure of the Republic of Srpska [2003] , Official Gazette of RS, No 58/2003, 85/2003, 74/2005, 63/2007, 105/2008– decision of the Constitutional Court, 45/2009 – decision of the Constitutional Court, 49/2009, 61/2013 and 109/2021 – decision of the Constitutional Court, Article 453a.

[194] ibid.

[195] The Law on Civil Procedure of the Federation of B&H [2003], Art 12; Law on Civil Procedure of the Republic of Srpska [2003], Art 12.

[196] Court of B&H, S1 3 P 027939 19 Pž od 3. 9. 2019.

[197] Karanikić-Mirić (2014), 73.

damage and the causal link between the anticompetitive act and the damage.[198] The lack of specific provisions in the Competition Act on civil proceedings concerning compensation of antitrust damages prevents private enforcement of competition law in Bosnia and Herzegovina. Parties hesitate to file a lawsuit to claim damages in civil proceedings because they are sceptical about the case's outcome.

10 Criminal Law Enforcement

The Criminal Act of B&H does not stipulate criminal offences related to competition infringements.[199] Besides the Criminal Act on the state level, three criminal laws exist at the entity level: the Criminal Act of the Federation of B&H,[200] the Criminal Code of the Republic of Srpska,[201] and the Criminal Act of Brčko District.[202] The Criminal Act of FB&H stipulated in Article 253 the criminal offence 'Creation of Monopolistic Position':

> A natural person within a legal person who agrees on restricting another legal or natural person in the free trade of goods or services within a specific area or with other legal and natural persons, or agrees on creating a monopolistic position of certain legal or natural persons on the market in another way, shall be punished by a prison sentence between six months and five years.[203]

The Criminal Code of RS does not prohibit monopolistic (restrictive) agreements. However, it lays down a criminal offence 'Agreeing on the Contest Outcome' in Article 239. A person who agrees on the outcome of a sports contest or any other contest shall be punished by a prison sentence ranging from six months to ten years. Article 239 of the Criminal Code of RS can be used to prosecute bid rigging.

B&H authorities have not prosecuted violators of the said provisions so far. Prosecutors' lack of knowledge about the harmful effects of acts restricting market competition and their lack of expertise in investigative techniques needed to prove these criminal offences represent the principal reasons for lenient criminal enforcement.

---

[198] The interview with an eminent law firm, which specialises in competition law, revealed that parties whose requests for proceedings were accepted by the CC and where the CC passed a decision confirming the violation that caused them damages do not pursue compensation in civil proceedings due to complexity of proving the damages.

[199] Criminal Act of BiH, Official Gazette of B&H, No 3/2003, 32/2003, 37/2003, 54/2004, 61/2004, 30/2005, 53/2006, 55/2006, 8/2010, 47/2014, 22/2015, 40/2015, 35/2018, 46/2021, 31/2023 and 47/2023.

[200] Criminal Act of FBiH, Official Gazette of FB&H, No 36/2003, 21/2004, 69/2004, 18/2005, 42/2010, 42/2011, 59/2014, 76/2014, 46/2016, 75/2017 and 31/2023.

[201] Criminal Code of RS, Official Gazette of RS, No 64/2017, 104/2018 – Constitutional Court decision, 15/2021, 89/2021 and 73/2023.

[202] Criminal Act of BD, Official Gazette of BD, No 19/2020.

[203] The Criminal Act of BD provides for an identical provision in Article 247.

11 Current Trends and Future Challenges to Enforcing Competition Law

There are many challenges that the CC is facing in the effective implementation of the competition law in B&H, especially after B&H was granted EU candidate status. The Competition Act should be amended to remove the aforementioned deficiencies and obstacles that prevent the efficient work of the CC and to improve the CC powers and capacities necessary for the performance of all activities entrusted by law to it. Namely, the specifics of competition law in B&H, recognised as legal anomalies also by the European Commission in the Progress Reports and discussed earlier, require adopting a new law on competition.[204] The CC decision-making, based on Article 11 (3) of the Competition Act, whereas it declares that a defendant had not violated the law if the CC did not adopt a decision within the specified time limit, prevents effective competition law enforcement and, consequently, causes great damage both to economic entities and to the entire economy. The principal reason for the CC's delay in completing investigations and decision-making lies in the "ethnic-based veto" incorporated in Article 24 of the Competition Act, which is also confirmed by our analysis of cases decided by the CC. The rules for appointing members of the Council as the decision-making body must be changed to ensure that the expertise and experience of candidates become the principal criterion for selecting the Council members. The provisions allowing for the "ethnic-based veto" must be removed from the new law.

The new law should also foresee the authority for the CC to impose structural and behavioural remedies to re-establish effective competition in the market in all forms of competition violations. More detailed procedural provisions are needed to protect parties' rights in proceedings before the CC. Special provisions are needed to regulate compensation for damages caused by competition law violations in civil court proceedings and to harmonise the B&H competition law with Directive 2014/104. Furthermore, the new law should enable natural and legal persons not being parties to the proceedings to submit an initiative for opening an investigation, as is the case, for example, in the Act on the Protection of Market Competition of the Republic of Croatia.[205] In addition, several bylaws should be amended to fully harmonise competition law with the EU *acquis*, especially bylaws on block exemption of certain categories of anti-competitive agreements.

With regard to judicial control of the CC decisions, it is necessary to introduce special provisions into the new law providing the Court of B&iH unlimited jurisdiction in cases where it decides upon the CC decisions imposing a fine or a periodic penalty payment to a defendant. As explained above, the Court of B&H has the power to decide on the legality of CC decisions. Only in limited circumstances can it

[204] In August 2020, the CC passed a Decision to appoint a working group to prepare a draft Law on Amendments to the Competition Act (2020).

[205] Act on the Protection of Market Competition of the Republic of Croatia - consolidated text, Narodne novine, No 79/09, 80/13, 41/21, Art 35.

adopt a decision altering the CC decision or replacing the CC's decision. As we mentioned earlier, the Court is entitled to issue a judgment replacing the CC decision only in cases where it has already annulled the CC decision and the CC did not follow the Court's instructions in the reopened proceedings. The existing powers of the Court of B&H are not compliant with Article 31 of Regulation 1/2003, according to which the court must have unlimited jurisdiction to review the competition authority's decision fixing the fine or periodic penalty payment.

Besides, since B&H does not have a long competition law legacy, it is necessary to raise public awareness of the importance of effectively implementing competition law. Given this, the promotion of competition should play a special role, which, according to the Competition Act, should be advocated by the CC. Continuous training and informing of economic operators and consumers through their associations is required concerning the basic categories of competition law, which opens the space for action by educational institutions. Training of the courts on issues concerning the application of competition law in administrative and civil proceedings is also necessary.

Furthermore, in light of the perceived activities of the competition authorities in the region, the CC should develop a practice of implementing sectoral analyses and guidelines that would facilitate the implementation of the law and understanding of its provisions by those who are to apply it.

CC needs stronger enforcement powers, especially regarding dawn raids. Under the current legal regime, the CC cannot conduct a dawn raid since the Competition Act does not stipulate which court is competent to issue a warrant allowing the CC officials to conduct the unannounced inspection of premises and objects of suspected competition law violators. Parties' procedural rights in proceedings before CC must be regulated in more detail to make the B&H competition law compliant with ECHR requirements.

12 Conclusion

The establishment and development of competition laws in transition countries have always been a difficult task for several reasons: weak economies, fragmented markets, existing ties between political and economic oligarchies, incumbent operators occupying national markets and preventing the rise of new competition, citizens' ignorance of the benefits of effective competition policy, etc. In Bosnia and Herzegovina, the situation is even more complicated due to the multiethnic structure of the state and unresolved issues concerning the competencies of the state-level and entity-level authorities. In these circumstances, enacting the Competition Act and establishing the Competition Council as the exclusive enforcer of competition laws must be assessed as a success in itself.

Regrettably, after the initial impetus given by establishing the basic normative-institutional competition protection framework, little has been done to harmonise B&H competition law with EU *acquis* further and strengthen the capacities of the

Competition Council and the courts to deal with competition law cases effectively. In the last 15 years, no progress has been made in improving the legislative framework and strengthening the Competition Council's independence and human and material resources. The advance of competition law requires outspoken support from the key political factors in B&H and meaningful external assistance to be provided by the EU. The B&H political elite must reach a consensus on eliminating procedural deficiencies in the present Competition Act and political influence in the appointment process of the members of the decision-making body. The EU institutions need to initiate and support the implementation of activities aiming at strengthening the capacities of the Competition Council and courts in charge of competition law enforcement and awareness-raising of state institutions, economic operators, legal professionals and citizens on the benefits of effective competition policy.

Table of Cases

Bosnia and Herzegovina

Competition Council, *Klas/Sprind,* UP 01-06-26-033-65-II/08, 6.04.2009

Competition Council, *Apatinska pivara a.d.,* 02-26-028-145-II/11, 04.09.2012, Official GazetteGazette of BiH, No 6/2013

Competition Council, *Bimal d.d.,* 02-26-1-09-14-II/13, 2013. Available at: https://bihkonk.gov.ba/datoteka/rjesenja-zahtjev-bimal-101013-bos.pdf. Accessed 16 February 2025

Competition Council, *Agrokor/Mercator,* UP 05-26-1-014-374-II/13, 10.6.2014

Competition Council, *OBN v Radio-Television of Bosnia and Herzegovina, Radio-Television of the Republic of Srpska, and Radio-Television of the Federation of Bosnia and Herzegovina,* UP 01-26-3-08-167-II/13, 14.09.2016. Available at: https://bihkonk.gov.ba/r-j-e-s-e-nj-e-o-nepostojanju-zloupotrebe-dominantnog-polozaja-privrednih-subjekata-radio-televizija-bosne-i-hercegovine-radio-televizija-republike-srpske/. Accessed 16 February 2025

Competition Council, *Telekom BH v. MTEL, Logosoft, Blicnet, Telrad&Elta Kabel,* UP 04-26-2-014-84/21, 4.04.2022

Competition Council, *Digital Asset Management d.o.o. Banja Luka v Raiffeisen Bank d.d. Bosna i Hercegovina, Branch Office Banja Luka,* UP 02-26-2-042-55/21, 16.11.2022. Available at: http://www.sluzbenilist.ba/page/PdfDownload?BrojIzdanja=13&NivoIzdavanja_FK=1&GodinaIzdanja=2023%D0%BF%D0%BE%D1%81-28/. Accessed 16 February 2025

Competition Council, *Telemach v. BH Telekom,* UP-01-26-2-018-173/17, 6.04.2023. Available at: http://www.sluzbenilist.ba/page/akt/Io1FF6s6Ngztz5k76kjn45hc=. Accessed 16 February 2025

Competition Council, *RTV BH, RTV FBH, RTRS and Media Pool,* UP-01-26-3-09-47/2023, 30.05.2023. Available at: https://bihkonk.gov.ba/rjesenje-po-zahtjevu-za-pokretanje-postupka-privrednog-subjekta-obn-d-d-sarajevo-protiv-privrednog-subjakta-media-pool-d-o-o-sarajevo-i-javnih-rtv-servisa-bhrt-ftv-i-rtrs/. Accessed 16 February 2025

Constitutional Court of Bosnia and Herzegovina, AP-2430/16, 15.09.2016. Available at: https://portalfo2.pravosudje.ba/vstvfo-api/vijest/download/78588. Accessed 16 February 2025

Constitutional Court of Bosnia and Herzegovina, SU-02-1056/21, 16.12.2021. Available at: https://www.ustavnisud.ba/bs/zakljucak-o-dostavljanu-odgovora-na-apelaciju-apelantima. Accessed 16 February 2025

Court of Bosnia and Herzegovina, *Molson Coors d.o.o. v. Competition Council of BiH*, S1 3 U 011234 14 Uvp, 3.10.2014

Court of Bosnia and Herzegovina, S1 3 U 013779 13 U, 16.11.2015. Available at: https://portalfo2.pravosudje.ba/vstvfo-api/vijest/download/78590. Accessed 16 February 2025

Court of Bosnia and Herzegovina, S1 3 U 013779 15 Uvp, 11.04.2016. Available at: https://portalfo2.pravosudje.ba/vstvfo-api/vijest/download/78589. Accessed 16 February 2025

Court of Bosnia and Herzegovina, *Polyclinic v. Competition Council of BiH,* S1 3 U 024742 18 U2, 5.04.2018. Available at: t https://portalfo1.pravosudje.ba/vstvfo-api/vijest/download/64680. Accessed 16 February 2025

Court of Bosnia and Herzegovina, *Telemach v. Competition Council of BiH*, S1 3 U 038507 21 Uvp, 23.02.2022

Court of Bosnia and Herzegovina, *Federal Ministry of Health v. Competition Council of BiH*, S1 3 U 035154 22 Uvp, 23.04.2022.

Court of Bosnia and Herzegovina, S1 3 P 027939 19 Pž od 3. 9. 2019, Bulletin of the Case Law, No 11/2021. Available at https://portalfo2.pravosudje.ba/vstvfo-api/vijest/download/85910. Accessed 16 February 2025

Brcko Arbitral Tribunal for Dispute Over the Inter-Entity Boundary in Brcko Area Award (1997) Available at: http://www.ohr.int/ohr_archive/1026-3/. Accessed 16 February 2025

High Representative's Decision on the Establishment of the Brcko District of Bosnia and Herzegovina (2000) Decision No 20/00. Available at: http://www.ohr.int/ohr_archive/odluka-visokog-predstavnika-o-uspostavqawu-brcko-distrikta-bosne-i-hercegovine/. Accessed 16 February 2025

Resolution CM/ResDH(2022)80 - Execution of the judgment of the European Court of Human Rights BIMAL d.d. against Bosnia and Herzegovina, adopted by the Committee of Ministers on 6 April 2022 at the 1431st meeting of the Ministers' Deputies

European Union

Judgment of 16 December 1975, *Suiker Unie and Others v. Commission*, C-40/73, Joined cases 40 to 48, 50, 54 to 56, 111, 113 and 114-73, ECLI:EU:C:1975:174

Judgment of 14 February 1978, *United Brands v. Commission*, C-27/76, ECLI:EU:C:1978:22

Judgment of 13 February 1979, Hoffmann-La Roche v. Commission, C-85/76, ECLI:EU:C:1979:36

Judgment of 17 February 1993, Chr*istian Poucet v Assurances Générales de France and Caisse Mutuelle Régionale du Languedoc-Roussillon*, joined cases C-159/91 and C-160/91, ECR 1993 I-00637, ECLI:EU:C:1993:63

Judgment of 19 January 1994, *SAT Fluggesellschaft mbH v. Eurocontrol*, ECR 1994 I-00043, ECLI:EU:C:1994:7

Judgment of 18 March 1997, *Diego Calì & Figli Srl v. Servizi ecologici porto di Genova SpA* (SEPG), ECR 1997 I-01547, ECLI:EU:C:1997:160Judgment of 25 March 1999, Commission, T-102/96, ECLI:EU:T:1999:65

Judgment of 19 February 2002, *J. C. J. Wouters, J. W. Savelbergh and Price Waterhouse Belastingadviseurs BV v. Algemene Raad van de Nederlandse Orde van Advocaten*, C-309/99, ECR 2002 I-01577, ECLI:EU:C:2002:98

Judgment of 7 January 2004, *Aalborg Portland A/S and Others v. European Commission*, Joined Cases C-204/00 P, C-205/00 P, C-211/00 P, C-213/00 P, C-217/00 P and C-219/00 P, ECLI:EU:C:2004:6

Judgment of 27 September 2006, *Dresdner Bank AG and Others v. European Commission*, Joined Cases T-44/02 OP, T-54/02 OP, T-56/02 OP, T-60/02 OP and T-61/02 OP, 27.09.2006, ECLI:EU:T:2006:271

European Court for Human Rights

Bimal d.d. v. Bosnia and Herzegovina, Judgment of 31 August 2021, Application No. 27289/17

Sejdić and Finci v. Bosnia and Herzegovina, Judgment of 22 December 2009, Applications Nos. 27796/06 and 34836/06

Socialist Federative Republic of Yugoslavia

Constitutional Court of Yugoslavia, 8.06.1988, Official Gazette of SFRY, No 51/1988,

Supreme Economic Court, Pkž-23/65, 31.05.1965

Supreme Economic Court, Pkž-22/64, 14.09.1974

Table of Legislation

Bosnia and Herzegovina

Administrative Proceedings Act, Official Gazette of B&H, No 29/02, 12/04, 88/07, 93/09, 41/13, 53/16

Competition Act, Official Gazette of B&H, No 30/01
Competition Act, Official Gazette of B&H, No 48/05, 76/07, 80/09
Criminal Act of BD, Official Gazette of BD, No 19/2020
Criminal Act of BiH, Official Gazette of B&H, No 3/2003, 32/2003, 37/2003, 54/2004, 61/2004, 30/2005, 53/2006, 55/2006, 8/2010, 47/2014, 22/2015, 40/2015, 35/2018, 46/2021, 31/2023 and 47/2023
Criminal Act of FB&H, Official Gazette of FB&H, No 36/2003, 21/2004, 69/2004, 18/2005, 42/2010, 42/2011, 59/2014, 76/2014, 46/2016, 75/2017 and 31/2023
Criminal Code of RS, Official Gazette of RS, No 64/2017, 104/2018 – Constitutional Court decision, 15/2021, 89/2021 and 73/2023
Decision on agreements with minor value, Official Gazette of B&H, No 86/05
Decision on annual work planning and the method of monitoring and reporting in the institutions of Bosnia and Herzegovina, Official Gazette of B&H, No 94/14
Decision on the definition of categories of dominant position, Official Gazette of B&H, No 18/06
Decision on group exemption of agreements between economic entities which are active on different levels of production or supply (vertical agreements), Official Gazette of B&H, No 18/06
Decision on group exemption of agreements between economic entities which are active on the same level of production or supply (horizontal agreements), in particular, concerning research, development and specialisation, Official Gazette of B&H, No 15/06
Decision on group exemption of agreements on distribution and repair of motor vehicles, Official Gazette of B&H, No 16/06
Decision on group exemption of agreements on the transfer of technology, licensing and know-how, Official Gazette of B&H, No 15/06
Decision on group exemption of insurance agreements, Official Gazette of B&H, No 15/06
Decision on the closer definition of the manner of periodic penalty payments [2006] Official Gazette of B&H, No 31/06
General Framework Agreement for Peace in Bosnia and Herzegovina (1995). Available at: http://ndcsarajevo.org/Dokumenti/Dejtonski-mirovni-sporazum.pdf. Accessed 21 February 2024
Law on Administrative Disputes (LAD), Official Gazette of B&H, No 19/2002, 88/2007, 83/2008, 74/2010
Law on Budget, Official Gazette of B&H, No 42/22
Law on Civil Procedure of the Federation of Bosnia and Herzegovina, Official Gazette of FB&H, No 53/2003, 73/2005, 19/2006 and 98/2015
Law on Civil Procedure of the Republic of Srpska, Official Gazette of RS, No 58/2003, 85/2003, 74/2005, 63/2007, 105/2008 – Constitutional Court Decision, 45/2009 – Constitutional Court Decision, 49/2009, 61/2013 and 109/2021 – Constitutional Court Decision
Law on Financing the B&H Institutions, Official Gazette of B&H, No 61/2004, 27/2008, 49/2009, 42/2012, 87/2012, 32/2013 and 38/2022
Law on Health Protection, Official Gazette of FB&H, No 46/2010, 75/2013

Law on Ministries and Other Administrative Bodies of Bosnia and Herzegovina, Official Gazette of B&H, No 5/03, 42/03, 26/04, 42/04, 45/06, 88/07, 35/09, 59/09, 103/09, 87/12, 6/13, 19/16 and 83/17

Law on Prevention of Money Laundering and Financing of Terrorist Activities, Official Gazette of B&H, No 47/2014 and 67/2016

Law on Public Radio-Television System of Bosnia and Herzegovina, Official Gazette of B&H, No 78/2005, 35/2009, 32/2010, 51/2015, 25/2016

Law on Trade, Official Gazette of FB&H, No 2/95, 19/96

Law on Trade, Official Gazette of RS No 16/96, 52/01

Law on Obligations [1978], Official Gazette of the SFRY, No 29/1978, 39/1985, 45/1989 - decision of the Court of Justice and 57/1989, Official Gazette of the RB&H, No 2/1992, 13/1993 and 13/1994 and Official Gazette of FB&H, No 29/2003 and 42/2011

Law on Obligations, Official Gazette of the SFRY, No. 29/1978, 39/1985, 45/1989 - decision of the Supreme Court of Justice and 57/1989 and Official Gazette of the RS, No. 17/1993, 3/1996, 37/2001, 39/2003 and 74/2004

Rulebook on Internal Organisation of the Competition Council of Bosnia and Herzegovina (2020) Available at: http://bihkonk.gov.ba/pravilnik-o-unutrasnjoj-organizaciji-konkurencijskog-vijeca-bosne-i-hercegovine/. Accessed 21 February 2025

Rules of Procedure of the Competition Council of Bosnia and Herzegovina (2006) Available at https://static.parlament.ba/doc/27977_poslovnik_o_radu_novi_ba-konkurencijsko%20vijece.pdf. Accessed 21 February 2025

Croatia

Act on Protection of Market Competition of the Republic of Croatia, Narodne novine RH, No 79/09, 80/13, 41/21

European Union

Commission Regulation (EC) No 2790/1999 of 22 December 1999 on the application of Article 81(3) of the Treaty to categories of vertical agreements and concerted practices [1999] OJ L 336

Commission Regulation (EU) 2022/720 of 10 May 2022 on the application of Article 101(3) of the Treaty on the Functioning of the European Union to categories of vertical agreements and concerted practices [2022] OJ L 134

Council Regulation (EC) No 139/2004 of 20 January 2004 on the control of concentrations between undertakings [2004] OJ L 24

Council Regulation (EC) No 1/2003 of 16 December 2002 on the implementation of the rules on competition laid down in Articles 81 and 82 of the Treaty [2003] OJ L 1

Directive (EU) 2019/1 of the European Parliament and of the Council of 18 December 2018 to empower the competition authorities of the Member States to be more effective enforcers and to ensure the proper functioning of the internal market [2019] OJ L 11

Interim Agreement on trade and trade-related issues between the European Community of the one part, and Bosnia and Herzegovina, of the other part [2008] OJ L 169/3

Notice on agreements of minor importance which do not appreciably restrict competition under Article 101(1) of the Treaty on the Functioning of the European Union (De Minimis Notice), OJ, 2014/C 291/01

Stabilisation and Association Agreement between the European Communities and their Member States, of the one part, and Bosnia and Herzegovina, of the other part [2015] OJ L 164

Germany

Act against Restraints of Competition (Gesetz gegen Wettbewerbsbeschrankungen-GWB), available at https://www.gesetze-im-internet.de/gwb/BJNR252110998.html

Socialist Federative Republic of Yugoslavia

Basic Law on Regulating Business Relationships in the Market [1962] Official Gazette of FPRY, No 28 /1962

Constitution of the Socialist Federative Republic of Yugoslavia [1963] available at http://mojustav.rs/wp-content/uploads/2013/04/Ustav-SFRJ-iz-1963.pdf. Accessed 21 February 2025

Law on Associations and Business Cooperation in the Economy [1960] Official Gazette of FPRY, No 28/1960

Law on Suppressing Unfair Competition and Monopolistic Agreements [1974] Official Gazette of SFRY, No 24/1974

Law on Amending and Supplementing the Law on Suppressing Unfair Competition and Monopolistic Agreements [1986] Official Gazette of SFRY, No 72/1986

Law on Trade in Goods [1967], Official Gazette of SFRY, No 1/1967

Law on Trade [1990] Official Gazette of SFRY, No 40/1990

References

Agency for Statistics of Bosnia and Herzegovina (2023) Gross Domestic Product by Production, income and Expenditure Approach. Available at: https://bhas.gov.ba/data/Publikacije/Bilteni/2023/NAC_00_2021_TB_1_BS.pdf. Accessed 16 Feb 2025

Biro Z (1976) Komentar Zakona o suzbijanju nelojalne utakmice i monopolisitičkih sporazuma. Belgrade

Ćatić Š (2019) Pravni izvori zabranjenih sporazuma kao nedozvoljenog oblika konkurencijskog djelovanja u pravu konkurencije na nivou Evropske unije i na nivou Bosne i Hercegovine. Anali Pravnog fakulteta u Zenici 23:289–310

CC (2009) Annual Report 2009. Available at: https://bihkonk.gov.ba/datoteka/izvjestaj_2009.pdf. Accessed 21 Feb 2025

CC (2012) Annual Report 2012. Available at: https://bihkonk.gov.ba/izvje%C5%A1%C4%87e-o-radu-konkurencijskog-vije%C4%87a-bih-za-2012-godinu/. Accessed 21 Feb 2025

CC (2013) Annual Report 2013. Available at: https://bihkonk.gov.ba/datoteka/Izvjestaj-o-radu-za-2013.pdf. Accessed 21 Feb 2025

CC (2014) Annual Report 2014 https://bihkonk.gov.ba/izvjestaj-o-radu-konkurencijskog-vijeca-bih-za-2014-godinu/. Accessed 21 Feb 2025

CC (2015) Annual Report 2015. Available at: https://bihkonk.gov.ba/datoteka/izvjestaj-o-radu-20151.pdf. Accessed 21 Feb 2025

CC (2016) Annual Report 2016. Available at: https://bihkonk.gov.ba/datoteka/izvjestaj-za-2016.pdf. Accessed 21 Feb 2025

CC (2017) Annual Report 2017. Available at: https://bihkonk.gov.ba/izvjesce-o-radu-konkurencijskog-vijeca-bosne-i-hercegovine-za-2017-godinu/. Accessed 21 Feb 2025

CC (2018) Annual Report 2018. Available at: https://bihkonk.gov.ba/nacrt-izvjestaj-o-radu-konkurencijskog-vijeca-bosne-i-hercegovine-za-2018-godinu/. Accessed 21 Feb 2025

CC (2019) Annual Report 2019. Available at: https://bihkonk.gov.ba/izvjestaj-o-radu-konkurencijskog-vijeca-bosne-i-hercegovine-za-2019-godinu/. Accessed 21 Feb 2025

CC (2020) Annual Report 2020. Available at: https://bihkonk.gov.ba/izvjestaj-o-radu-konkurencijskog-vijeca-bosne-i-hercegovine-za-2020-godinu/. Accessed 21 Feb 2025

CC (2021) Annual Report 2021. Available at: https://bihkonk.gov.ba/nacrt-izvjestaj-o-radu-konkurencijskog-vijeca-bosne-i-hercegovine-za-2021-godinu/. Accessed 21 Feb 2025

CC (2022) Annual Report 2022. Available at: https://bihkonk.gov.ba/hr/izvjestaj-o-radu-konkurencijskog-vijeca-bosne-i-hercegovine-za-2022-godinu-5/. Accessed 21 Feb 2025

Commission (2019) Commission Opinion on Bosnia and Herzegovina's application for membership of the European Union. SWD(2019) 222 final. Available at: https://neighbourhood-enlargement.ec.europa.eu/system/files/2019-05/20190529-bosnia-and-herzegovina-analytical-report.pdf. Accessed 21 Feb 2025

Commission (2021) Bosnia and Herzegovina 2021 report. SWD(2021) 291 final /2. Available at: https://neighbourhood-enlargement.ec.europa.eu/system/files/2021-10/Bosnia%20and%20Herzegovina%202021%20report.PDF. Accessed 21 Feb 2025

Commission (2022) Bosnia and Herzegovina 2022 report. SWD(2022) 236 final. Available at: https://neighbourhood-enlargement.ec.europa.eu/system/files/2022-10/Bosnia%20and%20Herzegovina%20Report%202022.pdf. Accessed 21 Feb 2025

Competition Council of BiH (2020) Budget Execution Report. Available at: http://bihkonk.gov.ba/izvjestaj-o-izvrsenju-budzeta-za-2020-godinu/. Accessed 21 Feb 2025

Council of Ministers of BiH Report on the work of the BiH Council of Ministers https://vijeceministara.gov.ba/akti/program_rada/Archive.aspx?langTag=bs-BA&template_id=92&pageIndex=5. Accessed 21 Feb 2025

Court of BiH (2024) Istorijat suda. Available at: https://www.sudbih.gov.ba/Content/Read/organigram. Accessed 21 Feb 2025

Draft Law on Amendments to the Law on Competition (2020). Available at: http://bihkonk.gov.ba/datoteka/rjesenje-zakon.pdf. Accessed 21 Feb 2025

European Council (2022) Conclusions from the meeting held on 15 December 2022. Available at: https://www.consilium.europa.eu/media/60872/2022-12-15-euco-conclusions-en.pdf. Accessed 21 Feb 2025
Hasić Z (2010) Uloga države u uređenju institucionalnog i pravnog okvira prava konkurencije u nekim razvijenim državama i u Bosni i Hercegovini. Univerzitetska hronika 3:23–29
Imamović-Čizmić K, Grbo Z (2018) Competition law in Bosnia and Herzegovina. Wolters Kluwer
Imamović-Čizmić K et al (2021) Competition law in Bosnia and Herzegovina - how ready we are for the challenges of the modern age? EU Comp Law Issues Challenges Ser (ECLIC) 5:176–196
Jerkić I (2018) Razmjena informacija među konkurentima, dogovori o cijenama ili elementima cijene – uloga strukovnih udruđenja i komora. International Conference of the Agency for Protection of Market Competition of Croatia. Available at: http://www.aztn.hr/ea/wp-content/uploads/2018/11/Razmjena-informacija-izme%C4%91u-konkurenata-Ivo-Jerki%C4%87.pdf. Accessed 21 Feb 2025
Karanikić-Mirić M (2014) Kolektivna zaštita potrošača u srpskom pravu. Anali Pravnog fakulteta u Zenici 14:57–83
Kulenović M (2016) Posebne mjere u kontroli koncentracija u konkurencijskom pravu EU i BiH. Društvena i tehnička istraživanja 2:119–145
Marković-Bajalović D (2020) Competition enforcement models in the Western Balkan countries: the rule of law still Terra Incognita? Yearb Antitrust Regul Stud 13(22):27–66. https://doi.org/10.7172/1689-9024.YARS.2020.13.22.2
Marković-Bajalović D (2022) The EU institutional model of competition law enforcement revisited: how much rule of law suffices? Pravni zapisi XIII(2):500–535. https://doi.org/10.5937/pravzap0-40075
Morait B (2014) Sloboda ugovaranja i pravo konkurencije u savremenoj sudskoj praksi. In: Marković G (ed) Zbornik radova Odnos prava u regionu i prava Evropske unije, Pravni fakultet Univerziteta u Istočnom Sarajevu, 33–49 Available at: https://bmoraitobligacije.com/sloboda-ugovaranja-i-pravo-konkurencije-u-savremenoj-sudskoj-praksi/. Accessed 21 Feb 2025
Poljić A (2014) Dominantan položaj u pravu konkurencije Bosne i Hercegovine. Anali Pravnog fakulteta Univerziteta u Zenici 13:117–134
Popović S (2023) EU candidate status of Bosnia and Herzegovina: undue reward or a boost for the reform process European Western Balkans. Available at: https://europeanwesternbalkans.com/2023/02/18/eu-candidate-status-of-bosnia-and-herzegovina-undue-reward-or-a-boost-for-the-reform-process/. Accessed 21 Feb 2025
Report on the budget execution of the CC and the Law on the Budget of the Institutions of Bosnia and Herzegovina and the international obligations of Bosnia and Herzegovina (2012). Available at: https://www.parlament.ba/law/LawDetails?lawId=675. Accessed 21 Feb 2025
Report on the work of the BiH Council of Ministers (2023). Available at: https://vijeceministara.gov.ba/akti/program_rada/Archive.aspx?langTag=bs-BA&template_id=92&pageIndex=5. Accessed 21 Feb 2025
Svetlicinii A (2013a) Expanding the definitions of 'undertaking' and 'economic activity': application of competition rules to the actions of state institutions in Bosnia and Herzegovina. Yearb Antitrust Regul Stud 6(8):11–33
Svetlicinii A (2013b) The Bosnia and Herzegovina Court quashes the no-infringement of the Competition Authority for the failure to conduct an efficient investigation *(Telekomunikacije)*. e-Competitions October 2013, Art. N° 64924
Trifković M (2006) Određivanje monopolisitičkih sporazuma u pravima Bosne i Hercegovine i Evropske unije. Pregled-časopis za društvena pitanja 4:63–91
Uzinidis D (2016) Propaedeutics in the theory of industrial organisation: the SCP (structure, conduct, performance) model. J Innov Econ Manag 2:197–215
Varadi T (1999) Competition law in socialist countries. Am J Comp Law 2:229–275

Dijana Marković-Bajalović is a Tenured Professor at the Union University School of Law in Belgrade. She obtained her PhD from the University of Belgrade Law School with the thesis "Market Power of Enterprises as the Subject of Anti-Monopoly Law" in 1999. Prof. Marković-Bajalović lectured Company, Commercial and Competition Law at the University of East Sarajevo School of Law from 2000 to 2020. She was a member of the Antimonopoly Commission of the Federative Republic of Yugoslavia from 1999 to 2003. She was elected Deputy Chairwoman (2006–2007) and Chairwoman (2007–2010) of the Commission for the Protection of Competition of the Republic of Serbia. From 2013 to 2016, she served as the Senior Legal Expert and Team Leader for the EU-funded project supporting the Competition Council of BiH. In 2017 and 2018, she advised the Competition Agency of Georgia as part of an EU-funded project. In June 2024, she was appointed as a Key Legal Expert within the Policy and Legal Advice Centre (PLAC IV) project, implemented in Serbia and funded by the European Union. The project aims to support the Serbian Government in harmonising legislation with the EU law, including competition and state aid law. Prof. Marković-Bajalović advised law offices on various competition law issues and served as an arbitrator in cases resolved by the Permanent Arbitration of the Republic of Serbia Chamber of Commerce, as well as an expert witness on competition law in an ICSID case. Prof. Marković-Bajalović has published numerous books and articles on various topics related to competition law.

Kanita Imamović-Čizmić is a Full Professor at the Faculty of Law, University of Sarajevo. She graduated from the Faculty of Law, University of Sarajevo. By defending her master's thesis entitled *Utjecaj pravne zaštite investitora na glavne aspekte efikasnosti tržišta hartija od vrijednosti* at the Faculty of Economics, University of Sarajevo in 2006, she obtained the title of Master of Economics. At the Faculty of Law at the University of Sarajevo in 2012, she defended her doctoral dissertation entitled "*The Modalities of Legal Regulation of Market Competition and Their Use in the Economy of Bosnia and Herzegovina*", earning the title of Doctor of Laws. She teaches courses in the scientific field of legal and economic science. Kanita has published several scientific papers and books. Some of the publications are: "Competition Law in Bosnia and Herzegovina" (Wolters Kluwer 2018, 2021 in co-authorship); "Legal and Politological Aspects of Competition in Bosnia and Herzegovina as a Paradigm of the European Integration Process", European Integration Studies 1(14):55–68, 2020; "Competition law in Bosnia and Herzegovina - how ready we are for the challenges of the modern age?", EU and Comparative Law Issues and Challenges Series (ECLIC) 2021, 5, pp. 176–196; "Effectiveness of public enforcement of competition law in Bosnia and Herzegovina"; "EU Antitrust: Hot Topics & Next Steps" International, Conference January 24–25, 2022 Prague, Czechia, Charles University - Faculty of Law; "The Artificial Intelligence and Competition Law Challenges for Bosnia and Herzegovina", European Integration Studies No. 16 / 2022, pp. 166–176.

Competition Law and Policy in Kosovo

Avdylkader Mucaj

1 Introduction

In post-1999 Kosovo, after the end of the war and the taking of Kosovo under international administration by the United Nations Interim Administration Mission (UNMIK),[1] many sectoral and sub-sectoral policies had begun to change. In the light of these developments, should be seen the introduction of competition legislation, namely Competition Law of 2004 (hereinafter LC of 2004).[2] This law, among other things, aimed to answer and facilitate two parallel processes that at that time were being led by the international community in Kosovo. The first was the change of the economic model, from the state-controlled one, where the presence of the state in the economy was high, to a free market economy, according to the standards of the European Union (EU), and the second aiming to increase competitiveness. These socio-economic changes are not at all easy to materialise and produce the intended results. However, what had facilitated this process was the fact that Kosovo was administered by the international community, and the popular and political will for the integration into the EU prevailed in Kosovo, thus not posing any opposition to such changes. The changes in the legislation occurred effortlessly. However, the same cannot be said for the effective enforcement.

This chapter will prove that after putting in place competition rules, the institutional chain responsible for the implementation of these rules, such as the Authority and the courts, proved the main and most difficult challenge to overcome. After the establishment of the Authority in 2008, it has been continuously followed by

[1] United Nations Mission in Kosovo (1999) Resolution 1244 (1999). S/RES/1244 (1999).
[2] Law no 2004/36 on Competition, Official Gazette 14/2007.

A. Mucaj (✉)
Pristina, Kosovo

J. Pecotić Kaufman et al. (eds.), *Competition Law and Policy in the Western Balkans*, European Union and its Neighbours in a Globalized World 22,
https://doi.org/10.1007/978-3-031-93756-9_4

challenges, both in terms of the staff recruitment as well as professional competences. This occurred for two main reasons: lack of political will to select experts in the field of competition, and second, limited human resources in the field of competition, who were educated or have working experience in the field of competition law. Nevertheless, this had a direct impact on the work of the Authority itself, which was followed with difficulty in the first cases. Another institutional challenge in the implementation of the competition law has been witnessed by the courts, which *prima facie* lack expertise in the field of competition law, as the cases discussed below shall confirm. As a consequence, competition cases in judicial review have mainly been judged based on the general administrative law rather than the competition law. In addition, during this time frame 2008–2022, the competent court for examining competition cases was changed three times.

2 Historical Development of the Competition Law in Kosovo

The first law on competition in Kosovo was introduced in 2004. However, it did not enter into force until 2007, the year in which it was published in the official gazette.[3] This law provided for the establishment of the Authority, as a competent institution for the enforcement of the Competition Law. The Authority was established by the Assembly of Kosovo in 2008.[4] Not much time had passed and the Law on the Protection of Competition was approved by the Assembly of Kosovo in 2010 (hereinafter LPC of 2010).[5]

The most significant change that the LPC of 2010 had brought was the amount of the fine that the Authority could impose on companies found to be in violation of the competition law, which was up to 10% of the annual turnover, the same as the practices of the EU. This was important alignment with the EU standards, since the LC of 2004, provided only for a maximum fine of EUR 100,000. Another change brought about by LPC of 2010 upon its amendment in 2014, was the lowering of the presumption of the dominant position to 25% market share.[6] Also, the LPC of 2010 changed the judicial review by the Supreme Court, in passing the judicial review of competition cases to the Administrative Court of Pristina.

The most recent legislation for the protection of competition is the Law on Protection of Competition of 2022 (hereinafter LPC of 2022).[7] This law also changed the competent court for judicial review of competition cases from the

[3] Ibid.

[4] Kosovo Competition Authority (2017).

[5] Law no 03/L-229 on Protection of Competition, Official Gazette No 88/2010.

[6] Law No. 04/L-226 On Amending and Supplementing the Law No. 03/L-229 On Protection of Competition, Official Gazette of the Republic of Kosovo / Nr.17/10.

[7] Law no.08/L-056 on Protection of Competition, Official Gazette No. 14/ 2022.

administrative court to the commercial court. The LPC of 2022 has provided for the first time in Kosovo the right to private enforcement of the competition law, thus completing the missing pillar. The previous legal framework had entirely been focused only on the public enforcement of the competition law, thus denying a right of compensation for damages caused by anti-competitive practices.

3 Relationship of Kosovo Competition Law with the EU

Albeit the establishment of the Authority had been an explicit request of the EU[8], and that the first two laws had transposed the administrative model of competition law enforcement, both in the normative and institutional aspects, in the first two laws there were not many references to EU law.

In the LC of 2004, in Article 23 (2) it was determined that: "All normative acts for the implementation of the present law shall be (i) consistent with the scope, language and purpose of the present law and (ii) otherwise consistent with the law and practice of the European Union regarding similar subject matter".[9] Whereas in Article 66 of the LPC of 2010 on implementation of the law stipulated as follows: "Implementation of this Law should be in conformity with European Union Directives on competition".[10]

As can be seen below, the LPC of 2022 has a broader reference to EU legislation, starting from the purpose of the law, thus trying to confirm the alignment of Kosovo's competition legislation with the *acquis communautaire*. Article 1 (2) lists the EU legal acts that have been transposed in the law, such as:

- Council Regulation (EC) No. 1/2003 of 16 December 2002 on the implementation of the rules on competition laid down in Articles 81 and 82 of the Treaty;
- Council Regulation (EC) No. 139/2004 of 20 January 2004 on the control of concentrations between undertakings (the EC Merger Regulation);
- Commission Regulation (EU) No 330/2010 of 20 April 2010 on application of Article 101 (3) of the Treaty on the Functioning of the European Union to categories of vertical agreements and concerted practices;
- Commission Regulation (EC) No 802/2004 of 7 April 2004 implementing Council Regulation (EC) No.139/2004 of 20 January 2004 on the control of concentrations between undertakings.[11]

[8] The 2008 EC Progress Report noted that "The Competition Commission (CC) is not yet operational. The assembly has yet to appoint the candidates selected for this commission. Kosovo needs to finalise the establishment of the CC, including the allocation of the necessary resources". Commission (2008), p. 37.

[9] LC of 2004, Art 23 (2).

[10] LPC of 2010, Art 66.

[11] LPC of 2022.

In addition, the LPC of 2022 in Article 70 (2) makes specific reference to the Stabilization and Association (SAA) between the European Union and Kosovo, by stating that "this law shall be implemented in accordance with the obligations of the Republic of Kosovo deriving from the Stabilization and Association Agreement with the European Union and the European Atomic Energy Community".[12]

The LPC of 2022 has made it mandatory for law enforcement bodies, which in this case is the Authority and the courts, to implement the provisions of the law in accordance with Kosovo's obligations under the SAA with the EU.[13] With the SAA, Kosovo has taken obligations to design and implement competition policies in accordance with those of the EU. The SAA requires Kosovo among others, to approximate the existing legislation to that of the EU as well as its effective implementation, anti-competitive agreements, abuse of a dominant position and concerted practices are incompatible with the SAA. In addition, Kosovo takes the obligation to ensure operationally independent authority to enforce competition law and policy for both private and public undertakings.[14]

4 Institutional and Normative Framework of Competition Authority in Kosovo

4.1 Establishment of the Authority

The LC of 2004 required the establishment of an independent regulatory body.[15] The Authority was established by the Assembly of Kosovo in 2008,[16] with responsibility for promoting competition among undertakings.[17] In Kosovo, however, a significant number of independent agencies have been established, be it under the supervision of the Kosovo Assembly or a particular Ministry, depending on the agency's scope. The establishment of these agencies with specific mandates, such as in the case of the Authority, is not proven to have resulted from the will and vision[18] of Kosovo's institutions. In this context, some agencies, as in the case of the Authority, the

[12] Ibid.

[13] Stabilisation and Association Agreement between the European Union and the European Atomic Energy Community, of the one part, and Kosovo, of the other part [2016] L71/3.

[14] Stabilization and Association Agreement, Articles 74–75.

[15] LC of 2004, Art 20(1); The Competition Authority (2023).

[16] LC of 2004.

[17] Art 21(1) of LC of 2004 stipulates that "The Kosovo Competition Commission shall have the responsibility and authority to enforce the present law and to promote competition among undertakings and consumer welfare in Kosovo".

[18] Muris noted that "the core mission [of the competition Agency] must derive from a vision of the institution clearly shared among and respected by constituents not just today but over long periods". Muris (2005), p. 167.

request for its establishment arose from the EU.[19] Hence, agencies are often neglected and lack necessary support from central institutions, specifically the Government and the Assembly. This is also proven by the fact that for nearly three years (2013–2016) the Authority was inactive. As noted by the 2016 EU Progress Report:

> After almost three years, in which the Kosovo Competition Commission (the decision-making body within the Authority) had not been able to fulfil its mandate due to the lack of a quorum, its five board members were finally appointed by the assembly in June 2016. Regarding implementation, due to the failure to nominate its members from 2013–2016, the Kosovo Competition Commission was not able to take any decisions and its activities were very limited, focusing mainly on judicial representation of previous cases.[20]

As noted in the 2014 EU Progress Report "The Competition Commission (the decision-making body within the Authority) has not been operational since November 2013 due to delays in the appointment of four out of five members whose mandate had come to an end. In the absence of a quorum (at least three members) of the Competition Commission, the Kosovo Competition Authority has not been able to fulfil its mandate".[21] Similarly, the 2015 EU Progress Report pointed out that "The Kosovo Competition Authority is still not operational, lacking a quorum since November 2013 due to delays in replacing five members of the Kosovo Competition Commission whose terms of office had ended. The Kosovo Competition Authority has thus not been able to carry out its duties as new investigations have to be approved by the Kosovo Competition Commission board".[22] As a result, the work of this Authority has been paralyzed for years.[23] In the absence of the Commission members, the Commission being the decision-making body can neither initiate investigations nor take decisions. Since 2013 when the mandate of the Commission members ended, there was media reporting on the issue, pointing out that this institution has been neglected by the Government and the Assembly and treated as an unimportant public body.

4.2 Authority Structure

The Authority consists of the Commission, which is a collegial body and decision-maker, as well as the Secretariat, which is composed of civil servants. The Secretariat of the Authority is an administrative body charged by law to perform

[19] Commission (2008), p. 37.

[20] Commission (2016), p. 47.

[21] Commission (2014), p. 34.

[22] Commission (2015), p. 41.

[23] Art 29 (2) of LC of 2004 requires that the quorum for Commission meetings and decision-making is at least three members of the Commission out of five. Decisions can be taken only with at least three affirmative votes.

monitoring and investigating cases to ensure free and effective competition in the market. The Secretariat consists of two departments: (i) the Legal and Administration Department and (ii) the Department for Market Supervision. The latter has four (4) divisions, namely: (a) Division for Prohibited Agreements, (b) Division for Dominant Position, (c) Division for Concentrations/Mergers and (d) Division of Analysis, Methodology and Exclusive Rights. Currently the Authority has 23 employees, whereas it is foreseen to reach 30. Six new recruitment positions, mainly inspectors, were approved in 2021.[24]

4.3 The Authority's Legal Mandate

Even though Kosovo recently enacted its third law in the field of competition, starting from the law of 2004, then in 2010 until the last one in 2022, the mandate of the Authority has mainly been the same and unchanged. The three competition laws had charged the Authority with the responsibility for implementing the law and competition rules in the main pillars such as: (i) anti-competitive agreements, (ii) concerted practices, (iii) abuse of a dominant position, and (iv) mergers. Whereas, state aid is within the competence of the Ministry of Finance, particularly state aid commission.

4.4 The Decision-Making Bodies Within the Authority

4.4.1 The Commission

The Commission is the only decision-making body within the Authority. The Commission is composed of five (5) members, including the President and the Vice President of the Authority appointed by the Assembly of the Republic of Kosovo. The Government, after holding a public competition, proposes the new Commission to the Assembly six (6) months before the end of the mandate of the Commission or immediately after the position of the member of the Commission is vacant. The mandate of the member of the Commission lasts five (5) years. A member of the Commission may be reappointed only once.[25]

According to the LPC of 2022 the Authority is an independent agency, accountable for its duties to the Assembly of the Republic of Kosovo. In addition, any political, public or private interference that may impair the independence or impartiality of the Authority is prohibited.[26] Given the fact that the Authority is

[24]Kosovo Competition Authority (2021), pp. 11–12.

[25]LPC of 2022, Art 22.

[26]LPC of 2022, Art 21.

responsible and reports its work only to the Assembly of Kosovo, the recruitment procedure had to be under the competence of the Assembly, together with the final selection. Currently, according to the legal framework into force, the recruitment procedures are managed by the Government and the qualified candidates are proposed to the Assembly for approval. If the recruitment procedures had been developed by the Assembly, as in many similar cases that the Assembly announces recruitment procedures for members of the boards of various regulators i.e. state aid commission members, potentially the selected members of the Commission within the Authority would have greater political independence. In the past, it has been proven that the nominees of the Government were appointed by the Assembly of Kosovo,[27] despite the fact that there were open dilemmas about political interference and the professional competence of some members proposed as members of the Commission.

The Assembly Committee on Economic Development, Infrastructure, Trade and Industry, in its meeting held on 26 April 2016, after reviewing the list of candidates for membership of the Commission proposed by the Government, estimated that most of the proposed candidates did not meet the condition of professional competence and as a result recommended not to appoint the propose candidates.[28] However, despite the recommendation of the Committee, the Assembly appointed the same candidates. This fact was, however, emphasised on the 2016 EU Progress Report for Kosovo.[29] In Addition, in its 2015 Progress Report the EU urged both the Assembly and the Government that the "appointments need to be made on the basis of professional qualifications and merit, not political patronage".[30]

4.4.2 Conditions for Being a Member of the Commission

A member of the Commission shall be appointed a person fulfilling the following conditions: (i) to be a citizen of the Republic of Kosovo; (ii) to have high qualifications in law, economics or equivalent field; and (iii) to have five (5) years of professional work experience. A person cannot be a member of the Commission if he/she: within the last two (2) years has been a member of the steering board or management of an enterprise or group of enterprises, in the last five (5) years has been sentenced by a final decision for a criminal offence of: official corruption, abuse of official duty, economic crimes and conflict of interest. During the exercise of mandate, a member of the Commission may not have a property interest,

[27] The Assembly of Kosovo, the Committee on Economic Development, Infrastructure, Trade and Industry, Procès-verbal of the meeting 17–26 April 2016 (Hereinafter: Procès-verbal of the meeting).

[28] Procès-verbal of the meeting 2016.

[29] Commission (2016), p. 47.

[30] Commission (2015), p. 4.

employment relationship or contractual relationship with an enterprise or group of enterprises, be a public official or be involved in political activities.[31]

Unlike the previous law, which required 7 years of work experience, the latter reduced it to 5 years of work experience. Nevertheless, the length of the work test may not be the most significant aspect, but the nature of the professional test, together with education or training in the field of competition, are essential and a prerequisite for a more effective implementation of the competition law by the Authority. Kosovo has had nearly 20 years since the adoption of its first competition law, although implementation only began after the Authority was established in 2008. Given that the country now should have human resources in the field of competition, an increase in the selection criteria for commission members would be justified. This was not the situation at the outset of the competition law enforcement.

4.4.3 Dismissal of the Commission Members

The Assembly or the Government shall propose the dismissal of a member of the Commission if: (i) that member is not in a state of health to perform duties for more than three (3) months and does not provide medical evidence that he will be able to perform duties during the next three (3) months; (ii) violates Article 23 of the LPC of 2022 concerning eligible criteria to be elected as a member of the Authority; (iii) is involved in a conflict of interest or in serious disregard of the duty of the Commission's member. The Commission's members may be dismissed by the Assembly with a majority vote of all deputies.[32]

4.5 The Administrative Procedure for the Implementation of the Competition Law in Kosovo

The LPC of 2022 stipulates that the Authority conducts the procedure in accordance with the provisions of this law. In the absence of the provisions determined by this law, the provisions of the relevant Law on General Administrative Procedure shall apply.[33] All public authorities in Kosovo are obliged to respect the Law on General Administrative Procedure during their administrative work, and that the procedural rules defined by special laws such as the competition law, cannot contradict the

[31] Ibid, Art 23.

[32] LPC of 2022, Art 24.

[33] LPC of 2022, Art 33.

principles of this law and cannot lower the level of protection of rights and legal interests of parties as granted by this Law.[34]

One aspect that needs further improvement in the work of the Authority, for the sake of effective enforcement of competition law as well as meeting the criteria stipulated in the Law in General Administrative Procedure, is better reasoning of its decisions. This is especially relevant, as the courts primarily focus their judicial review of administrative decisions on whether the reasoning aligns with the requirements of this law. Reasoning is one of the most important facets for the courts to consider. Similar reasoning has been given by the Court of Justice of the European Union in competition cases.[35] Such a requirement is necessary,[36] because only reasoning reveals to whether a decision is based and legal argument or has an element of arbitrariness or ungrounded judgment.

4.5.1 The Parties in the Procedure

The parties in the procedure are the enterprises against which the Authority conducts the investigation or the enterprises participating in concentration.[37] The proposal for initiating an investigation within the competence of the Authority can be submitted by any natural or legal person, professional association, association of enterprises, association of consumers, the Government and a central or local public administration body.[38] The Authority, however, may initiate proceedings *ex officio* to investigate prohibited agreements, abuse of a dominant position, and assess concentrations, even if the participants do not submit a request for authorization. If the concentration is found to have been carried out illegally, the decision to authorize it may be revoked or modified, and appropriate measures will be imposed from the Authority.[39]

Since the Authority can initiate proceedings based on requests or complaints from private or legal entities regarding alleged violations of competition law by one or more undertakings, it should promote proactive policies to encourage individuals and organizations to report suspected violations. This includes, among other things,

[34] Law No. 05/L-031 on General Administrative Procedure, Official Gazette of the Republic of Kosova / No. 20 / 21 June 2016, Art 2 (hereinafter: Law on General Administrative Procedure).

[35] According to EU case law, breach of procedural requirements gives rise to an action for annulment of Commission acts. See to that effect, Cauffman and Hao (2016) and the following cases: Judgment of 15 June 1994, *Commission v BASF and Others*, C-137/92 P, ECLI:EU:C:1994:247, para 41; Judgment of 15 June 1994, *Commission v BASF and Others*, C-137/92 P, ECLI:EU:C:1994:247, para 76; Judgment of 6 April 2000, P *Commission v Solvay,* Joined cases C-287/95 P and C-288/95 P, ECLI:EU:C:2000:189, para 45.

[36] Law on General Administrative Procedure, in Article 48 (2) stipulates that an insufficient, inappropriate, contradictory or incomprehensible reasoning shall be deemed as lack of reasoning.

[37] LPC of 2022, Art 34.

[38] LPC of 2022, Art 35.

[39] LPC of 2022, Art 36.

promoting a leniency program to facilitate the submission of such cases to the Authority.

After initiation of an investigation, the Authority shall submit the conclusion for initiating the procedure to the party against whom the procedure has been initiated or to the applicants who filed for permission to concentrate. Neither the LPC of 2010 nor the LPC of 2022 allow the parties in the procedure, against whom the Authority has issued a conclusion to initiate procedures against, to file an appeal against such a conclusion. The LPC of 2010 provided for the possibility of initiating a lawsuit in Court, but expressly denied the right to appeal.[40] While the LPC of 2022, in addition to denying the right to appeal against the conclusion, expressly prohibited the right to file a lawsuit in the competent court against the conclusion too, with which the Authority initiates the procedure against one or more undertakings.[41] The party against whom the procedure has been initiated shall submit remarks, information and documents for the case within the deadline set by the Authority.[42] This is a fundamental right for the parties in the procedure, which falls into the category of equality of arms, where the parties will have the opportunity from an early stage to present their evidence in support of their claims and opposition to those of the Authority. The Authority may request from the parties to the procedure and other natural and legal persons, associations of enterprises, associations of consumers, public bodies, the necessary information in any digital form, written remarks or verbal statements, as well as the provision of necessary data and documents.

4.5.2 Unannounced Inspections (Dawn Raids)

The Authority may, without notice, inspect the premises of the enterprise or other person under investigation if there is a risk of concealment or destruction of evidence. Before carrying out the unannounced inspection, the Authority shall request the competent court to authorise the officials of the Authority to enter the facility where the inspection will be carried out without notice. If there is a reasonable suspicion that the evidence in possession of the party to the procedure may disappear or be altered, the authorised Authority officials themselves or with the assistance of the police perform unannounced inspection and notify the person in possession of the building or items. Before carrying out the unannounced inspection, the authorised officials of the Authority shall show the party in the procedure or the owner of the facility the official identification card and the authorisation from the court for conducting the inspection.[43]

The Supreme Court, in 2021, accepted a request from the Authority to issue a legal opinion regarding the court's competence to issue an order authorising

---

[40] LPC of 2010, Art 35 (6).

[41] LPC of 2022, Art 66 (2.2).

[42] LPC of 2022, Art 38.

[43] LPC of 2022, Art 40.

members of the Authority to enter without prior warning the headquarters and any property and another facility of the enterprise that is used for carrying out business activities, in case there is a risk of concealment or destruction of evidence. The Supreme Court concluded that the Basic Court in Pristina is competent for issuing an order that authorizes members of the Authority to enter, without prior notice, the headquarters and any facility used by the enterprise for business activities if there is a risk of evidence being hidden or destroyed.[44]

The court of first instance (the administrative court) has raised a dilemma whether the order for unannounced inspections should be issued in criminal or administrative procedure. Through this opinion, the Supreme Court clarified that the order must be administrative, since the mandate of the Authority and the investigation in the field of competition is of an administrative nature and there is no logic for such an order to be criminal.

The Supreme Court had justified its opinion as follows:

> In the logic of this opinion is also the nature of the procedure that takes place before the Authority, which as a procedure has references in Law No. 03/L-229 on Protection from Competition and the Law on Administrative Procedure, respectively the Law on General Administrative Procedure. From this follows the understanding that the order authorising the members of the Authority to enter without prior warning or special permission, the headquarters and any property and other place of the enterprise that is used for carrying out business activities if there is a risk of hiding or destroying evidence, *it cannot be an action of the criminal procedure.* Even the imposition of a punitive measure, according to this law, is not a criminal but an administrative responsibility. The purpose of the order for entry without warning is in function of the administrative investigation that the Authority has as competence, for the implementation of the provisions of Law No. 03/L-229 on Protection from Competition, according to which punitive measures can be imposed, the legality of which will be assessed and ascertained according to the lawsuit in the administrative dispute before the competent court. The Supreme Court also assesses that it is neither usual nor logical to issue an order in criminal proceedings, at the request of an authority which is not authorised to investigate criminal offenses nor to file charges for criminal offences, therefore in this case the nature of the order and the competence of the court is interpreted in the light of the procedure for which the order is issued.[45]

According to the LPC of 2022, if there is a reasonable suspicion, the following premises may be subject to unannounced inspection: the building of the enterprise or group of enterprise for which no procedure has been initiated; the apartment or similar facility that has a connection with the member of the board of directors or the employee of the enterprise against which the procedure has been initiated; and the building of the other person. Such an inspection can be conducted against the will, if the enterprise, group of enterprises or the owner of the building refuses to allow the entry of authorized officials prevents viewing of business books or other documents or otherwise complicates the conduction of the unannounced inspection.[46]

---

[44] The Supreme Court of Kosovo, Guide approved at the General Session of the Supreme Court, held on 10 June 2021.

[45] Ibid.

[46] LPC of 2022, Arts 41–42.

4.5.3 Hearing Session

The Authority holds a hearing session in every proceeding. The Authority may exclude the public from the hearing session in order to maintain commercial secrecy. If none of the invited persons or their authorised persons appear at the hearing session, the Authority may adjourn the hearing session to another time. If the invited or their authorised persons do not appear at the hearing session even for the second time, the Authority shall hold the hearing session with the parties present or decide for itself according to the data and documents in its possession.[47]

In all cases where the Authority has developed investigative procedures and fined one or more enterprises for anticompetitive behaviour, hearing sessions were held with the parties to the procedure. There have even been cases where hearing sessions were held twice in the same case.

4.5.4 Determining the Conditions for Imposing a Fine

When it ascertains that the party in the procedure has disturbed the market competition or has violated the provisions of this law, the Authority shall submit to the party the notice for ascertaining the facts and the notice for the content of the decision taken on ascertaining the facts. The party is given the opportunity to provide comments and is presented with evidence on which the violation is found, a fine is imposed and the amount of the fine is determined. After the hearing, the Authority decides on the imposition of the fine, the amount of the fine and the manner and conditions of execution. The authority closes the procedure with the final decision that finds the violation and imposes the fine,[48] or determines that the competition has not been distorted.[49]

4.5.5 Fines

In accordance with the provisions of the LPC of 2022, both natural and legal persons can be fined if proved to have breached competition law. A fine of up to ten percent (10%) of the total turnover realised worldwide in the last year for which the financial report has been concluded shall be imposed on: (i) the enterprise or group of enterprises that enters into prohibited agreements or otherwise participates in agreements with which competition is distorted; (ii) abuses the dominant position; (iii) participates in prohibited concentration; (iv) does not submit to the Authority a request for permitting concentration and (v) does not act in accordance with the

[47] LPC of 2022, Art 48.

[48] LPC of 2022, Art 50.

[49] LPC of 2022, Art 55 (1.13).

decision of the Authority that imposes measures for restoration of competition or temporary measures.[50]

A fine of up to one percent (1%) of the total turnover realised worldwide in the last year for which the financial report has been concluded shall be imposed on the enterprise or group of enterprises that: (i) submits incorrect or false information to the Authority in the concentration assessment procedure; (ii) does not act upon the request of the Authority; (iii) obstructs the implementation of the order of the competent court; (iv) does not appear in the hearing according; (v) breaks the sealing imposed; (vi) gives inaccurate or misinformative data and documents or refuses to give a complete answer; and (vii) is not a party to the proceedings and does not act upon the request of the Authority.[51] The responsible person of the enterprise or state body shall be fined from EUR one thousand (1000) to EUR four thousand (4000) for any violation of the competition law.[52] There is still no recorded case where the Authority has imposed fines on a natural person or a responsible person of the enterprise or state body that have breached competition law.

4.6 *Yearly Budget of the Authority*

Similar to other public institutions, in the case of the Authority too, the budget is allocated by a special annual law, which is prepared by the Ministry of Finance, and after receiving the green light from the Government, it is passed to the Assembly for review and approval. The Law on Budget is one of those laws that always attracts debate in the Assembly and often undergoes changes from the version accepted by the Government. The annual law on budget lists the amount and categories for each public institution, including the Authority. Fines imposed by the Authority, are paid into the state budget or the state treasury. LPC of 2022 stipulates that:

> From the budget of the state shall be allocated sufficient funds for the needs of the Authority, including the employment of qualified professionals and the purchase of goods and services necessary for work. Administrative fees and fines collected by the Authority are deposited to the budget of the state.[53]

According to the Authority's annual reports 2017–2021, the Authority's budget was as shown in Table 1:

[50] LPC of 2022, Art 57.

[51] Ibid.

[52] Ibid.

[53] LPC of 2022, Art 21 (5–6).

Table 1 Kosovo Competition Authority Annual Budget 2017–2021

Year	Budget in EUR
2021	245,111.00
2020	296,263.16
2019	267,074.39
2018	267,074.39
2017	243,517.78

Source: Authority's annual reports 2017–2021

5 National Specifics that Differ from the EU Competition *Acquis*

Due to the fact that the LC of 2004 was approved at a time when Kosovo was still administered by the international community and the country had not declared its independence, the competition rules in this law were largely consistent with EU legislation, particularly in terms of definition of anti-competitive agreements, abuse of a dominant position and merger control. A similar model to that of the EU was adopted in relation to the institutional framework, where at the administrative level the competition legislation will be implemented by an independent agency, while judicial review of the authority's decisions was also ensured. However, the original competition legislation featured a maximum fine limit of EUR 100,000 rather than tying it to a percentage of the company's annual turnover, as is standard in EU practice. In the Law on Competition (LPC) of 2010, particularly following its amendment in 2014, the threshold for determining a dominant position was set very low, at only 25%. Another specific feature of the two aforementioned laws was the fact that the private enforcement of competition legislation was not included at all and was clearly not in line with that of the EU *acquis*. Here, the distinction lies in the fact that private enforcement was entirely absent from Kosovo's legal framework. It is only the LPC of 2022 which explicitly recognised the right of compensation for the damages caused as a result of anti-competitive behaviour. However, this pillar of competition law did not include the essential parts of the EU Directive 2014/104.

6 Application of National and EU Competition Rules by the Competition Authority and Discussion of the most Significant Cases

6.1 Anticompetitive Agreements

All competition legislations in Kosovo since 2004 prohibited anti-competitive agreements, as one of the main pillars of competition law and policy. In addition, the first case fined for breach of competition law were insurance companies for entering into an anti-competitive agreement, a case which shall be further discussed below. The Law on Protection of Competition of 2022, defines prohibited agreements as follows:

1. All agreements aimed at preventing, restricting or distorting competition in the relevant market shall be prohibited, and in particular those that:
   1.1. directly or indirectly impose purchase and sale prices or any other trading conditions;
   1.2. limit or control production, market, technical development or investments;
   1.3. share markets or sources of supply;
   1.4. implement unequal conditions to the same transactions with other commercial enterprises, consequently placing them in an unfavourable competitive position;
   1.5. condition the conclusion of the contract with the acceptance of additional obligations by contracting parties that by nature or commercial use are not related to the object of the contract.
2. Paragraph 1 of this Article does not apply to agreements whose entire duration meets all of the following conditions:
   2.1. contribute to the improvement of the production or distribution of goods or to the promotion of technical or economic progress;
   2.2. allow consumers a fair share of the benefit;
   2.3. do not impose restrictions on the enterprise that are not necessary for the achievement of the objectives of this paragraph;
   2.4. do not enable the enterprise to avoid competition for a significant part of the relevant products.
3. The enterprise or group of enterprises claiming compliance with paragraph 2. of this Article shall be borne the burden of evidence.
4. Agreements that are prohibited under paragraph 1. of this Article shall be null and void, unless they are excluded under paragraph 2. of this Article.[54]

6.1.1 The Insurance Companies Case

The first case in Kosovo where the Authority investigated anti-competitive agreements[55] was that of insurance companies in 2009.[56] In 2009, ten insurance

[54] LPC of 2022, Art 5.

[55] Kosovo Competition Authority, Decisions no 5/1 to 5/10 on the Agreement for Setting the Prices of Third Party Compulsory Motor Insurance Policies, Against Siguria, 27 December 2010.

[56] Mucaj (2020a); Mucaj (2020b). This case has been discussed in more detail in my previous research and publications.

companies[57] signed an anti-competitive agreement in Gjakova[58] in relation to insurance policies for compulsory third-party liability motor vehicle insurance. According to the contested agreement, the insurance companies agreed not to offer any kind of discount on the price of these services. The Authority managed to obtain a copy of the agreement in question and initiated investigations into all the insurance companies for entering into an agreement that violated the Law on Competition, specifically Article 3. The ten insurance companies were fined the sum of EUR 100,000 each.[59] The agreement in question, *inter alia*, included the term "[…] not to allow any kind of discount by insurance companies, to maintain the insurance market as it is currently".[60]

However, in this case, although the Authority possessed a copy of the anti-competitive agreement, which by object was clearly in breach of competition law, the Authority could not persuade the courts to win the case. In this case, ten (10) insurance companies were fined. Lawsuits in the court were filed separately by individual companies. Although in the same court, cases were reviewed by different judges, thus the same court reached contrary conclusions on the same issues. Here to say, one judge upheld the Authority's decision as grounded and lawful, whereas the majority judged the Authority's decisions as unlawful. It was the Court of Appeal which unified these cases, making the Authority to lose all of the court proceedings, since it requested the Authority, among other things, to prove if this agreement was signed by competent persons within the insurances companies, if formal procedures for reaching this agreement were respected such as stamped and sealed, to fined persons who signed by name and surname, and if such as agreement was implemented in practice or not. Almost all of these requirements were contrary to the logic and philosophy of competition law, which is less formalistic compared to other branches of law. For instance, the very last request, whether this agreement was implemented or not in practice proves this fact, since the competition law prohibits any agreement that has as its *object* or *effect* the destruction or restriction of competition. Unequivocally the object of this agreement was to limit competition, as a result, there was no needed to assess its effects.

---

[57] The names of the signatories for the insurance companies of the anti-competitive agreement. KS 'SIGURIA'; KS 'INSIG'; KS 'CROATIA SIGURIMI'; KS 'SIGAL'; KS 'SIGMA'; KS 'YLLIRIA'; KS 'GRAWE ELSIG'; KS 'KOSOVA E RE'; KS 'SIGKOS'; and KS 'DARDANIA'. Actually all the companies active in Kosovo at that time that were licensed by the Central Bank of Kosovo to practise insurance activities.

[58] The city of Gjakova is a city in western Kosovo with a population of around 95,000 inhabitants.

[59] Under the provisions of LC of 2004, Art 35(1) this was the maximum amount an undertaking could be fined if proved to have violated provisions of the Law on Competition.

[60] The Agreement of the ten insurance companies signed in Gjakova, 3 July 2009 (hereinafter: the contested agreement).

6.2 *Abuse of Dominant Position*

Abuse of dominant position has been prohibited in Kosovo since 2004, when the first law of competition was enacted, although not enforced prior to establishment of the Authority in 2008. The second case investigated by the Authority was abuse of dominant position, a case further elaborated below, known as a *Gekos* case. Article 9 of the LPC 2022 provides that:

1. Abuse of a dominant position is prohibited.
2. The enterprise or group of enterprises shall be considered to misuse its dominant position if:

   2.1. directly or indirectly impose an unfair purchase or sale price or other unfair trading conditions;
   2.2. restrict production, markets or technological development to the detriment of consumers;
   2.3. applies different conditions for equivalent transactions with other enterprises, putting them at a competitive disadvantage;
   2.4. conditions the conclusion of the contract with additional obligations that by nature or commercial use are not related to the object of the contract;
   2.5. impose prices or other conditions that have the purpose or effect of preventing the entry into the relevant market or the removal from the relevant market of specific competitors or their product;
   2.6. deny the other enterprise to access in return for adequate remuneration in the network or infrastructure, making it impossible for it to act as a competitor.

3. The Authority shall issue a sub-legal act for misuse of dominant position.

6.2.1 Gekos Case

Background of Gekos Case

The Government of Kosovo, after declaring its independence in 2008, took measures to combat the informal economy by initiating fiscalization across all businesses in the country.[61] This process required businesses to implement fiscal cash registers, with the Ministry of Economy and Finance overseeing the licensing of undertakings responsible for selling, installing, and maintaining Fiscal Electronic Devices (FEDs). The Ministry established a Commission that granted licenses to two undertakings—

[61] Government of Kosovo Decision of No 02/56 of 18 February 2009 on the Implementation of Fiscal Cash Registers throughout Kosovo (2009).

Gekos and Dukagjini—to handle these responsibilities in whole Kosovo's territory.[62]

Initiation of Investigations in the Gekos Case

The Authority launched an investigation after noticing that the licensed undertakings, namely Gekos and Dukagjini were subcontracting the sales, installing as well as maintaining of FEDs to a third company, called Enternet.[63] This raised concerns to the Authority, because Enternet was not licensed, and its activities in the market led to a lack of competition between the two licensed undertakings. In a hearing process,[64] after initiating of investigation, Gekos confirmed that it had a contract with Enternet, allowing the latter to make the sales and maintenance of FEDs on its behalf. Similarly, Dukagjini revealed that it was also planning to use Enternet for distribution due to its established network and professionalism in this field. Thus both undertakings admitted that Enternet played a key role in their operations of their duties, acquired via licensing process.

Authority's Decision in the Gekos Case

After the investigation, the Authority issued a decision fining Gekos for abusing a dominant position.[65] The Authority's legal reasoning was based on Kosovo's Competition Law, specifically Articles 15 (b) and (e), and Articles 13 and 17 of the Law on Administrative Procedure.[66] The Authority found that, despite the formal licensing of Gekos and Dukagjini, FED sales were carried out by Enternet, under the combined logo of the three entities.

In the reasoning regarding determining the dominant position the Authority, among other things deduced:

> Despite the fact that the two abovementioned undertakings [Gekos and Dukagjini] are licensed for the sale, installation, and maintenance of FEDs, according to contract Nr. 01/10 of 28.12.2009 for the sale, of FEDs between Gekos and Enternet, sales are carried out by Enternet, with the logo 'Dukagjini, Enternet, Gekos'. Dukagjini has not itself sold any FEDs at all, although it was licensed and had undertaken the obligation from the Ministry. This thereby enables Gekos to have a dominant position in the FED market in Kosovo, in breach of Article 14 of the Law on Competition.[67]

[62] Ministry of Economy and Finance Decision No KAF-11/2009 of 26 November 2009 and Ministry of Economy and Finance Decision No KAF-12/2009 of 26 November 2009.

[63] Kosovo Competition Authority (2010a).

[64] Kosovo Competition Authority (2010b).

[65] Kosovo Competition Authority (2010c).

[66] Law No 02/L-28 on Administrative Procedure, Official Gazette 8/2007 [hereinafter: Law on Administrative Procedure].

[67] Kosovo Competition Authority (2010c), p. 3.

The Authority's ruling was neither consistent nor well justified, since it's reasoning in the same part sometimes claims abuse of a dominant position and occasionally concerted practice, despite the fact that the alleged infringement in this case was abuse of a dominant position. Nevertheless, the Authority is not restricted to investigating abuse of a dominant position and concerted practices in a single case, but the case with GEKOS is different, since it was investigated merely for abuse of a dominant position and not for concerted practices. Therefore, the Authority's reasoning should have been focused and thoroughly arguing on the concept of the abuse of a dominant position only. In addition, the Authority's analysis can be criticized for lacking a thorough examination of how Gekos abused its dominant position and failed to establish whether Gekos engaged in anti-competitive behavior beyond simply holding a dominant position. Furthermore, the Authority did not adequately assess the role of Enternet, which, being closely connected to Gekos, might have benefitted from preferential treatment in the market. Such contradictions weakened the Authority's decision and led to doubts about its legal soundness, as will be evident in the court's assessment in the same case.

The Courts' Formalistic Approach to the Abuse of Dominant Position

The Court of First Instance of Pristina overturned the Authority's decision, citing violations of the Law on Administrative Procedure mostly.[68] The Court ruled that the Authority had failed to provide adequate reasoning for its decision and had relied on vague and general statements rather than specific evidence. The Court criticized also the Authority for not adhering to the objectivity principle, as it did not sufficiently verify the evidence or evaluate facts impartially. Furthermore, the Court found that the high market share held by Gekos was a consequence of the Ministry's decision to license only two operators, rather than the result of anti-competitive behavior by Gekos. What stands out in the court's decision is its emphasis on formal issues governed by the law on administrative procedure, largely overlooking the provisions of competition law. This approach clearly does not support the effective enforcement of competition law, as it prioritizes formal facets over the merits of the case.

The Court of Appeal upheld the decision of the Court of First Instance.[69] It noted that the Authority's ruling was legally unsound due to a lack of clear legal justification. The Authority's failure to specify the legal basis for its findings and its reliance on general references to laws instead of detailing the relevant facts were identified as major flaws in the ruling. The Court of Appeal emphasized that a legally binding decision requires a detailed and substantiated rationale. The Court of

[68] The Court of First Instance of Pristina – Administrative Department, Gekos Ruling No A181/2011 of 16 January 2015.

[69] Pristina Court of Appeal – Administrative Department, *Ruling on the Gekos case*, no AAnr.93/2015, 22 October 2015.

Appeal's approach mirrors that of the first instance, as the case was primarily examined through the lens of procedural law too. When critiquing the reasoning in the Authority's decision, the court's criticism is rooted in procedural law rather than competition law. While the judicial criticism of the Authority's reasoning appears valid, it would have been more appropriate if it had been focused broadly from the competition law prism.

The Supreme Court, after reviewing the case, found that the Authority's request for extraordinary review was unfounded.[70] The Court affirmed the findings of the lower courts, confirming that the Authority had failed to present a clear legal basis as well as reasoning for its decision. The Supreme Court concluded that Gekos and Dukagjini had imported FEDs from different manufacturers, but this deemed irrelevant to the primary issue of who was selling, insallin and maintaining FEDs in the relevant market. The Supreme Court dismissed the case, reinforcing the procedural shortcomings of the Authority's ruling, similarly to lower judicial instances.

The Gekos case, however, highlights significant procedural and substantive challenges in competition law enforcement in Kosovo. The Authority's decision was marred by vague legal reasoning, contradictions in its findings, and insufficient justification for its conclusions. The courts, particularly the Court of First Instance and Court of Appeal, emphasized the importance of clear, well-supported decisions in competition law cases. The failure to adequately justify the Authority's decisions ultimately led to the case being overturned. The decision underscores the need for competition authorities to provide comprehensive, clear, and legally grounded reasoning in their rulings to ensure that they can withstand judicial review at the end. According to settled EU case law, the Commission is obliged to state the reasons on which its decisions are based.[71] Yet, the Union courts have consistently held that the statement of reasons must state those reasons in a clear and unequivocal fashion, in such a way as to inform the persons concerned of the reasons for the measure and thus enable them to defend their rights and the court to exercise its supervisory jurisdiction.[72] The Union courts of their own motion enquire whether the statement of reasons is adequate.[73] Almost the same legal approach is required by the Law on Administrative Procedure in Kosovo. For this reason, observance of procedural rules is revealed to be one of the most important matters that the courts assess during judicial review of the Authority's decisions. According to the Law on Administrative Procedure Article 84(2) (d) every administrative decision must

[70]The Supreme Court of Kosovo Decision of 15 April 2016, *Ruling on the Gekos case*, ARJ-UZVP-no 45/2015.

[71]Judgment of 14 February 1990, *Delacre and Others v Commission*, C-350/88, ECLI:EU:C:1990:71, para 15; Judgment of 8 November 1983, *NV IAZ International Belgium and others v Commission*, Joined Cases 96–102, 104, 105, 108 and 110/82, ECLI:EU:C:1983:310, para 37.

[72]See Judgment of 29 February 1996, *Belgium v Commission*, C-56/93, ECLI:EU:C:1996:64, para 86; Judgment of 1 October 2009, *Commission v Council*, C-370/07, ECLI:EU:C:2009:590, para 37.

[73]See to that effect, Judgment of 20 February 1997, *Commission v Daffix*, C-166/95 P, ECLI:EU:C:1997:73, para 24; Judgment of 1 July 1986, *Usinor v Commission*, C-185/85, ECLI:EU:C:1986:276, para 19.

contain a clear statement of the legal basis.[74] The courts' approach, throughout the court hierarchy, has been that if the administrative decision does not state in a clear and unequivocal fashion the legal basis on which the ruling has been based, this is sufficient ground to set it aside for non-compliance with procedural standards and requirements. According to EU jurisprudence on the enforcement of EU competition rules, adopting an act without expressly indicating the relevant provision of EU law infringes the principle of legal certainty.[75] Observance of procedural rights appears to be an important prerequisite for the Authority's rulings to survive court scrutiny.

6.2.2 Oil Case

Background of the Case

At the beginning of 2019, a decade after the first case of anti-competitive agreement in the vehicles insurance sector, the Authority had started investigations for 16 oil derivatives companies[76] for suspicion of involvement in prohibited agreements and abuse of dominant position, contrary to competition law.[77] In the reasoning of the conclusion, the Authority emphasised the concerns raised by public opinion, through the media and civil society about their claims of anti-competitive agreements or concerted practices between companies that deal with the trading of oil derivatives in wholesale and retail of diesel and gasoline.[78] In relation to this, the Commission has decided to start the in-depth investigation procedure in the relevant market to prove the claim on the suspicions of whether there is an agreement, coordination, concerted practice or parallel behaviour in the market for fixing the prices of oil and gasoline between companies that are the subject of investigation for this case.

[74] Law on Administrative Procedure.

[75] See Judgment of 10 December 1985, *Stichting Sigarettenindustrie v Commission,* Joined Cases 240, 241, 242, 261, 262, 268 and 269/82, ECLI:EU:C:1985:488, para, 88; Judgment of 16 June 1993, *France v Commission*, C-325/91, ECLI:EU:C:1993:245, para 30.

[76] Alba Petrol Group Shpk, Alfa Trade Shpk, Al- Petrol Shpk, Benita Company Shpk, Ex -Fis Shpk, N.P.T. Fat Oil, Ip - Kos Shpk, Lab – Oil, N.P.T Ibrahimi, Petrol Oti Slovenija L.L.C, Patroni Shpk, Petrol Company, Veda-2 Petroll, Blu Oil Shpk, And Kastrati Group.

[77] Kosovo Competition Authority (2019).

[78] Ibid.

Decision of the Authority to Fine Companies in the Oil Case

Part of the investigation were 16 companies active in the derivatives market, and at the end of the investigation, 14 of them were fined,[79] while two of them were not.[80] Similarly, as in the past, despite the fact that the Authority had started investigations for several undertakings for the same grounds of investigation and in the same case, the decisions for finding violations and imposing fines were issued separately for each undertaking. This practice of the Authority for not joining the case, is resulting in negative consequences during the judicial examination, both in terms of time and merits. In the past, albeit the fact that all undertakings were fined at the same time, some court cases are pending years before others. This was proven in the case of insurance companies. Also in terms of merits, the case of insurance companies has shown an inconsistency on the part of the judiciary, since the cases from the court of first instance were decided for some companies in their favour, and for some others the Authority's decisions to be declared ungrounded, although it was the same case.

The main argument of the Authority for finding a violation of the law and competition rules by the 14 undertakings under investigation, was the fact that these companies had not reflected the decrees in the price of derivatives according to international bursa.[81] In this decision, the Authority claims that it has calculated the average prices for 2018 for each company, and the big difference of not reflecting the reduction in prices was mainly in November and December 2018, and that for the rest of the year this reduction was parallel.

In its decision, the Authority affirms that it has proven the existence of concerted practices, thus tacit collusion through economic and statistical analyses.[82]

In the justification of its decision, the Authority had the following main findings:

> While analysing and processing the data, we notice that from the month January to October the average gross profit/l was 0.09 cents/l, while for the months November and December the average gross profit/l was 0.14 cents/l. On this legal basis and the established facts, the Kosovo Competition Authority, estimates that undertakings set the selling price and the gross profit margin/l for in the months of November and December in coordination between themselves in breach of the Law on the Protection of Competition.
>
> The Authority finds that the companies that operate in the relevant market (retail sales) have not reflected in the way individual based on the sales price and gross profit/l for the month November and December, which means that the enterprises which are under investigations, had a gross profit/l of approximately 9% for the months January - October, while for the

[79] Authority Decisions of 6 May 2020: No 30/2020; No 31/2020; No 32/2020; No 33/2020; No 34/2020; No 35/2020; No 36/2020; No 37/2020; No 38/2020; No 39/2020; No 40/2020; No 41/2020; No 42/2020.

[80] Blu oil shpk and Kastrati Group.

[81] Authority Decisions of 6 May 2020: No 30/2020; No 31/2020; No 32/2020; No 33/2020; No 34/2020; No 35/2020; No 36/2020; No 37/2020; No 38/2020; No 39/2020; No 40/2020; No 41/2020; No 42/2020.

[82] Ibid.

month of November, they have coordinated achieved an average gross profit/l of 60% and for the month of December 124% in compared to the period January – October.[83]

Based on the aforementioned analyses, the Authority concluded at the end of the decision that these facts and analyses are *concerted practice* and qualifies as tacit collusion, by distortion of competition, in violation of Article 4 of the law on prohibited agreements or concerted practices.[84]

The Authority should be more consistent and argumentative in the reasoning part of its decisions.[85] This is vital for at least two reasons. First, based on the Law on Administrative Procedure, incorrect or/and contradictory reasoning of the administrative decision, is equivalent to the total lack of reasoning. Consequently an unreasoned administrative decision is illegal. Second, the courts in Kosovo in almost all competition cases during the judicial review have focused their review on compliance with the general law of administrative procedure.[86] In absence of a good reasoning, is a sufficient basis for the courts to overturn and declare Authority's decisions unlawful, even if the material law of competition has been correctly applied by the Authority. Therefore, it is crucial for the Authority to strictly comply with both administrative as well as competition legislation into force.

Also, the Authority's decision on the duration of the violation of the competition law by the companies involved in a period of only two months, seems to be in contradiction with the by-law of the Authority for the imposition of the fine.[87] In this regulation, the imposed sanction is calculated for the years that the company's activity had lasted in violation of the competition law. However, in this rule, there was no defined way of calculating and imposing the fine for the monthly period, as is the case here where the alleged violation lasted only two months. Faced with this fact, the Authority decided in its decision that "since the period of violation of this law is shorter than 6 (six) months, the Authority considers half a year and the penalty is applied to turnover for the period July – December 2018".

6.2.3 Mobile Telecom Serbia-MTS Case

At the end of 2023, the Authority, after conducting the investigative phase, took a decision to fine Mobile Telecom Serbia-MTS branch in Kosovo, in the amount of EUR 1,563,959.26, as a result of not submitting the notification for concentration.[88] According to Article 15 of LPC of 2010, concentration participants are required to submit to the Authority the objective of concentration if in a cumulative manner the

---

[83] Ibid.

[84] Ibid, p. 11.

[85] Mucaj (2020a, b).

[86] Mucaj (2020a, b).

[87] Administrative Instruction No. 01/2018 On the Criteria for the Pronunciation of Sanctions Administrative, 2018.

[88] Authority Decision No 120/23 of 18 December 2023.

following conditions have been fulfilled: determined incomes of all participating enterprises together, in international market, exceed EUR twenty (20) million, based on financial reports of the financial year preceding the concentration year, and if at least one of the participants is located in the Republic of Kosovo. According to the Authority's decision, MTS failed to notify concentration for buying 100% of undertakings VGN NET d.o.o, LIKA d.o.o, P.P.PKDS-IMPULS and Herc International d.o.o. In addition to imposing a fine, with the same decision MTS is obliged to submit a request for concentration to the Authority.

The economic activity of the MTS branch in Kosovo provides landline, mobile, internet and cable services in the northern part of Kosovo, specifically in the three municipalities inhabited by the Serbian majority. According to the Authority's assessment, as a result of the purchase of shares and the current concentration, there is less competition in the market and as a result the undertaking has been obliged to notify concentration. The Authority also assesses that in this case a strong dominant position has been created in the relevant market.[89]

The fine of MTS had aroused reactions of a political nature, starting from the fact that it was an undertaking originating from Serbia and that it offered its services mainly in the municipalities that are inhabited by the local Serb majority in Kosovo. However, the provisions of the competition legislation are binding on everyone without exception, and each undertaking operating in the Kosovo market is obliged to comply with. Otherwise, the Authority is obliged to act in accordance with the role it has as a watchdog in the field of competition. So far this is the highest fine issued for a company's failure to notify its concentration in Kosovo.

It remains for later research to assess the epilogue of this case from a judicial review, and it is also a good opportunity to evaluate the approach of the commercial court on how it will handle competition cases. In other words, if the same will continue the practice of the Administrative Court (which had competence in the field of competition) by judging the cases in the formal approach or change the practice by focusing more on the merits of the cases.

6.3 Merger Control

CL of 2022 also regulates merger control (the law refers to concentration) as one of the basic pillars of competition legislation, along with anti-competitive agreements and abuse of a dominant position. Below will be presented the main legal framework related to mergers, including prohibited concentrations, obligation to apply for permitting the mergers, application to merge, merger assessment, decision for mergers and measures after the illegal concentration.

Concentration is presented by the lasting change of control of enterprises when independent enterprises join together or parts thereof; one or more enterprises

[89] Ibid, 8.

acquire direct or indirect control over all or part of other enterprises, in particular by earning shares, by gaining the majority of voting rights and in other ways provided by the legislation in force.[90]

The acquisition of control, according to paragraph 1. of this Article, shall be made by the transfer of rights, by contract or in another way that enables the enterprises, alone or together, to exercise decisive influence over other enterprises on a permanent basis. The acquisition of control shall be made especially with a transfer of ownership or the right to use in whole or in part the assets of enterprises and transfer of rights or contracts that have a decisive influence on the composition, voting or decisions of the bodies of enterprises.

Concentrations that could significantly distort effective competition shall be prohibited, especially if such concentration results in the creation or strengthening of a dominant position.[91]

Concentration participants should ask the Authority in advance to allow them to achieve the intended concentration if the participants in the concentration have a total turnover of over twenty (20) million Euros in the international market and one concentration participant has a turnover of over one (1) million Euros in the domestic market or at least two (2) concentration participants have over three (3) million Euros turnover in the domestic market.[92]

The Authority shall initiate the concentration assessment procedure after receiving the full application. The applicant for the concentration permit has the burden of proving the beneficial effects of the concentration. The authority may require the applicant to submit the necessary documents and data for the assessment of the concentration. The Authority shall publish on its website a public announcement of the intended concentration. The public announcement shall include: (i) the names of the participants in the concentration and the type of activities performed by the participants in the concentration in the Republic of Kosovo; (ii) the nature of the concentration; (iii) call to enterprises, professional associations, employers' associations, consumer protection associations and other subjects who are not parties to the procedure, respectively competitors of the participants in the concentration, who are presumed to have knowledge of the relevant market reports, to provide remarks, thoughts and opinions about the possible effects of concentration; and (iv) the deadline for submission of remarks, thoughts and opinions, which may not be longer than fifteen (15) days.[93]

Concentration shall be considered permissible if the Authority based on the documents and data submitted by the Applicant or on the knowledge it possesses, considers that the intended concentration is not prohibited by Article 12 of this Law, and does not draw conclusions about the initiation of the concentration assessment procedure within thirty (30) days after receiving the full application for permitting

[90] LPC of 2022, Art 11.

[91] LPC of 2022, Art 12.

[92] LPC of 2022, Art 13.

[93] LPC of 2022, Art 17.

the concentration. The Authority shall conclude the initiation of the concentration assessment procedure if it considers that the concentration may impede effective competition in the relevant market, in particular by establishing or strengthening a dominant position. The conclusion shall be based on the documents and data submitted by the Applicant and on the knowledge possessed by the Authority. The Authority may approve, in whole or in part, the proposed measures, conditions and deadlines if it finds that they are sufficient to prevent the obstruction of effective competition in the relevant market. Within sixty (60) days after the conclusion for initiating the procedure the Authority with a decision shall: announce the concentration permitted; declare the concentration permitted if the measures, conditions and deadlines approved or set by the Authority are applied; declare the concentration prohibited.[94]

The Authority shall *ex officio* determine the measures, conditions and deadlines for the resetting the effective competition in the relevant market by a decision, when the concentration is carried out: contrary to the decision of the Authority announcing the concentration as prohibited or without submitting an application for permitting concentration. In such a scenario, the Authority can order the sale or transfer of acquired shares; prohibit or restrict the exercise of voting rights in the participating enterprises in the concentration; order the termination of the joint venture; prohibit other forms of gaining control that lead to illegal concentration; and impose a fine in accordance with this law.[95]

7 Enforcement and Sanctioning Statistics for the Period 2012–2022

The one-decade period covered by this research in the Western Balkan countries, reveals a limited number of cases in Kosovo, where the Authority imposed fines on enterprises for proven violations of competition law. To a large extent, this is related to the fact that in the period 2013–2016, the Authority was in the absence of its decision-making body, which is the Commission composed of 5 members, elected by the Assembly of Kosovo.[96] After the Commission members' mandate ended in 2013, the appointment of the new Commission members was only made in mid-2016.[97] As a result of this absence for years, many investigated cases were dismissed because the legal deadlines for review and decision-making had already passed. However, during the period from 2012 to 2022, the only significant case resulting in fines was the *oil* case. Although it was a single case, it involved

[94] LPC of 2022, Art 18.

[95] LPC of 2022, Art 20.

[96] Commission (2014) p. 1; p. 34.

[97] Commission (2016) p. 1; p. 47.

16 undertakings under investigation, 14 of them fined a total of more than 4,000,000.00 euros. This case is elaborated in more detail above.

8 Judicial Review

The adoption of laws in the field of competition in Kosovo, to a large extent with the standards of the EU, has not posed any difficulty, due to the fact that Kosovo had consistent aspiration for EU integration. In this light, the transposition of EU legislation for Kosovo in any sector, including the competition field, was never contested. However, as the above cases shown, what has proved challenging is the effective implementation of such legislation, both for the Authority and for the judiciary.

Since 2004, the court responsible for reviewing competition cases in Kosovo has changed three times. This could have been due to various factors, but the primary reasons appear to be, on one hand, the fact that after the end of the war in 1999, the judiciary in Kosovo was under the exclusive authority of UNMIK,[98] and on the other hand, the time it took for Kosovo to consolidate its judicial system following its declaration of independence in 2008, during which substantial changes occurred continuously.

In the first case of the prohibited agreement involving the insurance companies, the fined companies filed a lawsuit in the Supreme Court, while with the entry into force of the LPC of 2010, those cases were transferred to the Administrative Court of Pristina, according to this law. Whereas, in 2022, the Commercial Court was established in Kosovo by a special law,[99] and the competence to review competition cases has passed to the latter. For someone, the last change can be considered as an opportunity for the new court to put the implementation of the competition law on the right track, since the same cannot be said for the administrative court, since it mainly reviewed competition disputes from the formal and procedural facets of the administrative law, instead of competition law.

Judicial practice in the field of competition in Kosovo has passed a decade of experience, but achieving an effective enforcement, as the discussed cases proved, still remains an unachieved goal yet. The most obvious challenge remains the lack of sufficient knowledge of competition rules and policies on the part of the judiciary, inadequate training of judges in this field, as well as judging competition cases more based on procedural law rather than the substantive one. However, it remains to be seen whether the newly established Commercial Court shall handle competition cases in the right trajectory of public enforcement of competition law and policy in Kosovo.

---

[98] United Nations Mission in Kosovo (1999) Resolution 1244 (1999). S/RES/1244 (1999).

[99] Law No. 08/L-015 on Commercial Court, Official Gazette No. 7/ 2022 (hereinafter: Law on Commercial Court).

A recent development is the change of the competent court for examining competition cases, from the administrative court to the commercial court established in 2022. However, in order to address the challenges of stagnant and poor quality of jurisprudence, especially in business-to- business disputes (including competition cases), the Government of Kosovo has initiated the establishment of a Commercial Court, which took place in 2022. The Commercial Court shall have the competence to adjudicate competition law disputes, among its other powers. By its very nature, the purpose of establishing the Commercial Court was to increase the speed and quality in the handling of commercial cases, with a purpose to improve the business climate in Kosovo.

The distinctive aspect of this new court, initiated with the aim of improving the business environment in Kosovo, in a meaning that court cases from the economic field are resolved as quickly as possible for both local and international companies, is the fact that the appeals chamber there are intrigued within the same court. In contrast, the current judicial system in Kosovo has been organised in 7 courts of first instance and only one court of appeal, that has covered all other courts in Kosovo. However, economic cases, including competition disputes, will not be appealed to the court of appeal, but to the second level within the commercial court. It remains to be seen and evaluated in the future the approach of this court in competition cases, both in terms of the merits of the case reviews as well as in the time limits for deciding the cases.

The only two cases that have received epilogue hearing in court, is the case of the prohibited agreement between insurance companies,[100] the case of the FED that one company was fined for abuse of a dominant position and the other for concerted practices.[101] However, the court had decided these cases almost entirely in the procedural facets only and avoiding competition law. In the case of the prohibited agreement, even though the Authority had managed to ensure a copy of such an agreement, where the insurance companies had agreed to fix prices, the courts had not sustained the decision of the Authority arguing that the agreement was not signed by the competent persons in the hierarchy of the companies, i.e. the General Directors but by the directors of the branch of the companies and that the agreement was not implemented. If the judges had any basic competence in the field of competition, only the object of this agreement would be enough, without a need going to the effect. Such an approach of the judiciary in competition disputes also weakens the work and the role of the Authority, because it is difficult for the Authority to win cases, even when the violation of competition rules is clearly evident. However, the approach of the courts should not serve for the Authority as

[100] Supreme Court of Kosovo, Ruling on the Insig case, ARJ no 25/2016, 05 October 2016; Supreme Court of Kosovo, Ruling on the Grawe Elsig case, ARJ no 24/2016, 05 October 2016 and Supreme Court of Kosovo, Ruling on the Illyria case, ARJ no 38/2016, 23 January 2017.

[101] The Supreme Court of Kosovo, Ruling on the Gekos case, ARJ-UZVP-no 45/2015, 15 April 2016 and The Supreme Court of Kosovo, Ruling in the Dukagjini case, ARJ-UZVP no 50/2015, 27 April 2016.

an amnesty for the loss of cases in court, because the latter must take care in all stages the cases being investigated up to its final decisions.

9 Private Enforcement of Competition Law

Despite the fact that Kosovo has a competition law approved since 2004, until 2022 private enforcement was not guaranteed in the normative aspect, and therefore there was no case in court. New LPC of 2022 stipulates that the undertaking that violates this law must compensate for the damage it has caused to the other undertaking or to the other person.[102] Such compensation shall be awarded through the court.

The public enforcement experience has proven substantial challenges for the effective enforcement of completion law both from the Authority and the judiciary, the same is expected to be present in private enforcement as well, because this is a new legal institute in Kosovo. Thus, it will take time until this right is understood and enforced properly for all private parties who have suffered damages as a result of violations of the competition law. The positive side, however, rests on the fact that in the normative aspect, such a right is now guaranteed for the persons affected by anti-competitive infringements and that they will have the opportunity to seek compensation, in case their interests are damaged by the activity of enterprises in violation of the competition law. However, I must reiterate that this pillar of competition law did not include the essential parts of the EU Directive 2014/104.[103] Kosovo still needs to further align its competition legislation with EU standards, if it wants to fully transpose EU legislation.

10 Trends and Challenges for the Effective Enforcement of Competition Law

As the most significant recent developments in the field of competition that have been brought by the Law of 2022, it is the normative aspect of the private enforcement of competition on the one hand, as well as the collection of the fines imposed by the Authority, before the court decides on the case.[104] Before the entry into force

[102] LPC of 2022, Art 63 reads as follow: The enterprise that violates this law must compensate the damage caused to the enterprise or other person, in accordance with the legislation in force. Anyone whose legitimate interest is violated by a restrictive action from Article 5 or 9 of this law can request through the court: termination of illegal action and compensation for the damage caused.

[103] Directive 2014/104/EU of the European Parliament and of the Council of 26 November 2014 on certain rules governing actions for damages under national law for infringements of the competition law provisions of the Member States and of the European Union (Text with EEA relevance) [2014] OJ L 349/1.

[104] Skara (2023), pp. 171–176.

of this law, filing a lawsuit in court against the decision of the Authority, suspended the execution of the decision vis-à-vis the imposed fine. With the current law, the lawsuit in court against the decision of the Authority will not have a suspensive effect on fines, unless the court imposes a suspension measure against the Authority's decision. This mechanism will be a more powerful weapon in the hands of the Authority, in the implementation of the competition rules, but on the other hand, it may also undermine the legal security for the parties in the procedure. This is especially due to the fact that the average for resolving a court case in competition disputes in Kosovo is 8 years. Even if an undertaking in the end wins the case in the court and the many are returned, will not be the same effect and value of those many, after such a long period of time.

A constant challenge that has been facing the Authority since 2013 is the failure to complete the decision-making body, which is the Commission, on time. The appointment of the members of the Commission is done through the recruitment procedure announced by the Government, and the successful candidates are proposed by the Government to the Assembly of Kosovo for approval. In almost every case where the 5-year mandate of the Commission members ends, years pass until the election of new members or the continuation of the mandate of the current members. After the end of the mandate of the members of the Commission in 2013, the Government and the Assembly could not elect new members until 2016.[105] Since June 2021, when the mandate of the members of the Commission had ended, it took the Government and the Assembly almost 2 years to elect and complete the Commission with all the new members. This delay in the selection of members of the Commission as the decision-making mechanism of the Authority constitutes a handicap for the work of the Authority and the effective implementation of the competition law, whose decision-making is suspended in the absence of the Commission. Failure to timely appoint the members of the Commission, also risks the loss of legal deadlines in the cases under investigation, if the procedural actions are not carried out within the legal deadline. This leads to situations where from the time of receiving the conclusion for the start of the investigation to the decision being made by the Commission, deadlines are lost and the cases must be dismissed because there is a legal deadline within which a decision must be made from the time of the start of the investigation.

Another constant and significant challenge that has accompanied the work of the Authority is the insufficient and contradictory reasoning of its decisions. Such flaw has been evident in the cases of insurance companies that were fined for prohibited agreements, the case of *Gekos* fined for abuse of a dominant position, and the case of concerted practices in the *Dukagjini* case. Almost similar contradictions are also evident in the last case where 14 undertakings were fined, known as the *Oil* case. In this particular case, the Authority initiated investigation alleging that the companies under investigation are acting in violation of the competition law, since their activity may be qualified as a prohibited agreement and/or potential abuse of a dominant

[105] Commission (2016), p. 47; Commission (2015), p. 41.

position. However, at the end of the investigation, 14 of the 16 undertakings involved in the investigation, were fined for concerned practices and tacit collusion. There is clearly an inconsistency in the Authority's work regarding the definition of the legal basis vis-a-vis the reasoning of its decisions. An authoritative reasoning of the Authority's decisions is imperative and a prerequisite for these decisions to survive the court scrutiny in latter stages. It has already been stated several times that the courts in Kosovo, but this is also evident in many countries with a socialist background, that the main focus of the courts is on the formal and procedural aspects during the judicial examination. This may be also for the fact that the court lacks professional competence in many sectoral areas such as IP, energy, telecommunications as well as competition law. The same argument is supported by the practice so far in competition disputes, where the competition law has had an almost marginal role during the judicial review.

11 Conclusion

Similarly, to many countries with a socialist background, including but not limited to ex-Yugoslavia countries, after the war of 1999 Kosovo too, embraced gradually steps towards the free market economy, by adopting legislation as advised from the international community, including legislation in the field of competition. The time frame since the adoption of the first law is reaching two decades, since the first law dates back to 2004, although its implementation began only after the establishment of the Authority in 2008. The change in economic models, in many countries, has been proven that it is not so easy and fast, and that the case of Kosovo is no exception. This especially applies, if not for the normative aspect which is more accelerated, but for its full implementation and for such changes taking place. Such a scenario happened in Kosovo in the field of competition. The adoption of legislation based on the basic principles of European legislation occurred without any big challenge, but the same cannot be said for the implementation and achievement of the objectives for which the competition law was adopted.

The lack of competition culture in Kosovo was evident both in the institutional side, including the Authority where the staff had neither specific education nor working experience in the field of competition, and that the same stands for the judiciary too, since the judges who have reviewed competition cases did not have had any specific training in the field of competition either. The lack of basic knowledge related to the law and competition policies is also clearly observed in the business community, where almost without exception in all the investigated cases the representatives of the enterprises have claimed that they had no knowledge that such legal rules exist in Kosovo.

However, the Authority has recently been completed with its own decision-making body and the establishment of a new commercial court, responsible for reviewing competition cases too, is expected to be important prerequisites for the more effective implementation of the competition law in Kosovo in the near future.

Table of Cases

Authority

Authority Decision No 30/2020 of 6 May 2020
Authority Decision No 31/2020 of 6 May 2020
Authority Decision No 32/2020 of 6 May 2020
Authority Decision No 33/2020 of 6 May 2020
Authority Decision No 34/2020 of 6 May 2020
Authority Decision No 35/2020 of 6 May 2020
Authority Decision No 36/2020 of 6 May 2020
Authority Decision No 37/2020 of 6 May 2020
Authority Decision No 38/2020 of 6 May 2020
Authority Decision No 39/2020 of 6 May 2020
Authority Decision No 40/2020 of 6 May 2020
Authority Decision No 41/2020 of 6 May 2020
Authority Decision No 42/2020 of 6 May 2020
Authority Decision No 120/23 of 18 December 2023

CJEU

Judgment of 16 December 1975, *Suiker Unie and Others v Commission,* Joined Cases 40 to 48, 50, 54 to 56, 111, 113 and 114/73 ECLI:EU:C:1975:174
Judgment of 8 November 1983, *NV IAZ International Belgium and others v Commission*, Joined Cases 96–102, 104, 105, 108 and 110/82, ECLI:EU:C:1983:310
Judgment of 10 December 1985, *Stichting Sigarettenindustrie v Commission,* Joined Cases 240, 241, 242, 261, 262, 268 and 269/82, ECLI:EU:C:1985:488
Judgment of 14 February 1990, *Delacre and Others v Commission,* C-350/88, ECLI:EU:C:1990:71
Judgment of 16 June 1993, *France v Commission*, C-325/91, ECLI:EU:C:1993:245
Judgment of 15 June 1994, *Commission v BASF and Others*, C-137/92 P, ECLI:EU:C:1994:247
Judgment of 14 July 1994, *Arlette Grynberg and Eileen Hall v Commission*, T-534/93, ECLI:EU:T:1994:86
Judgment of 9 November 1995, *Atlanta Fruchthandelsgesellschaft and Others v Bundesamt für Ernährung und Forstwirtschaft*, C-466/93, ECLI:EU:C:1995:370
Judgment of 9 November 1995, *Atlanta Fruchthandelsgesellschaft and Others v Bundesamt für Ernährung und Forstwirtschaft*, C-466/93, ECLI:EU:C:1995:370
Judgment of 20 February 1997, *Commission v Daffix*, C-166/95 P, ECLI:EU:C:1997:73
Judgment of 1 July 1986, *Usinor v Commission*, C-185/85, ECLI:EU:C:1986:276

Judgment of 15 March 2000, *Cimenteries CBR and Others v Commission*, Joined Cases T-25/95, T-26/95, T-30/95, T-31/95, T-32/95, T-34/95, T-35/95, T-36/95, T-37/95, T-38/95, T-39/95, T-42/95, T-43/95, T-44/95, T-45/95, T-46/95, T-48/95, T-50/95, T-51/95, T-52/95, T-53/95, T-54/95, T-55/95, T-56/95, T-57/95, T-58/95, T-59/95, T-60/95, T-61/95, T-62/95, T-63/95, T-64/95, T-65/95, T-68/95, T-69/95, T-70/95, T-71/95, T-87/95, T-88/95, T-103/95 and T-104/95, ECLI:EU:T:2000:77

Judgment of 6 April 2000, P *Commission v Solvay,* Joined cases C-287/95 P and C-288/95 P, ECLI:EU:C:2000:189

Judgment of 29 February 1996, *Belgium v Commission*, C-56/93, ECLI:EU:C:1996:64,

Judgment of 1 October 2009, *Commission v Council*, C-370/07, ECLI:EU:C:2009:590

Judgment of 13 September 2010, *Éditions Odile Jacob v Commission*, T-279/04, ECLI:EU:T:2010:384

Judgment of 27 October 2011, *P Austria v Scheucher-Fleisch and Others,* C-47/10, ECLI:EU:C:2011:698

Judgment of 27 June 2012, *Bolloré v Commission*, T-372/10, ECLI:EU:T:2012:325

Judgment of 6 October 2015, *Post Danmark*, C-23/14, ECLI:EU:C:2015:651

Judgment of 15 December 2016, *Dimosia Epicheirisi Ilektrismou (DEI) v Commission*, T-169/08, ECLI:EU:T:2016:733

Commission

Commission Decision no 85/609/EEC *AKZO* [1985] OJ L374/1

Commission Decision no 89/22/EEC *BPB Industries pic* [1989] OJ L10/50

Commission Decision no 91/299/EEC, *Soda/Solvay* [1991] OJ L152/21

Commission Decision no 91/300/EEC, *Soda/ICI* [1991] OJ L152/40

Commission Decision no 98/531/EC, *Van den Bergh Foods Limited* [1998] OJ L246/1

Commission Decision no 2000/74/EC, *Virgin/British Airways* [2000] OJ L30/1

Commission Decision no 2002/405/EC, *Michelin* [2002] OJ L143/1

Kosovo

The Court of First Instance of Prishtina – Administrative Department, Gekos Ruling No A181/2011 of 16 January 2015

Supreme Court of Kosovo, *Ruling on the Gekos case*, ARJ-UZVP-no 45/2015 of 15 April 2016

Pristina Court of Appeal – Administrative Department, *Ruling on the Gekos case*, No AAnr.93/2015 of 22 October 2015.

Supreme Court of Kosovo, *Ruling on the Insig case*, ARJ no 25/2016, 05 October 2016.
Supreme Court of Kosovo, *Ruling on the Grawe Elsig case*, ARJ no 24/2016, 05 October 2016.
Supreme Court of Kosovo, *Ruling on the Illyria case*, ARJ no 38/2016, 23 January 2017.
Supreme Court of Kosovo, *Ruling on the Gekos case*, ARJ-UZVP-no 45/2015, 15 April 2016.

United States

Verizon Commc'ns Inc v Law Offices of Curtis V Trinko LLP 540 US 398 408 (2004)

Table of Legislation

EU

Council Regulation (EC) No 1/2003 of 16 December 2002 on the implementation of the rules on competition laid down in Articles 81 and 82 of the Treaty (Text with EEA relevance) [2003] OJ L 1/1
Council Regulation (EC) No 139/2004 of 20 January 2004 on the control of concentrations between undertakings (the EC Merger Regulation) [2004] OJ L24/1
Commission Regulation 330/2010 of 20 April 2010 on the application of Article 101(3) of the Treaty on the Functioning of the European Union to categories of vertical agreements and concerted practices [2010] OJ L102/1
Commission Regulation (EC) No 802/2004 of 7 April 2004 implementing Council Regulation (EC) No.139/2004 of 20 January 2004 on the control of concentrations between undertakings [2004] OJ L 133/1
Directive 2014/104/EU of the European Parliament and of the Council of 26 November 2014 on certain rules governing actions for damages under national law for infringements of the competition law provisions of the Member States and of the European Union (Text with EEA relevance) [2014] OJ L 349/1
Stabilisation and Association Agreement between the European Union and the European Atomic Energy Community, of the one part, and Kosovo, of the other part [2016] OJ L 71/3

Kosovo

Law No 02/L-28 on Administrative Procedure, Official Gazette 8/2007
Law no 03/L-229 on Protection of Competition, Official Gazette No 88/2010
Law no 2004/36 on Competition, Official Gazette 14/2007
Law No. 04/L-226 On Amending and Supplementing the Law No. 03/L-229 On Protection of Competition, Official Gazette of the Republic of Kosova / Nr.17/ 2014
Law No. 05/L-031 on General Administrative Procedure, Official Gazette of the Republic of Kosova / No. 20/2016
Law No. 08/L-015 on Commercial Court. Official Gazette No. 7/2022
Law no.08/L-056 on Protection of Competition, Official Gazette No. 14/2022

United Nation

United Nations (1999) Resolution 1244 (1999). S/RES/1244 (1999).

References

Administrative Instruction No 12/2009 on Amendment and Supplement of the Administrative Instruction No 06/2009 on the Use of Fiscal Electronic Devices, 17 September 2009. Available at http://www.atk-ks.org/wp-content/uploads/2017/10/Udhezim_Administrativ_12_20091.pdf
Administrative Instruction No. 01/2018 On the Criteria for the Pronunciation of Sanctions Administrative, 2018
Cauffman C, Hao Q (eds) (2016) Procedural rights in competition law in the EU and China. Springer
Commission (2008) Kosovo Progress Report 2008. Commission Staff Working Document. SEC (2008) 2697
Commission (2014) Kosovo 2014 Report. Commission Staff Working Document. SWD(2014) 306 final
Commission (2015) Kosovo 2015 Report. Commission Staff Working Document. SWD(2015) 215 final
Commission (2016) Kosovo 2016 Report. Commission Staff Working Document. SWD(2016) 363 final
Commission Notice on Immunity from Fines and Reduction of Fines in Cartel Cases [2002] OJ C45/3
Commission Notice on Immunity from Fines and Reduction of Fines in Cartel Cases [2006] OJ C298/17, 8 December 2006 and Amendments to the Commission Notice on Immunity from Fines and Reduction of Fines in Cartel [2006] OJ C256/1
Commission Notice on the non-imposition or reduction of fines in cartel cases [1996] OJ C207/4
Government of Kosovo Decision of No 02/56 of 18 February 2009 on the Implementation of Fiscal Cash Registers throughout Kosovo. Available at http://www.atk-ks.org/wp-content/uploads/2010/09/Vendimi_qeveris.pdf (in Albanian only)

Guidelines on the Applicability of Article 101 of the Treaty on the Functioning of the European Union to Horizontal Co-operation Agreements [2011] OJ C11/1

Kosovo Competition Authority (2010a) Conclusion for initiating the investigation into the enterprises Gekos and Dukagjini, 9 July 2010.

Kosovo Competition Authority (2010b) Records of hearings with the representatives of the enterprises Gekos and Dukagjini, at which they were present, 10 August 2010.

Kosovo Competition Authority (2010c) Decision on the concerted practice for the sale of fiscal cash electronic devices between enterprises Gekos and Dukagjini, 1 September 2010

Kosovo Competition Authority (2017) Annual Report 2017. Kosovo Competition Authority. Prishtina

Kosovo Competition Authority (2019) Conclusion for initiation of investigation against oil companies. Prishtina

Ministry of Economy and Finance Decision No KAF-11/2009 of 26 November 2009

Mucaj A (2020a) Antitrust law in Kosovo: challenges in following the EU enforcement jurisprudence. J Eur Compet Law Pract 11(3–4):166–172. https://doi.org/10.1093/jeclap/lpz069

Mucaj A (2020b) Competition law framework in Kosovo and the role of the EU in promoting competition policies in other countries and regions wishing to join the block. Yearb Antitrust Regul Stud 13(22):89. https://doi.org/10.7172/1689-9024.YARS.2020.13.22.4

Muris TJ (2005) Principles for a successful competition agency. Univ Chicago Law Rev 72:165

Skara G (2023) Reform of Kosovo competition law: closer to EU competition law. J Eur Compet Law Pract 14(3):171. https://doi.org/10.1093/jeclap/lpad013

The Assembly of Kosovo, the Committee on Economic Development, Infrastructure, Trade and Industry, Procès-verbal of the meeting 17–26 April 2016

The Supreme Court of Kosovo, Guide approved at the General Session of the Supreme Court, held on 10 June 2021

Avdylkader Mucaj obtained his PhD at the University of Ljubljana-Faculty on Law on European Law, whereas his thesis was entirely focused on competition law. Mr. Mucaj holds also an LL.M. in European Law from Stockholm University, Sweden. In addition, Mr. Mucaj also spent two years as PhD researcher in the field of EU Law at the Free University of Berlin, in Germany. Dr. Mucaj has published in the field of competition law, mostly reflecting competition law developments and enforcement in Kosovo, such as: 'Challenges in Following the EU Enforcement Jurisprudence' Journal of European Competition Law & Practice and "Competition Law Framework in Kosovo and the Role of the EU in Promoting Competition Policies in Other Countries and Regions Wishing to Join the Block" Yearbook of Antitrust and Regulatory Studies-YARS. Mr. Mucaj has participated in the e 6th Zagreb Competition Law and Policy Conference in Memory of Dr. Vedran Šoljan, Challenges to the Enforcement of Competition Rules in Central and Eastern Europe, 12–-13 December 2019, Zagreb, Croatia as well as the 7th Competition Law and Policy Conference "New developments and (old) challenges: are we ready for the new era?" organized from the University of Zagreb, Faculty of Economics and Business, presenting the paper and research: "The role of the judiciary on (none) effective enforcement of competition law in the new jurisdictions" 12–13 May 2022, Opatija Croatia. His current research interest is focused on public enforcement challenges of competition law in Kosovo; competition law in the digital markets; EU AI law; rule of law etc.

Competition Law and Policy in Montenegro

Nebojša Jovović

1 Introduction

Montenegro is a small country that today has an open economy.[1] In 1990's Montenegro began the process of economic transition from a centrally planned economy to a market-oriented economy. The transition to a free-market economy required a whole series of measures: the elimination of price controls, the introduction of effective functioning of private ownership (privatization), and a competitive market. In this sense, Montenegro prioritized the development of an economic system built on a dynamic and competitive market. This was especially pronounced after gaining independence in 2006.

Protection and development of market competition is a requirement for Montenegro, and other Western Balkan countries that aim to be part of the European Union (EU). In fact, they are required to send progress reports to the European Commission-Directorate-General (DG) for Competition. A very important segment for the Western Balkan countries is the creation of a market economy, which should be followed by increasing its productivity and competitiveness. Market opening and establishment of opportunities for free market entry is vital for state sustainable economic development.[2]

Accession negotiations between the EU and Montenegro were opened in June 2012 and all negotiation chapters were opened, of which negotiation chapter 8—Competition—was the last to be opened, in 2020. A competition policy adopted by the government should include both economic policies that enhance competition in

[1] According to Statistical Office of Montenegro (2020), Montenegro has an area 13,888 km^2 with 620,029 inhabitants.

[2] Monti (2002), p. 4.

N. Jovović (✉)
Agency for Protection of Competition, Podgorica, Montenegro

J. Pecotić Kaufman et al. (eds.), *Competition Law and Policy in the Western Balkans*, European Union and its Neighbours in a Globalized World 22,
https://doi.org/10.1007/978-3-031-93756-9_5

local and national markets, and competition law designed to stop anti-competitive business practices. The competition policy in Montenegro has gained in significance, in parallel with the acceleration of their EU accession process.

In accordance with its commitment to a market economy and EU membership, Montenegro developed legislation and policies on competition protection, in order to ensure that business entities can compete fairly and freely, which benefits consumers by providing greater choice and better prices. This type of legislation aims to prevent monopolies or other anti-competitive behaviour that can harm smaller businesses and reduce competition in the market. The goal of competition protection legislation and policy is to promote economic efficiency and fairness by regulating the behaviour of business entities on the market. This includes the prohibition of anti-competitive practices such as price fixing, abuse of dominant market positions and mergers that could lead to a reduction in competition.

Since 2006, Montenegro went through a significant transition in the field of competition protection and achieved significant progress in this sector. However, as in any country, there are challenges that must be overcome in order to ensure effective protection of competition and support sustainable economic development. In this chapter, we will explore the key concepts and principles of legislation and policy on competition protection in Montenegro. By the end of this text, readers will have a better understanding of competition legislation and competition protection policies in Montenegro.

2 Historical Development of the Competition Legislation in Montenegro

Montenegro established a competition protection system for the first time with the Competition Act from 2005,[3] which came into effect on January 1, 2006. Montenegro has made significant progress in developing the competition system based on the Competition Act since gaining independence in 2006. Competition law in Montenegro is based on the principles of EU legislation on the protection of competition and is largely harmonized with EU law through a series of harmonization measures. This alignment is crucial for Montenegro, as it aspires to integrate more and more into the EU. The first Competition Act prohibited anti-competitive (restrictive) agreements and practices, abuse of a dominant position, and established control of mergers (concentrations) that could significantly limit, prevent, or distort competition in the market.

According to the legal solutions from the Competition Act from 2005, the duty of protecting competition was first under the competence of the Ministry of Economic Development, that is, these tasks were performed in a narrower internal organisational unit within that ministry, the Sector for Protection of Competition,

[3]Competition Act [2005] Official Gazette of the Republic of Montenegro No. 69/05.

until establishing of the Administration for Protection of Competition, in accordance with the Act on Amendments to the Competition Act[4] and the Amendments to the Regulation on the Organization and Mode of Operation of the State Administration from 2007.[5] The Administration for the Protection of Competition performed these tasks until the registration of the Agency for the Protection of Competition (hereinafter referred to as MCA, in Montenegrin: *Agencija za zaštitu konkurencije*)[6] in the Central Register of Business Entities, that is, on February 8, 2013, in accordance with the Competition Act from 2012.[7] Only in 2013, by obtaining the legal status of an independent body with the status of a legal entity, did MCA gained organizational independence in the public administration system. The entry into force of the new Competition Act was accompanied by the adoption of new by-laws that regulated this area more closely.

Montenegro has improved its judicial system in order to ensure adequate investigation, and prosecution of cases related to competition protection violations. Until the reform of the misdemeanor system of Montenegro, created by the entry into force of the Act on Misdemeanors in 2011,[8] when the Misdemeanor Court and the High Misdemeanor Court of Montenegro (hereinafter referred to as High Misdemeanor Court) were established, authorized officials in the Administration for Protection of Competition conducted misdemeanor proceedings for competition infringements and directly imposed fines. After mentioned reform, the fining competences of the competition protection authorities remain only in initiation of misdemeanor proceedings before Misdemeanor Court and issuing misdemeanor orders. However, the Competition Act from 2012 introduces the institution of procedural fines, i.e. periodic fines, which MCA imposes in an administrative procedure to an undertaking for failure to provide data, obstruction of dawn raid, non-compliance with orders of MCA etc. In 2013, MCA gained the authority to conduct a dawn raid, that is, to collect data through dawn raid.

Until 2018, the MCA was headed by a director, who, in addition to management duties, made decisions in the field of protection of competition. As of 2018, when it comes to the organization itself, MCA, based on the Act on Amendments to the Competition Act 2018,[9] formed also a Council—a collegial body. The Council consists of the president and two members, which decides on procedures in the field of competition protection, on proposal of a decision by the director of MCA. On the other hand, director retained the powers in the management part, as well as the sactioning powers (issuing misdemeanor orders or submitting requests to initiate misdemeanor proceedings to the Misdemeanor Court).

[4] Act on Amendments to the Competition Act [2007] Official Gazette of Montenegro No. 37/07.

[5] Decree on Amendments to the Decree on the Organization and Mode of Work of the State Administration 2007 Official Gazette of Montenegro No. 6/07.

[6] The official website of the Agency for the Protection of Competition is www.azzk.me.

[7] Competition Act [2012] Official Gazette of Montenegro No. 44/12.

[8] Act on Misdemeanors [2011] Official Gazette of Montenegro No. 1/11.

[9] Act on Amendments to the Competition Act [2018] Official Gazette of Montenegro No. 13/18

The Competition Act was amended in 2018 in order to increase the jurisdiction of MCA and create better conditions for the opening of Negotiation Chapter 8—Competition. In addition, the Competition Act is aligned with the Act on Administrative Procedure,[10] which began to be applied on July 1, 2017. That was of great importance from a procedural point of view, given that the MCA, decides in areas related to the protection of competition in an administrative procedure. Also, in accordance with the amendments from 2018, MCA took over the duties of the State Aid Control Commission on 26 July 2018, with which, in addition to existing competencies, it also received tasks in the field of state aid control with expanded competencies when it comes to that area.

The latest amendments to the Competition Act from 2021,[11] which entered into force on January 8, 2022, did not deal with the material and procedural provisions of the Competition Act, but mainly concerned the organization of this institution in terms of the competence of the Council and the director of MCA, and the conditions for their appointment, providing a basis for further improvement of legal solutions.

3 Relationship of Montenegro Competition Act with the EU Law

The legal system of protection of competition in Montenegro is closely related to the legal system of the EU, since Montenegro strives to fully harmonize its laws with the EU law in preparation for possible future membership. According to the Constitution of Montenegro, confirmed and published international treaties and generally accepted rules of international law are an integral part of the internal legal order and have primacy over domestic legislation and are directly applied when they regulate relations differently from internal legislation.[12] In this regard, the Stabilisation and Association Agreement between the European Communities and their Member States, of the one part, and the Republic of Montenegro, of the other part[13] (hereinafter referred to as "SAA") and the Treaty on the Functioning of the European Union represent the foundations on which competition law rests in Montenegro. Also, both the MCA and the acting courts in Montenegro in their decisions, when taking positions in cases concerning the protection of competition, use the practice of the European Commission and EU courts often to represent the argumentation.

[10] Act on Administrative Procedure [2014] Official Gazette of Montenegro no. 56/14, 20/15, 40/16 and 37/17.

[11] Act on Amendments to the Competition Act [2021] Official Gazette of Montenegro No. 145/21.

[12] Constitution of Montenegro [2007] Official Gazette of Montenegro No. 1/07, Art 9.

[13] Act on the ratification of the Stabilisation and Association Agreement between the European Communities and their member states, on the one hand, and the Republic of Montenegro, on the other hand [2007] Official Gazette of Montenegro No. 7/07.

According to Article 73 (1) of SAA, the following are incompatible with the proper functioning of this Agreement, insofar as they may affect trade between the Community and Montenegro:

(i) all Agreements between undertakings, decisions by associations of undertakings and concerted practices between undertakings which have as their object or effect the prevention, restriction or distortion of competition;
(ii) abuse by one or more undertakings of a dominant position in the territories of the Community or Montenegro as a whole or in a substantial part thereof;
(iii) any State aid which distorts or threatens to distort competition by favouring certain undertakings or certain products.

In addition, Article 73 (2) of the SAA stipulates that:

> Any practices contrary to the mentioned Article shall be assessed on the basis of criteria arising from the application of the competition rules applicable in the Community, in particular from Articles 81, 82, 86 and 87 of the EC Treaty and interpretative instruments adopted by the Community institutions. Any practices contrary to this Article shall be assessed on the basis of criteria arising from the application of the competition rules applicable in the Community, in particular from Articles 81, 82, 86 and 87 of the EC Treaty and interpretative instruments adopted by the Community institutions.[14]

At the Intergovernmental Conference between Montenegro and the EU in Brussels (June 30, 2020) Montenegro opened negotiation Chapter 8—Competition, as the last negotiation chapter for Montenegro's accession to the EU. Montenegro has established close cooperation with the European Commission, which is responsible for implementing competition rules in the EU internal market. The European Commission provided technical assistance to Montenegro in the development of its competition law system of laws on competition protection.[15] In 2024, Montenegro has not yet met all the final criteria for closing Chapter 8—Competition.

In general, the system of regulations on the protection of competition in Montenegro is very important for its integration with the EU. By harmonizing its laws with those of the EU and closely cooperating with the European Commission, Montenegro strives to ensure that every participant operating in the Montenegrin market can compete under equal and fair conditions, which also apply to the internal EU market.

In 2022, MCA increased the number of competition and state aid investigations and established a general register of state aid to ensure better transparency and monitoring of public aid. According to the Montenegro 2022 Report of the European Commission,[16] when it comes to Chapter 8: Competition policy, Montenegro is moderately prepared in this area.

---

[14] Art. 73 (2) of SAA.

[15] IPA 2012, 2014, 2020 and twining light projects.

[16] Commission (2022) Montenegro 2022 Report. SWD (2022) 335 final.

4 Institutional and Normative Framework of Competition Authority in Montenegro

The institutional and normative framework is a crucial aspect of any country's governance, as it sets the foundation for regulating and overseeing various sectors of the economy. This is particularly important in the context of competition, where fair market practices and the prevention of anti-competitive behaviour are essential for promoting economic growth and protecting consumer interests. In Montenegro, the institutional and normative framework pertaining to competition is designed to ensure a level playing field for businesses and to protect the competitiveness of markets.

In this section, we will describe the institutional and normative framework for the protection of competition in Montenegro, taking into account the following topics: (i) powers of MCA; (ii) major substantive and procedural norms; (iii) investigative and sanctioning powers; (iv) the organisational structure; (v) budget and staff of MCA in the period 2012–2022.

4.1 *Competition Authority and Its Powers*

According to Article 73 (3–4) of the SAA:

> the parties shall ensure that an operationally independent authority is entrusted with the powers necessary for the full application of prohibition of practices that are incompatible with the proper functioning of this Agreement, insofar as they may affect trade between the Community and Montenegro (all agreements between undertakings, decisions by associations of undertakings and concerted practices between undertakings which have as their object or effect the prevention, restriction or distortion of competition; abuse by one or more undertakings of a dominant position in the territories of the Community or Montenegro as a whole or in a substantial part thereof), regarding private and public undertakings and undertakings to which special rights have been granted.

Pursuant to the requirements of Article 73 (4), in 2013, Montenegro established an independent authority for the protection of competition, named MCA. MCA is responsible for the protection of competition and state aid control. When it comes to matters of competition protection, in the first place, MCA, in addition to administrative and misdemeanor competences in the field of competition protection,[17] it is also responsible for giving opinions. Those opinions are issued on the application of regulations in the field of competition protection, as well as opinions regarding valid regulations that affect or may affect competition, monitoring and analysis conditions

[17] Approving implementation of concentrations, approving individual exemption of restrictive agreements from prohibition, taking measures against participants and associations of participants for violating competition on the market or taking measures in order to prevent the occurrence or cessation of injury, and eliminating harmful consequences for participants and consumers. Competition Act, Art 19 (2).

of competition on the market and the markets of individual economic sectors, and preparing the professional basis for drafting laws and by-laws in the field of competition protection. The ministry in charge of economic affairs has normative competence in terms of regulations governing the field of protection of competition in Montenegro.

4.2 Main Substantive and Procedural Norms, Investigative and Sanctioning Powers

When it comes to MCA competences in terms of protection of competition in the narrower sense, such as restrictive agreements, abuse of dominant position and concentrations, the director of MCA is authorized to propose administrative acts that decide on the approval of concentrations, determination of restrictive agreements and determination of abuse of a dominant position. On a director's proposal, the Council, as a collegial body of MCA, in accordance with the voting procedure, adopts an administrative act in a specific administrative matter. Issuing of opinions is passed the same way. The director of MCA is authorized to issue decisions on the initiation of investigation procedures for competition infringements, which means that the Council does not decide on the initiation of investigation procedures. Also, the Council does not have misdemeanor jurisdiction, given that the director issues misdemeanor orders and/or submits requests to initiate misdemeanor proceedings. Namely, Misdemeanors Court imposes fines, and decision of MCA on infringement of competition does not include a fine.

The procedure for issuing approval for the implementation of the concentration, as well as the procedure for individual exemption, is initiated at the request of the parties (undertakings). The aforementioned means that proceedings in these legal matters are initiated exclusively *ex privato*.

MCA initiates the procedure of examination of competition infringement *ex officio* and when, on the basis of submitted initiatives, information, documents, and other available data, it reasonably assumes the existence of competition infringement.[18] In accordance with this legal solution, the MCA initiates the procedure of examination of competition infringement exclusively *ex officio*. An initiative submitted *ex privato* cannot be an independent basis for initiating a competition infringement investigation procedure but only possibly a reason for MCA to initiate an investigation procedure if, on the basis of it, MCA reasonably assumes the existence of a competition infringement.

The party in the proceedings before the MCA is: (i) an undertaking who submitted a request for the issuance of an approval for the implementation of a concentration or a request for an individual exemption of restrictive agreement from the prohibition; (ii) an undertaking against whom investigation proceedings have been

[18] Competition Act, Art 28 (1).

initiated. In addition to prescribing who is to be considered a party in the proceedings before the MCA, the Competition Act explicitly states that the submitters of the initiative for examination of competition infringement, providers of information, documents, data, experts, and other interested persons, organizations whose analyzes are used in procedure, as well as state authorities and organizations that cooperate with MCA during the procedure, do not have the status of party.[19]

When it comes to dawn raids, the director of MCA issues a decision on dawn raids. Dawn raids, according to the Competition Act, can be carried out only after MCA initiates the examination procedure, which consequently means that the precondition for performing dawn raids is the well-founded assumption by MCA that a competition infringement has been committed. In performing a dawn raid, the authorized person of MCA has the right to:

- enter and inspect business premises, vehicles, land, and other facilities where the party or other undertaking performs activities or performs other business activities that result in the probability of violation of this law;
- review business books and other documents;
- copy or scan business documentation, and if this is not possible for technical reasons, temporarily seize business documentation for the time necessary to copy it;
- seal all business premises and business documents for the duration of the dawn raid, to the extent necessary for its implementation;
- take statements from the party's representatives or employees of the party, as well as documents on the facts related to the subject of dawn raid and make a record of it, and if a written statement is necessary, determine the date by which the statement must be delivered;
- perform other actions in accordance with the purpose of the investigation.[20]

A person who is not a party to the proceedings is obliged to allow dawn raids, when there is a well-founded suspicion that an activity is being carried out in his facilities or premises or that objects necessary for decision-making in the proceedings are found.

At the request of the MCA, in cases of obstruction or non-compliance with the orders of authorized persons in the execution of actions, the administrative body responsible for police affairs is obliged to provide assistance in the performance of certain actions in the procedure, especially in the collection of data by dawn raid and temporary confiscation of things in accordance with the law which regulates the powers and actions of the police.

In the period 2012–2022, MCA conducted six dawn raids; one in 2014, one in 2017, two in 2019 and two in 2022.

MCA does not have full sanctioning powers that is, it cannot directly impose fines on undertakings for competition infringement. In accordance with the regulations on

[19] Competition Act, Art 27.

[20] Competition Act, Art 30.

misdemeanors, by issuing a misdemeanor order, MCA can directly sanction the perpetrator of a competition infringement, i.e. an undertaking who has committed a competition infringement. However, with a misdemeanor order MCA can only impose the minimum prescribed fine. Only the competent Misdemeanor Court, i.e. the High Misdemeanor Court, can impose a fine in an amount higher than the minimum, considering the facts of the case, and especially mitigating and/or aggravating circumstances.

When it comes to the sanctioning powers of the competition authority, it is inevitable to mention the leniency program. The Competition Act, although narrowly, prescribes the special authority of the MCA against the participants of the restrictive agreement. If participant of the restrictive agreement comply with conditions from Competition Act, MCA may not submit a request for the initiation of misdemeanor proceedings or withdraw the already submitted request for the initiation of misdemeanor proceedings or propose to the court a milder punishment of the participant of the restrictive agreement. This special authority can be used if the participant of the agreement takes these steps: (i) first reports the existence of the agreement to MCA and submits valid evidence; (ii) provides MCA with evidence of the existence of the agreement, which at that time had certain knowledge but did not have sufficient evidence; (iii) reports the existence of another restrictive agreement in which he participates or has direct knowledge, and submits evidence. This special authority of ACP applies to all anticompetitive agreements. The leniency program does not apply to the participant of the agreement who initiated or organized the conclusion or implementation of the restrictive agreement. MCA may, in accordance with the application of the law regulating the misdemeanor procedure, propose to the participant of the restrictive agreement to enter into a plea agreement.[21] The leniency programme does not apply only to cartels, but to all types of anticompetitive agreement.

4.3 *Organizational Structure*

MCA was established as an independent body with the status of a legal entity that performs tasks established by the Competition Act. MCA is accountable to the Government for its work and reports to the Government and the Assembly annually. The bodies of MCA are the Council and the Director. The Council has a president and two members. The president and one member of the Council are appointed by the Government on the proposal of the body responsible for economic affairs, and the other member of the Council is appointed by the Government on the proposal of the state administration body responsible for state aid affairs. The president and members of the Council perform their functions in MCA professionally. The

[21] Competition Act, Art 69.

president and members of the Council are appointed for a period of four years and may be reappointed.

MCA is managed by a director appointed by the Council for a period of five years, based on a public competition and may be reappointed. Before the Competition Act was amended in January 2022, the director of MCA was appointed by the Government, on the proposal of the authority responsible for economic affairs, and the Council did not decide on the procedure for appointing the director of MCA.

The internal organization of MCA is divided into: (i) the Sector for Protection of Competition and (ii) the Sector for State Aid Control, along with the Service for General Affairs and Finance. The Sector for the Protection of Competition includes four departments: (i) the Department for the Determination of Restrictive Agreements, (ii) the Department for the Determination of Abuse of a Dominant Position, (iii) the Department for the Assessment of Concentrations and Individual Exemptions, and (iv) the Department for Sectoral Analysis. The State Aid Control Sector consists of two departments: (i) the Department for *Ex Ante* Control and (ii) the Department for *Ex Post* Control.[22]

4.4 Competition Agency Budget and Staff

The Competition Act stipulates that the funds necessary for the work of MCA in performing its tasks are provided from: (i) fees paid to MCA; (ii) budget of Montenegro; and (iii) other sources in accordance with the law.[23]

Fees are determined by the Tariff Book on the amount of fees to be paid in proceedings before MCA,[24] which MCA adopted with the consent of the Government. The established fees allow interested undertakings to, before submitting a specific request to the MCA, be informed of the amount of the fee they will bear for the issuance of the act by the MCA. Fees are recorded and placed on a separate account with the Central Bank of Montenegro. Although it is prescribed as the first source of its funds, MCA has never been a beneficiary. Namely, MCA did not have the possibility of disposing of the funds from the fees, because the said funds are under the jurisdiction of the ministry responsible for financial affairs.

Funds from the budget of Montenegro represent the main and for now the only source of funding for MCA, bearing in mind the unpredictability and uncertainty of funding from its own sources. In this regard, MCA does not have financial independence, it does not have a bank account, and it is fully financed from the budget of Montenegro.

[22] Regulations on internal organization and systematization of MCA No. 06-040/22-668/6 (2022).

[23] Competition Act, Art 24 (1).

[24] Tariff Book on the amount of fees to be paid in proceedings before MCA [2013] Official Gazette of Montenegro No. 14/13.

Table 1 MCA budget by year in the period 2013–2022 (in EUR)

Year	MCA Annual Budget
2013	221,618
2014	238,360
2015	305,287
2016	379,754
2017	484,734
2018	733,286
2019	795,506
2020	687,448
2021	632,806
2022	657,180

Source: Author's own calculation based on MCA's Annual Reports 2013–2022
The author did not present data on the amount of the budget for 2012, due to the organisational position of the Administration for the Protection of Competition, which ceased to operate in 2013

The source of funding for this institution is directly related to the legal status of its employees. The rights, obligations, and responsibilities of the president and members of the Council, the director, the deputy director and employees are subject to the regulations governing the rights, obligations, and responsibilities of civil servants and state employees, unless otherwise regulated by the Competition Act.[25] In this regard, employees in MCA are within the system of civil servants and state employees.

Table 1 shows a comparative overview of the annual funds that the MCA had available in the period 2013–2022. The budget in 2019 was the highest, due to the transfer of state aid mandate and employees who previously worked in the Ministry of Finance to the MCA.

It should be pointed out that one of the key assumptions for achieving complete independence of MCA is the establishment of a self-financing model. Self-funding is key to independence, efficiency, and integrity in market regulation. It enables unbiased decisions, efficient action, transparency, and progress in work. Stable and regular funding enables activity planning, investments in expertise, and capacity development in the long term. Continuity of funding is crucial for maintaining consistency in the application of competition laws and protecting competition in the long term.

Table 2 shows revenues by year that MCA realised on the basis of the fees stipulated in the Tariff Book on the amount of fees paid in the procedure before MCA for the protection of competition. Namely, the funds realized on this basis do not represent the property of MCA and they are disposed of by the ministry responsible for financial affairs, so MCA has no right to dispose of them. According

[25] Competition Act, Art 23a (1).

Table 2 Revenues of MCA based on the fees stipulated in the Tariff Book on the amount of fees to be paid in proceedings before MCA, by years in the period 2013–2022 (in EUR)

Year	Revenues
2013	200,490.86
2014	375,158.27
2015	500,418.38
2016	481,200.00
2017	487,817.73
2018	725,847.15
2019	911,510.33
2020	668,162.45
2021	1,031,376.22
2022	1,017,778.17

Source: Author's own calculation based on MCA's Annual Reports 2013–2022

Table 3 Number of employees (2013–2022)

Year	Number of employees
2013	12
2014	11
2015	13
2016	14
2017	17
2018	20
2019	28
2020	29
2021	28
2022	32

Source: Author's own calculation based on MCA's Annual Reports 2013–2022

to data in Tables 1 and 2 can be concluded that MCA continuously generates higher revenues than the available budget in the observed period.

Table 3 shows the trend of the number of employees in MCA by year. This number includes members of the Council (since 2018, when the Council was established) and the directors.

According to the data, it can be concluded that MCA is continuously increasing the number of employees. If we make a comparison with the bodies responsible for competition affairs in the EU, it is evident that there is a need for further increase of administrative and research capacities. In 2022, there has been an increase in the number of employees and this number is the highest since its establishment. However, it should be borne in mind that with the takeover of state aid control tasks in July 2018, there was also the takeover of employees from the State Aid Department within the Ministry of Finance in 2019, performing tasks in the field of state aid control. The number of case handlers in MCA is not explicitly separated in the annual reports.

5 National Specifics that Differ from the EU Competition *Acquis*

5.1 Peculiarities of the National Legal System that Significantly Differ from the EU Competition Acquis

Montenegro is a candidate for EU membership and is currently working on harmonizing its competition laws and policies with those of the EU. However, there are some specificities of the national legal system in Montenegro that differ significantly from the EU competition *acquis.* Along the most important peculiarities of the national legal system that significantly differ from the EU competition *acquis,* five main features can be distinguished:

(1) **Sanctioning powers**: Competition infringements in Montenegro are recognized as misdemeanors. Therefore, the qualification of a competition infringement as a misdemeanor entails the body i.e. court that has jurisdiction to punish undertaking for committed competition infringements. Namely, as previously mentioned, the MCA has only partial jurisdiction to sanction competition infringements as misdemeanours.[26] Also, in Montenegro, besides one general provision in the Competition Act, there is no special by-law act on leniency programs, which are common in the EU to encourage companies to cooperate with competition protection authorities in exchange for a reduction in fines or immunity from sanctions. In addition, there exists no by-law on calculating fines for infringements of competition, but it is up to the acting court to freely assess mitigating and/or aggravating circumstances when determining fines in each individual case.
(2) **Individual exemptions**: In Montenegro, the institute of individual exemption is still maintained in the procedure of submitting a request for approval of an individual exemption of restrictive agreement from the prohibition in cases where the agreement does not meet the requirements for block exemption and/or exemption based on the value of the agreement (*de minimis* exemption).[27] The burden of proving the fulfilment of the conditions for individual exemption

[26] See more about MCA's sanctioning powers in the section Institutional and normative framework.

[27] An agreement of small value according to Article 13 of the Competition Act is an agreement between undertakings whose total market share on the relevant market of products and services does not exceed: (1) 10% market share, when the agreement is concluded between undertakings operating at the same level production or trade (horizontal agreements); (2) 15% of the market share, when the agreement is concluded between undertakings operating at different levels of production or trade (vertical agreements); (3) 10% share of the relevant market for agreements in which it is not clearly defined whether they are horizontal or vertical. However, if the agreement contains conditions that directly or indirectly determine purchase or sale prices or other terms of trade, limits or controls production, the market, technical development or investments or divides the market or sources of supply, i.e. in cases where the agreement contains hard core restrictions, the possibility of applying the exemption based on the value of the restrictive agreement is excluded, regardless of whether the participants of the agreement meet the prescribed thresholds.

is on the applicants, according to Article 11 (4) of the Competition Act. The Rulebook on the Content and Method of Submitting Requests for Individual Exemption of Agreements from Prohibition[28] prescribes the content and method of submitting requests for individual exemption of agreements from prohibition. The term for which MCA can grant an individual exemption is up to five years from the date of issuing the decision on the approval of an individual exemption, with the possibility that the applicant can request an extension of the individual exemption no later than four months before the end of the established period for which the individual exemption was granted. The deadline for submitting a request for the extension of an individual exemption is exclusive and untimely requests are rejected.

(3) **Initiation of the procedure and thresholds for submitting applications for approval for the implementation of the concentration:** The Montenegrin legislator prescribed that the procedure for issuing approval for the implementation of the concentration is initiated only at the request of the party. In this regard, in the event of failure to submit a request for approval for the implementation of the concentration, MCA does not have the authority to ex officio initiate the procedure for the approval of the implementation of the concentration.

(4) **Initiation of the procedure for examination of competition infringement:** Until the entry into force of the Competition Act from 2012, procedures for investigating competition infringements could be initiated *ex officio* and *ex privato* (at the request of undertakings who are or may be infringed; chambers of commerce, associations of employers and entrepreneurs; associations consumer; body of state administration and local self-government). Since the entry into force of the above-mentioned law, the MCA competition infringement investigation procedure can be initiated only ex officio.

(5) **Legal assumption that the undertaking has a dominant position**: Another specificity of the national legal system in Montenegro refers to the criteria for assessing dominance on the relevant market. In the EU, dominance is assessed on the basis of market share and other relevant factors, such as barriers to entry and consumer preferences. In Montenegro, dominance is primarily assumed on the basis of market share, with a threshold of 50%. This means that a company with a market share of 50% or more can be considered dominant in the relevant market, regardless of other relevant factors (legal presumption).

In conclusion, although Montenegro is in the process of harmonizing its competition laws and policies with those of the EU, there are significant differences in the national legal system that need to be addressed. Harmonizing these differences will be an important step in ensuring equal conditions for doing business in Montenegro and promoting competition in the country.

[28] Rulebook on the Content and Method of submitting a request for an individual exemption of restrictive agreement from the prohibition [2013] Official Gazette of Montenegro No 18/13 and 53/20.

5.2 *Peculiarities of the National Legal System That Have Been Erased/Amended in the Process of Europeanization*

Europeanization represents the basis on which competition policy and law arose in Montenegro since it strove to establish a competition protection system that would be harmonized with the EU acquis.

In that process, the sanctioning policy stands out in particular. This policy has come a long way to get the form it has today, which is certainly not yet fully harmonized with the *acquis communautaire*. Thus, until the formation of MCA in 2013, it was prescribed that an undertaking would be fined for a competition infringement in the amount from 200-fold to 300-fold of the minimum wage in the Republic of Montenegro, and that responsible person in undertakings will be fined in the amount from 10-fold to 20-fold of the minimum wage in the Republic of Montenegro.[29] Interestingly, although the regulations on the protection of competition at the time recognized the abuse of a dominant position as a competition infringement, no fine was prescribed for this violation, but the competent authority could only determine the measures that undertakings are obliged to take in order to establish competition on the relevant market, eliminating the harmful consequences of abuse of a dominant position, in the form of ordering the division of participants, alienation of their property, or shares, termination of contracts or waiver of rights that give the possibility of decisive influence on the business of another participant in the market.[30]

6 Application of National and EU Competition Rules by the Competition Agency and Discussion of the most Significant Cases

The competition rules in Montenegro are governed mainly by the SAA and Competition Act. The application of national competition rules is based on EU rules, and Article 73 SAA that concerns anticompetitive practices is transposed into the Competition Act. The law prohibits acts or actions that infringe competition, such as: (i) agreements that prevent, limit, or distort competition; (ii) abuse of a dominant position; (iii) concentrations that prevent, limit, or distort competition or the free development of an open market economy, especially the creation or strengthening of a dominant position on the market. The process of harmonization

[29] Competition Act [2005] Official Gazette of the Republic of Montenegro No. 69/05 and Official Gazette of Montenegro No. 37/07, Arts 44 and 45.

[30] Competition Act [2005] Official Gazette of the Republic of Montenegro No. 69/05 and Official Gazette of Montenegro No. 37/07, Art 21.

and application of the *acquis* in the area of competition protection includes the adoption of EU competition protection regulations, directives, and guidelines.

6.1 Anticompetitive Agreements

The Competition Act (Article 8 paragraph 1), harmonized with Article 101 TFEU, also prohibits acts that have or may have as their object or effect the prevention, limitation, or distortion of competition on the relevant market. The Competition Act recognizes forms of anticompetitive agreements as written or oral agreements, contracts, certain provisions of contracts, express or tacit agreements, concerted practice, as well as decisions of associations of undertakings. Also, it is specifically defined that cooperation between undertakings without the conclusion of a formal or informal agreement, which aims to harmonize the business activities of competitors on the relevant market, and which can be achieved through direct or indirect contact between undertakings and which is not consequence of regular economic activity and independent business of undertakings can be a form of anticompetitive agreements.

The Competition Act divides restrictive agreements into horizontal and vertical agreements. Horizontal agreements are agreements between existing and/or potential undertakings operating at the same level of the production chain or supply chain, while vertical agreements are agreements on terms of procurement, purchase, sale, or resale between existing and/or potential undertakings operating at different levels of the production chain or supply chain.[31] This division is particularly significant due to the legal security of undertakings when it comes to the application of the group exemption and the exemption of agreements based on the value of the agreement (de minimis exemption), the assessment of which is required to be performed by undertakings. Namely, Competition Act divides market thresholds for application of de minimis exemptions, based on whether the anticompetitive agreement is vertical or horizontal. Also, different regulations on group exemptions are applied in cases of vertical and horizontal agreements.

When it comes to the institution of group agreements from prohibition (block exemption), seven regulations on group exemptions, taken from European legislation in this area, are in force: (i) Regulation on block exemption of vertical agreements from prohibition;[32] (ii) Regulation on the block exemption from the prohibition of horizontal agreements on research and development;[33] (iii) Regulation on block exemption from the prohibition of horizontal agreements on

[31] Competition Act, Art 10.

[32] Regulation on the group exemption of vertical agreements from the ban [2014] Official Gazette of Montenegro No. 13/14.

[33] Regulation on group exemption from the prohibition of horizontal agreements on research and development [2014] Official Gazette of Montenegro No. 13/14.

specialization;[34] (iv) Regulation on block exemption from the prohibition of agreements on the distribution of spare parts and servicing of motor vehicles;[35] (v) Regulation on the block exemption from the prohibition of technology transfer agreements;[36] (vi) Regulation on the block exemption from the prohibition of agreements in road, railway and inland water transport and consortium agreements in liner maritime transport;[37] and (vii) Regulation on the conditions, procedure, and criteria for block exemption from the prohibition of agreements in the insurance sector.[38] With the entry into force of Commission Regulation (EU) 2022/720 of 10 May 2022 on the application of Article 101(3) TFEU to categories of vertical agreements and concerted practices (VBER), there was a need to revise the existing Regulation on the block exemption of vertical agreements from the prohibition, in order to harmonize it with the VBER. Also, although Commission Regulation (EU) No 267/2010 of 24 March 2010 on the application of Article 101(3) TFEU to certain categories of agreements, decisions and concerted practices in the insurance sector (IBER), modelled on the Regulation on the conditions, procedure, and criteria for the block exemption from the prohibition of agreements in the insurance sector, ceased to be valid in 2017, the Montenegrin regulation regulating the block exemption of restrictive agreements in the insurance sector is still is in effect.

Restrictive agreements may be exempted from the prohibition if they contribute to the improvement of the production or distribution of goods or services, i.e. to the improvement of technical or economic development, at the same time allowing consumers a proportionate benefit resulting from them in the relevant market, provided that they only impose restrictions that are necessary to achieve the goals of the agreement and they do not allow participants to exclude competition on the relevant market or a significant part of it.[39] Below are discussed two significant cases related to restrictive agreements: "Lovćen" Insurance and "Sava Montenegro" case and the Driving Schools case.

---

[34] Regulation on group exemption from the prohibition of horizontal agreements on specialization [2014] Official Gazette of Montenegro No. 13/14.

[35] Regulation on group exemption from the prohibition of agreements on the distribution of spare parts and servicing of motor vehicles [2014] Official Gazette of Montenegro No. 13/14.

[36] Decree on the group exemption from the prohibition of agreements in road, railway and inland waterway transport and agreements on consortiums in liner maritime transport [2014] Official Gazette of the Republic of Montenegro No. 59/14.

[37] Decree on the group exemption from the prohibition of agreements in road, railway and inland waterway transport and agreements on consortiums in liner maritime transport [2014] Official Gazette of the Republic of Montenegro No. 59/14.

[38] Regulation on the conditions, procedure and criteria for group exemption from the prohibition of agreements in the insurance sector [2014] Official Gazette of Montenegro No. 52/14.

[39] Competition Act, Art 9.

6.1.1 "Lovćen" Insurance and "Sava Montenegro"

In the proceedings initiated against "Lovćen" Insurance and "Sava Montenegro" AD,[40] MCA established the existence of a restrictive agreement on the market for procurement of life and non-life insurance services of public companies of Montenegro in public procurement procedures: "Sava Montenegro" and "Lovćen" Insurance AD. These companies through direct exchange of data between March 2013 and April 2014 negotiated the conclusion of: i) Agreement on mutual relations for joint participation in the insurance market, ii) Agreement on joint bearing and distribution of risks for property insurance CGES Podgorica, and iii) Agreement on joint bearing and distribution of risks for property insurance of CGES Podgorica dated April 22, 2014.[41] MCA's position was that "Lovćen" Insurance and "Sava Montenegro" were obliged to act on the market and make business decisions exclusively independently, as well as to independently determine their prices, terms of cooperation with customers, i.e. purchasers in public procurement procedures, independently of their competitors. These insurance companies were not allowed to exchange business data and information, as direct or potential competitors, nor were allowed to conclude agreements on joint performance on the Montenegrin market, all of which, by the nature of the work and actions, directly affects competition, i.e. economic freedoms on this relevant market.

According to the position of MCA, the aim of concluding the aforementioned agreements was to eliminate mutual competition and directly determine the common price of the two largest competitors, with the ultimate goal of preventing, limiting and distorting competition on the relevant market, which consequently leads to limiting and controlling the market, its development and investments the market. The decision of MCA was confirmed by the Administrative Court of Montenegro (hereinafter referred to as Administrative Court).[42] The same was confirmed by the Supreme Court of Montenegro (hereinafter referred to as Supreme Court),[43] which rejected the request for an extraordinary review of the judgment of the Administrative Court. In the proceedings conducted before the Administrative Court, based on the lawsuits of "Lovćen" Insurance and "Sava Montenegro", assessing the legality of the contested decision, the Administrative Court found that the decision of MCA was unfoundedly challenged, and that MCA correctly decided when it determined that "Lovćen" Insurance and "Sava Montenegro" by agreeing, concluding, and executing the Agreement on mutual relations in the joint performance on the insurance market and the Agreement on joint bearing and distribution of risks for property insurance of CGES Podgorica, infringed competition referred to in Article 8 paragraph 1 point 1), 2), 3) of the Competition Act, and that these contracts were void and prohibited. Therefore, the court held that any agreement between

[40] MCA Decision No. 02-UPI-20/1- 15 of 3 March 2015.

[41] MCA Decision No. 02-UPI-20/39-15 of 24 July 2015.

[42] Judgement of Administrative Court U. No. 2259/2015 of 25 March 2016.

[43] Judgement of Supreme Court Uvp. No. 187/16 of 24 April 2016.

undertakings who are competitors and/or potential competitors constitutes a restrictive agreement, regardless of the purpose and/or consequences of concluding and/or implementing such an agreement, except in the case of exemption from the prohibition, in accordance with the provisions of the Act referring to agreements of small value, i.e. by-laws regulating the group or individual exemption of agreements from prohibition. MCA found that the aim of concluding the agreements in question was to eliminate mutual competition and directly determine the common price of the two largest competitors (over 55% of the market share), with the ultimate goal of preventing, limiting, and distorting competition on the relevant market, which could consequently lead to restrictions and control of the market, its development and investments in that market.

"Lovćen" Insurance and "Sava Montenegro" defended themselves arguing that MCA had to determine whether there were harmful effects in terms of the provisions of Article 8 paragraph 1 item 1), 2), 3) of the Competition Act. Regarding those allegations of the lawsuit, considering that it was pointed out in the administrative procedure, the defendant gave complete and well-founded reasons in the explanation of the disputed decision, which this court accepted in its entirety. Namely, it has been clearly established that agreements in this particular case are prohibited and void when their object or effect is or may be to prevent, limit or distort competition. Therefore, in procedures in which the existence of prohibited and void acts of undertakings is determined in terms of the mentioned legal norm, it is not necessary in each individual case to prove the existence of effects, i.e. harmful consequences of the agreements in question, but the harmfulness of such acts is assumed by the very purpose even when the consequences did not even occur. Prohibition and nullity by object or effect are prescribed alternatively, without disputing the possibility of their cumulation, in the case when such acts "have" or only "may have" the object "or" effect of preventing, limiting, or distorting competition on relevant market. This is how the position of the Administrative Court confirms the fact that joint agreements, and especially cartel agreements, are prohibited *per se*.

Exemption from the prohibition of agreements, which is within the competence of MCA, is prescribed as a possibility, but with the fulfilment of the cumulative conditions prescribed by Article 9 of the Act, whereby, in accordance with Article 12 paragraph 2 of the Act, the burden of proving the fulfilment of the conditions is the duty of the applicant. Bearing in mind the above, the Administrative Court found unacceptable the claims of "Lovćen" Insurance and "Sava Montenegro" that those agreements were exempted from the prohibition pursuant to Article 9 of the Competition Act.

In addition, requests were submitted against the aforementioned companies to initiate misdemeanor proceedings before the Misdemeanor Court. However, despite the decision of the Administrative and Supreme Courts, the Misdemeanor Court decided to suspend the proceedings due to the expiry of the statute of limitations for the initiation of misdemeanor proceedings against these two undertakings in relation to the Contracts from 2013, and in relation to the Contract from 2014 for reasons that at the time of conclusion, there was no corresponding by-law, i.e. the Regulation on conditions, procedure, and criteria for block exemption from the prohibition of agreements in the insurance sector. Although MCA appealed the decisions of the Misdemeanor Court in proceedings conducted against "Lovćen" Insurance company and the responsible person in it, as well as "Sava Montenegro" and the responsible person in it, the High Misdemeanor Court rejected the appeals and confirmed the position of the first instance court.

6.1.2 The Driving Schools Case

In the practice of MCA, there was a case of price fixing cartel agreement between driving schools in Nikšić, a municipality in Montenegro. In 2018, the MCA initiated the investigation of the competition infringement, i.e. the restrictive agreement between seven undertakings in the market for the provision of training services for all categories of vehicles by driving schools in the relevant geographic market of the territory of the Municipality of Nikšić. In the same year, the MCA issued the decision that the restrictive agreement - Decision on the new price list of training for all categories of vehicles, concluded by those participants in the market, was prohibited and void, and its further application and implementation was prohibited.[44]

Also, MCA ordered the participants of the agreement to determine decisions on service prices and terms independently of their competitors, in a clear and transparent manner, and to notify MCA of any change in decision or adoption of a new decision on the price list of services in the period of the next 2 years.

Namely, MCA determined that the goal of concluding the above-mentioned agreement was to eliminate mutual competition and determine a common price between competitors by direct agreement, with the ultimate object of preventing, limiting, and distorting competition on the relevant market, which could consequently lead to limiting and controlling the market, its development and investment in that market.

In this particular case, MCA found the existence of a common intention and the existence of a consensus of will for the direct contractual determination of training prices for all categories of vehicles. At the meeting of the Association of Driving Schools Nikšić, the participants of the agreement made a Decision on the new price list of training for all categories of vehicles, by agreement that determined the same price for relevant services. Additionally, all seven driving schools committed to continuous compliance with the agreed price list. MCA ordered the participants of the agreement to determine decisions on the price of services and conditions independently of their competitors, in a clear and transparent manner, and notify the MCA, in the period of the next two years, any change of decision or adoption of a new decision on service price list within seven days from the date of application. The parties did not file a lawsuit against this decision and it became final.

[44] MCA Decision No. 02-UPI-8/65-18 of 15 October 2018.

6.2 *Abuse of Dominance*

The Competition Act defines the conditions under which an undertaking can be considered dominant. An undertaking is assumed to have a dominant position on the product market if its share in the relevant market is greater than 50%. Considering the size of the territory, that is the market in Montenegro, the Montenegrin legislator determined that this threshold is 50% of the market share. It is assumed that two or more undertakings have a dominant position on the goods and services market if there is no significant competition between them and if their total share in the relevant market is greater than 60% (collective dominance). As the existence of a dominant position does not always have to depend on the market share of an undertaking, the Competition Act stipulates that a dominant position in the relevant market can also be held by a participant whose share on the relevant market is lower than 50%, whereby the evidence is taken into account other parameters.[45] Article 15 of the Competition Act, which defines types of abuses of dominance, is harmonised with Article 102 TFEU.

Interestingly, the Criminal Code of Montenegro foresees a prison sentence of three months to five years for the criminal offence of abuse of a monopolistic position, when a responsible person in a company or in another business entity causes a disturbance by abusing a monopolistic or dominant position on the market or concluding a monopolistic agreement on the market or put that entity in a privileged position compared to others, so that it achieves a financial benefit for that entity or for another entity or causes damage to other business entities, consumers or users of services.[46] This criminal offence qualifies as a criminal offence against payment transactions and business operations. The author is not familiar with any such cases.

The following shows two cases of abuse of a dominant position: "Vodovod i Kanalizacija" Budva case and "Luka Kotor" case.

6.2.1 "Vodovod i Kanalizacija" Budva Case

MCA was directly informed by the media about a significant increase in the price of water delivery services in the territory of the Municipality of Budva by the only company to perform this activity in that municipality - LLM "Vodovod i Kanalizacija" Budva. In accordance with the Act, the competence of the MCA includes, among others, proceedings against economic entities that, enjoying a dominant position on the market, can undertake the act of abuse by imposing

---

[45] Competition Act, Art 14.

[46] Art 270 of the Criminal Code of Montenegro [2003] Official Gazette of the Republic of Montenegro No. 70/03, 13/04, 47/06 and Official Gazette of Montenegro No. 40/08, 25/10, 32/11, 64/ 11 - second law, 40/13, 56/13, 14/15, 42/15, 58/2015 - second law, 44/17, 49/18, 3/20, 26/21 - correction, 144/21 and 145/21.

unreasonably high prices. This is a special case when the end customers are not able to replace the supplier, i.e. when the dominant participant equates to a monopolist in form, and there is no alternative for consumers. The Competition Act also applies to undertakings that perform activities of public interest, i.e. who are granted the right to perform certain activities by an act of the competent state authority, unless the application of the Act would significantly prevent the performance of those activities (the proof of which is the burden of undertakings).[47]

Bearing in mind that the companies in question are directly responsible only to the municipal management bodies, i.e. their founders, and that they operate independently on the market, no state authority had the power to investigate the reason for the significant increase in the price of water delivery services for households and the economy in these municipalities. In 2015, MCA initiated the procedure to determine the existence of the abuse of a dominant position by imposing unreasonably high prices, primarily for the purpose of exploiting consumers (exploitative abuse of a dominant position).[48]

Given that "Vodovod i Kanalizacija" Budva was the only business entity that performed a defined service of water supply and purification and disposal of waste water on the territory of the Municipality of Budva, during the procedure, MCA determined that "Vodovod i Kanalizacija" Budva, on the defined relevant market, enjoyed absolute dominant position in accordance with the Competition Act. MCA especially appreciated that the market share of "Vodovoda i Kanalizacija" Budva in the defined market was 100%, that there was no possibility of substitution of supply or demand, that customers had absolutely no possibility of changing suppliers regardless of the conditions, that there was no potential competition, bearing in mind the financial, regulatory, and technical barriers to entering the market, and the clear possibility of "Vodovod i Kanalizacija" Budva to dictate market conditions in relation to independently defined binding commercial conditions for the provision of the established service, and thus had a dominant position on the market for the provision of water supply and purification services and of wastewater disposal in the relevant geographical area of the Municipality of Budva.

By analysing the conditions of supply of the relevant product through the services of households and businesses in the area of other municipalities, it was established that "Vodovod i Kanalizacija" Budva established a special fee for reading the water meter on a monthly level. Business entities that perform the same type of activity in other specified areas (geographical markets) of neighboring municipalities were not familiar with that fee, nor did they determine it in a similar amount.

The shares for maintenance and reading of water meters in the average bill for the citizens of the Municipality of Budva were significantly higher than in other municipalities on the coast, which made a difference in the share of the special fee in the average bill for providing the average service of water supply and purification and removal of waste water in the Municipality of Budva, which was up to ten times

[47] Article 5 of the Competition Act.

[48] MCA Decision No. 02-UPI-32/1-15 of 6. April 2015.

higher for comparable economic entities that performed the same activity as "Vodovod i kanalizacija" Budva.

After the detailed analysis of factual situation, MCA issued a decision[49] that established that "Vodovod i Kanalizacija" Budva had a dominant position on the market for the provision of water supply and wastewater treatment and disposal services in the relevant geographic market of the Municipality of Budva. The company abused a dominant position by preventing, limiting, or distorting competition on the relevant market for water supply and wastewater treatment and disposal services in the territory of the Municipality of Budva, as the company brought decisions on the water supply and wastewater treatment and disposal services and immediately imposed an unreasonably high price for the service by directly determining a special monthly fee for maintenance and reading of the water meter in an inappropriately high amount of EUR 8,092 (including VAT), which was the obligation to pay in this amount conditioned as an additional obligation which, by its nature and purpose, was not related to the subject of the service.

By the same Decision, MCA prohibited any future action by which "Vodovod i Kanalizacija" Budva could prevent, limit, or impair competition by abusing a dominant position and ordered measures to be taken in accordance with the Act in proportion to the violation committed, in order to eliminate harmful consequences and establish effective competition on the market, as well as the deadline for its execution.

According to the judgement of the Administrative Court,[50] the lawsuit filed by "Vodovod i Kanalizacija" Budva, submitted for the annulment of the Decision of the Administrative Court, which established the abuse of the dominant position of "Vodovod i Kanalizacija" Budva, was rejected. Therefore, "Vodovod i Kanalizacija" Budva filed a request for examination of the court decision to the Supreme Court.

According to the assessment of the Administrative Court, MCA correctly determined that the obligation to accept the payment of "fees" in an inappropriate amount by the plaintiff represented an act of abuse of a dominant position, whereby "Vodovod i Kanalizacija", establishing an absolutely dominant position and the impossibility of consumers to change supplier, took advantage of such a position, which ensured the monopoly rent of the introduction of a special "fee". By determining the directly imposed unreasonably high price of water supply and purification and wastewater removal services in the territory of the municipality of Budva, by determining a special monthly fee for maintenance and water meter reading in an inappropriately high amount of EUR 8,092 (including VAT), as additional obligations "Vodovod i Kanalizacija" Budva violated the Competition Act.

Evaluating the legality of the contested judgment of the Administrative Court, the Supreme Court (in the third instance)[51] found that the judgment was rendered with

---

[49] MCA Decision No. 02-UPI-32/73-15 of 24 March 2016.

[50] Judgement of Administrative Court U. No. 1097/16 of 18 July 2017.

[51] Judgement of Supreme Court Uvp. No. 415/17 of 19 October 2017.

the correct application of substantive law to the established factual situation contained in the challenged decision and rejected as unfounded the request for examination of the court's opinion, which was submitted by "Vodovod i Kanalizacija" Budva.

Although "Vodovod i Kanalizacija" defended itself arguing that the local assembly of the Municipality of Budva gave its consent to the contested decisions, on the basis of which the relevant abuse of a dominant position was carried out, at the behest of the MCA, as well as the courts,[52] that fact was not important for a different course of action, bearing in mind that the Board of Directors of "Vodovod i Kanalizacija" Budva was the decision-maker of this undertaking.

On the other hand, taking into account the dual jurisdiction of MCA in procedures for determining competition infringements, requests were submitted against "Vodovod i Kanalizija" Budva and the responsible person (executive director) to initiate misdemeanor proceedings before the Misdemeanor Court. The Misdemeanor Court in Budva issued a decision[53] declaring "Vodovod i Kanalizacija" Budva guilty, as a legal entity and a responsible person in a legal entity, and determined a fine in the amount of 1% of the total annual income in the amount of EUR 61,553.22 for legal entity and a fine of EUR 1,000.00 for the responsible person in the legal entity. "Vodovod i Kanalizacija" Budva filed an appeal against that decision of the Misdemeanor Court, but the High Misdemeanor Court[54] rejected it as unfounded and confirmed the decision of the Misdemeanor Court.

6.2.2 "Luka Kotor" Case

In the most recent practice of MCA, in cases of abuse of a dominant position (related services), the "Luka Kotor" case stands out. After examining the Sea Pioneer Montenegro initiative, MCA initiated a procedure for investigating the competition infringement due to the well-founded suspicion that "Luka Kotor" abused its dominant position on the relevant market for the provision of port services—pilotage—on the relevant geographical market of the water area of the Port of Kotor—Municipality of Kotor. Luka Kotor is an undertaking that provides services for cruise ships, yachts and ships in the Bay of Kotor in Montenegro. In 2016, MCA established that "Luka Kotor" had a dominant position on the aforementioned relevant market and that this undertaking abused its dominant position, which prevented, limited or distorted competition by refusing to accept the maritime agency "BWA" LLM, the motor yacht "ALFA NERO" in the port of Kotor, due to the choice of the undertaking "Boka Pilot" to provide pilotage services in the port

[52] The Misdemeanor Court in Budva, the High Misdemeanor Court, the Administrative Court, and the Supreme Court.

[53] Decision of Misdemeanor Court PP. No. 163/17 of 20 November 2017.

[54] Decision of High Misdemeanor Court PP. No. 1810/17-2 of 28 December 2017.

of Kotor.[55] That way, Luka Kotor limited the provision of other port services in which way it clearly determined its business policy and prevented and limited the development of competition for pilotage services within the water area of the Port of Kotor. MCA provided an analysis of the market conditions for the provision of pilotage services in the geographical market of the Bay of Kotor, based on the data obtained, in 2015, it was found that the market share of "Luka Kotor" in the provision of pilotage services in the water area of the Port of Kotor was 98.15%, and in the provision of pilotage services in the territory of the Bay of Kotor 90.54%.

"Luka Kotor" submitted a lawsuit to the Administrative Court,[56] which partially accepted the lawsuit. The acting court confirmed the position of MCA on the existence of a dominant position of undertakings, referring to the definition of the European Court of Justice,[57] but annulled the positions of MCA related to the determination of the abuse of a dominant position and the ordered measures of conduct, and sent the case back for retrial. As for the reasons for partially accepting the lawsuit and cancelling the positions of the MCA, the acting court stated that it was not possible to establish in the specific case, i.e. to correctly determine the degree and dynamics of changes in the structure of the relevant market, the limitation and possibility of equal access to the market of new competitors, changes that limit the possibility of supplying the market based on the degree of convenience for consumers for the periods before and after the above events. The Administrative Court further stated that it cannot be concluded from the contested decision at that moment that the incident was followed by a change in the structure of the relevant market from the specified day, nor was there any reason in the contested decision regarding the limitation and the possibility of equal access to the market of new competitors, i.e. the change which limits the possibility of supplying the market based on the degree of convenience for consumers as well as other circumstances affecting competition. According to the judgment of that court, if the action was not continuous, if it was not a repetition of the same actions in a certain period or similar actions, which had the characteristics of abuse of a dominant position manifested by the direct or indirect imposition of unjustified buying or selling prices or other unjustified business conditions, as well as limiting the market in this case, the defendant's conclusion that the described event represents an abuse of a dominant position was called into question. In the renewed proceedings in 2019,[58] the MCA determined that "Luka Kotor", using its right of exclusivity as a "concessionaire" within the water area of the Port of Kotor, abused its dominant position by conditioning agents and shipping companies to hire the Port for pilotage services Kotor whenever "Luka Kotor" was the port of arrival and departure of the vessel, i.e. it has abused its dominant position, which prevented, limited or distorted competition on the relevant market of port services—pilotage—in the period from May 1, 2015,

[55] MCA Decision No. 02-UPI -81/67-15 of 25 October 2016.

[56] Judgement of Administrative Court U. No. 3944/2016 of 12 October 2017.

[57] Judgment of 14 February 1978, *United Brands v Commission*, C-27/76, ECLI:EU:C:1978:22.

[58] MCA Decision No. 01-UPI-81/141-15 of 2 October 2019.

i.e. the period from obtaining approval to perform pilotage for three pilothouses in the Bay of Kotor, until the fulfilment of the measures ordered by the MCA Decision from 2016, conditioned the provision of mooring services within the waters of the port of Kotor with the performance of port services—pilotage exclusively by the pilotage services of Port of Kotor.

Against that decision of MCA, "Luka Kotor" filed a lawsuit to the Administrative Court, which this time in 2021[59] rejected the lawsuit as unfounded and took the position that MCA acted correctly when it found that "Luka Kotor" had abused its dominant position by preventing, limiting or distorting competition on the relevant market of port services - pilotage. Therefore, according to the judgment of that court, MCA correctly determined that behaviour of "Luka Kotor" company, which culminated on July 7, 2015, indisputably proves that "Luka Kotor" linked the provision of mooring services and pilotage services, which represented an abuse of the dominant position.

In the misdemeanor proceedings that MCA initiated in 2015 before the Misdemeanor Court against "Luka Kotor" and the responsible person in that undertaking, the same court initially rejected MCA's request to initiate proceedings, and after the decision of the High Misdemeanor Court in the appeal procedure of MCA, which cancelled that decision and sent the case back for re-decision, acquitting "Luka Kotor". Again, in 2018, following the appeal of the MCA, the High Misdemeanor Court decided on the merits by accepting the appeal of the MCA, overturning the decision of the Misdemeanor Court and declaring "Luka Kotor" guilty of abuse of a dominant position and punishing it with a fine in the amount of EUR 27,249.54, while the responsible person in that undertaking was fined EUR 1,000.00.[60] High Misdemeanor Court also stated that Luka Kotor has a dominant position and determined that this undertaking abused its dominant position.

6.3 Merger Control

The request for approval for the implementation of the concentration is submitted under the condition that: (1) the joint total annual income of at least two participants in the concentration achieved on the Montenegrin market is greater than five million euros in the previous financial year; (2) the combined total annual income of the participants in the concentration achieved on the world market in the previous financial year is greater than 20 million euros, if at least one of the participants in the concentration achieved one million euros of income in the territory of Montenegro in that period.[61] The financial thresholds for the obligation to submit an application for approval for the implementation of the concentration are

[59] Judgement of Administrative Court U. No. 6009/2019 of 17 November 2021.

[60] MCA (2015, 2016, 2017, 2018).

[61] Competition Act, Art 50 (3).

set alternatively, i.e. it is sufficient for one of these two conditions to be met in order to exist an obligation of the undertaking to submit an application for the issuance of approval for the implementation of the concentration. The request is submitted within 15 days from the date of one of the following actions: (i) conclusion of the agreement or contract; (ii) publishing a public invitation, that is, an offer or closing a public offer; (iii) acquisition of control.[62]

Also, in the event that even though the financial thresholds have not been met, MCA may, after learning about the implemented concentration, order the participants in the concentration to submit a request for approval for the implementation of the concentration, if their joint share on the relevant market of Montenegro is more than 60%, whereby the burden of proving the joint market share of the undertakings in the concentration is on MCA.[63] If the undertaking does not submit a request for the issuance of approval for the implementation of the concentration within that period, the undertaking will be fined EUR 4000 to EUR 40,000.[64]

In situations where a participant in a concentration submits a request for approval for the implementation of the concentration and does not meet the prescribed financial thresholds for the existence of that obligation, MCA rejects such a request.[65]

The Montenegrin legislator prescribed that the procedure for issuing approval for the implementation of the concentration is initiated at the request of the party. In this regard, in case of failure to submit a request for the issuance of approval for the implementation of the concentration, MCA cannot ex officio initiate the procedure for the approval of the implementation of the concentration. However, in the event of the implementation of a concentration without the approval of the MCA, the MCA has authority to eliminate the consequences of the prohibited concentration, i.e. to determine the necessary measures and deadlines for the implementation of those measures (behavioral measures or structural measures), and in particular: (1) to order the disposal of the acquired shares or shares in the company; (2) to prohibit or limit the exercise of voting rights that give shares in the management of economic entities participating in the concentration, and to order the termination of control over the joint investment or other forms of acquisition of control from Article 16 of this law that led to the prohibited concentration.[66] Also, the Competition Act, under the provision related to prohibited concentration, prescribes that it is also prohibited to implement a concentration without the approval of MCA. In this regard, a penalty in the amount of 1% to 10% of the total annual income will be issued for the implementation of a prohibited concentration in the financial year prior the year when this misdemeanor was committed.[67]

---

[62] Competition Act, Art 58 (1).
[63] Competition Act, Art 50 (3).
[64] Competition Act, Art 68 (1).
[65] Competition Act, Art 56 (1).
[66] Competition Act, Art 58.
[67] Competition Act, Art 67 (1).

For deciding on requests for approval of the implementation of the concentration, fees were prescribed:

- for the issuance of approval for the implementation of the concentration in fast-track procedure, a fee is prescribed in the amount of 0.03% of the joint total annual income of all participants in the concentration achieved in the previous financial year, with the fact that the amount of the fee cannot exceed EUR 15,000.00;
- for the issuance of a decision on the approval of a concentration in the examination procedure and a decision on conditional approval of a concentration, 0.07% of the joint total annual income of all participants in the concentration achieved in the previous financial year, with the fact that the amount of compensation cannot exceed EUR 20,000.00;
- for the issuance of a decision on the rejection of the request for the issuance of approval for the implementation of the concentration in the case when it is determined that the concentration represents a prohibited concentration, EUR 1,000.00; and
- for the issuance of a decision on the rejection of the application for the issuance of approval for the implementation of the concentration in the case when the participants in the concentration do not meet the prescribed financial thresholds for the obligation to submit the application, EUR 600.00.[68]

MCA decides on the request for approval for the implementation of the concentration within the following deadlines:

(1) on the rejection of the application for the approval of the concentration if the financial thresholds are not met, within 25 working days from the date of submission of the application;
(2) on suspension of the procedure if the applicant withdraws the request, within 25 working days from the day of withdrawal;
(3) on the approval of a concentration when the assessment of the effects determines that the concentration does not significantly prevent, limit or distort effective competition, primarily by creating or strengthening a dominant position on the market, within 105 working days from the date of submission of the proper request;
(4) on the approval of the concentration with the imposition of additional measures, conditions and obligations that the participants in the concentration must perform before or after the implementation of the concentration, within 125 working days from the date of submission of the proper request;
(5) on the rejection of the request when the assessment of the effects determines that the concentration would significantly limit effective market competition on the relevant market, especially by creating a new or strengthening the existing

[68] Competition Act, Art 2 (1) item 6, 8, 9 and 10; Tariff Book on the amount of fees to be paid in proceedings before MCA [2013] Official Gazette of Montenegro No. 14/13.

dominant position, within 130 working days from the date of submission of the proper request.[69]

The Competition Act prescribes a positive presumption of silence of the administration, that is, in the event that MCA does not act within the prescribed deadlines, it will be considered that the implementation of the concentration has been approved.[70] According to the Act on Administrative Procedure,[71] which is the legal basis for proceedings before the MCA, when the administrative procedure is initiated at the request of a party (which is the case in the assessment of concentrations), and the public legal authority (MCA) does not pass and deliver the decision to the party within the prescribed or extended period deadline, the request will be deemed to have been adopted, if it is prescribed by a special law, in this case the Competition Act. In that case, the party has the right to ask the first instance or second instance public law authority to confirm that its request has been approved. The confirmation must contain all elements of the decision approving the party's request. If the public legal authority does not issue a certificate within seven days from the date of submission of the request for the issuance of the certificate, that is, if it does not pass a decision by which it subsequently decided on the party's request, the party may initiate an administrative dispute. The confirmation can be annulled or revoked in the same way as the decision.

We will describe the following merger control cases: Mercator CG/Franca, and CKB/SGB Montenegro.

6.3.1 "Mercator" CG/ "Franca" Case

Due to the great interest of the public in Montenegro and the significant impact that the concentration can have on consumers on the market of retail trade in food products in non-specialized stores mainly with food, drinks, and tobacco in the territory of Montenegro, the case of concentration was singled, that was resolved by the MCA in the examination procedure, and concerns the acquisition of control over the retail business of "Franca Marketi" LLM Bijelo Polje (Franca) by the Commercial Company for Trade and Services "Mercator-CG" LLM – Podgorica.[72] The Mercator retail chain consisted of 129 stores in 19 Montenegrin municipalities and Franca owned 67 stores on the Montenegrin market.

When determining the relevant market, MCA defined the relevant product market as the market for retail trade of food products in non-specialized stores, mainly food, drinks, and tobacco in the territory of Montenegro, as a broader relevant market, while as a narrower relevant market it defined municipalities where there is an

[69] Competition Act, Art 62 (3).

[70] Competition Act, Art 62 (5).

[71] Act on Administrative Procedure [2014] Official Gazette of Montenegro No. 56/14, 20/15, 40/16 and 37/17.

[72] MCA Decision No. UPI-04-354/22-100/19 of 28 March 2023.

overlap, namely the retail market of food products in non-specialized stores with mainly food, drinks, and tobacco in the territory of 16 municipalities in Montenegro.

Based on the analysis of the request and the documentation submitted to MCA by the applicant, as well as analyzing the data of the retail market of food and consumer goods, and assessing the effects, MCA determined that the implementation of the concentration in question did not lead to a significant prevention, limitation or disruption of effective competition in the wider relevant market - the market of retail trade of food products in non-specialized stores mainly with food, drinks, and tobacco in the territory of Montenegro. However, it determined that in the narrower relevant market - the market of retail trade of food products in non-specialized stores mainly with food, drinks, and tobacco in the territories of the Municipality of Plužine and the Municipality of Kolašin, "Mercator-CG" would fulfil the requirement for the legal presumption of a dominant position, after the implementation of the concentration. "Mercator-CG" proposed behavioural measures that MCA accepted, so in the examination procedure it conditionally approved the implementation of the concentration of undertakings, subject to the fulfilment of the proposed measures.

6.3.2 CKB/SGB Montenegro Case

Due to the perception that was created in the public, the concentration that also occupied the attention of the citizens of Montenegro, and due to the very specificity and significant influence that the banking system has in each country, concerns the acquisition of Crnogorska komercijalna banka a.d. Podgorica (CKB) over Societe Generale Banka Montenegro (SGB Montenegro), by purchasing 90.5578% of shares.[73] Before the transaction, SGB Montenegro was part of the Société Générale Bank group, while CKB was a part of the OTP group. MCA, especially starting from the activities and intentions of CKB, determined the relevant market as the market for the provision of all types of banking services, in the relevant geographic market of Montenegro. After that, MCA started analysing the market, and in cooperation with the Central Bank of Montenegro, other state authorities and participants in that market, collected documentation, information and data in order to correctly and completely determine the factual situation on the defined relevant market. At that moment, a total of 15 banks were operating in the territory of Montenegro. By analysing the market, MCA determined that the market share according to the amount of total assets of CKB was around 15.69%, and that SGB Montenegro was the second largest bank with a market share of 12.04%. By implementing the concentration in question, CKB would maintain its position as the most important bank in Montenegro, and would achieve a share of 27.73%. Analysis of the data and the HHI index showed that the market was moderately concentrated. In addition, it was estimated that at the lower level of the market, in the markets of retail banking and corporate banking, after the implementation of the concentration in question,

[73] MCA Decision No. 04-UPI-23/14-19 of 23 April 2019.

they would achieve a similar level of market share as in the overall market for the provision of banking services, approximately 30%.

In the end, as a result of MCA's assessment, and based on the fact that there is a merger of two banks with the largest individual market share, as well as the analysis of data obtained from the Central Bank of Montenegro, who is a regulator on the relevant market and to CKB, MCA determined that the relevant however, the concentration would not prevent, limit, or disrupt effective competition, i.e. create or strengthen a dominant position within the established relevant market. MCA additionally appreciated the expected effects and investments of CKB, especially when it comes to increasing the quality of services, increasing consumer choice, and lowering the price of the service, as well as the portfolio of existing service users participating in the concentration. It was resolved in such a way that MCA approved the concentration in question in a fast-track procedure.

7 Enforcement and Sanctioning Statistics for the Period 2012–2022

7.1 Enforcement Statistics

In relation to resolved cases in the period 2012–2022, eight procedures for determining abuse of a dominant position and thirteen procedures for determining restrictive agreements were completed. In relation to data from 2012, in accordance with the then Competition Act, which ceased to be valid on October 8, 2012, procedures for examining competition violations could be initiated *ex officio* and *ex privato*. Out of the total number of proceedings initiated in 2012, three proceedings were initiated *ex officio*, while the other three were initiated *ex privato*. The decrease in the number of competition infringement proceedings can be directly correlated with the Competition Act from 2012, according to which competition infringement proceedings can only be initiated *ex officio*. Table 4 shows the initiated and completed procedures for determining the violation of competition in the period 2012–2022.

In the observed period in Montenegro, we will analyse the decisions made regarding the competition infringement, decisions on measures taken and on mergers.

Out of a total of thirteen decisions relating to restrictive agreements, six decisions were related to cartels, of which four decisions were related to price fixing cartels and two decisions were related to bid rigging cartels.

Table 4 All decisions related to restrictive agreements and abuses of dominance (2012–2022)[a]

Year	Restrictive agreements	Abuses of dominance
2012	1	3
2013	1	1
2014	2	2
2015	1	–
2016	1	1
2017	–	–
2018	1	–
2019	1	1
2020	1	–
2021	3	–
2022	1	–
Total	13	8

Source: Author's own calculation based on MCA's Annual Reports 2012–2022

[a]Decisions that relate to the abuses of dominance and restrictive agreements include only substantive decisions, such as: infringement decisions, commitment decisions, decisions to suspend proceedings to determine competition infringement and decisions rejecting the request to determine competition infringement. Procedural decisions are not included in the number of decisions

7.1.1 Infringement Decisions

In Montenegro, in the observed period, out of total number of issued decisions, fourteen decisions were made that established competition infringements (restrictive agreement and abuse of a dominant position), and this number does not include the decisions of the MCA on determining the competition infringements that have been annulled by the Administrative Court.

7.1.2 Commitment Decisions

In the observed period, two commitment decisions were made by MCA, of which one decision was made in 2014 in the procedure related to the electronic communications sector, and the other in 2019 in the procedure related to the market for the sale of electronic devices in the territory of Montenegro.

7.1.3 Rejected Initiatives/no Infringement Decisions

In Montenegro, in the observed period, five decisions were made that suspended the procedure for determining the competition infringement, that is, rejected the request for initiation of determining the competition infringement.[74] Of the mentioned cases, the Urion and Montemedicom case stands out, where the MCA suspended the proceedings in 2020. Namely, in 2016, MCA issued the decision establishing a competition infringement (horizontal restrictive agreement) in case of Agreement on joint participation in the public procurement procedure of the Health Insurance Fund of Montenegro, between undertakings Urion And Montemedicom.[75] Administrative Court issued a verdict rejecting the lawsuit against MCA's decision, that is, it confirmed the legality of MCA's actions.[76] However, the Supreme Court, acting according to the extraordinary legal remedy, annulled the judgment of the Administrative Court in this case and sent it back to the Administrative Court for a new decision.[77] After that, the Administrative Court issued a new verdict in which it accepted the lawsuit, annulled the decision from 2016, and sent the case back to MCA for further proceedings.[78] In the retrial in 2018, the MCA issued a new decision by which it again determined the competition infringement.[79] After the parties again filed a lawsuit before the Administrative Court which accepted the lawsuits, annulled the new decision of the MCA, and sent the case back for a new decision,[80] the MCA suspended the procedure in 2020.[81]

As previously stated on several occasions, since the entry into force of the Competition Act from 2012, initiatives to initiate procedures for investigation of competition infringements do not have a binding character according to the Competition Authority, and the persons submitting the initiative do not have the status of parties to the proceedings, so MCA does not reject/adopt these initiatives. In observed period, before entry into force of the Competition Act from 2012, two decisions were issued in proceedings started by initiatives. Initiatives submitted before 2012 are not listed.

7.1.4 Individual Exemptions

Table 5 shows the growing trend of the number of individual exemptions in the period 2012–2022.

In 2022, MCA adopted ten individual exemption decisions. The exemptions came from different sectors and here we mention only a few of the more significant ones. For example, the MCA issued the individual exemption of the exclusive

---

[74] In accordance with the Competition Act [2005] Official Gazette of the Republic of Montenegro No. 69/05 and 37/07.

[75] MCA Decision No. 02-UPI-11/99-16 of 24 November 2016.

[76] Judgement of Administrative Court U. No. 4586/16 of 29 September 2017.

[77] Judgement of Supreme Court Uvp. No. 518/17 of 27 December 2017.

[78] Judgement of Administrative Court U. No. 7/18 of 09 February 2018.

[79] MCA Decision No. 02-UPI-11/129-16 of 23 March 2018.

[80] Judgement of Administrative Court U. No. 2727/18 of 11 June 2020.

[81] MCA Decision No. 04-UPI-11/151 -16 of 30 July 2020.

Table 5 Number of cases of individual exemptions (2012–2022)

Year	Number of cases
2012	1
2013	5
2014	3
2015	2
2016	-
2017	2
2018	3
2019	1
2020	1
2021	7
2022	10
Total	35

Source: Author's own calculation based on MCA's Annual Reports 2012–2022

Table 6 Number of resolved cases by year in concentration proceedings

Year	Number of cases
2012	11
2013	14
2014	19
2015	35
2016	29
2017	38
2018	48
2019	63
2020	53
2021	70
2022	68
Total	448

Source: Author's own calculation based on MCA's Annual Reports 2012–2022

distribution agreement between the Irish company Diageo Ireland Unlimited Company and the Montenegrin company Trebjesa Nikšić (which is part of the Molson Coors Group),[82] and also for Pepsi Cola bottling agreement between PepsiCo, Inc. (USA) and Knjaz Miloš (Serbia).[83]

Table 6 shows a comparative overview of the number of resolved cases in merger assessment procedures conducted before the MCA in the period 2012–2022. There is an evident growth trend and an increase in resolved procedures, which can be characterized by an increase in foreign investments in Montenegro, the openness of

[82] MCA Decision No. UPI-04-354/21-154/17 of 7 March 2022.

[83] MCA Decision No. UPI-01-354/22-49/11 od 29 September 2022.

Table 7 Overview of fines imposed by the Misdemeanor Courts of Montenegro in the period 2012–2022, based on requests for initiation of misdemeanor proceedings submitted

Year	Undertaking	Legal person (EUR)	Responsible person in legal person (EUR)	Type of infringement
2014	Pobjeda AD	36,428.97	1,000.00	restrictive agreement
	Šafran LLM	/	600.00	restrictive agreement
2017	Vodovod i kanalizacija LLM Budva	61,553.22	1,000.00	abuse of dominance
2018	Luka Kotor AD	27,249.54	1,000.00	abuse of dominance
2019	Urion LLM	6,020.78	1,000.00	restrictive agreement
	Montemedicom LLM	1,200.00	150.00	restrictive agreement
	Auto škola Zarubica Nikšić	500.00	200.00	restrictive agreement
2020	Auto škola Filip Nikšić	1,000.00	500.00	restrictive agreement
2022	Ksenija LLM	1,467.50	400.00	restrictive agreement
	Femić LLM	1,000.00	420.00	restrictive agreement
	Ronkula LLM	741.66	400.00	restrictive agreement
	Šćekić LLM	1,000.00	300.00	restrictive agreement
	Metović LLM	500.00	300.00	restrictive agreement
Total		138,661.67	7,270.00	

Source: Author's own calculation based on MCA's Annual Reports (2014, 2017, 2018, 2019, 2020, 2022)

the economy, but also by the strengthening of economic entities in Montenegro. It is expected that this trend will continue in the coming years.

Out of the total number of concentration cases, in the observed period, by final decision of MCA, one concentration was approved in the examination procedure (Phase 2) in 2021 and one examination procedure was initiated in 2022, and the rest of decisions are all reached in Phase 1.

7.2 Sanctioning Statistics

Table 7 shows the fines imposed by the courts for misdemeanors in Montenegro in the period 2012–2022, based on requests for initiation of misdemeanor proceedings

Table 8 Fines imposed due to untimely submission of the application for the issuance of approval for the implementation of the concentration 2012–2022 (in EUR)

Year	Undertaking	Responsible person in undertaking
2014	4,000	1,000
2019	8,000	2,000
2020	8,000	2,000
2021	4,000	1,000
2022	4,000	1,000
Total	28,000	7,000

Source: Author's own calculation based on MCA's Annual Reports (2014, 2019, 2020, 2021, 2022)

Table 9 Periodic fines imposed by MCA for the period 2013-2022 (in EUR)

Year	Periodic fines
2013	10,500
2014	39,000
2015	13,500
2018	5,000
Total	68,000

Source: Author's own calculation based on MCA's Annual Reports (2013, 2014, 2015, 2018)

submitted by MCA. The fines in each case was in minimal legal amount, with the assessment of mitigating circumstances by the acting courts.

In the observed period, when it comes to restrictive agreements, the total amount of fines for legal persons was EUR 49,858.91, and when it comes to abuse of a dominant position, the total amount of fines was EUR 88,802.76.

In the reporting period, there were a total of eight appeals against decisions of misdemeanour courts, concerning the amount of imposed fines, of which six appeals were approved by the High Misdemeanour Court and two appeals were rejected.

Table 8 shows the fines imposed due to the untimely submission of the application for the issuance of the approval for the implementation of the concentration. Out of the total number of fines imposed, in one case fine was imposed by the High Misdemeanor Court, while in the other cases MCA imposed the fines by issuing misdemeanor warrants.

Table 9 shows the total annual amounts of periodic fines imposed by MCA on undertakings in the period 2013–2022 due to non-fulfilment of obligations ordered by MCA, i.e. failure to provide data.[84]

As far as it concerns fines, by issuing misdemeanor warrants of MCA (in cases where proceedings did not go to court), were regularly collected. Also, there were no perceived problems in collecting periodic fines imposed by MCA.

[84]The competence to impose periodic financial penalties was obtained by the MCA upon the entry into force of the Competition Protection Act in 2012.

8 Judicial Review

A complaint can be filed with the Administrative Court against the decision of MCA in administrative proceedings, i.e. decisions on the approval of concentrations, individual exemptions and determination of competition infringement.[85] In accordance with the Act on Administrative Disputes, MCA is bound by the legal interpretation of the Administrative Court, as well as the remarks of that court regarding the procedure.[86] The following can be submitted against the legally binding decision of the Administrative Court: (i) a request for examination of the court decision; (ii) request to repeat the procedure. The Supreme Court decides on these legal remedies.[87] On the other hand, MCA submits a request for the initiation of misdemeanor proceedings to the Misdemeanor Court, i.e., issues a misdemeanor order. In case of issuing misdemeanour order, if an undertaking and/or responsible person in undertaking does not except it, it can request a court decision by the Misdemeanor Court upon same alleged misdemeanor. Against the decision of that court, an appeal can be filed with the High Misdemeanor Court.

According to previously mentioned, MCA initiates administrative proceedings for a competition infringement in order to establish the existence of that infringement and order measures to eliminate the consequences caused by that infringement. On the other hand, MCA participates in misdemeanor proceedings aimed at punishing undertakings who commit the competition infringement, due to the fact that in the system of Montenegro, competition infringements are considered misdemeanors. Punishment of undertakings due to a competition infringement before the Misdemeanor Court is preceded by the determination of liability determined by this court. The Misdemeanor Court is not bound by the decision of MCA.

According to the confirmed positions of the Administrative Court and the Misdemeanor Court, the results of the proceedings of another court[88] are irrelevant for their decisions. Especially taking into account the statute of limitations in misdemeanor proceedings (the statute of limitations for initiating the proceeding, as well as the statute of limitations for conducting the proceeding), which does not apply to the administrative procedure for determining the competition infringement conducted by MCA, practice has shown that in certain cases, even though MCA has established a competition infringement, undertakings who have committed a competition infringement avoid being fined. Also, as shown in the case of "Lovćen" Insurance and "Sava Montenegro", the interpretation of substantive provisions by the Misdemeanour Court and the High Misdemeanor Court differed from the interpretation of the Administrative Court and the Supreme Court.

In the period 2012–2022, 19 lawsuits have been filed against decisions of MCA in cases of restrictive agreements and abuses of dominance. Table 10 shows

---

[85] Competition Act, Art 64.

[86] Act on Administrative Disputes, Art. 56 (2).

[87] Ibid., art. 40.

[88] Judgment of Administrative Court U. No. 2259/2015 of 25 March 2016.

Table 10 Administrative disputes in relation to the MCA infringement decisions for the period 2012–2022

Administrative disputes	
Accepted lawsuits	3
Partially accepted lawsuits	2
Lawsuit rejected	8
Total	13

Source: Author's own calculation based on MCA's Annual Reports 2012–2022

administrative disputes in relation to MCA decisions (types of judgements), with the total number of judgements of the administrative court.

By comparing the data from Tables 4 and 10, it is clear that undertakings against whom procedures were conducted to determine the competition infringement used their right to legal protection and challenged the MCA decision before the Administrative Court. The data on the number of filed lawsuits exclusively refer to decisions on infringement of competition, while the number of lawsuits filed against decisions on initiation of proceedings *ex officio* and procedural decisions, as well as decisions on periodic fines, issued by the Competition Authority in the observed period, is not included in this data. Out of the total number of lawsuits filed, eight administrative disputes are ongoing (2023).

We want to discuss a case of the acting courts regarding the decision of MCA of approval of the concentration between KKR&Co LP - New York and M-Kabl LLM Podgorica. MCAapproved in an fast-track procedure the concentration of undertakings resulting from the acquisition of indirect control by the business entity KKR & Co. L.P., New York, through subsidiaries and affiliates, over the business entity "M-Kabl" LLM Podgorica, by purchasing a 100% share.[89] Undertakings "Crnogorski Telekom" and "Mtel", telecommunications companies and competitors of participants in concentration, filed lawsuits before the Administrative Court. In that lawsuits, it was pointed out, among other things, that substantive law was incorrectly applied and that the principle of legal certainty was infringed, as one of the basic legal principles, which oblige the authority to act in equal (predictable) ways in equal legal situations, and that decisions and actions in the procedure must be delivered in a way that will not cause uncertainty and doubts. In addition, they considered that the different interpretations in the defendant's decisions, with the same factual situation and unchanged legal regulations, directly infringed the rights of "Mtel" and "Crnogorski Telekom" as interested entities.

Answers to the lawsuits with case files and evidence of delivery of the disputed decision to the Prosecutors were submitted to the Administrative Court within the deadline set by law. In the same way, the MCA, after a detailed explanation of the case, proposed a verdict rejecting the claims due to the lack of active identification for conducting an administrative dispute and due to the untimely filing of the lawsuits, for the reason that the lawsuit of Mtel was filed after 70 days from the day of delivery of the decision to the party, while the claim of "Crnogorski Telekom"

[89] MCA Decision No. 02-UP-I-21/7-16 of 18 May 2016.

was filed after ninety days from the day of delivery to the party, i.e. after the deadline set by Article 16 of the on Administrative Disputes, which was the basis for rejecting them. On June 7, 2017,[90] the Administrative Court issued a Decision rejecting the lawsuits.

Against the Judgment of the Administrative Court by the business entity "Crnogorski Telekom" and "Mtel" requests were submitted to the Supreme Court for the review of the court decision - the decision of the Administrative Court from June 7, 2017. On October 12, 2017,[91] the acting court issued a judgment in which the requests for review of the court decision were adopted, the decision of the Administrative Court was revoked and the case returned to the Administrative Court on retrial and adjudication. The judgment of the Supreme Court found that decision of Administrative Court violated the rules of procedure, because the reasons for it were incomprehensible because the contested decision approved the concentration of undertakings, and the plaintiffs were indisputably market competitors of the participants who were approved for the concentration. Therefore, it is incomprehensible that they had no immediate legal interest that would justify conducting an administrative dispute.

In the retrial, appreciating the opinion of the Supreme Court expressed in its judgment, the Administrative Court determined that the filed lawsuits were untimely. Namely, from the case file and allegations of the lawsuits, as well as the words of the attorney at the hearing, it was established that the plaintiffs were not parties in the process of "concentration approval" of third parties, and that they received the decision in the process of the request for free access to information. In relation to the stated factual situation, and in connection with the regulations that were in force, the plaintiff's right to file a lawsuit started from the day the decision was delivered to the party in whose favor the decision was made, and as the decision was delivered on May 18, 2016, i.e. the same day when it was brought, these lawsuits filed on August 5, 2016 and August 29, 2016 by "Mtel" and "Crnogorski Telekom" were untimely.

Although in the end the lawsuits were rejected due to procedural reasons (untimeliness), this case is important from the point of view of the Supreme Court, which recognized the competitors of the participants in the concentration as interested parties and recognized their active party identification, because this was the first case in which the competitors (as persons who were not parties to the proceedings) contested the decision of MCA on the approval of the concentration.

[90] Decision of the Administrative Court U. No. 2357/16 of 7 June 2017.

[91] Judgment of the Supreme Court Uvp. No. 310/17 of 12 October 2017.

9 Private Enforcement of Competition Law

Compensation for damage caused by the acts and practices constituting impairment of competition established by MCA decision in accordance with Competition Act shall be exercised in a civil suit before a competent court.[92] With this, the Montenegrin legislator begins and ends the story related to private enforcement of competition law. It is concluded that the Competition Act enables that if MCA previously determines a competition infringement, only in that case the injured parties can claim compensation for damages through the so-called "follow-on lawsuits". There were cases in which in misdemeanor proceedings for conclusion of the same restrictive agreement, the Misdemeanour Court found guilty and punished the participants in that agreement, but the Administrative Court annulled the decision of the MCA in administrative procedure, in which was determined the restrictive agreement.[93] In view of this experience, this provision leaves the possibility that even if it is proven in the misdemeanor procedure that the undertakings have infringed competition rules, if the same is not proven in the administrative procedure, i.e. by the decision of the MCA, the injured party will not fulfil the condition for filing a lawsuit for compensation for damages. Explicitly binding the injured party to the prior determination of the competition infringement by MCA in order to file a claim for compensation of damages leaves no room for the injured party to independently prove the competition infringement and the damage caused to them in civil proceedings before the proceeding court (without a prior decision of MCA). Also, the current legal solution does not define whether the MCA's decision establishing a competition infringement must be final, so the question arises of the consequences of the cancellation of the MCA's decision and the success of injured persons in compensation proceedings. A scenario may occur in which the Administrative Court annuls MCA's decision and return the case for re-decision (e.g. due to procedural reasons or an incompletely established factual situation), then MCA re-conducts the procedure and establishes an infringement again, and after a renewed lawsuit, the Administrative Court confirms the decision of MCA, as was the case in the "Luka Kotor" case, described in Sect. 5.

There is a tendency to enact *lex specialis*, which would regulate the procedure for compensation for damages caused by competition infringement. So far, no procedures have been conducted in Montenegro for the compensation of damage caused by acts and actions that represent a competition infringement.

[92] Competition Act, Art 65.

[93] Urion and Montemedicom case, described in Sect. 5.

10 Current Trends and Future Challenges to Enforcing Competition Law

In recent years, Montenegro has made significant progress in implementing the Competition Act, and promoting the importance of competition in the market. However, there are challenges that must be addressed to ensure effective enforcement of competition law and support sustainable economic development.

In this sense, when talking about future challenges, the starting point is certainly Montenegro 2022 Report of European Commission, according to which when it comes to antitrust and mergers, it is said that in the coming year Montenegro should in particular further improve the track record in the areas of antitrust/mergers by providing appropriate staffing of the MCA, building up administrative capacities of the MCA and misdemeanor courts, further promoting the use of leniency policy and carrying out more in-depth investigations and on-site inspections.

Indeed, significant changes and improvements in 2022 are indicators of Montenegro's commitment to improving the competition area. The new management of MCA, director and governing body of MCA was appointed. During 2022, MCA initiated two new antitrust investigations, both in the area of restrictive agreements and both due to alleged horizontal collusion. In the first investigation, MCA investigates whether two oil companies operating on the Montenegrin market - INA Montenegro and Jugopetrol - colluded in connection with LNG prices in Montenegro. And in another case, MCA is investigating the Montenegrin Veterinary Chamber in connection with the price list of veterinary services that allegedly determines the minimum prices for such services.

Looking ahead, one of the main challenges for Montenegro will be the further development of its legislative framework on competition to full compliance with the *acquis* in this area. From the position of institutional capacities for the implementation of competition protection policy, the country will have to invest in the training and development of skills of the authority staff responsible for competition protection, and to ensure sufficient financial and technical resources in order to enable effective implementation of regulations in this area. In addition, it is necessary to raise awareness of the benefits of competition and the role of competition law in encouraging economic growth and innovation among businesses and consumers. Another challenge is to ensure the effective application of competition laws in practice. Montenegro will need to resolve issues related to the independence of MCA, including ensuring sufficient autonomy, primarily financial independence, and independence of political influence, as well as strengthening the legal framework for the implementation of the Competition Act.

Regarding the strengthening of the Misdemeanor Court, the training of all acting misdemeanor judges will be a big challenge for Montenegro due to the issue of the local jurisdiction of this court, as well as the fact that there is no specialized council for misdemeanors in the field of competition protection. Especially considering the fines imposed by the same court, which are presented in chapter 7, it can be concluded that this challenge remains one of the biggest when it comes to the enforcement of competition law. The modality of overcoming this challenge certainly remains the transfer of the sanctioning powers in the full sense to the jurisdiction of the MCA, whereby the MCA would in the first instance, when determining a competition infringement, independently impose fines for the same infringements. The Administrative Court in the second instance would decide on legal remedies by controlling the legality of the acts of the MCA.

Finally, as the country continues to pursue EU membership, it will need to ensure that its competition legal framework is fully aligned with the EU acquis and effectively implemented in line with EU standards.

Regarding trends in the implementation of the Competition Act in Montenegro, there is an increasing focus on digital markets. The growth of digital platforms and e-commerce has created new challenges for competition authorities, such as the need to deal with issues related to market power, data protection, and consumer rights. In this regard, the need is even greater to harmonize the existing Regulation on the group exemption of vertical agreements with the new VBER, which recognizes the importance of restrictive agreements on this market, together with the Digital Act.

Another trend is the increasing importance of cooperation between competition authorities in different jurisdictions. Multinational concentrations, cross-border cartels, as well as global anti-competitive practices, require cooperation between competition authorities in order to effectively enforce competition law. Montenegro has made efforts to increase cooperation with other competition authorities, both within the EU and globally, through its participation in various international organizations and initiatives.

11 Conclusion

EU rules protect free competition by enforcing antitrust regulations against restrictive agreements and abuse of dominant position, as well as regulating concentrations that impede effective competition. The rules also govern state aid control, allowing governments to grant aid only if certain conditions are met to prevent competition distortion. Montenegro has made significant progress in implementing competition laws and promoting competition in the market. However, there are challenges that need to be addressed for effective enforcement of competition laws and sustainable economic development.

Regarding antitrust and mergers, Montenegro's legislative framework aligns well with EU regulations. Amendments were made to the Competition Act in December 2021 to align it with the Act on State Administration. The Council of MCA is responsible for implementing the legal framework. It operates independently and has powers comparable to the European Commission in the area of antitrust and merges. Decisions are made by the MCA Council and can be appealed before the Administrative Court. Fines can only be imposed by misdemeanor courts. There is a leniency policy for self-reporting cartel members, but its implementation is hindered by low fines imposed by misdemeanor courts.

The MCA's administrative and financial capacities need strengthening, with vacancies in key positions. A new President and new members of the MCA Council were appointed in April 2022. In terms of implementation, the MCA issued decisions and initiated proceedings in the area of restrictive agreements. However, many cases faced acquittal or administrative disputes, leading to delays in completing cases and imposing fines. The number and amount of fines imposed by misdemeanor courts remained low. The MCA resolved two initiatives to investigate competition violations.

Cooperation between antitrust authorities in different jurisdictions is increasingly important. Montenegro has made efforts to enhance cooperation with antitrust authorities within the EU and globally through participation in international organizations and initiatives.

Future challenges for Montenegro include further developing its antitrust legislative framework, strengthening institutional capacity, investing in training and skills development of staff, and ensuring sufficient financial and technical resources for effective enforcement. Raising awareness of the benefits of competition and competition law among businesses and consumers is crucial. Independence of antitrust authority and the enforcement of competition laws need to be addressed, along with the focus on digital markets and addressing challenges related to market power, data protection, and consumer rights.

Aligning Montenegro's competition legal framework with EU standards is essential as the country pursues EU membership. Building professional, non-political institutions and establishing a national consensus are important for effective implementation. Raising awareness of the need and benefits of implementing regulations throughout society is necessary. Montenegro's commitment to these efforts will contribute to its European future.

Table of Cases

Agency for the Protection of Competition (MCA)

MCA Decision No. 02-UPI-20/1- 15 of 3 March 2015
MCA Decision No. 02-UPI-32/1-15 of 6. April 2015
MCA Decision No. 02-UPI-20/39-15 of 24 July 2015
MCA Decision No. 02-UPI-32/73-15 of 24 March 2016
MCA Decision No. 02-UPI -81/67-15 of 25 October 2016
MCA Decision No. 02-UPI-11/99-16 of 24 November 2016
MCA Decision No. 02-UP-I-21/7-16 of 18 May 2016
MCA Decision No. 02-UPI-8/65-18 of 15 October 2018
MCA Decision No. 02-UPI-11/129-16 of 23 March 2018
MCA Decision No. 04-UPI-23/14-19 of 23 April 2019
MCA Decision No. 01-UPI-81/141-15 of 2 October 2019
MCA Decision No. 04-UPI-11/151 -16 of 30 July 2020

MCA Decision UPI-04-354/21-154/17 of 7 May 2022
MCA Decision No. UPI-04-354/21-154/17 of 7 March 2022
MCA Decision No. UPI-01-354/22-49/11 od 29 September 2022
MCA Decision No. UPI-04-354/22-100/19 of 28 March 2023

European Union Court of Justice

Judgment of 14 February 1978, *United Brands v Commission,* C-27/76, ECLI:EU: C:1978:22.

Montenegro Courts

Judgment of Administrative Court U. No. 2259/2015 of 25 March 2016
Judgment of Supreme Court Uvp. No. 187/16 of 24 April 2016
Decision of the Administrative Court U. No. 2357/16 of 7 June 2017
Judgment of Administrative Court U. No. 1097/16 of 18 July 2017
Judgement of Administrative Court U. No. 4586/16 of 29 September 2017
Judgment of Supreme Court Uvp. No. 415/17 of 19 October 2017
Judgment of Administrative Court U. No. 3944/2016 of 12 October 2017
Judgment of the Supreme Court Uvp. No. 310/17 of 12 October 2017
Decision of Misdemeanor Court PP. No. 163/17 of 20 November 2017
Judgement of Supreme Court Uvp. No. 518/17 of 27 December 2017
Decision of High Misdemeanor Court PP. No. 1810/17-2 of 28 December 2017
Judgement of Administrative Court U. No. 7/18 of 09 February 2018
Judgement of Administrative Court U. No. 2727/18 of 11 June 2020
Judgment of Administrative Court U. No. 6009/2019 of 17 November 2021

Table of Legislation

Criminal Code of Montenegro [2003] Official Gazette of the Republic of Montenegro No. 70/03, 13/04, 47/06 and Official Gazette of Montenegro No. 40/08, 25/10, 32/11, 64/ 11 - second law, 40/13, 56/13, 14/15, 42/15, 58/2015 - second law, 44/17, 49/18, 3/20, 26/21 - correction, 144/21 and 145/21
Competition Act [2005] Official Gazette of the Republic of Montenegro No. 69/05
Constitution of Montenegro [2007] Official Gazette of Montenegro No. 1/07
Decree on Amendments to the Decree on the Organization and Mode of Work of the State Administration [2007] Official Gazette of Montenegro No. 6/07
Act on the ratification of the Stabilisation and Association Agreement between the European Communities and their member states, on the one hand, and the

Republic of Montenegro, on the other hand [2007] Official Gazette of Montenegro No. 7/07
Act on Amendments to the Competition Act [2007] Official Gazette of Montenegro No. 37/07
Act on Misdemeanors [2011] Official Gazette of Montenegro No. 1/11
Competition Act [2012] Official Gazette of Montenegro No. 44/12
Act on Administrative Disputes [2016] Official Gazette of Montenegro no. 54/16
Act on Administrative Procedure [2014] Official Gazette of Montenegro no. 56/14, 20/15, 40/16 and 37/17
Act on Amendments to the Competition Act [2018] Official Gazette of Montenegro No. 13/18
Act on Amendments to the Competition Act [2021] Official Gazette of Montenegro No. 145/21

References

Commission (2022) Montenegro 2022 Report. SWD(2022) 335 final
Decree on the group exemption from the prohibition of agreements in road, railway and inland waterway transport and agreements on consortiums in liner maritime transport [2014] Official Gazette of the Republic of Montenegro No. 59/14
MCA (2012) Annual report for 2012. Podgorica
MCA (2013) Annual report for 2013. Available at: https://azzk.me/docs/ostala%20dokumenta/Izvjestaj%20o%20radu%20Agencije%20za%202013%20godinu%2020.06.2014.pdf. Accessed 16 February 2025
MCA (2014) Annual report for 2014. Available at: https://azzk.me/docs/ostala%20dokumenta/Izvjestaj%20o%20radu%20Agencije%20za%202014%20godinu.pdf. Accessed 16 February 2025
MCA (2015) Annual report for 2015. Available at: https://azzk.me/docs/ostala%20dokumenta/Izvjestaj%20o%20radu%202015.%20za%20sajt%20-%20konacni.pdf. Accessed 16 February 2025
MCA (2016) Annual report for 2016. Available at: https://azzk.me/docs/ostala%20dokumenta/Izvjestaj%20o%20radu%20AZZK%20za%202016.pdf. Accessed 16 February 2025
MCA (2017) Annual report for 2017. Available at: https://azzk.me/docs/ostala%20dokumenta/Izvjestaj%20o%20radu%20AZZK%202017.pdf. Accessed Accessed 16 February 2025
MCA (2018) Annual report for 2018. Available at: https://azzk.me/docs/IZVJESTAJ_O_RADU_ZA_2018_GODINU_FINAL_sa_potpisom14062019.pdf. Accessed 16 February 2025
MCA (2019) Annual report for 2019. Available at: https://azzk.me/docs/Izvjestaj_o_radu_AZZK_ZA_2019_fin.pdf. Accessed 16 February 2025
MCA (2020) Annual report for 2020. Available at: https://azzk.me/docs/izvjestaj-o-radu-agencije-za-zastitu-konkurencije-za-2020-godinu.pdf. Accessed 16 February 2025
MCA (2021) Annual report for 2021. Available at: https://azzk.me/wp-content/uploads/2022/11/Izvjesta-o-radu-agencije-2021_compressed.pdf. Accessed 16 February 2025
MCA (2022) Annual report for 2022. Podgorica. Available at: https://azzk.me/wp-content/uploads/2024/01/Izvjestaj-o-radu-Agencije-za-zastitu-konkurencije-za-2022.-godinu.pdf. Accessed 4 June 2025
Monti M (2002) Foreword [in:] Competition policy in Europe and the citizen (Przedmowa, in: Polityka konkurencji w Europie a obywatel), European Commission, Luxembourg

Regulation on group exemption from the prohibition of agreements on the distribution of spare parts and servicing of motor vehicles [2014] Official Gazette of Montenegro No. 13/14

Regulation on group exemption from the prohibition of horizontal agreements on research and development [2014] Official Gazette of Montenegro No. 13/14

Regulation on group exemption from the prohibition of horizontal agreements on specialisation [2014] Official Gazette of Montenegro No. 13/14

Regulation on the conditions, procedure and criteria for group exemption from the prohibition of agreements in the insurance sector [2014] Official Gazette of Montenegro No. 52/14

Regulation on the group exemption of vertical agreements from the ban [2014] Official Gazette of Montenegro No. 13/14

Regulation on internal organisation and systematisation of MCA no. 06-040/22-668/6 from 25 August 2022. Available at: https://azzk.me/pravilnik-o-unutrasnjoj-organizaciji-i-sistematizaciji/. Accessed 16 February 2025

Rulebook on the Content and Method of submitting a request for an individual exemption of restrictive agreement from the prohibition [2013] Official Gazette of Montenegro No 18/13 and 53/20

Statistical Office of Montenegro (2020). Available at: https://monstat.org/uploads/files/publikacije/CG%20u%20brojkama%202020%20MNE.pdf. Accessed 16 February 2025

Tariff Book on the amount of fees to be paid in proceedings before MCA [2013] Official Gazette of Montenegro No. 14/13

Nebojša Jovović has been employed at the Agency for Protection of Competition in Montenegro since 2017, where he worked in the field of competition and state aid. Since April 2022, Nebojša has been the Director of the Agency. Prior to joining the Agency, he worked as an economic analyst and consultant. Alongside his extensive practical experience at the Agency, Nebojša has conducted in-depth research in the field of competition, culminating in his doctoral dissertation on a related topic. He is also an Assistant Professor at the Faculty of Economics and Business, Mediterranean University in Podgorica, where he teaches courses on finance, digital economy, and banking. In addition to his academic role, Nebojša has worked as a consultant in various economic sectors, contributing to financial analysis, investment projects, and environmental policy development within spatial planning projects. His consultancy experience further strengthens his multifaceted background and deep understanding of both theory and practice. He gained knowledge in the field of competition and state aid at numerous projects, seminars and trainings. Nebojša has made contributions to the academic world, authoring several monographs and publishing numerous scientific papers in prestigious journals.

Competition Law and Policy in North Macedonia

Goran Koevski, Borka Tushevska Gavrilovikj, and Darko Spasevki

1 Introduction

The effectiveness of competition protection is influenced by various factors, including market liberalisation, government policies, the work of competition authorities, and the legal framework.[1] Experts emphasise the importance of legislation in combating unfair competition, considering the impact of globalisation and harmonisation of legal regimes.[2]

The Republic of North Macedonia (MK) is a small economy, characterised by a limited number of market players and sources of supply in the key industries.[3] These country-specific factors are clearly of great importance when it comes to defining the priorities of competition law. The development of competition law in the MK is inextricably linked to the country's aspirations for membership in the European Union (EU). As outlined in this chapter, national competition law almost entirely incorporates the competition rules contained in the legal sources of the EU.

The period of harmonisation and transposition of Macedonian competition law with the EU law can be divided into two periods. The first period covers the time

[1] Tushevska (2020), p. 60.

[2] Ibid.

[3] ISO (2025).

G. Koevski · D. Spasevki (✉)
Faculty of Law "Iustinianus Primus", University "Ss. Cyril and Methodius", Skopje, North Macedonia
e-mail: g.koevski@pf.ukim.edu.mk; d.spasevski@pf.ukim.edu.mk

B. Tushevska Gavrilovikj
Faculty of Law, Goce Delcev University, Stip, North Macedonia
e-mail: borka.tusevska@ugd.edu.mk

J. Pecotić Kaufman et al. (eds.), *Competition Law and Policy in the Western Balkans*, European Union and its Neighbours in a Globalized World 22,
https://doi.org/10.1007/978-3-031-93756-9_6

before the signing of the Stabilization and Association Agreement (SAA) in 2001. The second period covers the time from the signing of the SAA in 2001 until today.

This chapter on MK, exploring competition law and policy, is structured to offer a comprehensive overview of the nation's competition law enforcement system. Commencing with an introduction, it navigates through the historical evolution of MK's competition law. The examination of the country's relationship with the EU includes an exploration of the legal basis and pertinent national cases shaping this interaction. The institutional and normative framework section scrutinizes the competition authority's powers, the judicial review system, and pivotal substantive and procedural norms. The national specifics subsection distinguishes peculiarities in the national legal system from the EU competition *acquis* and highlights modifications during the Europeanization process. The chapter proceeds to dissect the application of both national and EU competition rules by the CPC shedding light on enforcement patterns, fining policies, and crucial cases. Judicial review and private enforcement are discussed separately, emphasizing significant cases in each domain. The chapter culminates in addressing prevailing trends and anticipating future challenges in enforcing competition law in MK, encapsulating a comprehensive snapshot of the country's competition landscape.

2 Historical Development of the Competition Law in North Macedonia

The Law on Protection of Competition (hereinafter "Competition Act") currently in force in the MK dates back to 2010.[4] Prior to this law, the Law against Restrictions of Competition[5] from 1999 and the Law on Protection of Competition from 2005 were being applied.[6]

In terms of historical development, it is important to note that the 1991 Constitution of the MK,[7] contains the principles of "free market and entrepreneurship" and "equal treatment of market participants". Namely, Article 55 of the Constitution, specifically states that "[t]he freedom of the market and entrepreneurship is guaranteed".[8] Additionally, in this provision of the Constitution, it is emphasized that "the Republic guarantees an equal legal position to all parties on the market" and that "[t]he Republic takes measures against monopolistic positions and monopolistic

[4]Law on Protection of Competition [2010] Official gazette of the Republic of Macedonia Nos 145/10, 136/11, 41/14, 53/16, 83/18 and 208/2024.

[5]Law against Restrictions of Competition [1999] Official gazette of the Republic of Macedonia No. 80/1999.

[6]Law on Protection of Competition [2006] Official gazette of the Republic of Macedonia No 4/05, 70/06 and 22/07.

[7]The Constitution of the Republic of North Macedonia was adopted on 17 November 1991.

[8]Tushevska (2020), p. 44–45.

conduct on the market". The provision of Article 55 of the Constitution ends with a paragraph that regulates exemptions, and it provides: "[t]he freedom of market and entrepreneurship can be restricted by law, only for reasons of the defense of the Republic, protection of the natural and living environment or public health". The 1999 Law against Restrictions of Competition was a significant step towards further adopting competition law and promoting fair competition in the country. However, this law was later repealed and replaced by the 2005 Competition Act, which was a more comprehensive and modern body of law.

Although the 1999 Competition Act was not effectively enforced, it demonstrated the MK government's commitment to promoting fair competition and addressing unfair practices that could harm consumers and hinder economic growth.[9] The 2005 Competition Act further strengthened this commitment by providing a legal framework to prevent anti-competitive practices, promote market competition, and protect consumers' interests, thus seeking to develop a competitive market economy and promote sustainable economic growth.

The enactment of the 2010 Competition Act was aimed at improving the country's compliance with EU competition law. This law was also enacted to address the shortcomings of the previous 2005 Law. Since 2010, the Competition Act has been amended in 2011, 2014, 2016, 2018 and 2024.[10] The 2010 Competition Act aimed to harmonize MK's competition laws with the EU competition rules, including Articles 101, 102, and 106 of the Treaty on the Functioning of the European Union (TFEU). This was crucial to align MK's competition law framework with the principles and objectives of the EU competition law regime.

The 2010 Competition Act introduced new provisions and amended the existing ones, in order to enhance the effectiveness of the entire corpus of competition legislation. The 2010 Competition Act incorporated provisions related to anti-competitive agreements, abuse of dominance and merger control. The 2010 Law also provided for the establishment of a competition authority, (*Комисија за заштита на конкуренцијата*—Commission for the Protection of Competition (CPC)).[11] According to the 2010 Competition Act, the CPC would be responsible for enforcing the competition rules and investigating its infringements. Overall, the adoption of the 2010 Competition Act was a significant step towards achieving a better compliance with EU competition law and ensuring a more competitive market environment in MK. The following section provides a more detailed explanation of the process and methods involved in transposing European rules into MK law.

---

[9] Tushevska (2020), p. 44–45.

[10] The details of each amendment to the law are explained in Sect. 5.2 of this chapter.

[11] http://kzk.gov.mk/

3 Relationship of North Macedonian Competition Act with the EU Law

The impact of the EU competition law on the Macedonian one is quite clear and understandable, especially considering MK's candidate status for EU membership gained in 2005.[12] Essentially, the process of harmonizing and transposing EU law into the Macedonian legal system, as noted in the introduction, initially began in 2001 by signing of the SAA.[13] With Articles 68 and 69 of the SAA, MK has expressed its interest in aligning with the EU's competition legal regime. Article 69, titled "Competition and other economic provisions", in paragraph 1 stipulates that:

> [t]he following are incompatible with the proper functioning of the Agreement, in so far as they may affect trade between the Community and the FYROM:
>
> (i) all agreements between undertakings, decisions by associations of undertakings, and concerted practices between undertakings which have as their object or effect the prevention, restriction, or distortion of competition;
> (ii) abuse by one or more undertakings of a dominant position in the territories of the Community or of the former Yugoslav Republic of Macedonia as a whole or in a substantial part thereof;
> (iii) any public aid which distorts or threatens to distort competition by favoring certain undertakings or certain products.

Paragraph 2 states that: "[a]ny practices contrary to this Article shall be assessed on the basis of criteria arising from the application of the rules of Articles 81, 82, and 87 of the Treaty establishing the European Community".[14]

The importance of competition law for the EU integration, also derives from Article 68 of the SAA. According to this Article, competition law has priority in the EU approximation process. The SAA explicitly stipulates a proper timeframe for aligning Macedonian competition law with EU competition law. According to the formulation in Article 68, paragraph 3 of the SAA:

> Starting on the date of signing of the agreement and lasting as explained in Article 5 [of the SAA], the approximation of laws shall extend to certain fundamental elements of the Internal Market acquis, as well as to other trade-related areas, along a program to be defined in coordination with the Commission of the European Communities. The Former Yugoslav Republic of Macedonia will also define, in coordination with the Commission of the European Communities, the modalities for monitoring the implementation of legislation and law enforcement actions to be taken, including reform of the judiciary. Deadlines will be set for competition law, intellectual property law, standards and certification law, public procurement law, and data protection law. Legal approximation in other sectors of the internal market will be an obligation to be met at the end of the transition period.

---

[12] European Council (2005).

[13] Stabilisation and Association Agreement between the European Communities and their Member States, of the one part, and the former Yugoslav Republic of Macedonia, of the other part [2004] OJ L 84/13.

[14] Tushevska (2020), p. 47.

The Competition Act in MK is fully compliant with EU law on protection of competition, in terms of the relevant provisions of the TFEU and the relevant EU competition legislation such as:

- Council Regulation (EC) No 1/2003 of 16 December 2002 on the implementation of the rules on competition laid down in Articles 81 and 82 of the Treaty;
- Commission Regulation (EC) No 773/2004 of 7 April 2004 relating to the conduct of proceedings by the Commission pursuant to Articles 81 and 82 of the EC Treaty;
- Council Regulation (EC) No 139/2004 of 20 January 2004 on the control of concentrations between undertakings (the EC Merger Regulation);
- Commission Notice on the definition of relevant market for the purposes of Community competition law;
- Commission Notice on agreements of minor importance which do not appreciably restrict competition under Article 81(1) of the Treaty establishing the European Community (de minimis);
- Commission Notice on Immunity from fines and reduction of fines in cartel cases, and
- Guidelines on the method of setting fines imposed pursuant to Article 23(2)(a) of Regulation No 1/2003.

Additionally, the harmonization and transposition of EU law has been achieved by adoption of a series of by-laws. The following are the currently applicable by-laws:

- Regulation on Closer Conditions for Contracts of Minor Importance,[15] which transposes the Commission Notice on agreements of minor importance which do not appreciably restrict competition under Article 81(1) of the Treaty establishing the European Community (de minimis).
- Regulation on the Form and Content of the Notice of Concentration and the Necessary Documentation to be submitted Together with the Notice,[16] which transposes the Commission Regulation (EC) No 802/2004 of 7 April 2004 implementing Council Regulation (EC) No 139/2004 on the control of concentrations between undertakings.
- Regulation on Group Exemption of Certain Types of Insurance Contracts,[17] which transposes the Commission Regulation (EU) No 267/2010 of 24 March 2010 on the application of Article 101(3) of the TFEU to certain categories of agreements, decisions and concerted practices in the insurance sector.

[15] Regulation on Closer Conditions for Contracts of Minor Importance [2012] Official Gazette of the Republic of Macedonia no. 44/12.

[16] Regulation on the Form and Content of the Notice of Concentration and the Necessary Documentation to be Submitted Together with the Notice [2012] Official Gazette of the Republic of Macedonia no. 44/12.

[17] Regulation on Group Exemption of Certain Types of Insurance Contracts [2012] Official Gazette of the Republic of Macedonia no. 44/12.

- Regulation on Closer Conditions for Group Exemption of Certain Types of Horizontal Agreements for Specialization,[18] which transposes the Commission Regulation (EU) No 1218/2010 of 14 December 2010 on the application of Article 101(3) of the TFEU to certain categories of specialization agreements.
- Regulation on Closer Conditions for Group Exemption of Certain Types of Contracts for Transfer of Technology, for License, or for Know-How,[19] which transposes. The Commission Regulation (EC) No 772/2004 of 27 April 2004 on the application of Article 81(3) of the Treaty to categories of technology transfer agreements.
- Regulation on Group Exemption of Certain Types of Vertical Contracts,[20] which transposes the Commission Regulation (EU) No 330/2010 of 20 April 2010 on the application of Article 101(3) of the TFEU to categories of vertical agreements and concerted practices.
- Regulation on Group Exemption of Certain Types of Contracts for the Distribution and Servicing of Motor Vehicles,[21] which transposes the Commission Regulation (EU) No 461/2010 of 27 May 2010 on the application of Article 101(3) of the TFEU to categories of vertical agreements and concerted practices in the motor vehicle sector.
- Regulation on Closer Conditions for Group Exemption of Certain Types of Contracts for Research and Development,[22] which transposes the Commission Regulation (EU) No 1217/2010 of 14 December 2010 on the application of Article 101(3) of the TFEU to certain categories of research and development agreements.
- Regulation on Closer Conditions for Release or Reduction of Fines and Procedures under which the Commission for Decision-Making after an Offence Decides on Release or Reduction of Fines,[23] which transposes the Commission Notice on Immunity from fines and reduction of fines in cartel cases.

The CPC has also developed several guidelines for the application of the Competition Act in 2015. These include:

[18] Regulation on Closer Conditions for Group Exemption of Certain Types of Horizontal Agreements for Specialization [2012] Official Gazette of the Republic of Macedonia no. 44/12.

[19] Regulation on Closer Conditions for Group Exemption of Certain Types of Contracts for Transfer of Technology, for License, or for Know-How [2012] Official Gazette of the Republic of Macedonia no. 44/12.

[20] Regulation on Group Exemption of Certain Types of Vertical Contracts [2012] Official Gazette of the Republic of Macedonia no. 44/12.

[21] Regulation on Group Exemption of Certain Types of Contracts for the Distribution and Servicing of Motor Vehicles [2012] Official Gazette of the Republic of Macedonia no. 44/12.

[22] Regulation on Closer Conditions for Group Exemption of Certain Types of Contracts for Research and Development [2012] Official Gazette of the Republic of Macedonia no. 44/12.

[23] Regulation on Closer Conditions for Release or Reduction of Fines and Procedures under which the Commission for Decision-Making after an Offense Decides on Release or Reduction of Fines [2012] Official Gazette of the Republic of Macedonia no. 44/12.

- Guidelines for the method of calculating the fine imposed in accordance with the Competition Act;
- Guidelines for the release or reduction of the fine;
- Guidelines for defining a relevant market for the purposes of the Competition Act;
- Guidelines for the preparation of a non-confidential version of the Commission's decisions;
- Guidelines for the application of Article 7 of the Competition Act for horizontal cooperation agreements;
- Guidelines for vertical restrictions;
- Guidelines for the application of Article 7 paragraph (3) of the Competition Act;
- Guidelines for determining the cases in which, during the evaluation of the concentrations, the Commission will normally determine that they are in accordance with the Competition Act;
- Guidelines for the submission and completion of a concentration notification;
- Guidelines for possible changes and undertaking of obligations in relation to reported concentrations acceptable to the Commission in accordance with the Competition Act;
- Guidelines on restrictions directly related to and necessary for the implementation of the concentration;
- Guidelines for the assessment of horizontal concentrations for the purposes of the Competition Act;
- Guidelines for the assessment of vertical and conglomerate concentrations;
- Guidelines for the concept of concentration; and
- Guide for the detection of illegal agreements in the procedures for awarding public procurement contracts.[24]

The level of transposition of EU competition law into Macedonian law can be assessed through the special reports prepared by the EU. Specifically, the EU Progress Reports on MK's Chapter 8—Competition Policy are prepared annually to evaluate the country's progress in aligning with the EU competition *acquis*. These reports cover a wide range of issues, including the legislative framework, the functioning of relevant institutions, and the implementation of competition rules.

As a general observation, if we look at the latest Progress Report on MK from 2022,[25] it notes that the country is moderately prepared in the area of competition in principle. The phrase "moderately prepared" represents the EU's assessment of the overall situation with Chapter 8, Competition Policy, as of 2022.

Similarly, in 2021, there was a similar emphasis on the need to align implementing legislation, and the absence of a leniency policy towards whistle-blowers was also noted. The lack of capacity of the CPC was mentioned again, along with the concern that this could affect the independence and sustainability of

[24] Commission for the Protection of Competition (2021), p. 7.

[25] Commission (2022).

operations.[26] The number of merger decisions increased from 49 in 2019 to 60 in 2020, and three decisions were adopted on cartels and abuse of dominant position. The 2020 EU Progress Report highlighted the CPC's lack of administrative and enforcement capacity, both in terms of staff and budget.[27]

The EU Progress Report on MK for 2022 generally notes that: "[t]he legislative framework is broadly aligned with the EU acquis in the area of antitrust and mergers, but implementing legislation has yet to be aligned".[28] Regarding the CPC, which is responsible for implementing the Competition Act, the 2022 EU Progress Report notes a series of weaknesses, including the fact that the CPC continues to be understaffed, leading to a limited enforcement capacity. The CPC's annual budget also remains insufficient.[29] The 2022 EU Progress Report also highlights the need to increase on-site inspections and the use of the leniency instrument to strengthen enforcement. In addition, the 2022 EU Progress Report lists the following priorities for the next period: (i) strengthen the administrative and financial capacity of the national competition authority; (ii) increase the transparency of State aid granted by the government; and (iii) further align implementing legislation in the area of State aid and antitrust.[30]

4 Institutional and Normative Framework of Competition Authority in North Macedonia

4.1 Competition Authority: Organisation and Powers

The CPC, as defined by the Competition Act, has the status of an independent state authority, with a status of a legal entity.[31] With a team comprising of a President, four members, and technical support staff, the CPC operates within the framework mandated by the law.[32] Funded by the MK budget, the CPC is accountable to the Parliament of the MK. In accordance with the Competition Act, the CPC is obliged to submit an annual report to the Parliament no later than March 31st.

The CPC's responsibilities are multifaceted and far-reaching. At its core, this includes obligations for monitoring and enforcing the Competition Act, the Law on

[26] Commission (2021), pp. 73–74.
[27] Commission (2021), pp. 67–68.
[28] Commission (2022), pp. 73–74.
[29] Commission (2022). pp. 73–74.
[30] Commission (2022). pp. 73–74.
[31] Competition Act, Art. 26 (1).
[32] Competition Act, Art. 26 (1).

State Aid, and associated regulations.[33] The CPC mandate extends to conducting administrative and misdemeanor procedures.[34]

The President and members of the CPC are appointed and dismissed by the Parliament of the MK, based on a proposal from the Parliament's Committee for appointment and dismissal matters.[35] This tenure spans 5 years, with the possibility of renewal. The Competition Act mandates that the President and all members of the CPC must be professionally engaged in its work. This is a new requirement introduced in October 2024, which differs from the previous arrangement where only the President and two members were professionally engaged, while the other two could be external members.[36] When it comes to selecting CPC members, the Competition Act sets stringent criteria.[37] Citizenship, a clean record devoid of penalties or prohibitions—such as a court-imposed ban on performing a profession, activity, or duty—, relevant education, substantial work experience, and proficiency in foreign languages—these prerequisites ensure that the CPC's ranks are filled with accomplished experts. Notably, the President or a professionally engaged member must hold a bachelor's in law and have passed the bar exam.

The Competition Act reinforces the CPC's independence by barring its members from assuming certain roles during their tenure: no membership in Parliament, Government, or engagement in political parties or business associations that could pose conflicts of interest.[38] To preserve impartiality, the Competition Act restricts CPC members from making decisions regarding undertakings where they, their spouses, or direct lineage family members up to the first degree hold stakes or management positions.[39]

The operations of the CPC are governed by statutes and general acts.[40] The decisions are taken by voting as the CPC President and four members convene, with each member's vote carrying equal weight. Abstaining from voting is not permitted.[41] Transparency is very important for the CPC operations. The Competition Act mandates that specific decisions are published in the Official Gazette of the MK.[42] Beyond this, decisions, judgments, and notifications of concentrations are published on the CPC website.[43] The published text of decisions divulges the parties involved and the essential decision elements, ensuring that the CPC's work remains

---

[33] Competition Act, Art. 28 (1).
[34] Competition Act, Art. 28 (1).
[35] Competition Act, Art. 27.
[36] Competition Act, Art. 27 (4).
[37] Competition Act, Art. 27 (6).
[38] Competition Act, Art. 27 (7).
[39] Competition Act, Art. 27 (8).
[40] Competition Act, Art. 28 (8).
[41] Competition Act, Art. 28 (10).
[42] Competition Act, Art. 67 (1).
[43] Competition Act, Art. 67 (2).

accessible to public. The Competition Act ensures that business and professional secrets, in line with Article 57 of the Competition Act, remain confidential.[44]

In 2010, a pivotal moment arrived with the consolidation of administrative and misdemeanor procedures within the CPC. This monumental shift curtailed the time gap between identifying infringements and imposing administering fines. In the past, administrative and misdemeanor procedures stood separate. The administrative process took the lead in determining infringements, only to be followed by the misdemeanor procedure for the same violation of the law. The decisions made in both processes were subject to appeal before the Administrative Court and, ultimately, the Supreme Court, as prescribed by the 2005 Competition Act. However, this system proved to be inefficient.

Prior to November 2010, under the applicable Competition Act, the CPC conducted both administrative and misdemeanor procedures for the same behavior. This involved a two-step process: first, an administrative procedure to ascertain the violation of competition protection rules, and subsequently, a misdemeanor procedure to impose sanctions for the identified misconduct. This dual procedure proved to be inefficient and complex. The inefficiency stemmed from the fact that parties dissatisfied with the CPC's decisions in administrative proceedings could challenge them in the Administrative Court. Only after the administrative decision became legally effective could the CPC initiate a misdemeanor procedure, which concluded with a separate decision. Once again, the dissatisfied party could contest this decision in the Administrative Court and further appeal to the Supreme Court. This protracted process, from the occurrence of a Competition Act violation to the execution of the sanction, resulted in ineffective protection, prolonged legal uncertainty, and opportunities for abuse by participants in the procedure.

Recognizing these shortcomings and aligning with EU law, a new Competition Act was drafted in 2010. This legislation introduced a unified misdemeanor procedure, empowering the CPC to simultaneously determine both the violation of the Competition Act and the corresponding misdemeanor. This streamlined approach aimed to enhance the efficiency of competition law enforcement, reduce legal uncertainty, and curtail potential abuses of procedural positions. Such alignment arises specifically from the need to transpose the EU Regulation 1/2003.[45] Article 5, titled "Powers of the Competition authorities of the Member States," clearly states that competition authorities should also have the authority to impose fines, periodic penalty payments, or any other penalty provided for in their national law. The need to harmonize this part of the legal framework is also highlighted in the CPC's 2010 Annual Activity Report, which details the new law passed in 2010.[46]

[44] Competition Act, Art. 67 (5).

[45] Council Regulation (EC) No 1/2003 of 16 December 2002 on the implementation of the rules on competition laid down in Articles 81 and 82 of the Treaty [2003] OJ L1/1.

[46] Commission for the Protection of Competition (2010), p. 6.

The technical, legal, administrative, supervisory, financial, accounting, IT and other activities of the CPC are performed by the supporting staff of the CPC.[47] This service is overseen by the Secretary-General, who is appointed by the President of the CPC.[48] For the efficient performance of the work and tasks of the CPC, according to the type, scope, and degree of their complexity, five sectors are formed within the organization of the CPC.[49] Additionally, an independent unit is established for financial issues.[50] Within each of the sectors, units are formed as smaller organizational units.[51]

Table 1 presents an overview of the trends in the number of employees and the annual budget of the CPC from 2012 to 2022. Examination of these data provides valuable insights into the financial and staffing aspects of the organization over the years. The annual budget of the CPC experienced fluctuations throughout the period. Starting at over MKD 17.6 million in 2012, it showed a slight increase in 2013 before dipping to MKD 16.9 million in 2014. However, the budget gradually recovered in the subsequent years, reaching its peak at over MKD 23.3 million in 2020 before decreasing slightly to MKD 21.3 million in 2021, and increasing again to some MKD 2.3 million in 2022. Relatedly, most of the remarks in the respective

---

[47] Competition Act, Art. 29.

[48] Competition Act, Art. 29.

[49] Rules for the internal organization of the Commission for the Protection of Competition, Art. 4.

[50] Ibid.

[51] Here is an overview of the organizational structure of the CPC in accordance with Article 4 of the Rules for the internal organization of the commission for the protection of competition:

1. Sector for General and Legal Affairs
    1.1. Unit for General and Expert-Administrative Affairs
    1.2. Unit for Communication and Public Relations and Human Resources Management
2. Sector for Analysis and Assessment of Concentrations
    2.1. Unit for Market Research and Analysis
    2.2. Unit for Assessment of Concentrations
3. Sector for Misdemeanor Proceedings
    3.1. Unit for Misdemeanor Proceedings in the Field of Abuse of a Dominant Position and Concentrations
    3.2. Unit for Misdemeanor Proceedings in the Field of Prohibited Agreements and Minor Offenses Determined by the Law on Protection of Competition
4. Sector for State Aid Control
    4.1. Unit for State Aid Supervision
    4.2. Unit for State Aid Evaluation
5. Sector for International Cooperation, Monitoring, and Application of EU Law
    5.1. Unit for International Cooperation
    5.2. Unit for Monitoring and Application of EU Law
6. Unit for Financial Affairs

Table 1 The number of employees and the annual budget of the CPC (2012–2022)

Year	Annual Budget (in MKD)	Annual Budget (in EUR)[a]	Number of employees (incl. the President and two members[b])
2012	17,650,000	286,812.50	28
2013	18,767,351	305,973.46	28
2014	16,933,175	275,167.09	27
2015	17,784,337	288,526.48	29
2016	17,723,415	287,528.99	28
2017	18,856,000	306,430.00	27
2018	18,715,835	304,141.36	27
2019	21,340,595	346,084.68	26
2020	23,365,000	379,181.25	27
2021	21,331,510	346,635.64	27
2022	23,004,000	373,306.92	26

Source: Authors' own calculations based on CPC's Annual Reports 2012–2022
[a]Calculation based on average exchange rate for the relevant year
[b]Until October 2024, the Commission comprised two members who were full-time employees, two external members, and a President, with the external members not considered employed under the Commission's methodology and thus excluded from the table

reports from 2020, 2021, and 2022 are very similar, suggesting slow progress in competition law enforcement.

The number of employees, including the President and two members, remained relatively stable during the period, ranging from 26 to 29. There were minor fluctuations, but no significant upward or downward trend is apparent. This stability suggests that the CPC maintained a consistent workforce despite budgetary fluctuations, indicating efficient resource management or the presence of long-term employment strategies.

Analysing the data, it is interesting to note that there is not a clear correlation between the annual budget and the number of employees. In some years, like 2012 and 2013, the budget increased while the number of employees remained constant. Conversely, in 2014, a notable decrease in the budget did not result in a corresponding decrease in the workforce. This lack of direct correlation might imply that the CPC focused on optimising existing resources and improving operational efficiency rather than scaling up or down based solely on budgetary changes.

4.2 *Main Substantive and Procedural Norms*

4.2.1 Types of Violations of Free Competition under Macedonian Competition Law

When discussing Macedonian competition law, the 2010 Competition Act outlines three key areas where the principle of free competition may come under threat.

These are: prohibited agreements, decisions of associations of undertakings, and concerted practices; concentrations; and the abuse of a dominant market position. Essentially, these legal concepts align with those established by the EU competition law, emphasising MK's dedication to the harmonisation of the domestic legal framework in the European integration process.

At the core of this segment lies Article 7 of the Competition Act, a direct counterpart to Article 101 TFEU. Namely, this provision of the Competition Act states that any agreements between undertakings, decisions by associations of undertakings, or concerted practices that have the potential to distort competition are prohibited.[52] This prohibition extends to actions that:

i) directly or indirectly fix purchase or selling prices, or any other trading conditions.
ii) restrict or control production, markets, technical development, or investments.
iii) divvy up markets or sources of supply.
iv) apply dissimilar conditions to equivalent or similar transactions, putting trading partners at a competitive disadvantage.
v) impose supplementary obligations unrelated to the subject matter of the agreements on other parties as a condition for acceptance.

If such agreements, decisions, or individual provisions breach the rules of Article 7(1) of the Competition Act, they shall be rendered null and void.[53] The Competition Act introduces exceptions to this prohibition, particularly for agreements, decisions, or practices that foster the production, distribution of goods and services, or technological and economic development.[54] These exceptions come with specific conditions—they must ensure that consumers benefit proportionately, refrain from imposing unnecessary restrictions on the involved undertakings, and refrain from affording said undertakings the power to stifle competition in a substantial part of the relevant products or services.

Furthermore, Articles 8 and 9 of the Competition Act enumerate categories of agreements exempt from the purview of Article 7. These include contracts of minor importance and categories subject to group exemption. In a nutshell, an agreement of minor importance is one in which the combined market share of the parties and undertakings under their control does not exceed specific thresholds—10% for horizontal agreements, 15% for vertical agreements, or 10% in cases where classification as either horizontal or vertical is unfeasible. Agreements of minor importance also encompass scenarios where the market share of the undertakings has grown by less than 2% over two consecutive business years.

The Competition Act also extends this exemption through block exemptions to several categories of agreements, covering various fields such as distribution, research and development, specialization, technology transfer, licenses,

[52] Competition Act Art. 7 (1).
[53] Competition Act Art. 7 (2).
[54] Competition Act, Art. 7 (3).

know-how, insurance, and transportation.[55] These exceptions contribute to the Competition Act' balanced approach to competition regulation.

The Macedonian competition law places special emphasis on dominant market positions and their potential for abuse. The definition of what constitutes a dominant position in the market is found in Article 10 of the Competition Act. An undertaking is deemed dominant if it lacks competitors on the relevant market or, in comparison to its rivals, enjoys a leading position, particularly concerning market share, financial clout, access to supply sources or the market, associations with other undertakings, legal or factual barriers to entry, the capacity to dictate market conditions, and the capability to exclude competitors by seeking alliances with other undertakings.

The Competition Act introduces a presumption: if an undertaking's market share exceeds 40%, it shall be considered to possess a dominant position, unless the undertaking can conclusively prove otherwise.[56] Furthermore, the Competition Act holds that when two or more legally independent undertakings act or participate jointly on the relevant market, they may be deemed to jointly possess a dominant position.[57]

Article 11 of the Competition Act prohibits the abuse of a dominant position on the relevant market or a substantial portion of it. Such abuse encompasses actions such as:

i) imposing unfair purchase or selling prices, or other unjust trading conditions, whether directly or indirectly;
ii) curtailing production, markets, or technical development to the detriment of consumers;
iii) applying different conditions to equivalent or similar transactions, disadvantaging trading partners;
iv) imposing supplementary obligations unrelated to the essence of the agreements on other parties;
v) unjustified refusal to engage with other undertakings, influencing or persuading other entities to refrain from transacting with a particular undertaking with the intention of causing harm through deceit; and
vi) unjustified refusal to grant another undertaking access to its network or infrastructure facilities for reasonable compensation, potentially rendering the other undertaking unable to compete effectively.

Article 11 (3) of the Competition Act offers an exemption from this prohibition if the dominant undertaking can prove that concurrent usage of its network or infrastructure facilities is either infeasible due to operational or other legitimate reasons or is unjustified for valid reasons.

Economic concentrations are regulated in Articles 12–25 of the Competition Act, delineating notification obligations, assessment, and procedures. The most crucial provision in that regard is Article 14 of the Competition Act. Specifically, any concentration must be duly notified to the CPC under the following conditions:

[55] Competition Act, Art. 9 (1).
[56] Competition Act, Art. 10 (2).
[57] Competition Act, Art. 10 (3).

i) The cumulative turnover of all participating undertakings generated from the sale of goods and services worldwide, amounting to a minimum of 10 million euros in denar equivalence, based on the exchange rate applicable on the day of compiling the annual accounts, realized in the preceding business year. Additionally, at least one participant must be registered in the MK.
ii) The combined turnover of all participating undertakings, resulting from the sale of goods and services in the MK, reaching a minimum of 2.5 million euros in denar equivalence, according to the prevailing exchange rate on the day of annual account preparation.
iii) The market share of any participant exceeding 40%, or the collective market share of all participants in the concentration surpassing 60% in the year prior to the concentration.

Participants in the concentration are obligated to notify the CPC before implementing it. This notification should follow the procedural trajectory outlined in the merger agreement, the public announcement of a bid for purchasing or acquiring a controlling interest in a nominal capital undertaking, or when participants publicly declare their intent to participate in a public bid that would result in a concentration, all within the purview of the Competition Act.

Calculating aggregate turnover, as outlined in the Competition Act, is an important step in the concentration assessment process.[58] Namely, this aggregate turnover encompasses revenues arising from the sale of goods produced as part of an undertaking's regular operations, as well as revenues derived from services offered within the regular scope of operations.[59] These figures should account for the business year immediately preceding the concentration, after accounting for sales rebates (discounts) and the subtraction of Value Added Tax and other public taxes directly related to revenues. In case of related undertaking,[60] all related undertakings are treated as a single entity when calculating their aggregate turnover. When addressing the rules for calculations, Article 16(3) mandates that when computing aggregate turnover for related undertakings, revenues generated from the sale of goods and services among these related entities should not factor into the equation.

The Competition Act sets the rules for determining the impact of a concentration on effective competition.[61] Namely, the Competition Act prescribes specific factors that the CPC should take into account while evaluating whether a concentration significantly impedes competition on the market. These factors encompass the need to preserve and promote effective competition, the market position of the involved undertakings, the availability of alternatives for suppliers and users, the presence of legal or other barriers to market entry and exit, supply and demand trends, and consumer interests. Moreover, technological and economic development is relevant, but only when it directly benefits consumers and does not hinder competition.

A significant concept of Macedonian competition law, enshrined in the 2010 Competition Act, is the principle of "territorial effects of the law". Under this doctrine, the Competition Act and all its amendments apply to all actions or activities

[58] Competition Act, Art. 16.
[59] Competition Act, Art 16 (1).
[60] Competition Act, Art. 16 (2).
[61] Competition Act, Art. 17 (4).

that have an impact on the territory of the MK, even if they originate beyond its borders.

In the Macedonian Criminal Code,[62] there is a specific offense related to regulating competition and market freedom ('preventing, limiting, or distorting competition'). Article 283 of the Macedonian Criminal Code pertains to individuals within legal entities who engage in agreements or participate in actions that violate competition laws, with the intention to prevent, limit, or distort fair competition. If such actions result in significant financial gain or widespread damage, the responsible person within the legal entity may be subject to imprisonment for a period ranging from one to 10 years.[63] However, there is a provision for exemption from punishment if the responsible person actively contributes to the discovery of the illegal agreement, decision, or concerted behaviour.[64] This contribution must lead to a competition protection authority conducting an investigation and potentially granting an exemption or reducing fines imposed on the involved legal entity.[65]

Despite the provisions in the Criminal Code addressing the punishment of violations of competition law, the actual practice in the MK paints a different picture. According to relevant sources available to us, there is no established practice in the application of Article 283 of the Criminal Code. Consequently, from a practical standpoint, the sanctioning of competition violations is predominantly conducted through an administrative procedure under the jurisdiction of the CPC.

4.2.2 Misdemeanor Procedure under Macedonian Competition Law

According to the Competition Act, the misdemeanor procedure is conducted and the sanction imposed by the Commission for Misdemeanor Matters (*Комисија за одлучување по прекршок*) (CMM), a specialized working body of the CPC composed of the President and all CPC members, although prior to the October 2024 amendments, it consisted only of the President and two full-time elected members..[66] When deciding on an offense, the commission operates and makes decisions in sessions, requiring a majority vote from the total number of members. A member of the commission cannot abstain from voting.[67] Regarding the procedure, the CMM, while conducting the misdemeanor procedure, shall appropriately apply the

[62] Macedonian Criminal Code [1996] Official Gazette of the Republic of Macedonia No 37/96, 80/99, 4/02, 43/03, 19/04, 81/05, 60/06, 73/06, 7/08, 139/08, 114/09, 51/11, 135/11, 185/11, 142/12, 166/12, 55/13, 82/13, 14/14, 27/14, 28/14, 41/14, 115/14, 132/14, 160/14, 199/14, 196/15, 226/15, 97/17 и 248/18 and Official Gazette of the Republic of Macedonia No 36/23.

[63] Macedonian Criminal Code, Art. 283 (1).

[64] Macedonian Criminal Code, Art. 283 (2).

[65] Macedonian Criminal Code, Art. 283 (2).

[66] Competition Act, Art 30 (1).

[67] Competition Act, Art 30 (2).

provisions of the Law on General Administrative Procedure,[68] except if it is otherwise stipulated by the Law on Misdemeanors[69] and the Competition Act. Misdemeanor procedures before the CMM may be initiated in two ways: i) *ex officio*, at the request of the Secretary General of the CPC, or ii) upon the request of a natural or legal person with a legitimate interest in determining the existence of a misdemeanor.[70] The Competition Act acknowledges the right of response for the person against whom the procedure has been initiated.[71] In the Competition Act, it is highlighted that misdemeanor procedures before the CMM are not urgent, adhering to regular deadlines, not expedited ones.[72]

4.2.3 Investigative Powers of the Commission for Protection of the Competition and the System of Fines under Macedonian Competition Law

The system of fines is regulated in the Competition Act. Namely, if circumstances point to the possible distortion of competition, the CPC may conduct an investigation in a particular sector of the economy or a specific type of agreement in different sectors of the economy.[73] During the investigation, the CPC may request undertakings, through a procedural order, to submit data related to their economic and financial conditions, business relations, information on their statutes and decisions, the number and identity of persons affected by such decisions, and other data relevant to the investigation. No appeal or legal action on instituting an administrative dispute shall be allowed against the procedural order.

The Competition Act allows the CPC to issue procedural orders to undertakings, granting CPC-authorized personnel various access and inspection rights. These rights include unhindered access to premises, record examination, copying, temporary retention, sealing, explanations, and necessary actions. In cases of urgency where there is a risk of serious and irreparable damage to competition, the CPC may, *ex officio* and based on its initial information (*prima facie*) as to the existence of a misdemeanor offence, order interim measures to an undertaking that, by its conduct, may cause serious and irreparable damage to competition.[74]

Regarding sanctions, the most important provisions are to be found in Articles 59–66 of the Competition Act. Article 59 stipulates that CMM may impose a fine on an undertaking or association of undertakings, by means of a decision, in the amount

[68] Law on General Administrative Procedure [2015] Official Gazette of the Republic of Macedonia No. 124/2015 and 65/2018.

[69] Law on Misdemeanors [2019] Official Gazette of the Republic of North Macedonia No. 96/2019.

[70] Competition Act, Art 32 (1)

[71] Competition Act, Art 31 (6)

[72] Competition Act, Art 32 (7).

[73] Competition Act, Art 48 (1).

[74] Competition Act, Art 51 (1)

of up to 10% of the value of the total annual turnovers earned in the last business year, calculated in absolute and nominal amounts, for which the undertaking or association of undertakings has compiled an annual account, if it:

a) concludes a prohibited agreement or otherwise participates in an agreement, decision or concerted practices leading to a distortion of competition within the meaning of Article 7 of the Competition Act;
b) abuses its dominant position within the meaning of Article 11 of the Competition Act;
c) fails to act pursuant to the decision of the CPC referred to in Article 51 of the Competition Act; or
d) fails to act pursuant to the decision of the CPC referred to in Article 52 of the Competition Act.[75]

The commitment decisions have been included in Article 43 of the Competition Act since the introduction of the Act in 2010. When a competition-distorting action or omission occurs, the involved party can propose remedies to the CPC after proceedings begin but before a final factual report is submitted. If the violation is severe, these commitments are not accepted. Accepted commitments must be detailed with a deadline for completion, and evidence of fulfillment must be provided by the accused party. The process is paused pending the fulfillment of these commitments. If not met, proceedings continue. A failure to fulfill commitments can lead to the resumption of the procedure, but if successfully completed, the procedure is terminated without appeal rights. Based on information received from the CPC for the period 2012–2022, only one such case has been recorded.

As a standard for determining fines based on misdemeanor offences by undertakings or associations of undertakings, CMM considers the total annual turnover earned by the undertakings in the last business year. Article 16 of the Competition Act explicitly explains the meaning of 'total annual turnover.[76] In alignment with the 'scope of application' regime anticipated in Article 3 of the Competition Act,[77] the CPC imposes fines on the total annual turnover earned in the last business year, both nationally and internationally, if their effects are observed within the territory of the MK.

Articles 60, 61, and 62 from the Competition Act, refer to "serious misdemeanours under a procedure for assessing concentrations", and to fines addressed to associations of undertakings. In these three Articles, the fining policy for violation of competition rules has been incorporated.

[75] Competition Act, Art 59 (1).

[76] In Article 16, paragraph 1 of the Competition Act, the term 'aggregate turnover' is defined. It includes revenues generated from the sale of goods produced within the regular operation of an undertaking, as well as revenues from services provided within its regular operations. These revenues must have been realized during the business year preceding the concentration, with deductions for sales rebates (discounts) and the Value Added Tax, along with other public taxes directly related to the revenues.

[77] In Article 3, paragraph 1 of the Competition Act, this law applies to all forms of prevention, restriction, or distortion of competition (referred to hereinafter as 'distortion of competition') that have an impact on the territory of the Republic of Macedonia, even if they result from acts and actions carried out or undertaken outside the territory of the Republic of Macedonia.

Competition Act stipulates that the CMM can impose fines on undertakings or associations of undertakings up to 1% of their total annual turnover if they fail to comply with various obligations outlined in Articles 40, 48, and 49. These obligations include adhering to procedural orders, providing accurate data, allowing access and examination, and facilitating other necessary actions as per Articles 41 and 50. Refusal to explain certain facts or providing false information can also result in fines.[78]

The challenges highlighted in conducting dawn raids, as revealed in the interview with CPC representatives, underscore significant practical hurdles.[79] The inability to secure electronic evidence effectively due to constraints in printing and potential risks of data manipulation poses a serious obstacle. The absence of a consistent method for recording seized material further complicates the process, raising concerns about the accuracy of documentation. The ambiguity surrounding the examination of private emails on official accounts and the uncertainty regarding the search of phones and the timeframe for legal representation add layers of complexity to the procedure. Access to locked compartments, refusal of passwords, and unexplored areas like company vehicles and office sealing are also challenges. Furthermore, the legislation should address the challenge of regulating police assistance when exercising the powers of the CPC.

Based on the information outlined in the project "Technical Cooperation to the Commission for the Protection of Competition in North Macedonia" (implemented during the period 2019–2024 by the European Bank for Reconstruction and Development EBRD), one of the primary objectives was to provide in-house training on how to conduct effective dawn raids and document the pertinent procedures in a guidance document. This project approach is entirely aligned with and falls within the framework of the data and needs identified during the interviews with the CPC representatives.

When a misdemeanor offence is committed by an association of undertakings and relates to the activities of its members, the fine shall not exceed 1% of the aggregate annual turnover for procedural misdemeanors, and 10% for more serious misdemeanors.[80] This applies to each member of the association acting on the relevant market. When determining the fine, account shall be taken of: 1) the seriousness of the misdemeanor offence; 2) its the duration; and 3) the extent of distortion of competition and the effects caused by the misdemeanor offence.[81]

[78] Competition Act, Art 61 (1).

[79] Interview with a senior CPC representatives.

[80] Competition Act, Art 61 (1).

[81] Competition Act, Art 64 (1).

5 National Specifics that Differ from the EU Competition *Acquis*

5.1 Peculiarities of the National Legal System that Significantly Differ from the EU Competition Acquis

The MK, as a country with a small economy, bases both its competition policy and competition law on the EU values and practices. In essence, the state follows other countries in the region, which have fully or partially incorporated the European rules for the protection of competition. We are of the opinion that despite following EU competition law and practice, each country should adapt its legislation to the needs of the prevailing national circumstances, taking into account the needs of the business sector, the public sector and of course consumers as stakeholders. This, however, must be achieved within the framework of the existing EU rules, but, in any case, not to forget Gal's concept of "minimum efficient scale", and the importance of implementing proper competition policy in small market economies such as the Macedonian economy.[82]

According to our view, the direct incorporation of EU rules into national legislation would not *per se* mean success in ensuring a fair market competition. Just the opposite, the negative consequences of the automatic/mechanical implementation of the EU solutions can produce negative consequences in the economy. Therefore, our position is that there should be national peculiarities, which differ not only from the EU rules, but in general, peculiarities that represent specifics inherent to the national economy. For example, as a small market, with a few key industry sectors, competition law in the MK should pay attention to the merger control regime and have a more liberal legal regime regarding mergers and acquisitions of companies. The latter strive to provide space for realizing scale economies, so the enhanced production will lead to a decrease in unit costs.

Unfortunately, despite extensive efforts to align domestic laws with EU regulations, the main challenge lies in their effective implementation. A thorough analysis reveals that countries in the region strive merely to maximum harmonization of their national competition laws, considering it as a great success. This fact is supported by the latest report from the European Commission on MK, which acknowledges that the country achieved legislative progress. However, the primary obstacle is the practical application and enforcement of enacted legal norms. Additionally, it is crucial not to overlook the role of the CPC, which has a key role in implementing both legislation and national policies to safeguard competition.[83]

In terms of legislation, the MK has no rules that differ significantly from the EU legislation. As presented above, almost all actions in legislative policy are aimed at harmonizing national regulations with EU rules. This situation can be seen through

[82] Gal (2003).

[83] Commission (2022).

several instruments that are part of the competition protection legislation. For example, in this segment it is relevant to mention leniency program. This program, although implemented in the Macedonian legislation, is still unused, despite the opportunities it offers to either the business sector or the needs of the CPC. Hence, it is difficult to draw conclusions, when in essence, some of the rules are not yet applied, and in addition to this, the policies for the protection of competition are not deep and based on the real needs of business and the consumers. In this direction, our suggestions call for a deeper analysis of the market by the CPC, and adaptation of the legislation and policies to its needs.

5.2 *Peculiarities of the National Legal System that have been Erased/Amended in the Process of Europeanization*

The Competition Act has undergone four amendments since its adoption, respectively in 2011, 2014, 2016, and 2018. These modifications primarily concern administrative aspects and membership of the CPC. In 2011, the amendments integrated principles of administrative procedure, like "silence means approval", aligning it with the Law on General Administrative Procedure.[84] However, these provisions were later deemed impractical and were eliminated in 2016.[85]

On April 3, 2014, another amendment established procedures for electing the President and CPC members, along with eligibility criteria.[86] This amendment now requires that these officials must be Macedonian citizens, without recent convictions hindering their duties, possessing relevant education, a minimum of 5 years' professional experience, special knowledge in competition, business law, management, finance, and English language proficiency.[87] The law mandated psychological and integrity tests.

In March 2016, Competition Act amendments synchronized its provisions with those of the Law on General Administrative Procedure and further refined the qualifications for Commission members and President.[88] Notably, the requirement for integrity and psychological tests was removed. Additionally, Article 15 received amendments introducing paragraphs 5 and 6 to expedite administrative processes,

[84] Law on Amendments and Supplements to the Law on Protection of Competition [2011] Official Gazette of the Republic of North Macedonia No 136/11.

[85] Law on Amendments and Supplements to the Law on the Protection of Competition [2016] Official Gazette of the Republic of North Macedonia No 53/16.

[86] Law on Amendments and Supplements to the Law on Protection of Competition [2014] Official Gazette of the Republic of North Macedonia No 41/14.

[87] Art 27 (7) of the Law on Amendments and Supplements to the Law on Protection of Competition [2014] Official Gazette of the Republic of North Macedonia No 41/14.

[88] Law on Amendments and Supplements to the Law on the Protection of Competition [2016] Official Gazette of the Republic of North Macedonia No 53/16.

demanding financial statements and trade register extracts within 3 days for assessments of concentration.

On May 8, 2018, further amendments incorporated new prerequisites for CPC members and the President.[89] This new provision added APTIS (Certificate of proficiency in English) at least at a B2 level. Furthermore, a provision mandated that Presidents and members elected between the law's enactment and September 1, 2018, must fulfil the language proficiency requirement within 1 year. Failure to do so would result in the termination of their mandates.

6 Application of National and EU Competition Rules by the CPCs and Discussion of the Most Significant Cases

6.1 Application of National and EU Competition Rules by the CPCs

The SAA is the foundational legal framework governing the relations between MK and EU. MK committed to align its existing and future laws with EU standards, emphasizing proper implementation. Articles 68 and 69 of the SAA detail MK's obligations, specifically in relation to EU competition law. Article 69 identifies situations constituting competition law violations. The implementation of EU law within MK's national legislation, rooted in Articles 68 and 69, is vital for fostering a free and competitive market. The SAA's Article 68(1) underscores MK's duty to gradually align its laws with those of the EU, emphasizing the importance of approximation. Furthermore, Article 69(2) highlights the use of criteria from EU Treaty for assessing anti-competitive practices affecting trade between the parties.

Regarding the application of EU law, we can focus on two aspects. The first is the application of EU law by the courts of the MK, and the second is the application of EU law in procedures of the CPC.

The basis of this analysis derives from Article 118 of the Constitution.[90] The Constitutional Court's stance on international treaties, including the SAA with the EU, reflects a consistent approach. The Court, following a broad interpretation, refuses to review statutes and regulations for conformity with the SAA, relying on the argument that such assessments fall under the purview of the Parliament of the MK during the ratification process.[91] Even in cases like "Made in Macedonia,"

[89] Law on Amendments and Supplements to the Law on the Protection of Competition [2018] Official Gazette of the Republic of North Macedonia No 83/18.

[90] Article 118 of the Constitution reads: "International agreements ratified in accordance with the Constitution are part of the internal legal order and cannot be changed by law."

[91] The Republic of Macedonia, as a non-EU member, lacks an explicit constitutional basis for the application of EU law through a dedicated 'Europe clause,' a characteristic common among EU aspirant countries in Southeast Europe and their Central and Eastern European counterparts. While

where the Court could directly apply relevant SAA provisions, it refrained from doing so.[92] However, the Court grants indirect effect to SAA provisions and extends this approach to EU secondary law, such as directives and regulations. Despite acknowledging that EU directives are not sources of law in MK, the Court considers them in support of its legal standing. Notably, the Court exhibits a lenient stance towards laws transposing EU directives, consistently upholding their constitutionality, thereby adopting an EU-friendly approach.[93]

When we talk about the approach of ordinary courts, we must refer to the Law on Courts. Article 18 (4) of the Law on Courts stipulates that when a court perceives a conflict between domestic law and a ratified international agreement, it must apply the agreement's provisions if they can be directly enforced. Additionally, in specific cases, the court is mandated to immediately apply final decisions from international courts like the European Court of Human Rights or like the International Criminal Court. However, Article 18 (5) of the Law on Courts excludes the applicability of decisions from the European Court of Justice, signalling that the jurisdiction of the ECJ is not recognized in MK. This follows from the provision of Article 18 (5) of the Law on Courts, which reads: "...or to another court whose jurisdiction is recognized by the Republic of Macedonia."

Regarding the application of EU law, Georgievski et al. concludes in his research that ordinary courts, including the Supreme Court, are observed to lack the awareness and skills for direct application of EU and international law.[94] While these courts traditionally view the EU legal order as an extension of the international one, they have developed a favorable standard for the application of international treaties, notably in the context of the European Convention on Human Rights (ECHR).[95]

As per actual cases, the case of *Makpetrol* should be highlighted. In this case, the Supreme Court, aligned with lower courts, directly applied the Interim Agreement between Macedonia and the Communities in 2004, despite lacking ratification by the

Article 118 of the Macedonian Constitution grants ratified treaties direct applicability without requiring implementing legislation, there is a significant omission in Article 110 concerning the Constitutional Court's explicit authority to review the conformity of domestic laws with such treaties. This gap leads to anomalies in the Constitutional Court's practice in applying the general monist regime of Article 118. Georgievski et al. (2014), p. 117.

[92] Ibid.

[93] Macedonia's Constitutional Court typically treats ratified treaties and international law as secondary, persuasive authorities, using them for interpretation rather than direct application. This approach extends to sources of secondary EU law, with directives and regulations indirectly referenced, primarily in harmonization matters. In a recent case involving Article 68 of the SAA and the constitutionality of provisions in the Public Procurement Act, the Court used the SAA and Directive 2004/18/EC as key arguments. These international instruments were not merely supporting but played a central role in interpreting national law consistently with secondary EU law, emphasizing the Court's commitment to aligning national legislation with EU principles. Georgievski et al. (2014), p. 118.

[94] Georgievski et al. (2014), p. 127.

[95] Georgievski et al. (2014), p. 127.

Macedonian Parliament.[96] The Court invoked Article 118 of the Constitution, emphasizing a functional link between the Interim Agreement and the ratified SAA. The decision prioritized the Agreement over a conflicting Government regulation, treating it as if ratified through its functional link to the SAA.[97] This reflects the courts' early willingness to directly apply SAA provisions, exemplified by reliance on Article 5(4) of the Interim Agreement in prohibiting quantitative restrictions on trade between parties.[98]

The basis for the action of the CPC in the context of EU law is provided for in Article 3 (3) of the Competition Act, which regulates that "in the assessment of the forms of distortion of competition that may affect trade between the Republic of Macedonia and the European Communities, in accordance with Article 69 of the Stabilization and Association Agreement concluded between the Republic of Macedonia and the European Communities and their member-states, the criteria arising from the proper application of the rules regulating competition in the European Union shall be accordingly applied." Consequently, the CPC can apply the criteria derived from EU law when dealing with an anti-competitive practice which may impact MK's trade with the EU.

Regarding the application of the legal rule of Article 3 (3) of the Competition Act, several decisions of the CPC are noted, which have been judicially reviewed. The decisions of the Administrative Court reveal a substantial adherence to EU legal principles in the realm of competition law by the CPC.[99] Notably, the Court, in a 2012 judgment (U. no. 6218/2009), affirmed the direct application of EU competition rules in accordance with Article 69 of the SAA and based on Article 3(3) of the Competition Act.[100] Subsequent cases, such as the 2012 judgment (no. 6517/2009), further underline the Court's commitment to this approach. The Administrative Court again upheld the use of European competition law criteria by the Competition Authority, based on Article 3(3) of the Competition Act.[101] The decision of the Administrative Court in this case was later upheld in a judgment of the High Administrative Court on appeal. Concerning the essence of the dispute, it should be noted that in this case, the CPC, in its decision, refers to communications issued by the European Commission relevant to the application of competition rules in the telecommunications sector, based on Article 3(3) of the Competition Act. These

[96] Georgievski et al. (2014), pp. 111 and 122.

[97] Georgievski et al. (2014), pp. 111 and 122.

[98] The judgment, seen as bold from an EU integration perspective, demonstrated the Court's departure from national constitutional norms to achieve a Euro-friendly outcome. Despite a lack of detailed argumentation, the Court considered the Interim Agreement a ratified international agreement under Article 118, suggesting an eagerness for EU integration. While the judgment may lack strong legal foundation, it emphasizes the court's commitment to EU-friendly interpretations, particularly regarding trade-related provisions, contributing to Macedonia's alignment with EU principles and aspirations for integration. Georgievski et al. (2014), pp. 111 and 122.

[99] Ibid. p. 123.

[100] Ibid.

[101] Ibid.

findings, as highlighting the consistent application of Article 3(3) of the Law on Competition, show the compatibility between Macedonian and EU competition rules.[102] Georgievski underscores the Court's interpretation of the domestic rule in three court decisions as an enabling mechanism for applying EU requirements, reinforcing the interconnectedness of Macedonian and EU competition law. In essence, these judgments, not only validate the domestic legal framework but also emphasize the integral connection between Macedonian and EU competition law, promoting a unified and cooperative regulatory environment.

6.2 *Discussion of the most Significant CPC Decisions (2019–2022)*

In this subsection, we delve into all of the CPC's decisions in the period from 2019 to 2022. It is crucial to acknowledge that these CPC decisions may undergo further scrutiny within the judiciary. Unfortunately, we could not access data related to ongoing court proceedings for our research. An analysis of court decisions is presented separately in the subsequent section on judicial review.

The basis for determining penalties for prohibited agreements derives from Article 59(1) of the Competition Act, and prohibited agreements as such are determined in Article 7 (1) of the Competition Act. In the section on cases that establish the existence of prohibited agreements, the following cases can be highlighted.

In the case against Farma Trejd, a single-member limited liability company from Skopje, and Dr. Panovski, a joint-stock company from Skopje, the CPC determined that these two companies, operating in the field of pharmacy, acted contrary to the Competition Act in the way they negotiated prices for a call for awarding a contract for public procurement of insulin, glucagon, insulin needles, and strips for measuring sugar and insulin pumps with consumables for the period from August 2016 to August 2018, for the needs of the population of the MK, for the medicine with the generic name Human insulin.[103] Specifically, the two companies submitted offers with previously determined prices, which led to the distortion of competition. In the procedure of electronic auctions, they did not reduce the offered prices with the aim of distorting the competition through direct or indirect fixing of sales prices. In this case, the CPC imposed a fine of MKD 44,359,800.00 on the first company and a fine of MKD 65,230,700.00 on the second company.

In the case against Grozd, a joint-stock company from Strumica, the CPC determined that Grozd Strumica, in the period from 12 February 2015 to 18 March 2016, conditioned the conclusion of business cooperation agreements with buyers—distributors for the purchase and sale of non-alcoholic and alcoholic beverages in the

[102] Ibid.

[103] Commission for the Protection of Competition Decision No. 09-16/1 of 09.04.2019. Commission for the Protection of Competition (2019), pp. 9–10.

territory of the Republic of Macedonia.[104] This was done in a way in which the other contracting party was required to accept other contracting obligations, which, by their nature or in accordance with the commercial practice and customs, are not related to the subject of the contract. Namely, Grozd, in the business cooperation contracts, imposed prohibited provisions aimed at distorting the competition. In this case, the CPC imposed a fine of MKD 1,930,460.00.

In 2019, the CPC determined[105] that the Company for beer, malt, vinegar, alcoholic and non-alcoholic beverages, Pivara Skopje, a joint-stock company from Skopje, during the period from December 17, 2012, to April 18, 2016, included a prohibited provision in contracts for the sale and distribution of products concluded with independent distributors in the territory of the MK. The CPC found that these provisions affected the ability of distributors to determine the price at which they would sell the products to their customers, allowing Pivara Skopje to fix the retail price, which represented a severe restriction of competition and aimed to disrupt competition. In this case, Pivara Skopje was obligated to pay a fine of MKD 10,790,659.00.

The CPC, in the case against the company for printing, production, and services, Feniks Print, a single-member limited liability company from Kochani, and the company for the employment of disabled persons for printing newspapers, Evropa 92, a single-member limited liability company from Kochani, which operate in the market of printing materials and provide printing services in the territory of the MK, determined that from March 9, 2018, until the day of the decision, they continuously behaved in a coordinated manner with the aim of coordinating their behavior as competitors on the market, effectively participating in a cartel.[106] Fenix Print was sanctioned with a fine in the amount of MKD 28,188.00 while Evropa 92 received a fine in the amount of MKD 1,438,148.00.

In the case against the company for trade, production, and services, Promedika DOOEL Skopje, and the company for trade, production, and services, Neokor Medika DOO, the CPC determined that the two companies deliberately, through their behavior, led to the distortion of competition by participating in a cartel, which constitutes a violation of Article 59, paragraph (1), point 1) of the Competition Act in relation to Article 7, paragraph (1) of the Competition Act. In this case, the CPC imposed two fines: "Promedika DOOEL Skopje" was fined MKD 5,087,820.00 and "Neokor Medika DOO Skopje" was fined MKD 158,945.00.[107]

In 2021, the CPC examined the Agreement for the distribution of the Arena Sport channels, which included the broadcasting of UEFA Champions League and UEFA

---

[104] Decision No. 09-10/21 of 21.05.2019. Commission for the Protection of Competition (2019), pp. 9–10.

[105] Decision No. 09-15/12 of 21.11.2019. Commission for the Protection of Competition (2019), pp. 9–10.

[106] Commission for the Protection of Competition Decision no. 09-4/2 of 27.01.2020. Commission for the Protection of Competition (2020), p. 10.

[107] Commission for the Protection of Competition Decision no. 09-3/8 of 25.02.2020. Commission for the Protection of Competition (2020), p. 10.

Europa League matches for the seasons 2015/2016, 2016/2017, and 2017/2018, for the territory of the Republic of North Macedonia. This agreement was concluded between "Makedonski Telecom," a joint-stock company from Skopje, and "HD WIN," a limited liability company, for the period from August 10, 2015, to August 31, 2018. The CPC considered that this agreement led to a distortion of competition, to the detriment of other operators of public communication networks that transmit audio-visual content to end-users in the territory of the MK, as well as the end consumers. The CPC found that a prohibited provision was inserted into the contract, thus limiting the market for broadcasting or rebroadcasting the matches from the UEFA Champions League without any justified factual and legal reasons. Based on the above, the CPC determined a violation and imposed the following penalties: Makedonski Telekom was fined MKD 1,515,780.00 and HD WIN was fined MKD 1,515,780.00.[108]

In general, based on the analysis of the CPC's 2022 decisions, particularly in the section on prohibited agreements, it is evident that all cases are ones previously handled by the CPC but were sent back for further review due to administrative judiciary decisions that overturned the initial CPC rulings.[109] In a repeated procedure, it was determined that Makedonski Telecom AD Skopje and Arena Channels Group Limited Liability Company, in the period from 10 Aug 2015 to 31 Aug 2018, entered into an agreement for the distribution of Arena Sport channels. This agreement encompassed broadcasting UEFA Champions League and UEFA Europa League matches for the seasons 2015/2016, 2016/2017, and 2017/2018 in the MK. The CPC found that this resulted in disrupting competition in the broadcasting market, disadvantaging other operators of public communication networks. The companies inserted a prohibited provision into the contract without justified reasons, limiting the broadcasting market. Makedonski Telecom AD Skopje was fined MKD 1,515,780, and Arena Channels Group received a fine of MKD 1,288,413.[110] In another repeated procedure, it was established that Intellectual Services Company JAVOR-KOP DOOEL Skopje conditioned franchise agreements with franchisees on unrelated obligations on 29 occasions from 30.10.2011 to 01.09.2018. These obligations were not related to the contract's subject, leading to the CPC determining the existence of a prohibited agreement. No fine was imposed in this case, given the company's total annual income of EUR 0 in the previous financial year, 2021.[111] In the third case of a repeated procedure, the CPC determined that Pharma Trade DOOEL Skopje and Dr. Panovski Skopje, companies in the pharmaceutical industry, submitted offers with predetermined prices within a public procurement

[108] Commission for the Protection of Competition Decision no. 09-3/6 of 11.02.2021. Commission for the Protection of Competition (2021), p. 10.

[109] Commission for the Protection of Competition (2022), p. 9.

[110] Commission for the Protection of Competition Decision no. 09-11/2 of 15.3.2022. Commission for the Protection of Competition (2022), p. 10.

[111] Commission for the Protection of Competition Decision no. 09-24/1 of 20.4.2022. Commission for the Protection of Competition (2022), p. 11.

procedure, distorting competition. Dr. Panovski was fined MKD 1,288,413, and Pharma Trade DOOEL received a fine of MKD 44,359,800.00.[112]

In several of its decisions during the analyzed period of 2019–2022, the CPC found and sanctioned cases of prohibited decisions. In the section of cases that establish the existence of prohibited agreements, the following can be mentioned.

In 2021, the CPC determined that the Association of Private Doctors of the MK, as an association of enterprises in the sense of the Competition Act, made a prohibited decision in the period from 3 Oct 2012, to the day of the decision's adoption. The management board of the Association of Private Doctors of the Republic of Macedonia adopted a decision on 10 March 2012, which foresaw the price list for services for private patients and private services. This decision directly or indirectly fixed the sales prices of services for private patients and private services (services not financed by the state budget). The CPC considers that such a price list prevents, limits, or distorts competition and is an offence. The Association of Private Doctors of the MK has been fined in the amount of MKD 282,761.00.[113]

In another case, the CPC found that the Dental Chamber of Macedonia, as an association of enterprises in the sense of the Competition Act, made a prohibited decision on March 2, 2013. This decision involved the Rulebook on basic, protective (minimum) prices of services and products in dental health facilities in the MK, which patients pay with personal funds in full (services not financed by the state budget). In accordance with this decision, the CPC considers that fixing the sales prices on the market for services and products in dental health facilities in the MK, which patients pay with personal funds in full, prevents, limits, or distorts competition. For this offense, the Dental Chamber of Macedonia has been fined with a fine in the amount of MKD 20,000.00.[114]

In 2021, the CPC determined that a group of companies offering services in the vulcanization market in the city of Bitola[115] participated in a prohibited agreement and concerted conduct in February 2019. They introduced a price list for vulcanization services, which all the listed providers of vulcanization services endorsed, with the aim of distorting competition by directly fixing the sales prices of vulcanization services in the territory of the city of Bitola. As a result, the CPC has evaluated

[112]Commission for the Protection of Competition Decision no. 09-30 of 14.7.2022. Commission for the Protection of Competition (2022), p. 11.

[113]Decision no. 09-5/1 of 21.01.2021. Commission for the Protection of Competition (2021), pp. 10 and 12.

[114]Commission for the Protection of Competition (2021), p. 10.

[115]Namely this case involves the following companies: "Bikal" single member limited liability company, "Jambo pet", single member limited liability company, "Malakovski", single member limited liability company, "Pneumati" sole proprietor, Dragana Stojadin Trajkovska, "Tigar promet" single member limited liability company, "Techno coomerce", joint stock company, "Radial commerce" limited liability company, "Vulkanizer service champion", "Service bemve", "Goldstat Naumovski Stevko", limited liability company, "Washing cars Kiril", limited liability company, "Vulkanizer-Damper", "Vlkanizer MA-VI", "Vulkanizer- Autoperalna IGO-MIT", "Chasit Import-Export", single member limited liability company, and "Avram Import-Export", single member limited liability company.

this action as an offense, and individual fines with a total amount of MKD 121,700 were imposed, on all these companies.

The conclusion presented for the cases of prohibited agreements by the CPC in 2022 also applies to two decisions on prohibited decisions from the same year. Specifically, these two decisions involve the CPC reconsidering previous rulings, cases that were sent back for review due to decisions made by the administrative judiciary.

In the first case of a repeated procedure, it was determined that the Dental Chamber of Macedonia made a prohibited decision by implementing a Rulebook on reference, protective (minimum) prices of services and products in dental health facilities in the Republic of Macedonia. The CPC imposed a fine of MKD 20,000.00 on the Dental Chamber of Macedonia.[116]

In the second case of a repeated procedure, it is asserted that the Association of Private Doctors of the MK made a prohibited decision during the period from October 3, 2012, to the day of the decision's adoption. Consequently, the association was fined with an amount of MKD 282,761.[117] In the repeated proceedings by the CPC in 2022, which have been sent back for review due to decisions made by the administrative judiciary, regardless of whether the subject of the decision is a prohibited agreement or a prohibited decision, the CPC made the same decision as before in the initial ruling.

In terms of trends in CPC decisions, given the limited number of cases and the diverse range of offenses covered, it becomes challenging to form a definitive stance and offer explanations for the trends and preferences of the CPC. This challenge is heightened by the fact that over a 4-year period (2019–2022), the CPC issued 9 rulings on prohibited agreements (including 3 reconsiderations of the same cases), only 5 rulings on prohibited decisions (with 2 being reconsiderations of the same cases), and merely 2 cases related to the abuse of a dominant market position.

In the analysis of the individual CPC's decisions over this period, one decision stands out, which involves abuse of dominant position. Specifically, it concerns the decision in the case of *Makedonski Telecom*, in which a prohibited agreement was also established. According to the CPC's findings, Makedonski Telecom abused its dominant position by refusing to enter into a wholesale contract for the rebroadcast of the Arena Sport channels, including the rebroadcasting of matches from the UEFA Champions League and UEFA Europa League on the territory of the MK. This refusal was deemed unjustified and aimed at unfairly harming other companies. The CPC determined that in this case, Article 11, Paragraph (1) of the Competition Act, as well as Article 59, Paragraph (1), Point 2) of the Competition Act in relation to Article 11, Paragraph (2), Point 5) of the same law, were violated.

[116]Commission for the Protection of Competition Decision no.9-11 of 15.3.2022. Commission for the Protection of Competition (2022), p. 11.

[117]Commission for the Protection of Competition Decision no. 09-23 of 14.7.2022. Commission for the Protection of Competition (2020), p. 12.

Consequently, Makedonski Telecom AD Skopje was fined in the amount of MKD 826,788,000.[118]

In the concentration section, a penalty was imposed in 2021 on Gieseke Deverient GmBH[119] for failing to submit a notice of concentration to the Commission for the Protection of Competition, which is a violation under Article 60, Paragraph (1), Point 1) of the Competition Act. A fine of MKD 184,500 was imposed. The CPC also determined that Article 60, Paragraph (1), Point 2) of the Competition Act was violated, for which a sanction was imposed in the amount of MKD 123,000,000. The fine has been paid, and the decision is final and enforceable. Furthermore, the CPC in 2022 fined Mesna Industrija Braca Pivac DOO Croatia with a penalty amounting to MKD 857,055 for failing to submit a concentration notification and subsequently implementing it.[120]

Finally, in another case from 2020, for a minor type of offence, two misdemeanour fines were imposed on the Association of Private Doctors of the Republic of Macedonia for not providing requested data in a timely manner, as per Article 61, Paragraph (1), Points 1 and 2 of the Competition Act. The total amount of the fines in both cases was MKD 60,016.20.[121]

In general, there is no indication that the collection of fines is problematic in MK. When it comes to specific fine amounts, some annual reports detail how much was collected in a particular year, noting that this represents the total amount claimed for that case. Throughout the period of interest (2012–2022), there was only one instance where a fine was not collected due to the bankruptcy of the entity owing the fine. This applies only to penalties resulting from decisions that are final and enforceable, meaning no further appeal procedure is possible.

7 Enforcement and Sanctioning Statistics for the Period 2012–2022

This section explores the CPC enforcement of the Competition Act from 2012 to 2022. Table 3 outlines the number of misdemeanor decisions and the imposition of fines. Table 4 provides insight into the financial ramifications of these enforcement actions, detailing the fines imposed for various categories of offenses. It is important to note that the figures analyzed pertain to fines imposed by the CPC, which are subject to court proceedings where they can potentially be reduced or annulled. Such examples of a cartel include the case of Alkaloid Cons and

[118]Commission for the Protection of Competition (2021), pp. 10 and 12.

[119]Decision no. 09-1/4 of 18.02.2021. Commission for the Protection of Competition (2021), pp. 10 and 12.

[120]Commission for the Protection of Competition Decision no. 09-2/6 of 20.4.2022. Commission for the Protection of Competition (2022), p. 14.

[121]Commission for the Protection of Competition (2020), p. 10.

Table 2 Number of CPC decisions regarding concentrations (2012–2022)

Year	Unconditionally approved	Conditionally approved	Fall outside the scope of the law	Rejected and/or impermissible	Annulled previous decision
2012	22				
2013	17		1		
2014	29		1		
2015	40	1			1
2016	30			1	
2017	48			1	1
2018	60	1			
2019	50		6		1
2020	58	2	2		
2021	78		3		
2022	101				
Total	523	4	14	2	3

Source: Authors' own calculations based on CPC's Annual Reports 2012–2022

Dr. Panovski, for which the CPC issued decisions for the first time in 2012, and subsequently in 2014, 2015, and 2017. Another example is the case of EFT Makedonija LLC—Skopje, where the CPC first decided in 2014, and then again in 2017. Additionally, the case involving the Chamber of Dentists of MK can be highlighted, where the CPC's first decision was in 2015. Following an appeal from the chamber, the CPC issued further decisions in 2017, 2019, and 2022. In 2024, the case was still pending before the Higher Administrative Court. Unfortunately, the final court decisions that decide the specific cases were not available for this research. Additionally, the section presenting facts and figures includes Table 2, which pertains to the number of decisions regarding concentration approvals. The second part of this section provides an analysis of the most significant decisions made by the CPC in the last 3 years.

Table 2 provides a summary of the CCP's decisions on concentrations from 2012 to 2022, highlighting the number of approved, rejected, and annulled decisions. The number of approved decisions for concentrations shows an increasing trend over the decade. In 2012, there were 22 approved applications, and this number steadily rose each year, reaching 101 approvals in 2022. This consistent growth may indicate a more favorable environment for mergers and acquisitions or increased regulatory efficiency in reviewing applications.

Table 3 provides a concise overview of the number of misdemeanor decisions with fines imposed by the CPC from 2012 to 2022. This data allows us to gain insights into the regulatory actions taken by the Commission and the trends in different categories of offences. The data shows that the number of misdemeanor decisions related to prohibited agreements fluctuated during this period. The highest number of decisions was in 2012, with 5 cases, but there was a sharp decline in 2013 with only 1 case. Subsequently, the numbers remained relatively consistent, with occasional variations, indicating that this category of offences has not shown a

Table 3 Number of misdemeanour decisions with fines imposed by the CPC (2012–2022)

	2012	2013	2014	2015	2016	2017	2018	2019	2020	2021	2022	Total
Prohibited agreements (cartels) and decisions of associations	5 (0)	1 (0)	4 (4)	3 (3)	3 (0)	6 (0)	4 (0)	3 (0)	2 (2)	4 (1)	5 (0)	40 (10)
Abuse of dominant position	2	3	4	2	2	1	2	–	–	1	1	18
Total	*7*	*4*	*8*	*5*	*5*	*7*	*6*	*3*	*2*	*5*	*6*	*58*

Source: Authors' own calculations based on CPC's Annual Reports 2012–2022

Table 4 Fines imposed by CPC (2012–2022)[a]

Year	Fines (in MKD) Prohibited agreements and decisions of associations; (out of which for cartels)	Fines (in MKD) Abuse of a dominant market position	Fines (in EUR)[b] Prohibited agreements and decisions of association; (out of which for cartels)	Fines (in EUR)[b] Abuse of a dominant market position
2012	10,081.30; (0)	1951.21	163.82; (0)	31.71
2013	3414.63; (0)	8943.08	55.52; (0)	145.33
2014	3750,79; (3750,79)	24,441.46	60.94; (60.94)	397.17
2015	745,583.73; (745,583.73)	11,874.79	12,124.73; (12,124.73)	192.94
2016	158,601.62; (0)	136,005.30	2577.27; (0)	2211.08
2017	10,339,034.40; (0)	1951.21	168,016.31; (0)	31.71
2018	295,601.62; (0)	115,725.33	4803.02; (0)	1880.55
2019	1,988,806.81; (0)	–	32,331.61; (0)	–
2020	109,156.11; (109,156.11)	–	1774.10; (1774.10)	–
2021	56,194.65; (49,293.65)	13,443.70	913.65; (801.02)	218.48
2022	1,837,478; (0)	13,444	29,805.67; (0)	218.49
Total	15,547,704.66; (907,784.28)	327,779.38	252,626.64; (14,760.79)	5327.46
Grand total (Restrictive agreements + abuse of dominant position)	15,875,484.04		257,954.10	

Source: Authors' own calculations based on CPC's Annual Reports 2012–2022
[a]All values are nominal values
[b]Calculations are based on the average exchange rate for the relevant year

consistent upward or downward trend. In 2021, there was a notable decrease to just 1 case.

Table 4 presents data on the amounts of fines imposed by the CPC for various categories of offenses over a 10-year period from 2012 to 2022. The data reveals significant fluctuations in fine amounts, indicating varying levels of enforcement and changes in the types of offenses committed.

Table 5 includes two types of violations not covered in Table 3, specifically those that occurred under Article 60 of the Competition Act. First, these violations pertain to the procedure for evaluating concentrations on the following grounds: if a notification of the concentration is not submitted in accordance with Article 15 of the law, or if the concentration is implemented contrary to the law. Second, the section on Other Types of Offenses includes minor offenses, which involve situations where the requested data is not submitted, or where submitted data is incomplete or incorrect, or the conclusions are not acted upon, etc. The grounds for liability for minor offenses are detailed in Article 61 of the Competition Act.

Table 5 Number of misdemeanor decisions with fines (other than those included in Table 3) imposed by the CPC in the period 2012–2022

	2012	2013	2014	2015	2016	2017	2018	2019	2020	2021	2022	Total
Concentrations	3	–	2	–	–	–	–	–	–	1		6
Other types of offenses	–	–	–	–	2	–	1	–	1	–	1	5
Total	*3*	*0*	*2*	*0*	*2*	*0*	*1*	*0*	*1*	*1*	*1*	*11*

Source: Authors' own calculations based on CPC's Annual Reports 2012–2022

Table 6 Fines imposed by CPC, 2012–2022 (other than those in Table 3)[a]

	Fines (in MKD)		Fines (in EUR)[b]	
Year	Concentrations	Other types of offenses	Concentrations	Other types of offenses
2012	257,000	–	4165.40	–
2013	–	–	–	–
2014	1,353,000	–	21,978.60	–
2015	–	–	–	–
2016	–	116,600	–	1888.92
2017	–	–	–	–
2018	–	305,580	–	4951.40
2019	–	–	–	–
2020	–	60,162	–	974.63
2021	307,500	–	4981.50	–
2022	–	857,055	–	13,905.89
Total	1,917,500	1,339,397	31,125.50	21,720.84

Source: Authors' own calculations based on CPC's Annual Reports 2012–2022
[a]All values are nominal values
[b]Calculation based on average exchange rate for the relevant year

Essentially, in relation to the amounts of fines listed in Table 6, it can be observed that, given the lesser severity of these offenses, the CPC adheres to the legal minimum for fines, thus shaping its penal policy accordingly.

8 Judicial Review

According to Article 53(1) of the Competition Act, decisions issued by the CPC in administrative procedure are final. Legal action on instituting an administrative dispute before the competent court may be brought against such decisions. The legal action on instituting an administrative dispute shall be brought within 30 days of receiving the decision, and it shall not defer the enforcement of the decision.

In the judicial system, judicial authority is exercised by the first instance courts, the appellate courts, the Administrative Court, the Higher Administrative Court, and the Supreme Court.[122] In that sense, the administrative judiciary consists of the Administrative Court and the Higher Administrative Court.[123] The two courts are established and exercise judicial authority in the entire territory of the MK and are headquartered in Skopje. The Administrative Court has jurisdiction to rule on the legality of individual acts in electoral procedures, public appointments, and dismissals as mandated by law. It also resolves disputes related to concession and

[122]Law on Courts [2006] Official Gazette of the Republic of Macedonia No 58/06, 62/06, 35/08, 150/10, 83/18, 198/18 and Official Gazette of the Republic of Macedonia No 96/19, Art 22.
[123]ibid., Arts 25 and 25-a.

public procurement contracts involving state authorities, public entities, and municipalities.[124] Additionally, it examines acts of public power holders when no alternative legal protection exists for parties claiming violations of their rights or interests due to administrative actions or omissions.[125] The Higher Administrative Court acts as an appellate authority, reviewing decisions of the Administrative Court, including those related to competition law disputes initially decided by the Administrative Court as a first instance court.[126] Courts must publish legally binding decisions on the court's website within seven days from the day they become final, in a manner established by law.[127]

Additionally, in terms of transparency and monitoring systems for decisions throughout the entire sequence of proceedings, the absence of a publicly accessible platform for monitoring the decisions of the CPC and the courts should be highlighted. Such a sequence would start with a decision in one and the same case at the level of the CPC's decision, followed by the first-instance court (Administrative Court), and ultimately the second-instance court (Higher Administrative Court).

The judicial practice in the field of competition law can be presented in two periods. The first period covers the judicial review of the old Law on the Protection of Competition,[128] which was in force until 2010, while the second period presents the judicial practice according to the new Competition Act enacted in 2010. For the purposes of presenting the court cases from the first period, in accordance with the old law, analyses of law scholars,[129] along with partial and limited data available on the courts' websites, was taken into account.[130] The cited court rulings do not reference any CJEU practice, EU law provisions, or the SAA.

In the case of CPC v ZEGIN, a registered pharmaceutical company based in Skopje, the Administrative Court determined that ZEGIN's acquisition of shares in the "Gradska Apteka" chain, also registered in Skopje, violated the Law on Protection of Competition. The court's decision shows that ZEGIN failed to prove that its participation in the relevant market is 40% or less. The court concluded that total income should be calculated based on the entire retail sale of drugs and auxiliary drugs, rather than only from drugs co-financed by the state on the so-called positive list. It was further determined that drugs on the positive list cannot be considered a separate market. Additionally, the court found that ZEGIN did not provide evidence

---

[124] ibid., Art 34.

[125] Law on Courts, Art 34.

[126] Law on Courts, Art 34-a.

[127] Law on Courts, Art. 99 (5).

[128] Official gazette of the Republic of Macedonia No 4/05, 70/06 and 22/07.

[129] For an overview of the initial period when the old law applied to the court proceedings involving JPKD Komunalec Strumica, Macedonian Drivers Union, and Macedonian Telecom see Svetlicinii (2012a); Svetlicinii (2012b); Svetlicinii (2012c); Svetlicinii (2012d).

[130] Law on Courts, Art 99 (5); Administrative Court (2023). The Law on Courts mandates that courts must publish legally binding decisions on their websites within seven days of their finalization. The decisions of the Administrative Court and the Higher Administrative Court are accessible in the 'decisions' section.

of an analysis regarding planned research for market development, anticipated consumer benefits from price reductions, or proof that the concentration would result in a significant increase in operational efficiency due to ZEGIN's participation.[131]

The Supreme Court of North Macedonia, in the T-Mobile Macedonia case determined that the appeal filed by T-Mobile Macedonia against the decision of the Administrative Court was unfounded.[132] Simultaneously, the Supreme Court upheld the decision of the Administrative Court, which affirmed the CCPC's imposition of a fine on T-Mobile Macedonia. The CPC had imposed the fine based on its findings that T-Mobile Macedonia was charging for services that were not agreed upon or accepted by consumers. The Supreme Court accepted the CPC 's position that the announcement for the voicemail service is part of the service itself and is subject to the chargeable interval. As a result, the caller does not have the option to decide whether to leave a voice message without incurring charges. This means that costs are incurred by the caller, who was not informed in advance that they would be charged, even though the called number was unavailable. T-Mobile argued that, given how the service is offered, there is no abuse of a dominant position, as the service allows the called subscriber to choose whether to activate the 'voicemail' service. Once activated, the caller is charged as if they made a call to the T-Mobile network, while the called subscriber incurs no costs for either activation or listening. T-Mobile also contended that this method of activating and charging for the 'voicemail' service is common among other mobile operators in the T-Mobile Group. However, this argument was not accepted by the CPC or the court, as the CPC had evidence that T-Mobile Hungary uses a different system that aligns more closely with competition protection rules.[133]

In the Cosmofon AD case, the CPC identified an abuse of dominant position by the mobile operator, Cosmofon AD. The operator violated the Law on Protection of Competition by charging callers to a Cosmofon AD subscriber who had activated the "voicemail" service from the moment the voicemail was opened, including the chargeable interval for the voicemail notification. Such behaviour was prohibited by Article 14, paragraph 2, item 1 of the Law on Protection of Competition, as it constituted the direct imposition of unfair selling prices. The CPC's decision was appealed to the Administrative Court, which upheld the CPC's decision. The case was further appealed to the Supreme Court, which confirmed that the challenged judgment was correct and lawful. Neither the court nor the CPC accepted Cosmofon's position that it constitutes an additional retail service in this case. Both maintained the opinion that it is a wholesale service. This case closely resembles the T-Mobile case discussed earlier.[134]

In the field of electricity, an important decision was made in the case of EVN Macedonia, where the CPC determined that EVN Macedonia AD Skopje had abused

[131] Administrative Court of North Macedonia Decision No. 3147/2007.

[132] Supreme Court of North Macedonia Decision No. 249/2010.

[133] Supreme Court of North Macedonia, Decision No. 249/2010.

[134] Commission for the Protection of Competition Decision No. 07-7/2.

its dominant position in the relevant market between 2005 and 2008. The abuse took the form of including a manipulative expense of 6 denars in the monthly electricity bills of tariff consumers, which constituted the imposition of unfair trading conditions prohibited by the Law. The CPC considered this behavior as an offense under Article 47 of the Law on Protection of Competition. Both the Administrative Court and the Supreme Court upheld the CPC's decision, confirming its validity and lawfulness. In this case, EVN Macedonia AD, Skopje argued that there is already a decision by the Constitutional Court on the relevant question, according to which the Instructions for the implementation of unified operations of commercial services in the distribution subsidiaries of PE 'Electrostopanstvo na Makedonija'—Skopje were not found to be unconstitutional. These instructions regulate the cost of 6 denars in item 32. However, the Court and the CPC maintain that, while the proceedings before the Constitutional Court focused on the nature of the manipulative cost and its justification under the Law on Obligation Relations, the CPC concluded that EVN Macedonia AD, Skopje violated the Law on Protection of Competition by charging twice for the same service. The CPC did not address the justification for charging the manipulative cost itself.[135]

From the judicial practice during the second period, specifically following the adoption of the 2010 Competition Act, several notable judicial distinctions can be identified.

In the first case, Makedonski Telecom was required to pay a fine of MKD 1,801,194,000. The decision was confirmed by the verdict of the High Administrative Court. In this case, the Court and the CPC determined that Makedonski Telecom abused its dominant market position by refusing to allow two companies to use an asymmetric digital subscriber line. Makedonski Telecom argued that both the Court and the CPC should have ruled according to the Law on Protection of Competition, rather than the Law against Restriction of Competition. At the time the abuse occurred, the latter law was in effect, but a new law—the Law on Protection of Competition—had been enacted while the proceedings were ongoing. However, the Court and the CPC held that, in accordance with Article 51 of the Law on Protection of Competition, the Law against Restriction of Competition would apply to procedures initiated under the previous legislation.[136]

In the second case, the company for printing, production, and services FENIX PRINT, was required to pay a fine in the amount of MKD 28,188 and the company Evropa 92 Kocani was required to pay a fine in the amount of 1,438,148.00 MKD. The decision was confirmed by the verdict of the High Administrative Court. In this case, both the Court and the CPC found evidence of concerted behaviour between the two entities, as they participated in a cartel. It involved a public procurement procedure in which both entities submitted the same document, raising suspicions of a cartel. It was established that the companies share the same business premises and

[135] Commission for the Protection of Competition Decision No 07/51/1.

[136] High Administrative Court of the Republic of North Macedonia Decision No. 105/2020 of 16.06.2021.

have employees who perform duties for both entities. The argument that an error occurred during the preparation of the public procurement documents was not acceptable to the Court and the CPC, as the responsible individuals in both companies shared the same office, leading to the mix-up.[137]

In the third case, GROZD was required to pay a fine in the amount of MKD 1,930,460. The decision was confirmed by the verdict of the High Administrative Court. In this case, it is undisputed that the plaintiff had concluded business cooperation agreements with distributors during the specified period. The agreements included provisions requiring the buyer to distribute only the seller's products and to adhere to the seller's pricing policy, which applied to all distributors in Macedonia. The CPC and the Administrative Court found that these agreements aimed to restrict competition. The Higher Administrative Court considered the plaintiff's claims that the Administrative Court did not fully establish the facts of the case.[138]

In the fourth case, the association for the protection of musical copyrights ZAMP Skopje was obliged to pay a fine in the amount of MKD 1,748,620.00, while the Association for International Collective Management of Rights from Audiovisual Works AGICOA, Geneva, Switzerland, was obliged to pay a fine in the amount of MKD 4,541,700.00. The decision was confirmed by the High Administrative Court. In this case, the CPC initiated a procedure following a third-party report alleging that ZAMP violated competition law by conditioning discounts under a License Agreement on also signing a General License Agreement, despite the agreements covering different legal matters. The CPC found a misdemeanor offence, imposed a fine, and the court later confirmed the decision. The Higher Administrative Court reviewed the plaintiffs' claims that the CPC had procedural violations and misapplied substantive law, but found these arguments to be unfounded and not impactful on the decision. Additionally, the court dismissed the statute of limitations argument, noting that the time limits for misdemeanor prosecution in competition cases had not expired according to the relevant legal provisions.[139]

9 Private Enforcement of Competition Law

Despite the formal harmonization of its competition law with the EU *acquis*, the Macedonian legislator has not yet implemented provisions related to the compensation of damages caused by competition law violations. Regarding the compensation

[137] High Administrative Court of the Republic of North Macedonia Decision No. 91/2021 of 17.11.2021.

[138] High Administrative Court of the Republic of North Macedonia Decision No. 80/2021 of 06.09.2021.

[139] High Administrative Court of the Republic of North Macedonia Decision No. 86/2021 of 21.10.2021.

for the damage caused, the Competition Act contains a general provision which stipulates that if the damage is caused by any action that constitutes an offense under the Competition Act, the person who suffers damage may seek compensation in accordance with the law.[140]

In Macedonian legislation, the Law on Obligations is a *lex generalis* in terms of damage regulations, and in relation to the procedural aspects for compensation of damages, the provisions of the Law on Civil Procedure apply. However, the provisions of these laws are of a general nature and are not relevant for exercising the specific right to compensation in situations where individuals were harmed by competition law provisions infringement.[141] The collective redress mechanisms in the form of class action are also not included in the Law on Civil Procedure. The lack of special rules in this respect in the Competition Act inevitably deters the harmed parties from initiating court proceedings.[142] Due to this fact, it is recommended to implement a system of specific rules in the foreseeable future that will enable proper compensation for persons who are harmed by anticompetitive practices.

From the analysis of court decisions available on the internet portal of the courts, only one ruling was identified regarding the application of Article 58 of the Competition Act. The decision of the Basic Civil Court in Skopje on September 23, 2019, involved the plaintiff, Makedonski telekom, against the defendant, the Association for the Protection of Copyright and Music Rights.[143] The plaintiff sought compensation for damages amounting MKD 72 million, with Article 58 of the Competition Act being a key ground for the claim. The defendant argued that, given the initiation of proceedings before the Higher Administrative Court related to the decision of the CPC, the plaintiff's claim lacked a basis for compensation until the administrative court proceedings concluded and became legally binding. These administrative court proceedings were crucial in determining the alleged abuse of dominant position by the defendant.

The Basic Civil Court in Skopje accepted the defendant's arguments and rejected the plaintiff's lawsuit as unfounded. Against the judgment of the Basic Civil Court, the plaintiff appealed to the Court of Appeal. On April 1, 2021, the Court of Appeal rejected the appeal as unfounded.[144] This decision was later affirmed by the Supreme Court in a special proceeding initiated as an extraordinary right of the defendant before this court. In its decision from December 21, 2021,[145] the Supreme Court emphasized two key points. First, it stated that in order the decision of the CPC, establishing a violation by the defendant and abuse of a dominant position, to be considered, it must be final and binding. In this case, the procedure against the

[140] Article 58 of the Competition Act stipulates, "If damage is caused by an action that constitutes an offence under this law, the affected person may request compensation in accordance with the law".

[141] Koevski (2022), p. 68.

[142] Koevski (2022), p. 69.

[143] Decision TS-79/18 of 23.9.2019, Basic Civil Court, Skopje.

[144] Decision TSZ-387/20 of 01.4.2020, Court of Appeal, Skopje.

[145] Decision REV. no. 263/2021 of 21.12.2021, Supreme Court.

decision of the CPC was conducted within the framework of the local judiciary, and it is still pending. Thus, the Supreme Court sided with the reasoning of the lower courts. Secondly, although Article 58 of the Competition Act grants the right to request compensation for damage, the Supreme Court emphasized that this request should align with Article 141 of the Law on Obligations. The court argued that while the CPC's decision established the existence of misdemeanor offence, it did not determine the liability for damage. Moreover, both the Supreme Court and the lower courts held that the defendant lacked fault as a basis for liability for damage, rendering Article 141 (1) of the Law on Obligation Relations unfulfilled.

According to our opinion, those court attitudes should be reconsidered, since they are not aligned with the notion of private enforcement of the competition law.

10 Current Trends and Future Challenges to Enforcing Competition Law

Both in terms of potential legislative activities and in the application of existing legislation, it is undeniable that the MK will face significant challenges in the coming period. These challenges encompass a broad spectrum of issues, including private enforcement of competition law, the capabilities of the competent body, the CPC and the financial resources at its disposal. This comprehensive challenge has been addressed in specific segments within this chapter, especially pertaining to the application and implementation of competition law through the decisions of the CPC.

Therefore, in the interest of clarity and conciseness, the authors of this chapter have made a deliberate choice to focus on two primary future challenges. The first of these challenges centers on the promotion and implementation of the leniency program, a concept enshrined in the legislation but currently inactive. The second part of this chapter is dedicated to an in-depth analysis of prospective legislative initiatives aimed at aligning the nation's competition law with the standards and regulations of the EU, thus ensuring harmonization and compliance.

10.1 The Potential for a Leniency Program in the Macedonian Competition Law

The leniency program is a concept that is included in the Competition Act, which is indisputable, but unfortunately, this concept has no practical application.[146] The Competition Act explicitly provides for the concept of exemption or reduction of the

[146] For more on the concept of leniency in Macedonia, see Koevski (2022); Svetlicinii (2012e).

fines (leniency).[147] Also, the Competition Act, in the part titled "fine assessment," it is explicitly stated that the CMM within the CPC treats leniency as a mitigating circumstance in the assessment of the fine.[148]

What should be emphasized is that the leniency program refers only to the detection and prosecution of cartels and not to any other forms of distortion of competition.[149] According to the legal wording of Article 65 of the Competition Act, the CPC for deciding on a misdemeanor offence may grant full exemption from a fine to a company that has recognized its participation in a cartel constituting a violation of Article 59 paragraph (1) item 1) of the Competition Act. This is provided that the company first submits evidence that enables the CPC to initiate a misdemeanor procedure or complete an already initiated procedure with a decision that determines the existence of a misdemeanor offence.

The Competition Act also provides for the concept of a reduction in fines and the conditions that must be met to apply for it. If a company that has admitted its participation in a cartel does not meet the conditions for full exemption from the fine, the fine may be reduced if the company submits relevant evidence of decisive importance for determining the existence of a misdemeanor offence to the CPC.[150]

The 2012 Government Regulation outlines the leniency procedure's phases, including fine exemption requests and eligibility criteria. To obtain a fine exemption under Article 65, paragraph (1), item 1) or 2) of the Competition Act, a company must apply to the CPC, providing specific evidence: a) a statement acknowledging participation in the cartel, as per Article 3 and b) other cartel-related evidence dating back to the cartel's initiation.[151]

Article 5 sets conditions for exemption. The CPC may grant fine exemption under Article 65, paragraph (1), item 1) if it lacked evidence for a misdemeanor procedure. Exemption under Article 65, paragraph (1), item 2) is possible if the CPC lacked evidence, no prior exemption was granted, and the applicant provides compelling evidence dating back to the cartel.[152]

Companies seeking fine exemption under Article 65 of the Competition Act and Regulation 2012 must provide complete and timely information to the CMM. The proposed solution involves a marker system, allowing companies to reserve their

---

[147] Competition Act, Art 65.

[148] Competition Act, Art 64.

[149] Koevski et al. (2021), p. 71.

[150] To qualify for immunity or a reduction in the fine under Article 65, the undertaking must meet the following requirements cumulatively: immediately terminate its participation in the cartel after submitting the request, fully cooperate with the Misdemeanor Commission, submit necessary data promptly, not notify other participants in the cartel about the request for immunity or reduction, not disclose the existence or content of the request prior to submission, except to bodies responsible for sanctioning the cartel outside the Republic of Macedonia, and not destroy, conceal, or falsify relevant evidence used to establish facts of importance for the decision of the Misdemeanor Commission.

[151] Koevski et al. (2021), p. 72.

[152] Koevski et al. (2021), p. 72.

spot for fine exemption by submitting an intention notice. Upon receipt, CMM issues a certificate, preserving the spot for a specified period. If the formal exemption request is submitted within the deadline, it's considered filed on the certificate's issuance date. Failure to meet the deadline allows CMM to dispose of the submitted data. Article 8 of the Regulation outlines the entire CMM procedure.

In practice, a noticeable disparity exists between business operations and the approach of the CPC when it comes to the leniency concept. The research by Koevski, Tushevska Gavrilovikj, and Spasevski (2021) established that the CPC has not made any decisions on exemption from fines or fine reductions under Article 65 of the CPC in the past 10 years. Furthermore, the CPC has not received any request for exemption or reduction of the fine on the basis of cartel detection, i.e., in terms of Article 65 of the CPC, i.e., application for leniency program.[153]

Regarding the research on the attitudes of the business sector towards the leniency program, a questionnaire was sent to over 120 companies registered in the territory of MK. The research focused on gathering information about: (i) whether they have heard of the leniency program; (ii) if they are familiar with the benefits that leniency provides for its users; (iii) if they consider it a useful tool in the fight against cartelism; and (iv) if they would consider using this program. Twenty-seven companies showed willingness to answer the questions. Of these, eighteen had never heard of leniency, and nine companies said they knew the program but had little knowledge of its benefits.[154]

10.2 Future Legislative Expectations in the Process of Aligning Macedonian Competition Law with EU Law

Future transposition activities in domestic competition law must consider key EU documents, including Commission Regulation (EU) 2022/720 and the 2022 Guidelines on Vertical Restraints. These guidelines are vital for evaluating vertical agreements under Article 101 TFEU. Additionally, the Communication on collective agreements for solo self-employed individuals and the Commission Notice on informal guidance (2022/C 381/07) are crucial. These resources guide competition law application in specific cases, ensuring fairness and alignment with EU standards. Their consideration is vital for effective competition law implementation in MK, contributing to the nation's competitive future.

[153] Koevski et al. (2021), p. 78.

[154] Koevski et al. (2021), p. 79.

11 Conclusion

The basis of the competition law framework in MK is found in Article 55 of the Constitution, which promotes "free market and entrepreneurship" and "equal treatment of market participants". The fact that "freedom of the market and entrepreneurship" is one of the fundamental values of the constitutional order of the MK highlights the importance of "free competition" for the Macedonian economy and legal order in the MK.

Over the years since the adoption of the Constitution in 1991, which coincided with the acquisition of independence by the MK, three laws have been adopted regulating the protection of competition, namely: i) the Law against Restrictions of Competition of 1999, ii) the Law on Protection of Competition of 2005, and iii) the Law on Protection of Competition of 2010.

The 2010 Competition Act currently in force (along with its consecutive amendments), as well as the laws and by-laws regimes previously enacted in the field of competition, align with European rules pertaining to the protection of competition. The origin of this obligation lies in Articles 68 and 69 of the SAA, a fundamental document for the MK that regulates the accession process to the EU.

The Macedonian competition law is almost fully aligned with the relevant articles of the TFEU, as well as with other important sources of EU law. Compliance with the competition law regime in MK is noted in the EU Progress Reports for MK for 2022, 2021, and 2020. However, what these reports highlight as a weakness in the Macedonian competition law system is the lack of resources and capacities of the CPC from many different points of view. Namely, the European Commission reports indicate that the CPC is understaffed, leading to limited enforcement capacity. Many of the instruments that are at the CPC's disposal have not been used. The need to increase on-site inspections and the use of the leniency instrument to strengthen enforcement is also emphasized.

The consecutive amendments to the 2010 Competition Act until today, generally refer to issues with administrative nature. More preciously, the changes encompass provisions that regulate conditions that a certain individual must meet in order to be elected either as a president or as a member of the CPC. Additionally, the amendments refer to inter-institutional cooperation in terms of providing documents. In accordance with the competencies of the CPC, in the period of 2019, 2020, 2021 and 2022, the CPC acted in a dozen misdemeanor procedures, which represents a relatively small number of procedures. Based on the research conducted in this chapter we strongly believe that the CPC must focus on enhancing the implementation of procedures for the protection of competition law. The CPC serves as the driving force in the concept of protecting market competition. According to Macedonian law, in relation to the decisions of the CPC, an administrative dispute before the competent court may be brought against such decisions. The competent courts in that sense are the Administrative Court and the Higher Administrative Court.

Part of the entire concept of competition protection involves the question of private enforcement. Namely, it can be noted that this institution is absent in

Macedonian law (of course excluding the content of Article 58 of the Competition Act). In that sense, it should be mentioned that, there are no special rules regulating this mechanism in the Competition Act. From the available data on court internet portals, there is only one case about private enforcement. This case is analysed in this chapter. Of course, very important reasons for that are the legal inaccuracies regarding private enforcement.

The concept of leniency is regulated in accordance with the Competition Act. Unfortunately, from 2010 to 2020, for which data is provided, this concept has not been applied even once. For these reasons, it remains one of the future challenges and main priorities for enforcing competition law to be the application of this concept of leniency together with the need to introduce another equally important mechanism, which is private enforcement. As stated in this research itself, the main weaknesses of the Macedonian competition law system are accentuated by the absence of enforcement modalities and/or capacities for their application.

Finally, the protection of competition in any economy is a systemic issue that requires the involvement of various participants from both the public and private sectors. The key role in connecting them still belongs to the CPC, in accordance with the law, by-laws, and policies for competition protection, growth, and development in any economy, including MK. Given the importance of this issue, the budget should not be a constraint for the Macedonian government. If this situation does not change in terms of efficiency and effectiveness in competition, and if the level of education in business and the public sector regarding competition law does not improve, the conclusions in future reports by the European Commission will be identical every year. All of this implies stagnation in this field and the absence of economic progress for MK.

Table of Cases

Commission for the Protection of Competition

Commission for the Protection of Competition Decision No. U-5 n. 445/2012
Commission for the Protection of Competition Decision No. 09-10/21 of 21.05.2019
Commission for the Protection of Competition Decision no. 09-11/1 of 04.02.2021
Commission for the Protection of Competition Decision no. 09-11/4 of 10.09.2020
Commission for the Protection of Competition Decision No. 09-15/12 of 21.11.2019
Commission for the Protection of Competition Decision No. 09-16/1 of 09.04.2019
Commission for the Protection of Competition Decision no. 09-3/6 of 11.02.2021
Commission for the Protection of Competition Decision no. 09-3/8 of 25.02.2020
Commission for the Protection of Competition Decision no. 09-4/2 of 27.01.2020
Commission for the Protection of Competition Decision no. 09-4/29 of 28.06.2021
Commission for the Protection of Competition Decision no. 09-5/1 of 21.01.2021
Commission for the Protection of Competition Decision no. 07/51/1
Commission for the Protection of Competition Decision no. 07-7/2

Commission for the Protection of Competition Decision no. 09-2/6 of 20.4.2022
Commission for the Protection of Competition Decision no. 09-23 of 14.7.2022.
Commission for the Protection of Competition Decision no.9-11 of 15.3.2022
Commission for the Protection of Competition Decision no. 09-30 of 14.7.2022
Commission for the Protection of Competition Decision no. 09-24/1 of 20.4.2022
Commission for the Protection of Competition Decision no. 09-11/2 of 15.3.2022

North Macedonian Courts

Administrative Court of North Macedonia Decision No. 3147/2007. Available at: http://kzk.gov.mk/wp-content/uploads/2019/06/УС-Комисијата-против-Зеги н-ДОО-Скопје.pdf. Accessed 17 February 2025

Basic Civil Court, Skopje, Decision TS-79/18 of 23.9.2019, Available at: https://shorturl.at/FW458. Accessed 17 February 2025

Court of Appeal, Skopje, Decision TSZ-387/20 of 01.4.2020, Available at: https://shorturl.at/emnos. Accessed 17 February 2025

High Administrative Court of the Republic of North Macedonia Decision No. 105/2020 of 16.06.2021

High Administrative Court of the Republic of North Macedonia Decision No. 91/2021 of 17.11.2021

High Administrative Court of the Republic of North Macedonia Decision No. 80/2021 of 06.09.2021

High Administrative Court of the Republic of North Macedonia Decision No. 86/2021 of 21.10.2021

Supreme Court of North Macedonia Decision No. 249/2010

Supreme Court of North Macedonia, Decision No. 249/2010

Supreme Court of North Macedonia, Decision REV. no. 263/2021 of 21.12.2021, Available at: https://shorturl.at/nqwY7. Accessed 17 February 2025.

Table of Legislation

European Union

Commission Regulation (EU) 2022/720 of 10 May 2022 on the application of Article 101(3) of the Treaty on the Functioning of the European Union to categories of vertical agreements and concerted practices (Text with EEA relevance) [2022] OJ L 134/4

Council Regulation (EC) No 1/2003 of 16 December 2002 on the implementation of the rules on competition laid down in Articles 81 and 82 of the Treaty (Text with EEA relevance) [2003] OJ L 1/1

Commission Regulation (EC) No 773/2004 of 7 April 2004 relating to the conduct of proceedings by the Commission pursuant to Articles 81 and 82 of the EC Treaty (Text with EEA relevance) [2004] OJ L 123/18

Council Regulation (EC) No 139/2004 of 20 January 2004 on the control of concentrations between undertakings (the EC Merger Regulation) (Text with EEA relevance) [2004] OJ L 24/1

Council Regulation (EC) No 1/2003 of 16 December 2002 on the implementation of the rules on competition laid down in Articles 81 and 82 of the Treaty [2003] OJ L1/1.

Stabilisation and Association Agreement between the European Communities and their Member States, of the one part, and the former Yugoslav Republic of Macedonia, of the other part [2004] OJ L 84/13

North Macedonia

Constitution of the Republic of North Macedonia was adopted on 17 November 1991

Law against Restrictions of Competition [1999] Official gazette of the Republic of Macedonia No. 80/1999

Law on Amendments and Supplements to the Law on Protection of Competition [2011] Official Gazette of the Republic of North Macedonia No 136/11

Law on Amendments and Supplements to the Law on Protection of Competition [2014] Official Gazette of the Republic of North Macedonia No 41/14

Law on Amendments and Supplements to the Law on the Protection of Competition [2016] Official Gazette of the Republic of North Macedonia No 53/16

Law on Amendments and Supplements to the Law on the Protection of Competition [2018] Official Gazette of the Republic of North Macedonia No 83/18

Law on Courts [2006] Official Gazette of the Republic of Macedonia No 58/06, 62/06, 35/08, 150/10, 83/18, 198/18 and Official Gazette of the Republic of Macedonia No 96/19

Law on Courts [2006] Official Gazette of the Republic of Macedonia No 58/06, 62/06, 35/08, 150/10, 83/18, 198/18 and Official Gazette of the Republic of Macedonia No 96/19, Arts 25 and 25-a

Law on General Administrative Procedure [2015] Official Gazette of the Republic of Macedonia No. 124/2015 and 65/2018

Law on Misdemeanors [2019] Official Gazette of the Republic of North Macedonia No. 96/2019.

Law on Protection of Competition [2006] Official Gazette of the Republic of Macedonia No 4/05, 70/06 and 22/07

Law on Protection of Competition [2010] Official Gazette of the Republic of Macedonia Nos 145/10, 136/11, 41/14, 53/16, 83/18 and 208/2024

Macedonian Criminal Code [1996] Official Gazette of the Republic of Macedonia No 37/96, 80/99, 4/02, 43/03, 19/04, 81/05, 60/06, 73/06, 7/08, 139/08, 114/09, 51/11, 135/11, 185/11, 142/12, 166/12, 55/13, 82/13, 14/14, 27/14, 28/14, 41/14, 115/14, 132/14, 160/14, 199/14, 196/15, 226/15, 97/17 и 248/18 and Official Gazette of the Republic of Macedonia No 36/23

Rules for the internal organization of the commission for the protection of competition, available at http://kzk.gov.mk/wp-content/uploads/2022/12/Pravilnik-za-vnatreshna-organizanza-na-KZK.pdf. Accessed 16 February 2025.

References

Administrative Court (2023) Judicial Portal of the Republic of North Macedonia. Available at: http://www.vsrm.mk/wps/portal/usskopje/sud/odluki/!ut/p/z1/jZDBCoJAEIafxYNXZ8K0tdtaJpkVZJLtJTRsM8wttXz9LLsEpc1thu_jZ35gEADLwnvCwzIRWZjW-5bpOwPHes8cobucDQjSuW-5vj11tIUKmxeg2_0-khm6xFuZSC0ckLVB0Z4gsH_8FuDp44-h-PZbgM581hXRAC0vOsB4KqKmLppFKuHA8vgQ53Gu3PL6fCzLSzGUUcaqqhQuBE9jZS_OMn5TjqIoIfgkwSuucDn7foAnLb27B0ol6QEyjVCC/dz/d5/L0lHSkovd0RNQU5rQUVnQSEhLzROVkUvZW4!/. Accessed 16 Feb 2025

Commission (2021) North Macedonia Report 2021. SWD(2021) 294 final

Commission (2022) North Macedonia Report 2022. SWD(2022) 337 final

Commission for the Protection of Competition (2010) Annual report on the work of the Commission for the Protection of Competition for 2010. Available at http://kzk.gov.mk/category/godishni-izveshtai/. Accessed 16 Feb 2025

Commission for the Protection of Competition (2019) Annual report on the work of the Commission for the Protection of Competition for 2019. Available at http://kzk.gov.mk/category/godishni-izveshtai/. Accessed 16 Feb 2025

Commission for the Protection of Competition (2020) Annual report on the work of the Commission for the Protection of Competition for 2020. Available at http://kzk.gov.mk/category/godishni-izveshtai/. Accessed 16 Feb 2025

Commission for the Protection of Competition (2021) Annual report on the work of the Commission for the Protection of Competition for 2021. Available at http://kzk.gov.mk/category/godishni-izveshtai/. Accessed 16 Feb 2025

Commission for the Protection of Competition (2022) Annual report on the work of the Commission for the Protection of Competition for 2022. Available at http://kzk.gov.mk/category/godishni-izveshtai/. Accessed 16 Feb 2025

European Council (2005) Република Македонија на патот кон ЕУ. Available at: https://www.sobranie.mk/r-makedonija-na-pat-kon-eu.nspx. Accessed 7 Oct 2023

Gal MS (2003) Competition policy for small market economies. Harvard University Press, Cambridge

Georgievski S, Cenevska I, Presova D (2014) Application of the Law of the European Union in the Republic of Macedonia, "European Union Law Application by the National Courts of the EU-Membership Aspirant Countries from South-East Europe". Centre for SEELS

ISO (2025) MK: North Macedonia. Available at: https://www.iso.org/obp/ui/#iso:code:3166:MK. Accessed 16 Feb 2025

Koevski G (2022) Compensatory damages from the viewpoint of the competition law in the European Union and the Republic of North Macedonia. Revija Kopaonička škola prirodnog prava, Broj 1/2022, Godina IV

Koevski G et al (2021) The concept of leniency in the Republic of North Macedonia, EU and comparative law issues and challenges series (ECLIC 5), pp 60–84

Regulation on Closer Conditions for Contracts of Minor Importance [2012] Official Gazette of the Republic of Macedonia no. 44/12

Regulation on Closer Conditions for Group Exemption of Certain Types of Horizontal Agreements for Specialization [2012] Official Gazette of the Republic of Macedonia no. 44/12

Regulation on Closer Conditions for Group Exemption of Certain Types of Contracts for Transfer of Technology, for License, or for Know-How [2012] Official Gazette of the Republic of Macedonia no. 44/12
Regulation on Closer Conditions for Group Exemption of Certain Types of Contracts for Research and Development [2012] Official Gazette of the Republic of Macedonia no. 44/12
Regulation on Closer Conditions for Release or Reduction of Fines and Procedures under which the Commission for Decision-Making after an Offence Decides on Release or Reduction of Fines [2012] Official Gazette of the Republic of Macedonia no. 44/12
Regulation on Group Exemption of Certain Types of Contracts for the Distribution and Servicing of Motor Vehicles [2012] Official Gazette of the Republic of Macedonia no. 44/12
Regulation on Group Exemption of Certain Types of Insurance Contracts (2012) Official Gazette of the Republic of Macedonia no:44/12
Regulation on Group Exemption of Certain Types of Vertical Contracts [2012] Official Gazette of the Republic of Macedonia no. 44/12
Regulation on the Form and Content of the Notice of Concentration and the Necessary Documentation to be Submitted Together with the Notice [2012] Official Gazette of the Republic of Macedonia no. 44/12
Svetlicinii A (2012a) The Macedonian High Administrative Court upholds the Competition Authority's infringement decision concerning an abuse of dominant position on the funeral services market (JPKD Komunalec Strumica). e-Competitions May 2012, Art. N° 49033
Svetlicinii A (2012b) The Macedonian High Administrative Court upholds the CPC's infringement decision finding an abuse of dominant position on the funeral services market (JPKD Komunalec Strumica), e-Competitions May 2012, Art. N° 49153
Svetlicinii A (2012c) The Macedonian High Administrative Court upholds the decision of the Competition Authority concerning anticompetitive practices on the market for mandatory technical certification of motor vehicles (Macedonian Drivers Union), e-Competitions November 2012, Art. N° 50562
Svetlicinii A (2012d) The Macedonian High Administrative Court upholds the decision of the Macedonian Competition Authority prosecuting the incumbent telecom operator for establishing high prices for its digital lines leased to the rival Internet providers (Macedonian Telecom), e-Competitions November 2012, Art. N° 50877
Svetlicinii A (2012e), The Macedonian Govement regulates leniency under the new competition act, e-Competitions March 2012, Art. N° 47333
Tushevska B (2020) Competition law in the Republic of North Macedonia - 20 years of Competition law in Republic of North Macedonia. pravni Vjesnik, god. 36 br. 3-4

Goran Koevski is a Law Professor and Researcher at the Iustinianus Primus Faculty of Law, Ss. Cyril and Methodius University, offering 30 years' continuous experience in developing and reforming business law in North Macedonia. He is involved in improving national business environment by actively participating in background examination of the underlying policies and the drafting of legislative acts directly related to business law. He has been conducting research visits at many renown universities and institutes such as Columbia University School of Law in New York City, etc. He lectures company law, commercial law, competition law and corporate governance courses on graduate, postgraduate and doctoral level.

Borka Tushevska Gavrilovikj is a Full Professor at the Faculty of Law at the state university Goce Delchev in the Republic of North Macedonia. She is a lawyer with a master's thesis and a doctorate in the field of business law. In her academic career, she wrote several scientific and professional papers, two monographs and two university textbooks. In the last decade, she has participated in several scientific research projects, scientific and professional debates, workshops, etc. In the last few years, her academic occupation refers to competition law and competition policy.

Darko Spasevki is a Full Professor at Iustinianus Primus Faculty of Law, Ss. Cyril and Methodius University in Skopje, Macedonia, and has been with the faculty since 2008. He teaches Business Law at the undergraduate level and International Business Law, Bankruptcy Law, Business Law Applied Program, and E-Commerce Law at the postgraduate level. His business law courses also cover competition law. Prof. Spasevski has undertaken study visits to prestigious institutions worldwide, including Ludwig Maximilian University of Munich, Leibniz University of Hanover, University of Turin, Civil Law Foundation in Paris, Moscow State University "Lomonosov," Universität des Saarlandes, Faculty of Law in Podgorica, Weiser Center for Europe and Eurasia, and William Davidson Institute at the University of Michigan. He is an alumnus of the DAAD (Germany) and State Department (USA).

Competition Law and Policy in Serbia

Veljko Milutinović and Vuk Leković

1 Introduction

This chapter presents a brief history, trend of development, state of alignment with the European Union ("EU") and other interesting aspects of competition law enforcement in Serbia. Some particularly illuminating cases will be discussed, to show how the relatively young Commission for Protection of Competition (*Komisija za zaštitu konkurencije* "CPC")[1] has grown, matured and become a relevant player in Serbian business and policy-making.

The purpose of the chapter is to introduce the reader to the workings of a relatively young, Western Balkan competition authority, and the challenges it faces towards becoming a fully EU-compatible National Competition Authority. As will be seen below, while the system is largely aligned with the EU system, there are some national peculiarities, particularly in the spheres of extraterritorial merger control and the still-existing prior notification/individual exemption regime. The chapter will conclude with general trends and future challenges facing the CPC and the Serbian competition law system.

The chapter is divided into eleven sections, including the present Introduction. In Sect. 2, a brief account will be given of the historical development of competition law in Serbia. In Sect. 3, the relationship between the Serbian legal system and Serbian competition law with EU law will be explained. Section 4 will be dedicated to the institutional and normative framework that governs Serbian competition

[1] https://www.kzk.org.rs.

V. Milutinović
Faculty of Business Studies and Law, Union Nikola Tesla University, Belgrade, Serbia

V. Leković (✉)
Gecić Law Firm, Belgrade, Serbia

J. Pecotić Kaufman et al. (eds.), *Competition Law and Policy in the Western Balkans*, European Union and its Neighbours in a Globalized World 22,
https://doi.org/10.1007/978-3-031-93756-9_7

enforcement, while Sect. 5 will discuss and elaborate the national specifics that differ from the EU competition *acquis* or that have been erased/amended in the process of Europeanization. Section 6 will be devoted to the application of national and EU competition rules by the competition agencies and discussion of the most significant cases. Meanwhile, Sect. 7 will deal with some enforcement and fining statistics, to give a quantitative image of the situation in Serbia. Section 8 will address issues related to judicial review of competition authority decisions, while Sect. 9 will deal with private enforcement. Section 10 will lay out some current trends and future challenges to enforcing competition law, while a conclusion will be offered in Sect. 11.

2 Historical Development of Competition Law in Serbia

While the current Competition Act harks back to 2005, with a new law in 2009 and minor amendments in 2013, the idea that competition should be fair and open is quite an old one in Serbian (previously Yugoslav) legal thinking.

The very first Constitution of the post-World War II Communist Yugoslavia (1946) states, in its Article 18(4), that:

> The existence of private monopolistic organizations, such as cartels, syndicates, trusts and similar organizations formed for the purposes of dictating prices, monopolizing the market and damaging the interests of the people's economy is prohibited.

Thus, it is clear that the framers of the Constitution must have been aware of the dangers of monopolies and cartels. It is notable that the provision prohibited *private* monopolies and cartels. Thus, it did not fetter the authority of the central planning organs in making *public* monopolies. Throughout its existence, however, Communist Yugoslavia aimed at maintaining some form of competition, mainly through the competition of state-owned (or, to use the correct terminology, state or socially owned) undertakings. In the subsequent Constitutions of 1963 and 1974, explicit anti-monopoly provisions were suspiciously absent. Yet, a prohibition on contracts leading to or exploiting a monopoly reappeared in the Law on Obligations, in 1978 and which, in its relevant parts, remains valid law to this day.[2]

Prohibitions on monopolies made a comeback in the Constitution of Serbia of 1990,[3] and the Constitution of the Federal Republic of Yugoslavia of 1992 (the "rump" Yugoslavia that lasted from 1992 to 2003, consisting only of Serbia and

[2] Law on Obligations (1978) Official Journal of the SFRY, nos. 29/78, 39/85, 45/89-decision of the Constitutional Court and no. 57/89, Official Journal of the FRY no. 31/93, Official Journal of Serbia-Montenegro no. 1/2003 – Constitutional Treaty and the Official Gazette of the Republic of Serbia no. 18/2020) Article 14.

[3] Art 64(3) of the Constitution of Serbia (1990) made the creation of monopolistic positions unconstitutional.

Montenegro).[4] The current Serbian Constitution of 2006 contains a similar prohibition in Article 84.

It was not until 1996 that the first anti-monopoly legislation was passed. It was called the Antimonopoly Law, and was enacted at the federal level, to implement the constitutional prohibition on monopolies:

> The first Antimonopoly Commission was established in 1999, pursuant to the Antimonopoly Law. Practically, the implementation of this law had been postponed until the setting up of the Antimonopoly Commission. The Antimonopoly Commission was established as an administrative body of a collective nature, attached to the Federal Ministry for Internal Trade of the former Federal Republic of Yugoslavia. The president and six members were appointed and dismissed by the federal government. Therefore, the Antimonopoly Commission was not considered an independent and autonomous entity, but rather an administrative organ of the state administration.
>
> The Antimonopoly Commission also comprised a Technical Service and was entrusted, inter alia, with issuing decisions regarding the abuse of monopolistic and dominant position, and evaluation of the existence of a monopolistic agreement.
>
> Overall, due to several unsolved material issues and procedural difficulties, the first Antimonopoly Commission was practically inoperable. It ceased its activities on 4 February 2003, when the Constitutional Charter of the State Union of Serbia and Montenegro came into force. It continued to exist as the state administrative body of the Republic of Serbia, and its Technical Service was taken over by the Ministry of Trade, Tourism, and Services of the Republic of Serbia (currently the Ministry of Internal and External Trade), within which it continued to operate as the Antimonopoly Department.[5]

The vaguely worded "monopolistic" situations gave way, in 2005, to the first EU-based Competition Act ("2005 Act"),[6] which copied substantive EU law almost verbatim, especially what are now Articles 101 and 102 of the Treaty on the Functioning of the EU ("TFEU"), and some of the relevant EU case law. Likewise, the substantive EU law on mergers was transposed into Serbian law by the same act. The 2005 Act also established the CPC, which is operational to this day. As will be seen below, the major difference with the EU model, and a major flaw in the first law, was that the CPC could not issue fines on its own. Instead, it had to go through the misdemeanour court system, which made fining all but impossible. This mistake was corrected in the 2009 Competition Act ("2009 Act"),[7] which maintained most of the substantive provisions of the 2005 Act, while making major improvements in terms of procedure and remedies. Minor amendments were also made in 2013, to improve the functioning of the CPC. Interestingly, while the Antimonopoly Commission never really did anything of note, it did provide the first employees of what would become the CPC.

[4] Article 74(2) of the Constitution of the Federal Republic of Yugoslavia (1992) contained an almost identical prohibition as in the Serbian Constitution of 1990.

[5] Milutinović and Jovanić (2010), pp. 80–81.

[6] Competition Act [2005] *Official Gazette of the Republic of Serbia*, No. 79/2005.

[7] Competition Act [2009] Official Gazette of the Republic of Serbia, Nos 1/2009 and 95/2013 (hereafter 2009 Act).

In addition, it is noteworthy that in Serbia antitrust infringements are recognized in criminal legislation. Namely, the Penal Code[8] stipulates two criminal offences related to antitrust infringements: (i) Article 228—Abuse Concerning Public Procurement, and (ii) Article 229—Conclusion of a Restrictive Agreement. In both cases the offender shall be punished with imprisonment of 6 months to 5 years.

3 Relationship of Serbian Competition Law with the EU Law

The Stabilisation and Association Agreement ("SAA") is an international treaty which entered into force on September 1, 2013, granting Serbia the status of an associated country to the EU.[9] The two most significant commitments that Serbia has taken over with the signing of the SAA are to (i) establish a free trade zone and (ii) align domestic legislation with the EU. Serbia agreed to ensure that its existing laws and future legislation will gradually be made compatible with the EU *Acquis* and that such laws will be properly implemented and enforced. In that vein, one of the areas which should be harmonized is competition law and policy. Both sides are bound by competition rules based on EU law, relating to behavior that may affect trade between the EU and Serbia. In other words, to foster economic cooperation and attract investors from the EU, it is inevitable to establish a level playing field that should be equal for all undertakings.

In particular, Article 73(1) of the SAA stipulates that the following are incompatible with the proper functioning of this Agreement, insofar as they may affect trade between the EU and Serbia:

(i) all agreements between undertakings, decisions by associations of undertakings and concerted practices between undertakings that have as their object or effect the prevention, restriction or distortion of competition;
(ii) abuse by one or more undertakings of a dominant position in the territories of the Community or Serbia as a whole or in a substantial part thereof;
(iii) any State aid which distorts or threatens to distort competition by favouring certain undertakings or certain products.

Paragraph 2 sets forth that any practices contrary to Article 73 shall be assessed based on criteria arising from the application of the competition rules applicable in the EU, in particular from what are now Articles 101, 102, 106 and 107 of the TFEU and interpretative instruments adopted by the EU institutions. Therefore, it

[8] Penal Code [2005] Official Gazette of the Republic of Serbia, Nos 85/2005, 88/2005 - cor., 107/2005 - cor., 72/2009, 111/2009, 121/2012, 104/2013, 108/2014, 94/2016, 35/2019 and 94/2024.

[9] Stabilisation and Association Agreement between the European Communities and their Member States of one part, and the Republic of Serbia, of the other part [2013] L 278/16.

unequivocally confirms that Serbian courts and the CPC are obliged to follow the case law of the European Commission ("EC"), the General Court and the Court of Justice in their decisions and judgments concerning the abuse of dominant position and restrictive agreement cases. It is important to note that Serbia does not have separate sets of rules for cross-border and purely internal cases. According to Article 2 of the 2009 Act, the competition rules apply to conduct which has an effect on trade in Serbia. Thus, cases with an international dimension are covered, provided that there is also an effect on the Serbian market.

Considering the obligation stemming from Article 73 of the SAA, it is commonplace for the CPC to rely on EU case law as a crucial point of reference in its decisions. Reference to EU case law is also very helpful for undertakings, their advisors and a broader audience to become more familiar with the rich and longstanding practice of the EC and the EU courts, having in mind the relatively nascent nature of CPC which is still *de facto* constituting itself through its everyday practice, often facing a lack of experience in more complex investigations.

Regarding the abuse of dominance position cases, in *Niš Ekspres,*[10] discussed further below, the CPC cited - the *1998 Football World Cup*,[11] in determining how the party in question imposed unfair trading conditions through the discrimination of end users. Also, in *Inter Tours Plus*, which concerns the exploitation of end users by charging unreasonably high prices, the CPC referred to (i) *United Brands Company vs. Commission* and (ii) *Scandlines Sverige AB vs. Port of Helsingborg.*[12] Another abuse of dominance case where the CPC referred to EU case law is the *Frikom* case, discussed below. In ascertaining that the party in question imposed on its downstream counterparties several anti-competitive provisions aiming to exclude its competitors from the market, the CPC cited (i) *Van den Bergh Foods Ltd* and (ii) *Langnese-Iglo GmbH.*[13]

Concerning restrictive agreement cases, it is noteworthy that the CPC has a valid track record in catching and prosecuting resale price maintenance ("RPM") provisions.[14] This type of infringement is by far the most common type of cases conducted by the CPC in comparison to abuse of dominance and cartels. In all RPM cases, the CPC referred to the EU Vertical regulation[15] in order to justify that RPM provisions are considered 'hardcore' vertical restrictions that do not enjoy a

[10]Decision no. 5/0-02-290/2020-3 of 24 December 2021.

[11]Commission Decision of 20 July 1999, *1998 Football World Cup,* Case IV/36.888.

[12]Decision no. 5/0-02-90/2017-131 of 23 October 2017; Judgment of 14 February 1978, *United Brands v Commission*, C-27/76, ECLI:EU:C:1978:22; Decision of 23 July 2004, *Scandlines Sverige AB v Port of Helsingborg,* Case COMP/A.36.568/D3.

[13]Decision no. 5/0-02-329/2012-16 of 19 November 2021.

[14]Decision no. 4/0-01-65/2022-11 of 19 August 2022, *S1;* Decision no. 4/0-01-176/2021-35 of 2 July 2021, *Comtrade*; Decision no. 4/0-01-177/2021-26 of 2 July 2021, *Roaming*; Decision no. 4/0-02-89/2017-31 of 1 December 2017, *N Sport.*

[15]Commission Regulation (EU) No 330/2010 of 20 April 2010 on the application of Article 101(3) of the Treaty on the Functioning of the European Union to categories of vertical agreements and concerted practices [2010] Commission Regulation (EU) No 330/2010.

block exemption under the said regulation. Moreover, in *S1*, *Roaming* and *Comtrade*,[16] the main reason for initiating the probe was that prices of consumer electronic products had been 13% higher in Serbia than in the EU. Based on this, the CPC suspected that the parties, present on the upstream market, imposed RPM provisions and caused significantly higher retail prices in Serbia, which led to an investigation, culminating in a finding of infringement with, sadly, token fines.

4 Institutional and Normative Framework of Competition Authority in Serbia

4.1 Powers of the Authority

The CPC is imbued with roughly the same powers as the EC when pursuing competition cases. To be more specific, the CPC is authorized to investigate, prosecute, and fine undertakings for infringements of the competition rules, i.e. antitrust and merger control but not state aid. It is also authorized to impose behavioural and, exceptionally, structural remedies.

The power to investigate includes the power to request information from the parties, as well as from third parties and government authorities.[17] It also includes the power to conduct announced inspections on site,[18] as well as unannounced inspections ('dawn raids')[19] which may, exceptionally, include searches outside of office premises.[20] Strictly speaking, all investigations of infringements are launched *ex officio*,[21] in the sense that, even if the CPC acts based on a complaint, the complainant is not a party,[22] and merely has the right to be informed not to participate in the proceedings. All investigations are launched by the President of the CPC.[23]

The power to prosecute means the power to determine whether an infringement has occurred. This is done by looking at the evidence collected from the parties and/or third parties, as well as considering any submissions from the parties. This work is performed by the case handlers, in cooperation with the Member of the Council appointed as rapporteur, who then together prepare a report and a draft decision for the Council.

[16] Decision no. 4/0-01-176/2021-35 of 2 July 2021, *Comtrade*; Decision no. 4/0-01-177/2021-26 of 2 July 2021, *Roaming*.

[17] 2009 Act, Arts 44, 48 and 49.

[18] 2009 Act, Art 52.

[19] 2009 Act, Art 53.

[20] 2009 Act, Art 54(3).

[21] 2009 Act, Art 35.

[22] 2009 Act, Art 33(2).

[23] 2009 Act, Art 35(2).

The power to impose penalties and remedies rests with the Council.[24] By default, every finding of infringement must result in fines, which amount to up to 10% of the annual turnover of the guilty undertakings in Serbia in the previous calendar year.[25] It may also result in behavioural remedies, the most common of which is the cease-and-desist remedy,[26] ordering the undertakings not to continue or repeat the impugned behavior. Behavioural and even structural remedies may also be accepted in a commitment decision, where the Council accepts commitments by the parties in lieu of a finding of infringements and pauses the proceedings,[27] to observe the behaviour of the parties. In extreme cases, where fines and behavioural remedies are insufficient, in the sense that the very structure of an undertaking creates anticompetitive results, the extreme measure of structural remedies (e.g. the breakup of a company) may be imposed.[28]

As well as all these final, definitive measures, the CPC has the power to impose interim measures to prevent imminent irreparable damage,[29] as well as to charge procedural penalties (similar but not identical to periodic penalty payments), for non-compliance with orders, e.g., to provide information.[30]

Last but not least, the CPC has the power to grant immunity and leniency from fines to cartel members who volunteer information that the CPC could not otherwise obtain or could obtain with great difficulty,[31] in a manner very similar to the one seen at the EU level.

4.2 Internal Organization and Election

The Serbian legislator has opted for a collective decision-making body, instead of a single director. Thus, decisions on infringements, and phase-two merger decisions, as well as on some budgetary and soft law issues are made by the Council of the CPC (*Savet Komisije za zaštitu konkurencije*).[32] Why the body was not simply called the Commission (*Komisija*) with five Commissioners (*Komesari*), is not clear, but this paradoxical naming has remained from the original 2005 Act until today.

The Council of the CPC consists of five members, of which at least two must be lawyers and at least two economists.[33] They are appointed by the Parliament for a

[24] 2009 Act, Art 22(1).
[25] 2009 Act, Art 68.
[26] 2009 Act, Art 59(1).
[27] 2009 Act, Art 58.
[28] 2009 Act, Art 59(3).
[29] 2009 Act, Art 56.
[30] 2009 Act, Art 70.
[31] 2009 Act, Art 69.
[32] 2009 Act, Art 22(2).
[33] 2009 Act, Art 23(2).

five-year term, which can be renewed indefinitely, upon an open competition, where qualified individuals (those with experience in competition or EU law matters, according to the law) are interviewed by a parliamentary committee and then voted on by the plenum of the Parliament. The President, while a member of the Council, is appointed from a separate list, whereby candidates for the Council must state in their application if they are also applying for the position of President, or only for the position of President.[34] The institution of the President of the CPC was introduced via the 2009 Act. The original, 2005 Act had the institution of President of the Council of the CPC, who was elected by the Council itself.[35] Thus, the position of the President was much weaker under the original regime, in the sense of being dependent on the consent of the Council. Thus, decision-making was more democratic.

The President of the CPC presides over the sessions of the Council, as a first among equals and does not have a deciding vote.[36] On a day-to-day basis, the cases are managed by the Expert Service, which should be under the direction of the Secretary of the CPC.[37] In practice, this post has been vacant for more than a decade, and the President acts as the *de facto* head of the Expert Service, through his exclusive power to hire, fire and impose disciplinary measures on Expert Service staff. The Expert Service staff need to meet the same basic criteria as members of the Civil Service, even though they are not members of it and their labour relations with the CPC are regulated by the general labour rules.[38] They also follow the hierarchy used by the Civil Service, with the same titles (Advisor, Senior Advisor, etc.).

4.3 Procedure

The powers of the President of the CPC are enormous, with a great concentration in the hands of one person. For one, the President decides all phase-one merger cases (which means almost all of the merger cases) alone.[39] The President alone has the power to initiate proceedings and order dawn raids, without consulting the Council. As was stated above, through the power to hire, fire and impose discipline on the Expert Service, the President *de facto* controls most of the procedures.

Due to the ostensible independence of the Expert Service, Members of the Council are usually brought before a *fait accompli* even in cases where they are involved. Apart from the President, all four common Members work as *rapporteurs*

[34] 2009 Act, Art 23(4).
[35] 2005 Act, Art 46.
[36] 2009 Act, Art 25(4).
[37] 2009 Act, Art 26(3).
[38] 2009 Act, Art 26(2) and (3).
[39] 2009 Act, Art 37(2).

in individual cases of suspected infringement and phase-two merger control.[40] The cases are assigned by the President. The Members report to the Council on the progress of cases and make recommendations on what decisions should be taken. In practice, how much power a rapporteur will have over the case handlers in the cases allocated to him or her depends on his or her personal relations and political weight. It also depends on whether they receive support from the President.

All final decisions on infringements and phase-two merger control are made collectively, by a simple majority of the Members of the Council. For a session to be valid, a majority of the total Members must be present at the Council session. As political appointees who change over time, they often act as a counterbalance to the permanence of the Expert Service.

The pre-procedure is controlled entirely by the President. When a suspected infringement needs to be investigated, he or she consults the head of the sector which has competence (infringements or mergers), plus any other persons he may have in his or her confidence, including, at times, individual Council Members. The President is the sole decision-maker as to whether to initiate proceedings and, if so, what fact-finding measures are appropriate, including, if he or she deems it necessary, dawn raids. Proceedings for infringement are opened by a decision of the President and closed by a decision of the Council. The Council may decide that there is an infringement, that there is no infringement or that the proceedings should be paused and commitments from the parties be accepted. The amount of the fine and the scope of any other remedies (behavioural or structural) is determined by the Council, normally at the suggestion of the rapporteur and the Expert Service.

The procedure itself is a hybrid of the Competition Act and the Law on General Administrative Procedure ("LGAP"),[41] which acts as a subsidiary law for all matters not explicitly regulated by the 2009 Act.[42] The LGAP limits the powers of the CPC in practice, by providing parties with rights such as the right to be heard, the right to impartiality, the right to a reasonable length of proceedings and other rights that are not regulated or not well-regulated by the 2009 Act.

Under the Law on Administrative Review and the 2009 Act,[43] administrative judicial review falls before the Administrative Court, for all final decisions of the CPC. From the Administrative Court, an extraordinary legal remedy exists before the Court of Cassation, acting as the supreme court of the land. In practice, the review of the courts is limited to matters of procedure, and the substance of competition claims is rarely mentioned and even then indirectly, whereby it is presented as a failure to adequately collect evidence.

[40] 2009 Act, Art 25(1).

[41] Law on General Administrative Procedure [2016] Official Gazette of the Republic of Serbia Nos 18/2016, 95/2018 – authentic interpretation and 2/2023 – decision of the Constitutional Court.

[42] 2009 Act, Art 34.

[43] Law on Administrative Review [2009] *Official Gazette of the Republic of Serbia* No. 111/2009; 2009 Act, Art 72.

Table 1 Dawn raids carried by the CPC for the period 2012–2021

Year	Number of dawn raids
2012–2014	/
2015	4
2016	/
2017	10
2018	11
2019	2
2020	18
2021	6
2022	/
Total	51

Source: Authors' own calculation based on CPC Annual Reports (2013, 2014, 2015, 2016, 2017, 2018, 2019, 2020, 2021)

4.4 Dawn Raids and Fines

The original 2005 Act did not allow for dawn raids to be conducted by the CPC acting alone. Instead, the CPC would have to obtain a judicial warrant for such a raid.[44] Under the current law, the CPC carries out dawn raids on its own authority,[45] with judicial warrants required solely for private premises and even then only when the owner of the premises objects to the raid.[46] The assistance of the police may be sought and obtained.[47] The power to conduct dawn raids is used by the CPC extensively and dawn raids have, in recent years, become more of a norm than an exception. Namely, between 2012 and 2022, the CPC carried out 51 dawn raids (see Table 1).

As far as fines are concerned, the 2009 Act contained a provision similar to the EU one, allowing the CPC to fine undertakings up to 10% of their turnover. Without further explanation, that provision could be deemed to refer to global turnover. Sadly, and as a great setback for deterrence, the legislator amended the provision in question in 2013, and limited fines to 10% of turnover in Serbia, making the system far less intimidating for foreign firms, and discriminating, *de facto*, against domestic firms.[48] As will be seen below, the amount of fines expressed as a percentage of Serbian turnover has been very far below the 10% mark, with fines usually not exceeding 1 or 2%. In recent years, under the current Council of the CPC, fines have reached ridiculously low levels, expressed sometimes as tenths of a percent, for serious infringements.

[44] 2005 Act, Art 62.

[45] 2009 Act, Arts 53 and 54.

[46] 2009 Act, Art 54(3).

[47] 2009 Act, Art 50.

[48] 2009 Act, Art 68.

4.5 Budget and Staff for 2012–2022 Period

The funds for the functioning of the CPC are provided in accordance with the 2009 Act from the CPC's revenues generated by performing its tasks. The financing of the CPC is an important segment of institutional capacity and one of the basic conditions for independence from executive power. The funds are provided exclusively from revenues generated by performing the CPC's tasks, especially from: (i) fees paid in accordance with the 2009 Act, (ii) donations, except for donations from undertakings to which the 2009 Act applies; (iii) revenue from the sale of the CPC's publications; (iv) other sources in accordance with the 2009 Act.

The CPC's revenues mainly consist of funds generated from fees for issuing a clearance decision to notified concentrations, in phase I or after an in-depth investigation, from issuing decisions on requests for exemptions from restrictive agreements, and from issuing acts related to the Bankruptcy Act, in accordance with the relevant bankruptcy legislation.[49] If the annual calculation of the CPC's income and expenses determines that the total revenues are greater than the expenses incurred, the difference, after setting aside funds for reserves, is paid into the budget of Serbia. According to the annual report for 2021, the CPC's revenue amounted to RSD 607.92 million, where 98,76% was generated from fees for issuing a clearance decision to notified concentrations (see Table 2).

The Rulebook on Internal Organization and Job Classification determines that 70 job positions have been classified in the Expert Service. The organizational units are: (i) the President's Cabinet, (ii) the Concentration Investigation Sector, (iii) the Restrictive Practice Division, (iv) the Legal Affairs, Domestic and International Cooperation Sector, (v) the Economic Analysis Sector, (vi) the Material-Financial Affairs Sector, and (vii) the Normative-Legal, Personnel and General Affairs Sector. The CPC has seen a steady increase in the number of employees on a yearly basis (see Table 3). This trend indicates a growing demand for their services and a need for more resources to effectively carry out their duties.

[49] Following the enactment of the Law on Amendments and Supplements to the Bankruptcy Law ("Official Gazette of the Republic of Serbia," No. 113/2017), the Commission provides opinions solely for bankruptcy proceedings that were not concluded prior to the effective date of this law, namely, before December 25, 2017. These opinions are issued in accordance with the provisions of Articles 132, 135 and 157 of the Bankruptcy Law ("Official Gazette of the Republic of Serbia," No. 104/2009, 99/2011 - other law, 71/2012 – decision of the US, 83/2014). In the opinions of the Commission, which are provided based on the aforementioned provisions of the Bankruptcy Law, it is particularly emphasised that a purchaser of the bankrupt debtor, who acquires ownership and control over the bankrupt debtor through acquisition, is obligated to submit a concentration notification if the conditions prescribed by Article 61 of the Competition Act are met.

Table 2 Revenues of the CPC in the period 2012–2021

Year	Revenue in RSD	Revenue in million EUR[a]
2012	312,702,500	2,763,627
2013	280,868,000	2,483,695
2014	325,355,500	2,773,197
2015	324,725,400	2,689,686
2016	359,297,700	2,917,930
2017	419,383,800	3,454,519
2018	472,760,000	3,996,785
2019	523,275,500	4,439,842
2020	395,068,800	3,359,750
2021	607,888,600	5,169,989
2022	750,848,000	6,391,346

Source: Authors' own calculation based on CPC Annual Reports 2012–2021

[a]Calculations are based on the estimated average exchange rate for the relevant year

Table 3 Number of employees by year in the period 2012–2022

Year	Number of employees
2012	32
2013	33
2014	31
2015	39
2016	42
2017	45
2018	53
2019	56
2020	55
2021	57
2022	58

Source: Authors' own calculation based on CPC Annual Reports 2012–2022 [The number of employees includes those Members of the Council of the CPC who have signed employment contracts; some Members (usually university professors) may sign a manager's agreement instead due to their obligations to their university and will not be counted as employees. To the best of the author's knowledge, all current Members are employees]

5 National Specifics that Differ from the EU Competition *Acquis*

5.1 Peculiarities of the National Legal System That Significantly Differ from the EU Competition Acquis

5.1.1 Individual Exemption

Article 11 of the 2009 Act provides exemptions to certain restrictive agreements. These exemptions apply to agreements if four conditions are fulfilled, i.e., they (i) improve production and trade or contribute to technical or economic progress, (ii) provide consumers with a fair share of benefits, (iii) do not impose restrictions on undertakings that are not necessary for achieving the objectives of the agreement and (iv) do not exclude competition in the relevant market or in its substantial part.

If the agreement is not covered by de minimis or a block exemption, it must be notified for an individual exemption. At the time of writing, the following block exemption regulations are in force:

(i) Regulation on Agreements on Specialization Between Undertakings Operating on the Same Level of Production or Distribution Chain Exempted from Prohibition,[50]
(ii) Regulation on Agreements Between Undertakings Operating at the Different Level of Production or Distribution Chain Exempted from Prohibition,[51] and
(iii) Regulation on R&D Agreements Between Undertakings Operating on the Same Level of Production or Distribution.[52]

The CPC is authorized to grant an individual exemption upon the request of the parties to a restrictive agreement. The duration of the individual exemption can be no more than eight years. An extension of the duration of the individual exemption may be obtained based on a special request, which must be filed no later than two months prior to the expiry of the initial period.

The 2009 Act establishes a fixed sixty-day deadline for issuing a decision on individual exemptions. Regrettably, there is neither a penalty for non-observance of this deadline nor a non-opposition ("silence of the administration") procedure, so, in practice, the notifying parties must wait much longer. Also, it is noteworthy that the CPC has the prerogative (i) to revoke the decision on the individual exemption if the

[50] Regulation on Agreements on Specialization Between Undertakings Operating on the Same Level of Production or Distribution Chain Exempted from Prohibition [2010] Official Gazette of the Republic of Serbia, no. 11/2010.

[51] Regulation on Agreements Between Undertakings Operating at the Different Level of Production or Distribution Chain Exempted from Prohibition [2010] Official Gazette of the Republic of Serbia, no. 11/2010.

[52] Regulation on Research and Development Agreements Between Undertakings Operating on the Same Level of Production or Distribution [2010] Official Gazette of the Republic of Serbia, no. 11/2010.

conditions under which the exemption is granted are substantially altered or (ii) to annul such decision if it is based on incorrect or false information or if the exemption is misused.[53]

The CPC has published Guidelines on the Application for an Individual Exemption,[54] wherein it explicitly stated that the parties to the agreement would be fined if the CPC instituted an investigation concerning such agreement, even if the agreement in question fulfilled the condition for exemption. In other words, a failure to notify the agreement could amount to a competition infringement and, therefore, lead to a fine of up to 10% of the parties' annual Serbian turnover in the previous year.

Unfortunately, the current state of play is that the total lack of publication of individual exemptions (in contrast to infringement decisions, which are published), represents a significant obstacle to transparency and free access to information on key decisions of the CPC. In other words, this type of practice produces some degree of legal uncertainty since the parties to the agreement are not always sure whether to notify agreements or not. In that vein, the Foreign Investor Council[55] in Serbia issued a recommendation that the CPC should publish issued opinions and decisions on individual exemptions, in order to improve transparency and predictability of decisions.

5.1.2 Mergers

The 2009 Act regulates merger control procedures and provides for mandatory pre-merger notification of concentrations that meet certain thresholds which are based on the combined turnover of the merging undertakings in Serbia and worldwide. If the thresholds are met, the merging undertakings must notify the CPC.

According to Article 61 of the 2009 Act, a concentration must be notified to the CPC if, alternatively:

> The total annual revenue of all undertakings in the concentration on the world market in the previous financial year exceeds EUR 100 million. Additionally, at least one undertaking in the concentration in the market of the RoS must have revenue exceeding EUR 10 million;
>
> The total annual revenue of at least two undertakings in the concentration achieved on the market of the RoS is greater than EUR 20 million in the previous financial year. Additionally, at least two undertakings in the concentration in the market of the RoS have revenue exceeding EUR 1 million in the same period.

Once the notification is received, the CPC will review the merger to determine whether it would significantly restrict competition in the relevant market. The CPC will consider a variety of factors, including market share, barriers to entry, and the potential impact on consumers. If the CPC determines that the merger would

---

[53] 2009 Act, Art 60 (5).

[54] Guidelines on the Application for an Individual Exemption (2010).

[55] Labus and Foreign Investors Council (2021), p. 101.

Table 4 Number of concentrations approved by CPC for the period 2012–2022

Year	Total no. of concentrations	Phase II concentrations	No. of approved extraterritorial concentrations
2012	96	2	56
2013	94	3	62
2014	97	6	51
2015	101	/	55
2016	109	2	73
2017	139	1	84
2018	158	1	105
2019	169	3	119
2020	120	1	88
2021	211	2	144
2022	253	/	171
Total	1395	21	1008

Source: Authors' own calculation based on CPC Annual Reports 2012–2022

significantly restrict competition, it may prohibit the merger or require the undertakings to take certain measures to address the competition concerns. It is important to note that failure to notify the CPC of a qualifying merger can result in significant fines of up to 10% of the total revenue generated in Serbia.

The vast majority of concentrations cleared by the CPC are foreign-to-foreign transactions ("FtF"). These types of concentrations refer to mergers or acquisitions outside the territory of the country where the competition authority is located, in this case Serbia. FtF transactions are subject to merger control, provided any of the turnover thresholds stipulated in Article 61 of the 2009 Act are met.

A domestic effects doctrine has not yet been adopted by the CPC, although the 2009 Act applies to concentrations that have or might have effects on competition in the territory of Serbia. However, the current decisional practice does not support the view that a transaction (besides meeting thresholds) must also have an effect on competition in Serbia in order to trigger a filing obligation. Hence, FtF transactions that meet turnover thresholds trigger a filing obligation in Serbia, and the CPC regularly reviews and clears them in Phase I.

The CPC earns RSD 2,930,000 (approx. EUR 25,000) per approved extraterritorial concentration, in accordance with the Tariff for the Amount of Fees for Services Provided by the CPC (see Table 4).[56]

[56] Tariff on the Level of Compensation for Activities within the Competence of the CPC (2011).

5.2 *Peculiarities of the National Legal System That Have Been Erased/Amended in the Process of Europeanization*

The initial drafting of the 2005 Act was aimed at making the law constitutionally and legal-system compliant. That is why the fining was to be done by misdemeanour courts, as administrative bodies cannot, as a rule, issue fines. This system proved woefully inadequate in practice and had to be changed in the 2009 Act to an EU-like system of direct fining by the CPC. Some fining issues were not clear at all, such as the leniency procedure, while others remained open even after the 2009 Act, such as settlement procedures. Both leniency and settlement were brought in line with the EU *Acquis* through the practice of the CPC over the years.

5.2.1 Fines Issued by the Commission for Protection of Competition

As was mentioned in the Introduction, the 2005 Act provided that fines had to be issued by a misdemeanour court, with the CPC pressing charges. There were many problems with that solution from the outset, and, to the knowledge of the authors, no fines were actually issued during the period until the enactment of the 2009 Act.

First of all, there was a conflict of laws, between the 2005 Act and the Misdemeanour Act.[57] Under the latter act, the maximum fine that could be imposed amounted to 2,000,000 RSD,[58] which was, at the time, roughly equivalent to EUR 23,500. This was very meagre indeed compared to the very high fines, amounting even to millions of Euros, that was envisaged by the 2005 Act. As a matter of conflict resolution, the Misdemeanour Act seemed to limit the legislator, as it provided that the amount of up to 2,000,000 RSD is the maximum that could be prescribed by *legislation*.[59]

Furthermore, misdemeanour courts were very poorly equipped to assess a complex area such as competition law. Under the Serbian justice system, these courts are tasked with assessing minor infringements of law and order, such as traffic offences, careless trash disposal and the like. In no way were they prepared, nor was any serious effort made to prepare them for such complex cases.

The 2009 Act was a major reform insofar as it allowed the CPC to impose fines on its own. Many lawyers have doubted the constitutionality of this provision, as a determination of charges in the absence of an impartial tribunal. Yet, none have succeeded so far. The Administrative Court, which is in charge of conducting judicial review of CPC decisions, and the Constitutional Court, as the highest interpreter of the Constitution, have never overruled the legislator's decision to grant fining powers to the CPC *as such*.

[57] Misdemeanour Act, *Official Gazette of the Republic of Serbia* Nos br. 101/2005, 116/2008 and 111/2009.

[58] Misdemeanour Act, Art 35.

[59] Misdemeanour Act.

Regretfully, in recent years, the CPC has taken upon itself to issue fines far below deterrence levels, which may give rise to various theories. Thus, despite the best efforts to "Europeanize" Serbian competition law, the problem lies, as it often does, in the execution of the harmonized solutions. Even if it had the will to impose stronger fines, deterrence of large multinational companies is severely hampered by the fact that, following the 2013 amendments, the 2009 Act provides, in its Article 68(1), that fines are to be imposed as a percentage (maximum 10 per cent) of the *Serbian turnover* of the guilty parties. Thus, fines based on a percentage of global turnover are impossible, unlike in the EU.

5.2.2 Settlement Procedure

Neither the 2005 nor the 2009 Act (as amended), provide for a settlement procedure. There is, furthermore, no secondary legislation adopted under the 2009 Act to regulate this field. Instead, during the 2014–2019 Council, an informal mechanism was developed, based on the CPC's own 2011 Guidelines on Fines,[60] without changing the aforementioned. What the Council did, in fact, was to grant maximum points under the Guidelines to parties willing to settle, under the following headings envisaged under the Guidelines: stopping anticompetitive behaviour; taking active measures to remove the consequences of an infringement and voluntary cooperation with the CPC for the purposes of a faster, more efficient, and more economical termination of the proceedings.[61]

This is a rare, if not unique example of the CPC creating a new practice with legal and financial consequences but with no an explicit footing in primary or secondary legislation. In that respect, it is quite brave and is very much unlike the remainder of the Serbian public sector, which tends to support the thesis that what is not *explicitly* envisaged by the law cannot exist. Through the creative use of an existing set of guidelines, the 2014–2019 Council Members managed to introduce a European (originally US) legal institute and facilitate the closure of cases. Once the CPC has enough evidence to present a prima facie strong case but has not really completed its work, it can offer the parties an opportunity to save time and money by not opposing the procedure.

This informal rulemaking has one setback, however. Settlements are not legally binding on the parties, and they remain free to appeal any final decision taken by the CPC. In practice, this does not tend to be the case; still, the possibility remains that the CPC could go through the effort of reaching a settlement, only to have its decision annulled on the merits in subsequent judicial review.

[60] 2011 Guidelines on Fines (2011).

[61] 2011 Guidelines on Fines (2011), p. 3.

5.2.3 Modernized Leniency Procedure

The original 2005 Act envisaged a leniency procedure, but only in passing and in very bad phrasing. The provision is worth reproducing in full:

> A fine shall not be imposed on a participant in an agreement within the meaning of Article 7(1) of this act, nor to the responsible person, if the participant has reported to the CPC the existence of the agreement and its participants before proceedings have been initiated against him.[62]

This was the entire "leniency programme" from 2005 to 2009. No secondary legislation or guidelines were adopted. Unsurprisingly, it was not used much. That is, until 2009, when the new Act was about to come into force, when more than a hundred applications were filed within the space of two months. What was the catch? The Act did not provide that only one participant can get immunity from fines, nor that the immunity/leniency applicant should not be the 'ringleader'. Thus, some enterprising lawyers filed more than a hundred applications, mainly for resale price maintenance clauses between their clients and their distributors, in some cases promising that both parties would be immune, as the law was not clear that it applied only to cartels. This was done by enterprising lawyers, who approached large supermarket and food distribution chains, which apparently had a myriad of resale price maintenance clauses in their contracts with suppliers/distributors. The idea was to obtain leniency for both parties to a vertical price maintenance agreement, as the 2005 Act did not know the concept of a 'ringleader' and did not exclude them from leniency explicitly.

In one case that the CPC chose to examine, it showed that it would not allow this 'abuse of law' to pass. Two parties, a coffee producer and a supermarket chain, were fined 2% and 1.5% of their turnover respectively, for resale price maintenance. According to the CPC, the supermarket chain filed for leniency just one day before the 2009 Act came into force and had to have known that there would be no time for the CPC to open proceedings under the old Act. While following the rules of procedure set out in the old Act, the substantive provisions of the new Act of 2009 were applied. It was found that the supermarket chain, which had applied for leniency, was, in fact, the initiator of the resale price maintenance agreement and that both it and the coffee producer, who had not filed for leniency, should be fined. Thus, the attempt to cheat the law was thwarted.[63]

Today, Article 69 of the 2009 Act (the relevant provision is still in force, after the 2013 amendments), provides for two levels of protection: immunity, for the first party to come forward, and leniency, i.e. a reduction in fines, for subsequent parties, provided that they have given the CPC information it did not have before. Crucially, neither immunity nor leniency applies to a party that was the initiator ('ringleader') of the restrictive agreement.

[62] 2005 Act, Art 71(5).

[63] Decision n. 4/0-02-64/12-69 of 20 September 2012.

Therefore, since 2009, the Serbian leniency system is broadly aligned with the EU one, and there are relatively detailed guidelines on the application of Article 69 and thus, the leniency programme, in force since 2010.[64]

5.2.4 'Backsliding' Under the 2009 Act

Having said all the above, it cannot be said that the 2009 Act has been a total improvement over the 2005 one. As was mentioned previously, most of the power is concentrated in the hands of one person: the President. A procedural provision that was very useful and democratic under the 2005 regime was a provision for oral hearings to be held before the Council, whenever the parties had opposing interests, experts or witnesses had to be heard, or when the Council found it appropriate. Therefore, the Council, in addition to exercising the power of appointment and dismissal of the President (then the Presiding Member of the Council), had the power to hear the parties directly, and the procedure was far more transparent, fair and democratic. As the system stands today, Members of the Council, aside from the President and, to a greater or lesser extent, the Member acting as *rapporteur*, are kept pretty much in the dark until they are brought before a *fait accompli*, where they can either believe the version of events presented to them by the Expert Service-or not, and vote on a decision they may know very little about.

Another significant backslide, which is not in accordance with EU law, is that the persons who file a complaint to the CPC (complainants) are no longer parties under the 2009 Act. They merely have the right to be informed what the CPC is doing about the complaint, once, within 15 days of filing.[65] However, even this provision is not always respected by the CPC, and cases have been known where complaints have been filed with no response for two years.

Under the 2005 Act, as parties, complainants could see the evidence for themselves (subject to confidentiality limitations) and be part of the oral hearing, which enabled more robust and fair decision-making by the CPC. This suppression of rights was done quietly, by eliminating the opening of proceedings "upon request" of the complainants,[66] in favour of proceedings that are opened *ex officio* only,[67] whereby the complainants are relegated to the role of informants or concerned members of the public.

The concentration of power in the hands of the President, the exclusion of oral proceedings and the exclusion of complainants are significant steps back away from the EU model and contribute negatively to the quality of decision-making. Their only redeeming virtues are that they save time for the CPC, and somewhat limit the

[64] Leniency programme in Serbia (2010).

[65] 2009 Act, Art 35(4).

[66] 2005 Act, Art 58.

[67] 2009 Act, Arts 33 and 35 in conjunction with Article 36: in merger proceedings, the party filing a merger application remains a party (otherwise there would be no parties…).

flow of confidential information (by not giving complainants any information at all, except whether proceedings have been opened or not, which is something they would find out on the CPC's website anyway, in due time). Thus, the story of "improving" the Serbian Competition Act is one of Europeanization, but also one of procedural 'backsliding' at the expense of justice and fairness.

6 Application of National and EU Competition Rules by the Competition Agencies and Discussion of the Most Significant Cases

6.1 *Anticompetitive Agreements*

6.1.1 Konica Minolta and Others

In September 2019, the CPC concluded that Konica Minolta, alongside Original, Mikops, Birotehnika, Birodeveloping, Birolinija, Dikti Line, and Biro Print Sistemi, engaged in collusive tendering practices.[68] Specifically, it was established that these entities coordinated their participation in public and other procurement processes for acquiring Konica Minolta office equipment.

This case marked the inaugural application of the leniency program since its introduction in 2009. Subsequent to a disclosure from one of the implicated parties, the CPC conducted raids on the premises of all involved parties. The investigation uncovered email correspondences confirming their agreement to collude in public procurement activities. Dawn raid involved making forensic images of computer hard drives and collecting other evidence of collusion in the tender preparation process.

The emails disclosed a common practice where one party would notify Original, the exclusive Konica Minolta distributor in Serbia, about the preparation of a specific tender and their intended bid for a particular client. These communications often included references to ongoing relationships with the client, previous equipment sales, or existing service obligations. Typically, companies like Birodeveloping, Mikops, and Dikti Line would communicate with Original to disseminate tender information. On one occasion, this role was undertaken by Birolinija. Notably, upon receiving such information, parties rarely responded electronically, though Birotehnika occasionally acknowledged with a simple "ok."

The email exchanges further indicate an understanding among the parties to regard certain clients as exclusive, thus reserving them for future procurements. This led to a pattern where the same party recurrently submitted bids to a specific client over time, often as the sole bidder from this group, thereby securing contracts. The parties' awareness of this arrangement was evident in their queries about who

[68] Decision no. 4/0-02-56/2019-64 of 27 September 2019, *Konica Minolta and others.*

was managing a particular client, aimed at deciding whether to bid or abstain based on the client's perceived ownership.

Moreover, the emails revealed a strategy where the parties would coordinate on tender preparations, agreeing to present supporting or service bids to create a semblance of competition. Generally, one entity would act as the primary bidder, instructing others to submit higher-priced bids or abstain altogether. This approach was designed to enhance the primary bidder's competitive appearance, bolstering their likelihood of contract acquisition, while maintaining the illusion of a competitive tender process.

The CPC granted the cartel participant full immunity from the fine because it had self-reported and handed over evidence before the CPC knew about this infringement.

6.1.2 Vital-Victoriaoil Case

In 2017, the CPC ascertained that two edible sunflower oil market competitors, Vital and Victoriaoil, had concluded a restrictive agreement that limited edible oil production and prevented competition in the market.[69] The relevant market was determined as the production of edible sunflower oil in Serbia. Both parties were fined 0.33% of the total annual turnover generated in 2014 on the Serbian market, which amounted to SD 22,980,000 (approx. EUR 190,000) for Victoriaoil and SD 8,466,500 (approx. EUR 70,000) for Vital.

Before initiating the investigation, the CPC had legitimate concerns that the parties had concluded a restrictive agreement since it had found that its competitor produced and bottled refined edible sunflower oil Vital.

The cooperation agreement was concluded between direct competitors. Namely, it had foreseen that Victoriaoil (i) produces the edible sunflower oil under the name of Vital and (ii) sells that oil to Vital.

During the investigation, the CPC collected relevant information from all undertakings present on the market. The requested information included production capacities, total oil production, production for other oil mills and private brands, data on oil prices, production costs, sunflower purchases, etc. Based on this information, the CPC calculated data on the capacity utilization of all undertakings, including the parties.

The main ground for the CPC to find infringement was that Vital could entrust the filling operations to Sunce, its related party. In other words, Sunce had the necessary capacities to produce edible sunflower oil. It means that Vital was able to avoid revealing confidential information related to the technological and financial capacities of the oil mill to Victoriaoil, its direct competitor. Therefore, appreciating all the available documentation, the CPC considered that the agreement in question was not necessary for the continuation of the basic activity of Vital.

[69] Decision no. 4/0-02-58/2017-1 of 13 March 2017.

To date, it was the first and only restrictive agreement type of case where the CPC found an infringement by effect, not by object and therefore conducted a detailed economic (econometric) analysis of adverse effects on the market in question. In that vein, the CPC determined that Victoriaoil's market share increased in the period when the agreement was in force. Further, the CPC concluded that the agreement in question (i) negatively affected wholesale and retail prices, (ii) brought no consumer benefits, (iii) increased Herfindahl–Hirschman Index (HHI) from 3097 to 3982, and (iv) contributed to sensitive information exchange between competitors.

Finally, it is noteworthy that the parties argued the definition of the relevant market. Namely, their line of argumentation was that the relevant market is defined narrowly and should include animal fat as well. However, the CPC stated that pork fat and sunflower oil are not considered to be substitutes due to the following reasons (i) sunflower oil and pork fat have different composition, (ii) the nutritional value of these products is different, and (iii) pork fat can be used as a substitute only in case of thermal food processing.[70]

6.1.3 Roaming Electronics and Comtrade Distribution

Two years ago, the CPC conducted and completed two similar investigations regarding RPM on the consumer electronics market. In the first case, the CPC sanctioned Roaming Electronics, the importer and distributor of consumer electronics under the following brands: LG, Samsung, Philips, Hisense, TCL, Metz, Huawei, Realme, and PlayStation, and four retailers of such products (XLS, Gigatron, Emmezeta, and Technomedia).[71] Another case refers to Comtrade Distribution and its retailers[72] (Tehnomija, Gigatron, Tehnomedija, Emmezeta, and XLS), which pertains to the same type of breach on the same product market, regarding Tesla electronic appliances.

The trigger for instituting investigations in both cases was the fact that the CPC had analyzed the prices of consumer electronics products on Eurostat and found that the prices in Serbia had been 13% higher than in the EU. In addition, the CPC determined that all retailers applied similar or identical prices. After that, a dawn raid was conducted at the premises of all the abovementioned undertakings.

In the Roaming Electronics case, based on e-mails acquired during dawn raids, the CPC concluded that the objective of the undertaking in question was to maintain retail prices at the agreed level, thus maintaining the agreed margin and preventing price competition between retailers. Retailers strictly followed the recommended prices, either under pressure from other competing retailers (which was typically exercised through the supplier - Roaming Electronics) or lured by special benefits offered in case of adherence to the recommended prices, or simply following their

[70] Peterhof (2018).

[71] Decision no. 4/0-01-177/2021-26 of 2 July 2021.

[72] Decision no. 4/0-01-176/2021-35 of 2 July 2021, *Comtrade*.

own business interests not to lower prices, assuming that other retailers will behave in the same manner.

The same type of infringement and similar facts of the case were ascertained in the *Comtrade Distribution* case, although it appears that it was less apparent that the objective of RPM was to prevent unilateral price cuts in this case. However, this was of no relevance to the outcome since it was sufficient to determine that retailers' pricing policies were not independent and that retail prices were subject to monitoring and analysis by Comtrade Distribution.

The transparency of the market contributed to the conclusion that recommended prices were mandatory, as it facilitates monitoring of all prices (especially in the case of online sales) and enables parties to react in case of any deviation from the agreed prices. This was additionally made more accessible by using special software for monitoring and analyzing retail prices implemented by upstream parties, Roaming Electronics and Comtrade Distribution.

In both cases, the CPC has explicitly determined that defining and communicating recommended prices between undertakings can amount to price collusion and, therefore, to a restrictive agreement without examining the adverse effects of such behavior on the market. In other words, recommended prices, which are generally permitted under both the EU and the Serbian competition legal framework, under certain circumstances, are no longer considered recommended but rather mandatory for the retailers if they have incentives or pressures from upstream undertakings to follow the prices. In addition, it is worth noting that the CPC referred to the EU Vertical Guidelines in its reasoning.

With respect to fines, it must be noted that they are extremely low given (i) the market position of the upstream parties, (ii) the fact that RPM is qualified as a severe type of infringement according to the 2009 Act, and (iii) the fact that the CPC found aggravating circumstances in both cases. Namely, the CPC imposed fines on Roaming Electronics and Comtrade Distribution that amount to 0.2% of their respective annual revenues, whereas the legal maximum is 10%. Moreover, in both cases, the CPC failed to provide a detailed rationale for the methodology used for calculating fines, as required by the Guidelines on fines (which was also the case with some previous decisions).

Although the fines are not negligible in absolute terms, it is questionable whether they are sufficient to have a deterrent effect, given that conduct that breaches the 2009 Act can be very lucrative. One can only speculate on the reasons behind this recent trend of lenient penalties and whether this is a deliberate attempt to implement antitrust laws in a way that does not cause too much "harm" to the undertakings.

6.2 *Abuse of Dominance Position*

6.2.1 Frikom Case

In 2012 the CPC found that Frikom, a producer of frozen goods in Serbia, abused its dominant position in the wholesale market of industrial ice cream.[73] The fine was RSD 341,130,000 (approx. EUR 3 million), i.e., 4% of relevant turnover. The relevant market was defined as market of industrial ice cream in Serbia.

The CPC ascertained that supply agreements concluded between Frikom as producer and retailers/customers contained the following anticompetitive provisions: (i) RPM, (ii) tying provisions, which required retailers/customers to purchase exclusively from Frikom and prohibited them from selling competing products, including exclusivity regarding the use of refrigerator space and shelf or shop space (non-compete), (iii) a requirement that retailers/customers purchase from the Frikom product range only, (iv) excessive damages in case of breach of any contract clauses by retailers/customers, (v) the unilateral right for Frikom to terminate the supply agreement with an inappropriately short notice period for breach of contract by the retailer/customers, and (vi) application of different commercial terms and conditions to the same business relationships with different retailers/customers.

The CPC explained that Frikom's goal was to develop an already firmly established and matured customer network and to oblige customers to exclusively purchase the relevant product from Frikom, which appears in the role of both manufacturer and supplier concerning those customers. Practically, this meant pushing existing competitors out of the market and creating significant entry barriers for new competitors, while at the same time strengthening their dominant position in the market.

Frikom was always aware of its market position and that its brand is a "must-have" product for any customer. Based on these circumstances, Frikom built its business policy of tying customers and imposing business conditions, which included, in some cases, an explicit ban on doing business with other Frikom competitors. With the strength of its negotiating power, which is primarily based on market power and the fact that long-term consumer habits and preferences have made its ice creams become "must stock items", Frikom, at the same time, offered incentives and rewards to its retailers/customers, but also contracted "sanctions" (usually twice the amount of incentives and rewards) if they violated the contractual obligations, especially in terms of prices.

Given that Frikom represented an "unavoidable trading partner" for every retailer/customer, even for large "Key customers," it easily concluded contracts with retailers/customers who, in return, renounced cooperation with Frikom's competitors. The effects were apparent, as previously described in this rationale.

With respect to RPM provisions, the CPC pointed out that by preventing price competition between different Frikom retailers/customers, it also prevented more

[73] Decision no. 5/0-02-329/2012-16 of 19 November 2012.

efficient retailers from entering the market or from reaching the appropriate level at lower prices. The previously described mainly occurs when the manufacturer himself carries out distribution, i.e., when it acts as a supplier to his retailers, as Frikom did; RPM can prevent or significantly hinder the entry into the market and the spread of distribution formats based on low prices.

Concerning the EU competition law perspective, the CPC referred to the EU Vertical regulation and the EU Vertical Guidelines, as well as the case law of the EU courts.[74]

Afterward, Frikom challenged the CPC's decision before the Administrative Court, the Supreme Court, as well as the Constitutional Court,[75] but in all three cases the claim was dismissed.

6.2.2 Niš Ekspres

It is interesting to consider the case of *Niš Ekspres*, the latest in a 'trilogy' of cases concerning abuses by bus stations in Serbia.[76] This decision, issued in 2021, is a culmination of a trend of investigating and/or punishing cases that primarily have to do with discrimination between consumers, rather than between undertakings. The CPC seems to have a particular aversion to cases of consumer discrimination and "money for nothing" cases, where higher prices are charged for no additional value.

In the case at hand, Niš Ekspres was, at the same time, both a provider of bus station services and of bus transportation, regionally and nationally. It was the licensed operator of the only bus station in the city of Niš, Serbia's third largest city, located in the southeast of the country. Unlike bus stops, of which there were many in and around Niš, of bus stations there was only one. Following a long saga, with several commitment offers and two administrative court judgments (where the CPC's decisions were annuled due to insufficiently clear calculation of fines), the CPC found that Niš Ekspres had abused its dominant position by charging different prices for the same service offered to different classes of passengers.

The Relevant Market

The CPC defined the relevant market as the market for access to bus station platforms on the territory of the City of Niš, where Niš Ekspres was found to have a 100% market share, as the sole operator.

---

[74] Van den Bergh Foods Ltd v Commission and Langnese Iglo GmbH v Commission.

[75] Odbija se kao neosnovana ustavna žalba privrednog društva „Industrija smrznute hrane Frikom" d.o.o. izjavljena protiv rešenja Saveta Komisije za zaštitu konkurencije broj 5/0-02-329/2012-1 od 19. novembra 2012. godine, presude Upravnog suda U. 17578/12 od 12. marta 2013. godine i presude Vrhovnog kasacionog suda Uzp. 181/13 od 6. februara 2014. Godine (only in Serbian).

[76] Decision No. 5/0-02-90/2017-131 *Inter Turs Plus*, of 23 October 2017; Decision no. 5/0-02-117/07-1 *BAS* of 16 February 2007.

Access to platforms meant access to the arrival/departure platforms of the bus station. Bus stations, in turn, were distinguished by the range of services that they offer, and which bus stops do not, such as: reservation of tickets, seating accommodation, toilets, information desks, luggage safe-keeping, etc.

On such a relevant market, Niš Ekspres was found to have a monopoly, as only it could provide access to its own platforms. Platforms were used by two main groups: one, by passengers departing from or arriving at the station, and two, by persons accompanying or awaiting the former group (non-passengers). A fee was charged for access to the platform, for all passengers and non-passengers.

Competition Concerns

Niš Ekspres was accused of abusing its dominant position in two main ways, both of which were discriminatory towards passengers and/or non-passengers.

First, the fees charged to passengers had varied according to the length of their envisaged journey. The CPC found that there is no difference between providing access to the platform for a passenger travelling 50 km and providing access to the platform to a passenger travelling 500 km. The service was the same: waiting for the bus and boarding it, or, for arriving passengers, disembarking the bus.

Second, Niš Ekspres charged one platform access fee to passengers who booked through its own system (at the ticket counters) or had a Niš Ekspres monthly card, and another to non-passengers and passengers who bought tickets on the bus itself, without a monthly card. The platform fee charged to the former was lower than the one charged to the latter.

In the second form of discrimination, there was a discrimination between undertakings, albeit indirectly. Some competitors of Niš Ekspres who drove their own bus routes to and from the bus station merely paid the service of parking the bus, and did not provide Niš Ekspres with their price lists, thus disabling Niš Ekspres from selling the tickets on its counters and charging a 9 per cent commission. The passengers of these operators were penalized by paying the higher (non-passenger) price of access to the platform.

In its decision, while acknowledging the potential of the second form of behaviour as being able to affect competitors, the CPC based its reasoning mainly on the rare and somewhat outstanding the EC decision in *1998 World Cup*,[77] holding that discrimination by a dominant firm can constitute an abuse even when only consumers and not competitors are affected. This line of thinking was not overturned in either of the judicial review cases that had intervened since the original proceedings were opened in 2017.

[77] Commission Decision of 20 July 1999, *1998 Football World Cup*, Case IV/36.888.

Resolving Competition Concerns

In addition to imposing a fine on Niš Ekspres, the CPC ordered the company to charge non-discriminatory prices to all persons getting access to the platforms and provide the CPC with a price list of services every six months for a period of two years.

By this decision, the CPC, as mentioned above, put a final touch on a long course of eliminating discrimination and excessive pricing by various bus stations in Serbia. In that sense, it ties in well with the 2017 *Inter Turs Plus* decision, where the CPC found that another combined bus transport/bus station operator charged excessive station fees to bus companies, as compared to other stations in the country and as compared to the costs of providing the service. It also ties in well with the very early *BAS* decision,[78] adopted under the 2005 Act, whereby the Belgrade Bus Station was found to have abused its dominant position by charging different platform access fees for passengers and non-passengers. While the main reasoning is the same, the difference between *BAS* and *Niš Ekspres* is enormous, in retrospect, as the former is far less detailed, far less reliant on EU legislation and case law. The intervening fourteen years have led to sharper responses from accused undertakings, judicial review by the Administrative Court and, overall, a higher level at which the competition enforcement 'game' is being played.

6.3 Merger Control

6.3.1 Holcim Ltd - Lafarge SA

In 2014 the CPC was notified by Holcim Ltd, a world-renowned cement producer, of its intention to acquire Lafarge SA, another multi-national cement giant. Holcim Ltd had four local subsidiaries in Serbia: Holcim Srbija d.o.o., Holcim agregati a.d., Ecorec d.o.o., and AGG proizvodnja d.o.o.; while on the other hand Lafarge SA had two local subsidiaries – Lafarge Beočinska fabrika cementa d.o.o. and Beo eko korak d.o.o.[79]

On a preliminary note, the CPC ascertained that the structure of the market for the production and sale of cement has only three participants, two of which are parties to the concentration, with the third one being "Titan" d.o.o. The market in question was, therefore, highly concentrated, as indicated by the value of the HHI which was 3600 before the concentration, and 6700 after.

The CPC also found that the parties to the concentration would take up more than 70% of the market after the transaction. Finally, the CPC found that the parties are active on two more markets: aggregates market and concrete market. The cement

[78] *Decision no. 5/0-02-117/07-1 of* 16 February 2007, *BAS.*

[79] Decision no. 6/0-02-504/2014-115 of 19 December 2014.

market and the aggregates market are upstream markets for the concrete market, and can, therefore, influence the formation of the price of concrete.

The Relevant Market

The CPC found that there were three relevant markets on which the parties were operating, which were mainly the cement market—where the parties gain most of their revenue, and subsidiarily the aggregates market—where the parties gain little revenue and the concrete market where the parties gain a minor part of their revenue but represent above 20% of supply on the territory of Belgrade. As to the relevant geographic market for cement, the CPC concluded that it is the market of the Republic of Serbia.

The CPC found that the relevant geographic market for aggregates was local but did not analyze it any further because the parties had little revenue on that market. The CPC accepted Holcim's definition of the relevant geographic market for concrete which is narrower than the usually used national market. The local market is determined based on the time needed to transport concrete to the final buyer, which is usually about 90 min. In defining relevant markets, the CPC took into account the case law of the EC, but explicitly references.

Competition Concerns

The main concern of the CPC was that the implementation of the concentration would transform the market structure which exhibited traits of an oligopoly, into an asymmetrical duopoly where one market participant would have almost four times the market share of the other. This would further limit competition in an already highly concentrated market. Furthermore, the vertical effects of the present concentration would impact the concrete market, since the cost of cement represents between 60% and 70% of the price of concrete. Because of all this, the CPC commenced phase II of the investigation into this concentration. In order to carry out the transaction in compliance with 2009 Act, Holcim proposed to sell the entirety of its business operations in Serbia.

Resolving Competition Concerns

The CPC accepted Holcim's proposal for the sale of the entirety of its business. Holcim proposed two manners by which the sale would be carried out:

(1) Direct sale of 100% of the business (which consists of four related companies and their property including factories and stone quarries), or
(2) The parties may establish a joint holding company to which they would transfer their entire business. After that, the parties would sell a controlling equity share

of their business, after which they would sell the rest of the capital via an initial public offering including a Preferential Subscription Rights Initial Public Offering; or via spinoff which would include direct transfer of shares to its owners in exchange for their equity participation in Holcim or Lafarge (as the case may be) and in combination with the listing of shares in one or more renowned stock exchange markets.

The CPC accepted the measures proposed by Holcim because it estimated that those measures are suitable for promoting a market structure that would not reduce the number of market participants, and would in turn enhance competition, at least on the cement market. Therefore, the CPC found that such a structural measure would solve all the relevant competition concerns related to the present concentration.

6.3.2 SBB—IKOM

In 2017 the CPC conditionally approved a transaction between the Serbia broadband - Srpske kablovske mreže d.o.o ("SBB") and Interaktivne kablovske objedinjene mreže - I.KOM d.o.o ("IKOM").[80] At the time of transaction, SBB was a dominant cable operator, while IKOM was the fourth largest cable operator.

The Relevant Market

The CPC found that the concentration in question affects the following retail markets: (i) fixed telephony, (ii) fixed broadband, and (iii) pay-TV. On the other hand, the relevant geographic market was defined as the city of Belgrade. In determining the relevant geographic market, the CPC decided the territory where the activities of merging firms overlapped.

Competition Concerns

The Competition concerns arose only in terms of a pay-TV market since the combined market share of merging firms in fixed telephony and fixed broadband were not significant and could not restrict, distort, or prevent competition in said markets. The CPC performed a 6-month, phase II investigation to assess the likely market impact of concentration on the pay-TV market in Belgrade.

As is ordinary in phase II proceedings, the CPC issued extensive requests for information to merging firms and other interested third parties, seeking among other things, internal documents, views of the boundaries of the relevant markets, the

[80] Decision no. 6/0-03-01/2017-26 of 13 March 2017.

Table 5 Number of decisions taken by the CPC for the period 2012–2022

Type of case	Number of decisions
Abuse of dominant position	6
Restrictive agreements (cartels)	18 (9)
Mergers	1304
Commitment decisions	11
Initiatives received	440

Source: Authors' own calculation based on CPC Annual Reports 2012–2022

projected effect of hypothetical price increases, the characteristics and dynamics of the affected market, and the competitive effect of the transaction under investigation.

Resolving Competition Concerns

The CPC concluded that the transaction was likely to restrict, distort or prevent competition on the pay-TV market in Belgrade, because the merged entity would have an estimated local market share of 60–70%, based on its number of subscribers and revenue. It, therefore, conditioned its approval on SBB committing to (i) divest cable infrastructure where there was overlap between SBB and IKOM, (ii) submit a report to the CPC any time it changed the retail prices of its media content distribution service package, providing its reasons for the price change for a period of two years, and (iii) offer to all IKOM customers the option to enter into either an open-ended subscription contract or a fixed-term subscription contact, both on the same terms offered to existing or prospective SBB customers.

7 Enforcement and Sanctioning Statistics for the Period 2012–2022

7.1 Enforcement Statistics

Table 5 provides the number of decisions taken by the CPS for the period 2012–2022, whereas Table 6 provides the enforcement data.

The table contains only publicly available information. With respect to mergers, authors count only cases where the CPC cleared transactions.

Table 6 CPC Enforcement data (2012–2022)

Type of case	Abuse of dominant position	Restrictive agreements (cartels)	Mergers	Commitments decisions	Initiatives received
2012	2	/	94	/	19
2013	/	/	91	/	33
2014	1	/	91	2	38
2015	/	2 (2)	101	/	43
2016	1	2 (1)	111	2	32
2017	1	3 (2)	139	/	82
2018	/	2 (1)	159	1	97
2019	/	1 (1)	175	4	42
2020	1	4 (2)	121	/	32
2021	/	3 (0)	213	2	22
2022	2	3 (1)	253	2	23
Total	8	20 (20)	1548	13	463

Source: Authors' own calculation based on CPC Annual Reports 2012–2022

Table 7 Fines per year imposed by CPC (2012–2022) for restrictive agreements and abuse of dominance position cases

Year	Fines (in RSD)	Fines (in EUR)[a]
2012	1,074,582,469.42	9,450,202
2013	–	–
2014	20,795,296.35	171,933
2015	35,048,208.36	288,178
2016	341,772,985.55	2,768,065
2017	86,417,467.62	729,446
2018	66,021,643.14	558,606
2019	60,006,647.36	510,304
2020	62,995,954.18	535,771
2021	79,087,482.66	672,627
2022	60,460,627.36	515,348
Total	1,887,188,782	16,200,480

Source: Authors' own calculation based on CPC Annual Reports 2012–2022

[a]The amount for each year is calculated by aggregating the total sum of fines in Serbian dinars, followed by dividing that cumulative amount by the average exchange rate of the Euro on December 31st of the respective year

7.2 Sanctioning Statistics

The amounts of fines presented in Tables 7 and 8 were imposed by the CPC before the court's proceedings. The CPC does not publish the cases in which the appeals are successful and therefore fines are set aside.

With respect to enforceability of fines, it is noteworthy that parties are obliged to pay fines in the deadline determined by the CPC which may not be shorter than three months nor longer than one year from the date of receipt of the decision. In addition,

Table 8 Fines per year for gun-jumping and failure to notify cases imposed by CPC (2012–2022)

Year	Fines (in RSD)	Fines (in EUR)[a]
2012–2016	–	–
2017	6,618,800.43	55,869
2018–2020	–	–
2021	11,760,351.6	100,020
2022	–	–

Source: Authors' own calculation based on CPC Annual Reports 2012–2022, which means they do not include outcomes of possible proceedings before the Administrative Court, where some of these fines may have been annulled. Administrative Court decisions are generally not available to the public

[a]The amount for each year is calculated by aggregating the total sum of fines in Serbian dinars, followed by dividing that cumulative amount by the average exchange rate of the Euro on December 31st of the respective year

together with initiating a lawsuit, parties can opt to request the postponement of the execution before the CPC until the Court's ruling if the execution of decision would (i) cause irreparable damage to the prosecutor, and (ii) lead to the bankruptcy or termination of business operations of the prosecutor, provided that the delay is not against the public interest.

Considering all of the data with respect to the CPC's enforcement, it is evident that unfortunately focus is still on phase I mergers. On the other hand, restrictive agreement cases are much more frequent than abuse of dominance cases, mainly due to lack of capacity to perform complex economic analyses.

8 Judicial Review

Review of the CPC's decisions is carried out by the Administrative Court ("Court"), which was established in January 2010, as a result of judicial reform in Serbia. It is composed of 52 judges. The 2009 Act just says that a claim may be submitted before the Court against the final decision of the CPC. In reviewing the CPC's decisions, the Court is only bound concerning the amount of the fine, since it is obliged to examine the fine in accordance with the 2009 Act. An action for judicial review does not automatically suspend the enforcement of the fine or other remedies, though the CPC and the Court may decide to suspend them. Normally, the CPC grants a stay of payment of fines pending the outcome of the judicial review.

It seems that the Court has unlimited jurisdiction. However, in practice, the Court is not willing to decide on the merits and take the role of the CPC, but only checks the legality of the CPC's decisions, namely lack of competence, infringement of an essential procedural requirement, infringement of the 2009 Act or of any rule of law relating to their application, or misuse of powers by the CPC.

Finally, the last stage of protection for parties is lodging an extraordinary legal remedy against the Court's judgments to the Supreme Court of Cassation ("Supreme Court"). It is to be noted that neither the Administrative Court nor the Supreme Court are obliged to publish their judgments, in these or any other matters. Occasionally, they publish completely anonymized and abridged versions of their judgments, to state an important principle of the law, albeit not competition law.

The Court is overwhelmed with significant cases of different legal natures and only a small portion of them refer to competition law. Also, given how cases are allocated to judges (by a type of lottery), the current state of play is that the Court, unfortunately, does not have judges who specialize in competition matters. This means that judges of the Court still lack comprehensive knowledge in the areas of competition law and economics to be able to interpret and examine the CPC's arguments and decisions in detail.

Judgments of the Court often lack detailed reasoning and consideration of the merits of the case, limiting their scope only to reiterating the CPC's findings and consideration of the fundamental procedural issues, without analysing the parties' arguments in dispute. Also, cases are, as a rule, decided on the basis of failures of domestic administrative law, not competition law, as the Serbian Law on General Administrative Procedure is drafted in such a way that it is almost always possible to find that an administrative authority has violated it. Thus, decisions tend to get quashed on the minutest of details of procedure. This is a serious shortcoming, as it prevents a confrontation of opinions, a comprehensive and adequate control of the CPC's decisions, and the development and harmonization of practices with EU standards (which is a requirement of the SAA), while it also jeopardizes further appeal proceedings in cases when an extraordinary legal remedy is lodged. Detailed reasoning of the Court's judgments, with a particular consideration of arguments and evidence presented by the parties to the proceedings, is of considerable importance for establishing judiciary oversight of the CPC's work. Otherwise, the CPC would be in a position to misuse its powers and independence.[81]

Not all judgments of the Court and the Supreme Court are publicly available, and those that are, are redacted in terms of information about parties' names. In that vein, we can only assume which cases judgments refer to. On the other hand, judgments are limited to reviewing the legality of the CPC's decisions and there is no case where the Court or the Supreme Court took a different position than the CPC in terms of merits. In other words, if said courts quash the CPC's decisions, it is only on the basis of procedural issues.

[81] Labus and Foreign Investors Council (2021), p. 104.

9 Private Enforcement of Competition Law

The 2009 Act seemed to be acting in line with the times (considering the publication of the EC's *White Paper on Damages* in the previous year[82]) and introduced an explicit private enforcement provision. Namely, under Article 73 of the 2009 Act (as it stands to this day):

> Compensation for damages incurred by acts and activities that represent a competition infringement in the sense of this act, which have been established by a decision of the CPC, may be obtained in a civil claim before the competent court.
>
> A decision of the CPC within the meaning of paragraph 1 of this article does not create a presumption that damage has occurred; instead, it must be proven in proceedings before a court.

For its time, this was a welcome provision, introducing, at least, the notion that competition infringements may cause recoverable damages. However, even at the time of enactment, in 2009, the provision was behind the relevant EU jurisprudence (post the *Courage* judgment of 2001),[83] which provided that damages may be sought by the parties independently and in the absence of a decision by a competition authority ("stand-alone claims"). Instead, the 2009 Act provides explicitly only for so-called "follow-on claims," i.e. claims based on a decision adopted in public enforcement. While stand-alone claims are not explicitly excluded, their position is made dubious by the failure to include them specifically in the Act. The authors are aware of at least one case, in which one of them was involved, where a civil court refused to hear a competition claim specifically because the issue "fell within the jurisdiction of the CPC." A decision of the CPC was held to be a *question prejudicielle* to the civil claim, and, since the CPC had never opened proceedings, the civil case led to nowhere.

As of 2025, more than eight years after the adoption of the EU Damages Directive,[84] this position is untenable. No effort has been made to incorporate the Directive into Serbian law, and private enforcement has no specific delineation as it does in the EU: the definition of what damages are covered, whether interest is included, a specific provision for stand-alone claims, the existence of presumptions, the position of so-called indirect purchasers and many more.

Somewhat luckily for private plaintiffs, the general rules on damages claims in Serbia are similar to what was laid down in the EU, insofar as damages may include actual damages and lost profits, and commonly include pre-judgment interest. This is, however, where harmonization with the EU stops.

---

[82] European Commission (2008).

[83] Judgement of 20 September 2001, *Courage Ltd v Bernard Crehan and Bernard Crehan v Courage Ltd and Others*, C-453/99, ECLI:EU:C:2001:465.

[84] Directive 2014/104/EU of the European Parliament and of the Council of 26 November 2014 on certain rules governing actions for damages under national law for infringements of the competition law provisions of the Member States and of the European Union [2014] OJ L 349/1 (Antitrust Damages Directive).

It is suggested that, for the benefit of enforcement in general, stand-alone claims be allowed explicitly, thus relieving the CPC of its near-monopoly on competition enforcement. It is clear that the CPC, like any other competition agency, never has enough human resources to catch and prosecute all infringements. Also, the civil courts could act as a controlling factor, picking up cases that the CPC unjustly dismissed. Certainly, like in the EU, the relationship between civil judgments and public enforcement decisions would have to be regulated. On that point, the Serbian Competition Act does not even make it explicit that CPC findings are binding on the courts, as to the existence of an infringement.[85] Rather, using the regular constitutional division of powers, civil courts may reach completely different results on the merits to those reached by the CPC. This makes the impact of CPC decisions much weaker.

Last but not least, it would be most useful if an obligation were introduced, similar to the EU, that competition cases be specially registered and publicized by the civil courts.[86] As the system stands, it is impossible to determine how many cases have been brought, if at all. One of the authors was involved in one follow-on case, where, although the civil court deferred to the decision of the CPC and took the infringement more-or-less as a given, the claim failed on the grounds of failure to prove a causal link between infringement and damage, and failure to quantify damages. It would be interesting and, indeed, educational to have such decisions published for a wide audience.

To sum up, much remains to be done in the field of private enforcement in Serbia. This includes a clear relationship between CPC decisions and civil proceedings, the clear legislative statement that courts can act on their own when there is no CPC case, as well as the need to introduce collective actions into Serbian civil law.

10 Current Trends and Future Challenges to Enforcing Competition Law

The current trend under the current Council of the CPC is for the CPC to issue ridiculously low fines in competition cases, which are far below anything that could be called dissuasive. Encouragingly, however, the CPC has recently decided to grapple with the digital world, having conducted a market analysis and opened

[85] Contrast with Article 9 (1) of the Antitrust Damages Directive which provides that: "Member States shall ensure that an infringement of competition law found by a final decision of a national competition authority or by a review court is deemed to be irrefutably established for the purposes of an action for damages brought before their national courts under Article 101 or 102 TFEU or under national competition law."

[86] Article 15(2) of the Regulation 1/2003 provides that: "Member States shall forward to the Commission a copy of any written judgment of national courts deciding on the application of Article [101] or Article [102] of the Treaty. Such copy shall be forwarded without delay after the full written judgment is notified to the parties."

proceedings in the case of food delivery apps. International relations, from their all-time high in 2014–2019, are now at an all time low, with fewer interactions with other competition authorities and international organizations and projects. In the past, joint conferences and exchanges of staff have provided much-needed knowledge and best practices.

Many future challenges lay ahead. One of them is the qualification of the Members of the Council, the majority of whom are not EU law or competition experts, contrary to the provisions of the law. Another is hiring more expert staff. A legal challenge is the concentration of too much power in the hands of the President, who takes decisions on phase I mergers alone, initiates proceedings in abuses and restrictive agreements alone, and hires and dismisses employees alone. This has left the Council virtually powerless until brought before the fait accompli of a prepared decision and makes the system very undemocratic.

Major challenges remain in alignment with the EU Acquis. The rules on settlement should be formalized, so as to be more predictable, and the general rules on fines should be changed in such a way as to disallow fines of less than one tenth of a per cent. Also, the process of alignment with new EU rules on vertical agreements and horizontal cooperation has not even begun, and neither has the process of alignment with EU law on private damages actions, as per the 2014 EU Damages Directive, now almost a decade old.

Perhaps the most work needs to be done with the courts reviewing CPC decisions. Their decisions should be published, as should decision of civil courts deciding damages and other civil claims. This would require an amendment to the general system of publication of judgments but would massively improve transparency. Special training on competition law should be provided to civil, administrative and Supreme Court judges.

11 Conclusion

In the span of less than eighteen years, the Serbian competition regime has come a long way, towards Europeanization and standardization. A significant body of case law and personal expertise has been built up, and the law has been modernized significantly at least once, in 2009. Overall, there have been some very high quality decisions in some difficult cases, such as the *Vital/Victoria* case mentioned above.

The years since the enactment of the 2009 Act and, in particular the period 2014–2019 have seen a modernization of practices, with commitment, settlement, and leniency decisions becoming important and relatively predictable tools to make better use of the CPC's limited resources. The authority has enough power to investigate, prosecute and punish infringements of the competition rules.

Nevertheless, the past years have also seen some significant 'backsliding', both legislative and practical. The serious reduction of the role of the Council under the 2009 Act is an example of the former. The serious reduction in fines for serious infringements that is observed in recent practice is an example of the latter. A notable reduction in transparency was seen in the CPC's stopping the publication of individual exemption decisions, thus defying the very purpose of predictability and legal certainty that an individual exemption system (now obsolete in the EU) is meant to provide.

Overall, the CPC remains in a fragile position. While significant knowledge and established practice have been accumulated, more reform of the competition rules is necessary, and a more strict and disciplined approach to detecting and punishing infringements is called for. Private enforcement is in a particularly dire state, with no legal certainty as to the relationship between public and private enforcement, and no explicit provision for stand-alone civil actions, which would boost the impact of the competition rules in the real world.

To sum up, a lot has been done, and yet a lot still remains to be done in the Serbian competition law system.

Table of Cases

European Commission

Commission Decision of 20 July 1999, *1998 Football World Cup,* Case IV/36.888.

Decision of 23 July 2004, *Scandlines Sverige AB v Port of Helsingborg,* Case COMP/A.36.568/D3

Court of Justice of the EU

Judgment of 14 February 1978, *United Brands v Commission*, C-27/76, ECLI:EU:C:1978:22

Judgement of 20 September 2001, *Courage Ltd v Bernard Crehan and Bernard Crehan v Courage Ltd and Others*, C-453/99, ECLI:EU:C:2001:465

Commission for Protection of Competition

Decision n. 4/0-02-64/12-69 of 20 September 2012. Available at: https://kzk.gov.rs/kzk/wp-content/uploads/2012/11/Resenje-Idea-Grand-20.09.2012.pdf. Accessed 17 February 2025

Decision no. 4/0-02-56/2019-64 of 27 September 2019, Konica Minolta and others, Available at:https://kzk.gov.rs/kzk/wp-content/uploads/2019/10/27-09-2019-56-Resenje-o-povredi-konkurencije-Original-Konica-Minolta-i-ostali.pdf. Accessed 17 February 2025

Decision no. 4/0-01-176/2021-35 of 2 July 2021, *Comtrade*, Available at: https://kzk.gov.rs/kzk/wp-content/uploads/2022/01/re%C5%A1enje-02-07-2021-ComTrade.pdf. Accessed 17 February 2025

Decision no. 4/0-01-177/2021-26 of 2 July 2021, *Roaming*, Available at: https://kzk.gov.rs/kzk/wp-content/uploads/2022/01/RESENJE-ROAMING.pdf. Accessed 17 February 2025

Decision no. 4/0-01-65/2022-11 of 19 August 2022, *S1*, Available at: https://kzk.gov.rs/kzk/wp-content/uploads/2022/09/Resenje-SF1_Coffee.pdf. Accessed 17 February 2025

Decision no. 4/0-02-58/2017-1 of 13 March 2017. Available at: https://kzk.gov.rs/kzk/wp-content/uploads/2017/04/Victoria-Vital16_3_20171.pdf. Accessed 17 February 2025

Decision no. 4/0-02-89/2017-31 of 1 December 2017, *N Sport,* Available at: https://kzk.gov.rs/kzk/wp-content/uploads/2017/12/R-40-02-892017-312.pdf. Accessed 17 February 2025

Decision no. 5/0-02-117/07-1 *BAS* of 16 February 2007. Available at: https://kzk.gov.rs/kzk/wp-content/uploads/2018/10/Resenje-BAS.pdf. Accessed 17 February 2025

Decision no. 5/0-02-290/2020-3 of 24 December 2021. Available at: https://kzk.gov.rs/kzk/wp-content/uploads/2021/02/Resenje-Nis-ekspres-.pdf. Accessed 17 February 2025

Decision no. 5/0-02-329/2012-16 of 19 November 2012. Available at: https://kzk.gov.rs/kzk/wp-content/uploads/2014/03/povreda-konkurencije-frikom.pdf. Accessed 17 February 2025

Decision no. 5/0-02-329/2012-16 of 19 November 2021. Available at: https://kzk.gov.rs/kzk/wp-content/uploads/2014/03/povreda-konkurencije-frikom.pdf. Accessed 17 February 2025

Decision No. 5/0-02-90/2017-131 *Inter Turs Plus*, of 23 October 2017. Available at: https://kzk.gov.rs/kzk/wp-content/uploads/2020/01/Resenje-InterTursPlus1.pdf. Accessed 17 February 2025

Decision no. 5/0-02-90/2017-131 of 23 October 2017. Available at: https://kzk.gov.rs/kzk/wp-content/uploads/2020/01/Resenje-InterTursPlus1.pdf. Accessed 17 February 2025

Decision no. 6/0-02-504/2014-115 of 19 December 2014. Available at: https://kzk.gov.rs/kzk/wp-content/uploads/2014/12/Holcim-Lafarge-6-0-02-504-2014-115.pdf. Accessed 17 February 2025

Decision no. 6/0-03-01/2017-26 of 13 March 2017. Available at: https://kzk.gov.rs/kzk/wp-content/uploads/2017/03/01-26-SBB.pdf. Accessed 17 February 2025

Judgement of the Constitutional Court no. Už-3003/2014 of 20 June 2016. Available at: https://sirius.rs/praksa/ipbbGg. Accessed 17 February 2025

Table of Legislation

EU

Directive 2014/104/EU of the European Parliament and of the Council of 26 November 2014 on certain rules governing actions for damages under national law for infringements of the competition law provisions of the Member States and of the European Union [2014] OJ L 349/1

Council Regulation (EC) No 1/2003 of 16 December 2002 on the implementation of the rules on competition laid down in Articles 81 and 82 of the Treaty [2003] OJ L 1/1

Commission Regulation (EU) No 330/2010 of 20 April 2010 on the application of Article 101(3) of the Treaty on the Functioning of the European Union to categories of vertical agreements and concerted practices [2010] OJ L 102/1

Stabilisation and Association Agreement between the European Communities and their Member States of one part, and the Republic of Serbia, of the other part [2013] L 278/16.

Serbia

Competition Act [2005] Official Gazette of the Republic of Serbia No. 79/2005

Competition Act [2009] Official Gazette of the Republic of Serbia Nos 1/2009 and 95/2013

Constitution of Serbia [1990] Official Gazette of the Republic of Serbia No 1/1990

Law on Administrative Review [2009] Official Gazette of the Republic of Serbia No. 111/2009; 2009 Act

Misdemeanour Act, Official Gazette of the Republic of Serbia Nos 101/2005, 116/2008 and 111/2009

Law on General Administrative Procedure [2016] Official Gazette of the Republic of Serbia Nos 18/2016, 95/2018 – authentic interpretation and 2/2023 – decision of the Constitutional Court

Law on Obligations [1978] Official Journal of the SFRY, nos. 29/78, 39/85, 45/89-decision of the Constitutional Court and no. 57/89, Official Journal of the FRY no. 31/93, Official Journal of Serbia-Montenegro no. 1/2003 – Constitutional Treaty and the Official Gazette of the Republic of Serbia no. 18/2020

Regulation on Agreements Between Undertakings Operating at the Different Level of Production or Distribution Chain Exempted from Prohibition [2010] Official Gazette of the Republic of Serbia, no. 11/2010

Regulation on Agreements on Specialization Between Undertakings Operating on the Same Level of Production or Distribution Chain Exempted from Prohibition [2010] Official Gazette of the Republic of Serbia, no. 11/2010

Regulation on Research and Development Agreements Between Undertakings Operating on the Same Level of Production or Distribution [2010] Official Gazette of the Republic of Serbia, no. 11/2010

Constitution of the Federal Republic of Yugoslavia [1992] YUG-1992-C-29669

Law on Amendments and Supplements to the Bankruptcy Law [2017] Official Gazette of the Republic of Serbia No. 113/2017

References

CPC (2012) Annual Report. Available at: https://kzk.gov.rs/kzk/wp-content/uploads/2013/05/GODISNJI-IZVESTAJ-O-RADU-KZK-za-2012-godinu.pdf. Accessed 17 February 2025

CPC (2013) Annual Report. Available at: https://kzk.gov.rs/kzk/wp-content/uploads/2014/06/Izvestaj-o-radu-za-2013-godinu.pdf. Accessed 17 February 2025

CPC (2014) Annual Report. Available at: https://kzk.gov.rs/kzk/wp-content/uploads/2015/04/godisnji_izvestaj_kzk_2014.pdf. Accessed 17 February 2025

CPC (2015) Annual Report. Available at: https://kzk.gov.rs/kzk/wp-content/uploads/2016/05/godisnji-izvestaj-kzk-2015.pdf. Accessed 17 February 2025

CPC (2016) Annual Report. Available at: https://kzk.gov.rs/kzk/wp-content/uploads/2017/05/gior2016.pdf. Accessed 17 February 2025

CPC (2017) Annual Report. Available at: https://kzk.gov.rs/kzk/wp-content/uploads/2018/05/Godisnji-izvestaj-KZK-za-2017-godinu.pdf. Accessed 17 February 2025

CPC (2018) Annual Report. Available at: https://kzk.gov.rs/kzk/wp-content/uploads/2019/06/GI-2018-srb1.pdf. Accessed 17 February 2025

CPC (2019) Annual Report. Available at: https://kzk.gov.rs/kzk/wp-content/uploads/2021/02/2019-Godišnji-izveštaj-o-radu-MI-BS-final.pdf. Accessed 17 February 2025

CPC (2020) Annual Report. Available at: https://kzk.gov.rs/kzk/wp-content/uploads/2021/10/Godisnji-izvestaj-KZK-2020-Fin-20210225.pdf. Accessed 17 February 2025

CPC (2021) Annual Report. Available at: https://kzk.gov.rs/kzk/wp-content/uploads/2023/02/Izvestaj-o-radu-KZK-za-2021-godinu1.pdf. Accessed 17 February 2025

European Commission (2008) White paper on damages actions for breach of the EC antitrust rules. COM (2008) 165 final

Guidelines on Fines (2011). Available at: http://www.kzk.org.rs/kzk/wp-content/uploads/2011/08/NOVE-SMERNICE-MAJ-2011.pdf. Accessed 17 February 2025

Guidelines on the Application for an Individual Exemption (2010). Available at: http://kzk.gov.rs/kzk/wp-content/uploads/2011/08/UPUTSTVO-Podnosenje-zahteva-za-pojedinacno-izuzece-restriktivnih-sporazuma-od-zabrane.pdf. Accessed 17 February 2025

Labus M, Foreign Investors Council (2021) White Book: Proposals for Improvement of the Business Environment in Serbia. Foreign Investors Council

Leniency programme in Serbia (2010). Available at: http://www.kzk.org.rs/kzk/wp-content/uploads/2011/08/Smernice-za-primenu-cl-69-i-uredbe-o-oslobadjanju.pdf. Accessed 17 February 2025

Milutinović V, Jovanić T (2010) Serbia's new law on protection of competition: innovations and challenges for a young competition regime. In: Campbell D (ed) Comparative yearbook of international business. The Hague Kluwer Law International

Odbija se kao neosnovana ustavna žalba privrednog društva „Industrija smrznute hrane Frikom" d.o.o. izjavljena protiv rešenja Saveta Komisije za zaštitu konkurencije broj 5/0-02-329/2012-1 od 19. novembra 2012. godine, presude Upravnog suda U. 17578/12 od 12. marta 2013. godine i presude Vrhovnog kasacionog suda Uzp. 181/13 od 6. februara 2014. Godine (2014). Available at: https://sirius.rs/praksa/ipbbGg. Accessed 17 February 2025

Peterhof (2018) Vital - Victoria Oil Case. Available at: https://www.competitioneconomics.org/dyn/files/basic_items/713-file/B.2.%20Sunflower%20Oil%20-%20D.%20Loncar.pdf. Accessed 17 February 2025
Tariff on the Level of Compensation for Activities within the Competence of the Commission for Protection of Competition (2011). Available at: http://www.kzk.gov.rs/kzk/wp-content/uploads/2011/07/Tariff.pdf. Accessed 17 February 2025

Veljko Milutinović is an Associate Professor at the Faculty of Business Studies and Law, Union Nikola Tesla University, Belgrade. Veljko has been active in the field of competition and regulatory law since 2003, as a researcher, lawyer, professor, and consultant. Veljko was a Member of the Council of the Serbian Commission for Protection of Competition (2014–2019). He has been highly active as a consultant in EU and UN projects in Serbia, on a variety of matters ranging from freedom to provide services to construction and infrastructure. Experience in renewable energy and international business law. Experience in a senior public sector position, consulting (EU, UN) and university teaching. As a university professor, he taught business law, international business law, EU law, competition law and international civil aviation law. Veljko obtained his Ph.D. in EU and US competition law from the European University Institute in Florence, while he obtained his LL.B in English Law from the University of Essex and his LL.M from the University of Bristol. He has written numerous publications on issues of competition and EU law, including a distinguished monograph on the private enforcement of EU competition law. Veljko is fluent in English, Serbian, Greek and Italian, with a passive knowledge of French.

Vuk Leković practices law as an attorney and is affiliated with the Gecić Law firm, located in Belgrade. His primary focus lies in the field of Competition Law, where he provides regular counsel to clients involved in high-stakes antitrust cases across various Western Balkans jurisdictions. Other areas of expertise include Regulatory matters, Administrative Law, Public Procurement and Insurance Law. Prior entering the bar, Vuk worked at the Serbian Competition Authority (NCA) and the National Bank of Serbia (NBS). At the NCA, he was an independent advisor in the investigation of competition infringements. During this period, he completed a one-month training program at the Japan Fair Trade Commission. During his four-year tenure at the NBS, Vuk held the position of Associate for regulatory improvement within the Insurance Supervision Department, and he also worked as a Legal Affairs Associate in the Procurement department. He was also a member of the working group that drafted the Compulsory Traffic Insurance Act and the Voluntary Pension Funds and Pension Schemes Act. Vuk's academic credentials include an LL.M. in Business Law, which he obtained in 2016, and an LL.B. degree earned in 2014, both from the University of Belgrade, Faculty of Law. Moreover, he holds licenses as a Public Procurement Officer and a Bankruptcy Trustee. He is a member of the Belgrade Bar Association.

Competition Law and Policy in the Western Balkans: Comparative Assessment

Jasminka Pecotić Kaufman, Gentjan Skara, and Alexandr Svetlicinii

1 Introduction

This chapter offers a comparative assessment of the development of competition law systems in the Western Balkans (WB) countries (Albania, Bosnia and Herzegovina (B&H), Kosovo,[1] Montenegro, North Macedonia, and Serbia) from the 1990s to the present. It builds on preceding national chapters that provide detailed accounts of developments in individual jurisdictions. Our findings are substantiated by empirical data on the institutional capacities of national competition authorities (NCAs) and their enforcement records during the period 2012–2022, as presented in the national chapters.

We aim to present original insights into the dynamics of WB competition systems' evolution, primarily driven by the internalisation of EU competition rules at the national level within the context of EU enlargement.[2] This chapter's

[1] Some authors of this chapter considered it important to include the following statement: "This designation is without prejudice to positions on status, and is in line with UNSCR 1244 and the ICJ Opinion on the Kosovo declaration of independence".

[2] For a broader discussion on the relevant challenges see Džankić et al. (2019). For challenges related to building a competition culture in post-socialist jurisdictions and effectively aligning

J. Pecotić Kaufman
Faculty of Economics and Business, Department of Business Law, University of Zagreb, Zagreb, Croatia

Robert Schuman Centre for Advanced Studies, European University Institute, Florence, Italy
e-mail: jpecotic@net.efzg.hr

G. Skara (✉)
Department of Law, Epoka University, Tirana, Albania
e-mail: gskara@epoka.edu.al

A. Svetlicinii
Faculty of Law, University of Macau, Macao SAR, China
e-mail: alexandrs@um.edu.mo

J. Pecotić Kaufman et al. (eds.), *Competition Law and Policy in the Western Balkans*, European Union and its Neighbours in a Globalized World 22,
https://doi.org/10.1007/978-3-031-93756-9_8

comparative analysis follows the structure of the national chapters, organized into the following sections: i) historical outline and legislative development, ii) institutional framework, iii) application of EU law by NCAs and national courts, iv) national peculiarities, v) enforcement and fines, vi) judicial review, and vii) private enforcement.

2 Historical and Legislative Developments of Competition Law in the Western Balkans

Similar to other ex-socialist countries in Central and Eastern European countries (CEE), the introduction of competition law systems in the WB countries was, in a broader sense, part of the democratic and economic transition. The primary impetus for establishing and improving competition law frameworks in WB countries came from the EU rapprochement process within the context of the Stabilization and Association Process (SAP) in the early 2000s. These incentives were largely exogenous, driven by the intention of those countries to eventually become EU Member States.

Building coherent competition law frameworks was a gradual process. Initial attempts to establish effective competition law systems had somewhat limited success. First-generation antitrust laws, adopted in the mid/late-1990s or early/mid-2000s, depending on the jurisdiction, were either not enforced in practice (e.g. Albania) or provided for no sanctions or very low sanctions (e.g. B&H, Albania).

The second generation of competition legislation, adopted by most WB countries in the mid-2000s, was developed within the context of EU accession. Alignment with the EU *acquis* became a requirement under the respective Stabilization and Association Agreements (SAA). Consequently, these second-generation laws were more comprehensive, particularly concerning investigative powers of NCAs.

Experience gained by NCAs and courts in applying these laws led to further refinements through amendments, which granted NCAs direct fining powers (e.g., the 2009 Competition Act in Serbia)[3] and clarified investigative and sanctioning procedures. The introduction of new investigative tools, such as dawn raids, and various sanctions and remedies for competition infringements, was approached cautiously in some jurisdictions. In Albania, due to its long history of dictatorship, the parliament was wary of potential state power abuse,[4] perceiving imported EU legal solutions as paradoxically conflicting with the democratisation process.

judicial review with EU law standards see Pecotić Kaufman (2021), Pecotić Kaufman and Šimić Banović (2021), Pecotić Kaufman (2023) and Svetlicinii (2018).

[3] See Svetlicinii (2012a).

[4] See the chapter by Gentjan Skara, Pranvera Këllezi and Bojana Hajdini, Competition Law and Policy in Albania.

In many WB countries, modern institutional frameworks for enforcing competition rules required replacing ineffective state bodies responsible for first-generation competition laws. These departments, located within ministries of economy/trade and other government-subordinated institutions, were gradually replaced by independent competition authorities under the second-generation laws (e.g., Albania, Montenegro, Serbia).

In terms of their competences, WB countries opted for dedicated NCAs that exclusively enforce competition rules (i.e. anticompetitive agreements, abuse of dominance, merger control). The exceptions are Montenegro and North Macedonia, where NCAs also monitor state aid.[5] Notably, Albania's first-generation competition legislation included consumer protection and unfair competition rules.

Developing competition law systems in WB jurisdictions to align with the EU model and focus on effective enforcement has been challenging. In most WB countries, the EU accession process unfolded amid numerous legislative reforms, particularly in North Macedonia, where the third-generation competition legislation was amended four times. Frequent legislative changes arguably distracted from enforcement and hindered NCAs from building a credible enforcement record. In some WB jurisdictions, aligning with the EU *acquis* presented challenges in optimally adapting the domestic legal order to EU legal transplants.[6] Additionally, long-term institutional instability in some WB countries prevented effective enforcement of competition rules.[7]

3 WB Competition Authorities: Institutional Design, Resources, and Powers

3.1 Institutional Design

While institutional design varies from country to country, most WB NCAs have collegiate decision-making bodies, typically called "commission" or "council", consisting of five (Albania, Kosovo, North Macedonia, Serbia) or six members (B&H). In Montenegro, a dual model has been preserved, possibly a remnant of the pre-2018 regime under which a director headed the NCA. As of 2018, the Montenegrin NCA has (a) a decision-making collegiate body, consisting of a

[5] In Croatia, before EU accession, the NCA was also responsible for enforcing state aid rules. For more details, see Pecotić Kaufman (2022).

[6] See the chapter by Gentjan Skara, Pranvera Këllezi and Bojana Hajdini, Competition Law and Policy in Albania.

[7] See the chapters by Dijana Marković-Bajalović and Kanita Imamović-Čizmić, Competition Law and Policy in Bosnia and Herzegovina, Avdylkader Mucaj, Competition Law and Policy in Kosovo.

president and two members, and (b) a director, who has both a managing role and is involved in preparing decisions to be adopted by the council.[8]

Although some WB NCAs initially started as non-independent bodies within government ministries, they evolved into independent institutions, i.e., separate legal entities with formal independence guaranteed by law. The members of the decision-making body are appointed by parliament in most jurisdictions (Albania, Kosovo, North Macedonia, Serbia) or by the government (Montenegro, B&H). The NCAs submit annual reports to their respective parliaments and in Montenegro, also to the government.

3.2 Resources: Budget and Staff

Adequate funding for NCAs is a prerequisite for effective enforcement. Most WB NCAs are funded from the state budget. Serbia is an outlier in this respect, with funds for the NCA provided almost exclusively from its revenues generated by performing its functions, primarily from merger fees. In 2021, 98.76% of the total revenues of the Serbian NCA came from this source. In Montenegro, the law provides that NCA funding may come from several sources (collected fees, state budget, other sources), but in practice, the NCA is fully financed from the state budget.[9]

The dynamics of budget allocations for WB NCAs over the years are mostly similar. Generally, the budgets have increased over time, peaking in 2018 for Albania, in 2019 for Montenegro (due to the transfer of the state aid mandate to the NCA), or in 2020 for North Macedonia (the increase in budget not related to the increase in the number of employees). Thereafter, the budgets have fallen slightly. In contrast, B&H data shows no overall increase in the NCA budget in the relevant period (2011–2022), remaining almost constant. The number of NCA staff was gradually increasing over the 2012–2021/2022 period (Albania, Montenegro, Serbia), while in some countries no increase was observed (B&H, North Macedonia).

Table 1 shows data related to NCAs budgets, in absolute terms and in relation to population and to NCA staff. To better relate the data for a particular nation, we also show the Western Balkan Average. In addition, we show Western Balkan Average Excluding Serbia, as Serbia is a major outlier in a number of data points, including NCA's budget, country population, and nominal GDP. Since the economic development levels of the WB countries are relatively similar, the ranking in Table 1 seems to indicate fundamental differences in NCA budgeting between countries.

The data presented in Table 1 shows that Montenegro and Serbia have a noticeably higher NCA budget per citizen, and that Serbia accounts for the majority of the total budget for competition authorities in the region. We note that one of the

[8] See the chapter by Nebojša Jovović, Competition Law and Policy in Montenegro.

[9] Ibid.

Table 1 WB NCAs budgets and staff

Country	NCA budget in EUR	Total population	NCA budget in EUR per citizen	Number of total NCA staff	NCA budget in EUR per staff member	Note
Montenegro	657,000	619,000	1.06	32	20,531.25	Data for 2022 (inclusive of state aid mandate)
Serbia	5,170,000	6,800,000	0.76	57	90,701.75	Data for 2021 (expert service staff only)
Albania	710,000	2,800,000	0.25	46	15,434.78	Data for 2022
B&H	633,000	3,300,000	0.19	25	25,320.00	Data for 2021
North Macedonia	340,000	2,100,000	0.16	27	12,592.59	Data for 2021 (inclusive of state aid mandate)
Kosovo	245,000	1,900,000	0.13	23	10,652.17	Data for 2021
Western Balkans Average	**1,292,500**	**2,919,833**	**0.43**	**35**	**29,205.42**	
Western Balkans Average Excluding Serbia	517,000	2,143,800	0.36	31	16,906.16	

Source: Authors' own compilation

constraints when comparing WB NCAs' budgets relates to the fact that some NCAs (Montenegro, North Macedonia) perform state aid control in addition to competition enforcement, and information distinguishing between funding for different mandates is not available.

3.3 Powers

The use of inspection powers varies significantly between jurisdictions. In some WB countries, the power to conduct dawn raids is used extensively, while in others, its use is limited. In Albania, where we observe a disproportionately higher number of dawn raids than in other WB countries, 253 dawn raids were conducted over six years (2017–2022), averaging 42 dawn raids per year. In Serbia, 51 dawn raids have been conducted over ten years (2012–2021),[10] averaging five per year. In Montenegro, the NCA conducted six dawn raids over eleven years (2012–2022),[11] averaging 1.8 per year.

In some jurisdictions, a judicial warrant is necessary for inspecting both business and private premises (B&H and Kosovo), while in others, it is needed only for inspections of private premises, provided the owner objects to the raid (Serbia). In Montenegro, no court warrant is needed for conducting dawn raids.

In most WB jurisdictions, NCAs have the direct power to impose fines on undertakings for competition law infringements. However, in Montenegro, the NCA may impose a minimum fine, while higher amounts can only be imposed by the misdemeanour courts.[12] In some WB jurisdictions, individuals or responsible persons are also subject to fines (e.g. Albania, B&H, Kosovo). As WB countries follow EU rules as a model, the maximum fine for competition infringements that the NCA may impose on undertakings is set at 10% of the annual turnover. However, as noted in Serbia, the fines are usually far below the 10% mark.[13] The level of fines actually imposed has generally been quite low in WB countries, although there are significant variations across the region.[14]

Leniency is generally available in WB jurisdictions (Albania, Montenegro, North Macedonia, Serbia), but it is rarely or never used in practice. In some countries such as Montenegro, not only cartel members but also parties to any anti-competitive agreement may benefit from a leniency programme.[15]

4 Application of EU Law by NCAs and National Courts

In the context of the European integration process, the WB countries underwent fundamental political, economic, and legal transformations. Due to the conditionality mechanism, they had to undertake reforms and, most importantly, approximate their domestic legislation with the EU *acquis* and ensure their proper implementation.

[10] See the chapter by Veljko Milutinović and Vuk Leković, Competition Law and Policy in Serbia.

[11] See the chapter by Nebojša Jovović, Competition Law and Policy in Montenegro.

[12] See the chapter by Nebojša Jovović, Competition Law and Policy in Montenegro. Serbia abandoned the competence of misdemeanour courts to impose fines for competition law infringements in 2009. See the chapter by Veljko Milutinović and Vuk Leković, Competition Law and Policy in Serbia. Similarly, Croatia discontinued the misdemeanour courts system in 2009 Pecotić Kaufman (2022), while Slovenia still retains it Vlahek (2024).

[13] See the chapter by Veljko Milutinović and Vuk Leković, Competition Law and Policy in Serbia.

[14] For similar comments concerning Croatia, see Pecotić Kaufman (2022). More details on fines imposed by WB NCAs see infra, Sect. 6.2.

[15] See the chapter by Nebojša Jovović, Competition Law and Policy in Montenegro.

As the EU perspective became evident with the Thessaloniki Summit in 2003, declaring that "the future of the Balkans is within the European Union",[16] all WB countries have signed the SAAs, modelled after the 'Europe Agreements' concluded with the CEEs that joined the EU in 2004.[17] Unlike the CEEs, including Croatia, which had a 'European clause' in their constitutions regulating the status of EU law in the internal legal order prior to EU accession,[18] the WB countries' constitutions do not contain any special provisions providing for the application of EU law in the domestic legal order.[19] The SAA is considered an international treaty rather than a domestic legal provision on application of EU law.[20]

In general, all the WB countries, except for B&H, have explicitly adopted a 'monist' approach regarding the applicability and status of ratified and promulgated international treaties.[21] According to the monist approach, the SAA, as an international treaty, can be directly applied by national courts without prior adoption of any implementing legislation and has supremacy over domestic legislation, with a superior status to national legislation in the domestic hierarchy of norms. The situation regarding the effect and status of international treaties in B&H is unclear, as B&H's constitution adopted a combination of monistic and dualistic approaches. The monistic approach relates to legal sources of international law with direct effect specified in the constitution, whereas a moderate dualistic approach covers other legal sources of international law.[22] So far, there have been no constitutional court decisions discussing the status of the SAA in the legal systems of the WB countries.

From the perspective of the WB legal systems, the SAA is considered an international treaty that, once ratified and published in the official journal, has supremacy over domestic legal norms. From the EU perspective, the SAA represents the legal basis for the WB countries' association with the EU.[23] The WB SAAs aim at: (1) develop political dialogue between the EU and signatory countries; (2) gradually harmonise national legislations of signatory countries with the EU *acquis*; (3) improve economic relations between the two sides; (4) gradually developing the free trade zone between the two sides; and (5) encourage regional cooperation within the Stabilisation and Association Process.[24]

---

[16] Commission (2003).

[17] Blockmans and Lazowski (2006), p. 3.

[18] Albi (2005), p. 41; Bačić (2014), pp. 80–81.

[19] Nevertheless, in some countries like Serbia, domestic legislation refers explicitly to EU rules. For instance, the Act on Foreign Trade stipulates that foreign trade is regulated "in accordance with the EU rules." Vukadinović et al. (2014), p. 143.

[20] Skara and Hajdini (2021), Georgievski et al., (2014), pp. 102–113; Vukadinović et al. (2014), p. 143; Meškić and Samardžić (2014), pp. 63–66; Kostić-Mandić (2014), p. 133.

[21] Caka (2014), Meškić and Samardžić (2014), Georgievski et al. (2014), Vukadinović et al. (2014), Kostić-Mandić (2014), Zyberi and Sali (2015).

[22] Meškić and Samardžić (2014), p. 63.

[23] The SAA is concluded base on Article 217 TFEU and is signed by the EU and Member States on the one hand and candidate countries on the other hand.

[24] SAA with Albania, Art 1(2); SAA with North Macedonia, Art 1(2); SAA with Kosovo, Art 1(2); SAA with Serbia, Art 1(2); SAA with B&H, Art 1(2); SAA with Montenegro, Art 1(2).

The common characteristic of the WB countries' competition law is the influence of EU law in drafting national legislation. Particularly, national competition rules on restrictive agreements, abuse of dominant position, and merger control are modelled after Articles 101 and 102 TFEU and the EU Merger Regulation. In addition, the European Commission's soft laws in the competition law area have been transposed by WB NCAs through notices and guidelines to increase the level of harmonisation.

Furthermore, the WB SAAs contain an identical provision on competition policy, including state aid rules. According to this provision,

> the following shall be incompatible in so far as they may affect trade between the Community and [WB country]:
>
> (1) all agreements between undertakings, decisions by associations of undertakings and concerted practices between undertakings that have as their object or effect the prevention, restriction or distortion of competition;
> (2) abuse by one or more undertakings of a dominant position in the territories of the Community or of [WB country] as a whole or in a substantial part thereof;
> (3) any State aid which distorts or threatens to distort competition by favouring certain undertakings or certain products.[25]

Despite the harmonization obligations undertaken by WB under the respective SAAs, their approaches towards the application of EU competition rules or interpretation of national competition rules in light of EU law and jurisprudence differ. For example, jurisdictions like B&H and Kosovo have included references to the EU *acquis* or SAA provisions in their national competition legislation.

For instance, Article 43 (7) of the B&H Competition Act states that "Competition Council, for the purpose of assessment of a given case, can use the case law of the European Court of Justice and the decisions of the European Commission". By introducing this provision, the B&H legislator increases the clarity for the Competition Council to consider the Court of Justice of the European Union (CJEU) cases or Commission decisions. In the case of Kosovo, the LPC of 2022 has a broader reference to EU competition regulations.[26]

Additionally, Article 70 (2) of the LPC of 2022 makes specific reference to the EU/Kosovo SAA by stating that "this law shall be implemented in accordance with the obligations of the Republic of Kosovo deriving from the Stabilization and Association Agreement with the European Union and the European Atomic Energy

[25] SAA with Albania, Art 71 (1); SAA with North Macedonia, Art 69 (1); SAA with Kosovo, Art 75(1); SAA with Serbia, Art 73(1); SAA with B&H, Art 71(1); SAA with Montenegro, Art 73(1).

[26] Article 1(2) of the LPC makes reference to the following EU competition regulations: (i) Council Regulation (EC) No. 1/2003 of 16 December 2002 on the implementation of the rules on competition laid down in Articles 81 and 82 of the Treaty [2003] OJ L1/1; (ii) Council Regulation (EC) No. 139/2004 of 20 January 2004 on the control of concentrations between undertakings (the EC Merger Regulation) [2004] OJ L 24/1; (iii) Commission Regulation (EU) No 330/2010 of 20 April 2010 on the application of Article 101 (3) of the Treaty on the Functioning of the European Union to categories of vertical agreements and concerted practices [2010] OJ L 102/1 (no longer in force); iv) Commission Regulation (EC) No 802/2004 of 7 April 2004 implementing Council Regulation (EC) No.139/2004 of 20 January 2004 on the control of concentrations between undertakings" [2004] OJ L 133/1 (no longer in force).

Community". By emphasising SAA obligations in the LPC of 2022, the Kosovo NCA and courts can interpret national competition rules in accordance with EU law.[27]

Based on the experience of CEE countries,[28] the WB courts have applied EU law at the pre-accession stage, either by applying the particular source of EU law (direct applicability) or by using EU law as a tool for interpretation and application of domestic legal rules (judicial harmonisation). For instance, in several decisions, the Constitutional Court of Albania made direct references to EU law as a persuasive source of law to support the court's decision.[29] In these decisions, it invoked the SAA provisions and EU law to disapply national law that was found incompatible with EU law. However, the Constitutional Court of Albania did not explain why it relied on EU law or the place of EU law in the Albanian legal system.

In the case of B&H, the Constitutional Court interpreted market freedom in light of the *Schul* case,[30] stating that "the substantive notion of a "single market" implies that the internal market of B&H should be created by repealing all technical, administrative and other measures".[31] Similarly, Montenegrin and Serbian courts have referred to EU law on several occasions in the area of public law or civil law.[32]

The SAAs with WB countries contain a provision stipulating that any anti-competitive practices that may affect trade between the EU and the respective WB country shall be assessed "based on criteria arising from the application of the competition rules applicable in the Community", particularly from Articles 101, 102, 106 and 107 TFEU and the "interpretative instruments adopted by the Community institutions".[33] This provision requires the NCAs to asses any practice that may affect trade between the EU and the respective WB country in light of EU competition law, the CJEU jurisprudence, the Commission's decisions in competition cases, and various soft law measures, namely the Commission Guidelines and Notices.[34] For this reason, competition law has been considered a "privileged area"

---

[27] See the chapter Avdylkader Mucaj, Competition Law and Policy in Kosovo.

[28] Albi (2005), pp. 52–53; Albi (2007), p. 39; Kühn (2005a), p. 55; Kühn (2005b), p. 563; Meškić and Samardžić (2014), pp. 69–70; Lang and Mataija (2014), pp. 95–96; Georgievski et al. (2014), p. 122; Vukadinović et al. (2014), p. 150; Pecotić Kaufman and Butorac Malnar (2016), pp. 346–348; Emmert (2004), Cseres (2008), Cseres (2014), Balan (2021).

[29] Judgment of 24 July 2009, Albanian Constitutional Court, V-24/09, [2009] OJ 119; Law 97/2013 On audio and audio-visual media services in the Republic of Albania [2013] OJ 37/1497; Judgment of 27 July 2016, Albanian Constitutional Court, V-56/16, [2016] OJ 152; Judgment of 21 March 2014, Albanian Constitutional Court, V-14/14, [2014] OJ 50.

[30] Judgment of 5 May 1982, *Schul,* C-15/81, ECLI:EU:C:1982:135, para. 33.

[31] Judgment of Constitutional Court of B&H, U 68/02 cited in Meškić and Samardžić (2014), pp. 66-67. For more on the application of CJEU jurisprudence before the Courts of B&H, Constitutional Court of B&H see Meškić and Samardžić (2014), pp. 69–70; Čolaković (2014), pp. 71–76.

[32] Georgievski et al. (2014); Kostić-Mandić (2014), Radovanovic et al (2014), p. 150.

[33] SAA with Albania, Art 71 (2); SAA with North Macedonia, Art 69 (2); SAA with Kosovo, Art 75(2); SAA with Serbia, Art 73(2); SAA with B&H, Art 71(2); SAA with Montenegro, Art 73(2).

[34] Cremona (2003), pp. 269–271; Skara (2022), p. 223.

in the SAA, as it requires the applicability of the EU competition *acquis* before the accession of the WB countries to the EU.[35]

In light of the aforementioned SAA requirement, the WB NCAs have occasionally relied on EU law, the CJEU case law, and the Commission's soft law. Generally, the NCAs do not mention EU law or the SAA provisions among the legal grounds for their decisions. Most of the time, EU law is referred to for the purpose of interpreting national competition law. For instance, in Albania and B&H, NCAs have relied on EU secondary legislation, soft laws, and CJEU cases to define restrictive agreements or abuse of dominant position. Moreover, in many merger cases, the Albanian NCA has referred to the European Commission's practice to define the relevant product market, albeit not necessarily explaining the reasons for its reliance.[36]

National courts also relied on SAA provisions to interpret domestic competition law. As discussed in the B&H chapter, the B&H Competition Act, adopted before the ratification of the SAA, contains one provision enabling the NCA to 'take into account the practice of the ECJ and the decisions of the European Commission' when deciding a case.[37] Pursuant to this requirement, in the *ASA Auto* case,[38] the Court of B&H found an abuse of dominant position following the legal test laid down in the *IMS Health* judgment.[39]

In another decision, the Constitutional Court of Albania assessed the compatibility of domestic law in light of Articles 70 and 71 of the SAA.[40] The Constitutional Court was asked to declare the unconstitutionality of two Council of Minister Decisions, which created a concession contract for fuel marking and monitoring services in Albania. In its reasoning, the Albanian Constitutional Court noted the importance of Article 71 of the SAA[41] and referred to the CJEU case law when a certain activity was given by the public authority to a company with exclusive rights.[42]

---

[35] Meškić and Samardžić (2014), pp. 69–70; Lang and Mataija (2014), pp. 95–96; Georgievski et al. (2014), p. 122; Vukadinović et al. (2014), p. 150; Pecotić Kaufman (2022); Pecotić Kaufman and Butorac Malnar (2016), pp. 350–353.

[36] For more on this argument, see the chapter by Gentjan Skara, Pranvera Këllezi and Bojana Hajdini, Competition Law and Policy in Albania.

[37] Competition Act of B&H, Art 43.

[38] Court of B&H, decision No. S1 3 U 005412 10 Uvl, 15.3.2012., M.R.M. Ljubuški/ASA Auto d.o.o. Sarajevo (ASA Auto).

[39] Judgment of 29 April 2004, *IMS Health.*, C-418/01 [2004] ECLI:EU:C:2004:257.

[40] Judgment of 21 March 2014, Albanian Constitutional Court, V-14/14, [2014] OJ 50.

[41] In para 31, the Constitutional Court noted that "under the Stabilisation and Association Agreement, practises contrary to Article 71 (competition and other economic provisions) are assessed based on criteria arising from the application of the competition rules applicable in the Community, in particular Articles 81 82, 86 and 87 of the Treaty establishing the European Community, and interpretative instruments used by Community institutions". Judgment of 21 March 2014, Albanian Constitutional Court, V-14/14, [2014] OJ 50, para 31.

[42] Judgment of 18 March 1997, *Cali v. Servizi ecologici porto di Genova SpA*, C-343/95, ECLI:EU:C:1997:160, paras 16-23; Judgment of 19 January 1994, *SAT Fluggesellschaft mbH v Eurocontrol,*

5 National Peculiarities

While the process of harmonisation with the EU competition law *acquis* is currently progressing in each of the covered WB jurisdictions, all of them have retained certain national peculiarities that can be organised into the following broader groups. The first group of divergences is due to the historical reliance on market regulation by state authorities, which was common in socialist economies, and the initially limited understanding of the functionalities of competition law in a market economy. These factors have been especially visible in the first editions of the national competition legislation adopted in the 1990s when most of the studied jurisdictions commenced their market economy reforms. Gradually, with the accumulation of the enforcement experience and intensification of the EU harmonisation processes, most of the WB countries have eliminated these divergencies through legislative amendments or complete overhauls of their competition law enforcement systems.

The second group of national peculiarities is related to the legal traditions that are deeply rooted in the covered legal systems and pertain to the separation of powers between administrative and judicial branches, as well as the organisation of the investigative and sanctioning proceedings.[43] These factors originate from the laws underpinning the organisation of the judiciary, administrative law and administrative procedure, judicial review, and imposition of sanctions. As a result, they have persisted over a longer period of time, as their elimination would require more substantial changes in the national legal systems that several of the studied jurisdictions are not willing to implement. The ensuing analysis will elaborate on these two groups of factors and their evolution in the selected WB jurisdictions.

5.1 Peculiarities of the National Legal Systems that Significantly Differ from the EU Competition Acquis

The first group of factors related to the market regulation by the state authorities was reflected, among other things, in the initial positioning of the NCAs in WB jurisdictions. Like many other sectoral regulators and administrative authorities, these NCAs were incorporated into the governmental structures and subordinated to a higher-level authority such as the ministry of economy. For example, in Albania, the 1995 competition legislation placed the NCA under the authority of the Minister of Economic Cooperation and Trade. Subsequently, during the process of the SAA negotiations, the law was changed, and the Albanian NCA acquired the status of an independent administrative agency.

C-364/92, ECLI:EU:C:1994:7, para 30; Judgment of 19 May 1993, *Paul CORBEAU, C-320/91*, ECLI:EU:C:1993:198, para 14.

[43] Bernatt et al. (2018), Botta and Svetlicinii (2015).

The long-lasting tradition of state regulation in WB economies resulted in limited knowledge about the functionalities of competition law in a free market economy. The lack of understanding of the competition law concepts resulted in incoherent and, at times, dysfunctional legislation. These deficiencies are especially visible in the example of B&H. Its 2005 legislation extended the application of competition law to the actions of public authorities without clarifying whether the exercise of rule-making or rule-implementing powers could also be curtailed by competition law. As a result, it took several years of inconsistent enforcement practice and judicial review until the courts settled the matter by clarifying that public authorities are subject to competition law only when they enter into commercial transactions.[44]

Furthermore, when drafting the national equivalent of Article 101 TFEU, the B&H legislators used the connector "and" instead of "or", making the anticompetitive object and effect of an agreement between undertakings or decision of an association of undertakings a cumulative requirement for finding an infringement. This significantly increased the burden of proof incumbent on the NCA and resulted in an enforcement practice whereby the NCA assumed the illegality of the anticompetitive practices expressly listed in the legal provision. This prevented the development of enforcement practices that could address anticompetitive practices not expressly covered by the respective legal provision.

The second group of divergencies is rooted in the respective legal traditions of the WB jurisdictions and relates to the organisation of the judiciary, general principles or administrative law, and administrative procedures. For example, commitments and settlements are novel legal concepts for the administrative law systems of the covered jurisdictions. As a result, as the examples of B&H and Serbia demonstrate, in the absence of explicit legislative procedures, the NCAs conduct informal consultations with the parties under investigation and then insert the agreed "commitments" or "settlements" in the infringement decision in the form of an order or recommendation of the NCA. Several WB jurisdictions, including B&H, Montenegro and Serbia, decided to preserve the availability of individual exemptions, allowing the undertakings to clear their agreements under a distinct procedure while further adding to the workload of the respective NCAs.

However, the most pronounced effect on competition law enforcement in the WB region stems from the tradition of administrative law and the organisation of the judiciary. All of the selected jurisdictions, except Albania, inherited the Yugoslavian administrative law enforcement system based on the misdemeanour proceedings conducted by the courts. As a result, the administrative agencies, including the NCAs, were not authorised to impose sanctions for violation of competition rules. This has created a significant impediment to the efficiency of competition law enforcement, which had to be carried out through a dual system of administrative

---

[44] Svetlicinii (2012a, b, c 2013a, b). However, the recent judgment of the Court of B&H from 2022 again caused controversy regarding the application of competition rules to public bodies. Court of B&H, *Federal Ministry of Health v. Competition Council of & BiH,* S1 3 U 035154 22 Uvp, 21.04.2022.

and misdemeanour courts: the former reviewing the infringement decisions issued by the NCA and the latter deciding on the penalties to be imposed for competition law violations.

While most of the WB jurisdictions have moved to reform this system, at least in the field of competition law enforcement, Montenegro still preserves this dual-track system where the diverging assessments by misdemeanour and administrative courts result in a situation where undertakings found in violation of competition rules manage to avoid penalties for these violations.

5.2 *Peculiarities of the National Legal Systems that Have Been Erased or Amended in the Process of Europeanization*

All the aforementioned peculiarities of the national competition law systems in the WB jurisdictions have undergone substantial amendments in harmonisation with the EU *acquis,* guided by the requirements of the respective SAAs. For example, Albania's SAA was concluded in 2006, entered into force in 2009, and was followed by the amendment of competition legislation in 2010. However, due to a lack of expertise in competition matters, the Albanian legislators and the NCA have simply "copy-pasted" numerous provisions from the European Commission's notices and guidelines in their national equivalents, leaving it for the enforcement and judicial review practice to clarify the understanding of various novel legal concepts.[45]

In B&H, the harmonisation process has been delayed due to the country's compliance with ECtHR's ruling.[46] Thus, the respective SAA was concluded in 2008 but not ratified until 2011 and entered into force only in 2015. As a result, the 2001 competition law, which was B&H's first post-Yugoslavian competition legislation, was not harmonised with the EU *acquis* and contained numerous lacunae. The current competition legislation was adopted in 2005 and sought to follow the *acquis* but incorporated a number of aforementioned divergencies. In 2006, the B&H passed several block exemption regulations, transposing the EU equivalents into national competition law. Currently, they remain valid and await an update in light of the subsequent revisions of the EU block exemption regulations and guidelines.

Kosovo had a series of competition legislation (passed in 2004, 2010, and 2022), which was continuously harmonised with the EU *acquis* by enhancing the NCA's sanctioning powers (fines calculated as a percentage of annual turnover), amending presumptions related to dominance and market power, introducing private

[45] See the chapter by Gentjan Skara, Pranvera Këllezi and Bojana Hajdini, Competition Law and Policy in Albania.

[46] *Sejdić and Finci v. Bosnia and Herzegovina*, European Court of Human Rights, Judgment of 22 December 2009, Applications Nos. 27796/06 and 34836/06.

enforcement, etc. The latest competition legislation of 2022 transposed several EU regulations and, in line with the SAA, provided for the interpretation of competition law in accordance with SAA obligations.

In Montenegro, the competition law of 2005 was amended in 2012, establishing an independent NCA and introducing the administrative penalties that it could adopt without recourse to the misdemeanour courts. In 2018, legislative amendments transformed the NCA into a collegiate body and increased the fines to be imposed by misdemeanour courts. Thus, the gradual harmonisation of competition legislation with the EU acquis removed several earlier divergencies while preserving the dual-track judicial system (administrative and misdemeanour courts) that continues to affect the enforcement of competition law in Montenegro.

Likewise, North Macedonia has reformed its competition law system three times (in 1999, 2005, and 2010), with minor legislative amendments taking place in 2011, 2014, 2016, 2018 and 2024. The respective changes were introduced, among others, due to the approximation of competition legislation with the EU *acquis*. The harmonisation process has also been accomplished by the adoption of several secondary regulations and guidelines based on their EU equivalents. As a result, recent Commission reports on North Macedonia reflect satisfaction with legislative harmonisation while demanding more attention to the technical capacity of the NCA to enforce the law.[47]

In Serbia, the 2005 competition legislation copied the EU substantive rules almost verbatim, achieving a significant degree of approximation with the EU *acquis*. Then, in 2009, Serbia moved away from the dual-track judicial review system, authorising the NCA to impose fines and having the administrative courts review the infringement decisions and the imposed penalties. The legislative amendments also introduced the leniency system, which was actively used in the early period following its adoption.

This brief overview draws a picture of the continuous legislative approximation with EU standards, which has taken place in all of the covered WB jurisdictions. The national competition laws have undergone several rounds of amendments and overhauls, which gradually removed major divergencies and national peculiarities from these competition law systems.

6 Enforcement and Fines for the Period 2012–2022

6.1 Enforcement

In this section, we compare the enforcement activities of WB competition authorities during the period 2012–2022. As the national chapters in this volume show, competition authorities in all WB jurisdictions make efforts to identify and sanction

[47] Commission (2022).

competition law infringements. However, enforcement intensity varies across the region.

To be able to deliver relevant findings, we established a common methodological framework for collecting and analysing national data. However, achieving perfect uniformity of datasets was impossible, and national chapters vary somewhat in the level of detail, and availability of certain types of data. While granular enforcement data was obtained for most WB countries, access to enforcement data was challenging in others. For Kosovo, only partial data was available.

In our comparative analysis below, we address (a) merger control, (b) restrictive agreements, (c) abuse of dominant position, and (d) fines. Finally, we offer some concluding remarks on enforcement and fines. We focus on national-level quantitative data and do not qualitatively assess enforcement decisions by NCAs.

6.1.1 Merger Control

Merger control by WB NCAs steadily intensified during the 2012–2022 period. The total volume of merger decisions increased significantly when comparing the first and last years of this period: over 500% in Montenegro, over 400 % in Albania, around 360% in North Macedonia, and over 100% in Serbia. B&H is an exception in this regard; in this country, the number of merger decisions remained relatively stable.

Unsurprisingly, and likely due to its economic size, Serbia was the most productive jurisdiction in terms of the total number of merger decisions, with 1,395 merger decisions (out of which 899 were foreign-to-foreign transactions). North Macedonia (527) and Montenegro (448) also had relatively high numbers, followed by Albania (219) and B&H (160).

A clear majority were adopted in Phase 1, with WB NCAs having little experience with merger remedies. At the same time, merger control in some WB jurisdictions has tested their ability to intervene in high-profile and politically sensitive cases.[48]

6.1.2 Restrictive Agreements

Enforcement related to restrictive agreements, measured by the number of decisions, was stable in many WB countries during most of the relevant period (2012–2022), however with relatively small numbers of NCA decisions adopted annually. Exceptionally, in Albania, we note a significant increase in enforcement activity in recent years, at much higher levels than in other WB countries. More than half of all NCA decisions related to restrictive agreements, that were adopted between 2012 and

---

[48] See the chapter by Dijana Marković-Bajalović and Kanita Imamović-Čizmić, Competition Law and Policy in Bosnia and Herzegovina.

2022, relate to cases closed in 2021 and 2022. Conversely, in B&H, we note a slowdown in the number of decisions related to restrictive agreements since 2019, while the number of the abuse of dominance decisions in that country were increasing.

Concerning the total number of decisions related to restrictive agreements in the relevant period, most decisions were adopted in Albania (102),[49] followed by B&H (63), Montenegro (48),[50] North Macedonia (40), and Serbia (18).

Three WB jurisdictions, Albania, Montenegro, and Serbia continue to maintain a system of individual exemptions for restrictive agreements, meaning that undertakings have the possibility of confirming compliance of their contractual arrangements with competition rules by submitting them to the competition authority. More than 70% of all decisions related to restrictive agreements adopted by the Montenegrin competition authority in the 2012–2022 period relate to individual exemption decisions. On the other hand, only a minority of those in Albania relate to individual exemptions (around 10%).

Concerning cartel enforcement in the 2012–2022 period, national chapters only partially provide relevant data. While North Macedonia and Montenegro on average 1 in 4 decisions related to restrictive agreements concerned cartel infringements in Serbia, some 50% of all decisions regarding restrictive agreements were cartel decisions.

6.1.3 Abuse of Dominant Position

We now turn our attention to the decisions related to the abuse of a dominant position adopted by competition authorities in WB jurisdictions during the relevant period (2012–2022).[51] In some countries, we see a relatively high total number of decisions (77 in Albania, 54 in B&H), while in other countries, we observe a lower total number of unilateral conduct cases (18 in North Macedonia, 6 in Serbia, and 8 in Montenegro). In Albania, the country with the highest total number of the abuse of dominance cases among WB countries, the increase in prosecutions against unilateral conduct is a relatively recent occurrence, with almost three-quarters of all abuse decisions adopted in 2018–2022, with particularly strong enforcement in 2021 and 2022. In B&H and North Macedonia we observe consistent enforcement throughout the relevant period, with at least one abuse decision adopted each year, for the most years. In Serbia, abuse of dominance decisions were adopted relatively sparsely, while in Montenegro, most such decisions were adopted in earlier years, i.e. between 2012 and 2014.

[49] This figure includes 12 individual exemption decisions.

[50] This figure includes 35 individual exemption decisions.

[51] See also Svetlicinii (2012d), Svetlicinii and Botta (2015).

6.1.4 Antitrust Enforcement Track Record in Western Balkan Jurisdictions

Without exception, WB NCAs' investigations concerning antitrust infringements, i.e. restrictive agreements and abuse of dominance, are initiated ex officio, and the NCAs are not obligated to respond to complaints. In some countries, such as Montenegro and Serbia, earlier legislation granted complainants more procedural rights when initiating cases, but this model was later abandoned (in 2012 in Montenegro, and in 2009 in Serbia), removing the duty of the NCA to start a case upon complaint. Arguably, in Montenegro, the decrease in the number of infringement proceedings after 2012 can be directly related with this change. Therefore, in most WB jurisdictions, with the exception of B&H, it is the NCAs that shape their own enforcement record, rather than being driven by complaints.

Concerning the total number of antitrust decisions (restrictive agreements and abuse of dominance) adopted by WB competition authorities in the relevant period (2012–2022), the highest number of such decisions was adopted in Albania (179), followed by B&H (117), North Macedonia (58), Montenegro (56), and Serbia (24).

Comparing the enforcement intensity against restrictive agreements with the enforcement intensity against abuse of dominance, we note a clear preference for enforcement against restrictive agreements in most countries. This preference is most pronounced in Montenegro (86%), Serbia (75%), and North Macedonia (69%). Conversely, this preference is present but less significant in Albania (57%) and B&H (54%).

We observe that the enforcement track record against restrictive agreements is more stable over the relevant period when compared to the track record against the abuse of dominance, where decisions are more sporadic in most WB jurisdictions.

In Table 2, we offer comparative data on the numbers of NCAs' antitrust decisions, relating them to nominal GDP and population, and combining them with the number of NCA staff and budget to gain further insights. As in Table 1, we also present the Western Balkans Average to better contextualize the data for each nation.

In absolute terms, the most antitrust decisions were delivered in Albania (179) and B&H (117). Albania remains top-tier in relative terms, with over 6 decisions per 100,000 citizens and nearly 11 decisions per a billion euros of GDP. B&H leads in NCA efficiency with almost 5 decisions per NCA staff member, while Serbia leads in NCA funding with nearly EUR 91,000 per NCA staff member (see Table 1). Serbia remains an outlier with the lowest number of antitrust decisions per 100,000 citizens (0.35 decisions), per nominal GDP (0.46 decisions per a billion euros), and per NCA staff member (0.42 decisions). However, as we do not qualitatively assess enforcement decisions by NCAs, broader conclusions based solely on quantitative national enforcement data are hard to draw.

Montenegro is a significant outlier in the number of NCA staff per 100,000 citizens, with over 5 staffers per 100,000 citizens, while the rest of the region's NCAs employ around one staffer per 100,000 citizens.

Table 2 NCA antitrust decisions, budget and staff in relation to nominal GDP and population

Country[a]	Number of antitrust decisions[b] (2012–2022)	Nominal GDP in billion EUR[c]	Number of antitrust decisions per 100,000 population	Number of antitrust decisions per nominal GDP in billion EUR	Number of antitrust decisions per NCA's staff	Number of NCA staff per 100,000 population
Montenegro	56	5.4	9.05	10.37	1.75	5.17
Serbia	24	52.1	0.35	0.46	0.42	0.84
Albania	179	16.3	6.39	10.98	3.89	1.64
B&H	117	20.2	3.55	5.79	4.68	0.76
North Macedonia	58	12.6	2.76	4.60	2.15	1.29
Western Balkans Average (w/o Kosovo)	**87**	**21.3**	**3.89**	**5.87**	**2.32**	**1.82**
Western Balkans Average (w/o Kosovo) Excluding Serbia	102.5	13.6	4.60	6.96	2.70	2.01

Source: Authors' own compilation

[a] Kosovo excluded as only partial data available

[b] Substantive decisions related to anticompetitive agreements and abuse of dominant position

[c] World Bank's World Development Indicators supplemented with information from the International Monetary Fund's World Economic Outlook Database for the GDP figures in euros for the year 2022

6.2 *Fines*

In most WB countries, competition authorities can directly impose fines for breaches of competition rules. However, in Montenegro, fines are imposed by misdemeanour courts following the NCAs request based on its infringement decision. This setup arguably influenced the intensity of sanctions, as courts typically imposed fines at the minimum legal amount, with mitigating circumstances regularly taken into account.

However, unlike in other WB countries, in Montenegro, natural persons, i.e. responsible persons, were routinely fined alongside legal persons for competition law infringements by the misdemeanour courts. Montenegro is a clear outlier in this respect. No fines were ever imposed on individuals, for example, in Albania or Kosovo during the 2012-2022 period, although this possibility is regulated by their laws.

Competition authorities can impose fines for antitrust infringements, as well as for gun jumping or failure to notify mergers, or for procedural offences, such as unwillingness to provide data to the authority or obstruction of dawn raids. Generally, WB jurisdictions lack other types of sanctions, such as disqualification of directors or exclusion from public tenders.

The total amount of substantive, procedural and merger-related fines imposed by WB competition authorities (not adjusted for appeals) during 2012–2022 varies across the region. Serbia imposed the highest total fines (EUR 16.2 million), followed by North Macedonia (EUR 15.9 million). In Albania, total fines amounted to 4.5 million EUR, and in B&H to EUR 3.3 million. The lowest total fines in the relevant period were in Montenegro (approx. EUR 242,000).

Significant differences exist between WB jurisdictions regarding the types of competition law breaches for which fines were imposed. In some countries, fines mostly relate to antitrust infringements, such as in Serbia and Albania. In Serbia, only a small portion of the total fines were for merger-related and procedural issues (EUR 155,000 out of EUR 15.2 million). Similarly, in Albania, most fines were for antitrust infringements, with a tiny portion for mergers and procedural matters (EUR 79,000 out of EUR 4.5 million). However, Albania mentioned significant collection challenges, even for fines confirmed in appeal proceedings.[52]

In Montenegro, there was a more balanced distribution between fines for antitrust infringements (approx. EUR 139,000) and merger-related and procedural matters (approx. EUR 103,000, mostly for failure to provide data). In contrast, in B&H, most of the fines were related to mergers and procedural breaches, with only a small portion of fines concerning antitrust infringements.

Data for North Macedonia shows that during the relevant period, out of approx. EUR 15.9 million in total fines, some EUR 900,000 were for cartel infringements and over EUR 330,000 for abuse of dominance. In fact, most fines imposed for antitrust infringements in this jurisdiction relate to prohibited agreements and decisions of associations of undertakings, excluding cartels.

During the period 2012–2022, WB countries showed different dynamics in the intensity of fines. In Serbia, we observe relatively consistent levels of fines for antitrust infringements, particularly from 2018 to 2022, with an average annual total of around EUR 550,000. Before 2018, there were higher fluctuations in fine amounts depending on the year.

In North Macedonia, total fines grew strongly from 2012 (EUR 12,000) to 2017 (over EUR 10 million—the highest annual amount ever). Consistent fining followed, with totals ranging from approx. EUR 70,000 in 2021 to approx. EUR 2 million in 2019 and 2022.

In Montenegro, total fines decreased during the relevant period for both legal and natural persons. The highest fines were imposed between 2014 and 2018. Thereafter, we observe a significant decrease both for legal and natural persons.

[52] See the chapter by Gentjan Skara, Pranvera Këllezi and Bojana Hajdini, Competition Law and Policy in Albania.

During the relevant period (2012–2022), fines for gun jumping or failure to notify mergers were a constant phenomenon in almost all WB countries, with the total amounts varying: approx. EUR 155,000 in Serbia, EUR 56,000 in Albania, EUR 35,000 in Montenegro, and EUR 31,000 in North Macedonia. In fact, in B&H, most fines imposed by the competition authority during the relevant period were fines for failure to notify a concentration, with only a minority of fines related to abuses of dominance or restrictive agreements.

Occasionally, WB competition authorities issued procedural fines, usually related to failure to provide data to the authority. Montenegro imposed most such fines, followed by North Macedonia and Albania. In the latter jurisdiction, fines were also imposed for obstructing inspections, which was not observed in any other WB jurisdiction.

6.3 Concluding Remarks

Despite a relatively low total number of antitrust decisions compared to other WB countries, Serbia has the highest total amount of fines imposed for competition law breaches (EUR 16.2 million) in the 2012–2022 period. Most of this amount relates to fines imposed for antitrust infringements, with only a minor amount (EUR 150,000) imposed for gun jumping and failure to notify mergers. If we divide the total fines for antitrust infringements by the total number of antitrust decisions, Serbia ranks first with an average fine of approx. EUR 667,000 per decision. North Macedonia comes second with approx. EUR 274,000 per decision, Albania comes third with an average fine of approx. EUR 25,000 per decision, and Montenegro comes fourth with an average fine of approx. EUR 2500 per decision.

Our data suggests that competition authorities in Serbia, Albania, and North Macedonia are primarily focused on sanctioning substantive infringements, rather than procedural or merger-related breaches of competition rules, unlike the B&H competition authority, which mainly imposes fines for gun jumping in merger cases. Additionally, there seems to be an overall decrease in the total fines imposed in B&H during the 2012–2022 period.

Throughout the relevant period (2012–2022), there is a consistent enforcement track record in Albania, Serbia, and North Macedonia, both in terms of the number of antitrust decisions (restrictive agreements and abuse of dominance) and imposed fines. In Montenegro, the most intensive antitrust enforcement period was between 2012 and 2014, with almost half of all antitrust decisions during the relevant period (2012–2022) being adopted in those three years. This is consistent with the observation that in Montenegro most fines have been imposed between 2014 and 2018, which accounts for the time lag between competition authority's decision and misdemeanour courts' decision on fines. For B&H, we note that while the competition authority has been adopting antitrust decisions, there has been no focus on imposing more significant fines for antitrust infringements in this jurisdiction.

7 Judicial Review

When it comes to the role of judiciary in competition law enforcement in general and the judicial review of NCAs' decisions in particular, all WB jurisdictions surveyed in the present volume exhibit several common features that can be summarised as follows. First, most of WB judicial systems initially implemented a dual-track judicial review whereby administrative courts reviewed infringement decisions issued by the NCAs, while misdemeanour courts decided on the penalties to be imposed on the undertakings concerned. All the selected jurisdictions except Montenegro have moved away from this system, entrusting their NCAs to impose fines for competition law infringements.

Second, none of the jurisdictions established or designated specialised courts that would hear only competition law cases. While the administrative review of the NCAs' decisions has been gradually centralised in a particular administrative court, there is no specialisation of judges, who decide all kinds of administrative cases, including those related to competition law enforcement.[53]

Third, the aforementioned lack of specialisation, generally insufficient knowledge about competition law specifics, and modest enforcement records of the NCAs have resulted in inconsistent judicial review practices plagued with incoherent reasoning (or lack thereof) and an unwillingness of the courts to engage with substantive assessment of the anticompetitive practices, narrowing the review to procedural matters related to the conduct of investigations and satisfaction of the evidentiary burden.

For example, the courts in Albania have exhibited a "euro-friendly" approach following the entry into force of the respective SAA and have interpreted domestic competition legislation in light of EU law.[54] At the same time, delays in the resolution of judicial review cases due to a shortage of judges were noted as among the most significant problems affecting Albanian competition law enforcement at the time of writing. Even though the administrative review of the NCA's decisions is centralised in the hands of the Administrative Court in Tirana and the Administrative Court of Appeals in Tirana, the judges are frequently unable or unwilling to provide adequate reasoning as to why certain practices should be considered as abusive or anticompetitive, while the high standard of proof expected from the NCA complicates the discovery and prosecution of cartels.[55]

A similar situation is noted in B&H, where the administrative review of the NCA's decisions is equally centralised in the Court of B&H (including the first and second instance of review). Despite this centralisation, the lack of specialisation of judges in competition cases and the lack of clarity in legislative provisions have

---

[53] For similar challenges in Croatia, see Pecotić Kaufman (2023, 2024).

[54] See the chapter by Gentjan Skara, Pranvera Këllezi and Bojana Hajdini, Competition Law and Policy in Albania.

[55] See the chapter by Gentjan Skara, Pranvera Këllezi and Bojana Hajdini, Competition Law and Policy in Albania.

resulted in inconsistent judicial practices, introducing confusion into competition law enforcement.[56] The review does not allow the court to issue a decision on the merits; it only returns the case to the NCA for repeated investigation. Only on the second attempt can the court take its own decision on the merits and replace the NCA's assessment. This procedural deficiency has delayed the NCA's finalisation of cases.

In Kosovo, the lack of knowledge of competition law and minimal enforcement record of the NCA, coupled with the continuous re-organisation of the judicial system, has created a situation where the courts have not accumulated any consistent enforcement practice. Judges tend to review NCA decisions primarily on procedural grounds without entering the merits of the NCA's competitive assessment (or lack thereof).[57]

In Montenegro, judicial review involves two types of courts: the administrative courts reviewing the infringement decisions adopted by the NCA and the misdemeanour courts hearing the requests for sanctioning undertakings found in violation of competition rules. This results in a certain disconnection between the two types of proceedings, as the courts are not bound by each other's findings. As a result, some undertakings found in violation of competition law, as confirmed by the administrative courts, have managed to avoid sanctions by lodging successful defences before the misdemeanour courts.

In North Macedonia, judicial review of NCA's decisions was entrusted to the administrative courts with the possibility to appeal to the Supreme Court. The selected overview of judicial practice in the respective chapter suggests that the administrative courts have routinely accepted the substantive assessments of the NCA and its interpretation of competition rules, leading to a high ratio of NCA's decisions being upheld.[58] Without referring to EU competition law concepts or CJEU jurisprudence, the North Macedonian courts permitted the NCA to shape competition law standards in this jurisdiction.

Although after the 2009 competition legislation, the Serbian NCA no longer has to conduct misdemeanour proceedings before the courts, the centralisation of judicial review has not resulted in the specialisation of judges, as cases are distributed randomly. As a result, the judicial review is continuously focused on procedural aspects, with courts unwilling to second-guess the substantive assessment of the NCA. The lack of sufficient reasoning in judgments and insufficient transparency in the publication of judgments do not permit the formation of a consistent judicial review practice.[59]

---

[56] Svetlicinii (2013c, 2014a, b, 2015).

[57] See the chapter Avdylkader Mucaj, Competition Law and Policy in Kosovo.

[58] Svetlicinii (2009, 2010, 2012e).

[59] See the chapter by Veljko Milutinović and Vuk Leković, Competition Law and Policy in Serbia.

8 Private Enforcement of Competition Law

While public enforcement of competition rules in WB countries is present and developed, the situation with private enforcement is quite the opposite: under-regulated and under-developed. All the WB countries provide the possibility of private enforcement of competition rules but have opted for different regulations. For instance, the B&H Competition Acts do not stipulate provisions that regulate the right for compensation for infringement of competition rules. The claim for damages caused by infringement of competition law is considered a lawsuit based on civil delict, in line with the general provisions of the Law on Obligations.[60]

On the other hand, all other countries' competition acts contain just one vague or several provisions for the private enforcement of competition rules. Some countries, like Albania, Kosovo, North Macedonia, and Serbia regulate the right to seek damages due to infringement of competition rules. Montenegro's Competition Act contains only one vague provision regulating the right to seek damages due to infringement of competition rules.

Regarding standing to claim compensation, WB countries have different regulations. The Serbia and Montenegrin Competition Acts explicitly refer to only follow-on claims, where the injured parties can claim compensation for damages for infringement of competition rules based on the Serbian or Montenegrin NCA decision of infringement of competition rules.[61] Stand-alone actions are not recognised by the B&H, Kosovo, North Macedonia, Montenegro, and Serbian Competition Acts.[62] Conversely, Albanian Competition Law recognises both follow-on and stand-alone actions.

Finally, save for the Albanian Competition Act, which explicitly refers to the competent court, other WB countries' Competition Acts remain silent. In this context, other substantive and procedural rules concerning actions for damages for infringement of competition law are regulated by the provisions of the Civil Code or Law on Obligations and the Code of Civil Procedure.

[60] Law on Obligations, Official Gazette of the SFRY, No 29/1978, 39/1985, 45/1989 - decision of the Court of Justice and 57/1989, Official Gazette of the RBiH, No 2/1992, 13/1993 and 13/1994 and Official Gazette of FBiH, No 29/2003 and 42/2011; Law on Obligations, Official Gazette of the SFRY, No. 29/1978, 39/1985, 45/1989 - decision of the Supreme Court of Justice and 57/1989 and Official Gazette of the RS, No. 17/1993, 3/1996, 37/2001, 39/2003 and 74/2004. For a discussion of similar challenges in pre-accession period in Croatia see Pecotić Kaufman (2012). For experience of Croatia after EU accession see Pecotić Kaufman (2021).

[61] Law on Protection of Competition [2012] Official Gazette of Montenegro No. 44/12 as amended, Art 65; Competition Act [2009] Official Gazette of the Republic of Serbia Nos 1/2009 and 95/2013, Art 73.

[62] See the chapters by Gentjan Skara, Pranvera Këllezi and Bojana Hajdini, Competition Law and Policy in Albania; Dijana Marković-Bajalović and Kanita Imamović-Čizmić, Competition Law and Policy in Bosnia and Herzegovina, Avdylkader Mucaj, Competition Law and Policy in Kosovo; Nebojša Jovović, Competition Law and Policy in Montenegro; Veljko Milutinović and Vuk Leković.

Looking at the WB countries' authors, only Serbia and North Macedonia has reported a case on private enforcement of competition rules.[63] In North Macedonia case, Makedonski Telekom, relying on Article 58 of the Competition Act, sought compensation for damages amounting to MKD 72 million against the defendant, the Association for the Protection of Copyright and Music Rights. The Basic Civil Court in Skopje and then the Court of Appeal rejected the plaintiff's lawsuit as unfounded.[64] The Court of Appeal's decision was later affirmed by the Supreme Court in a special proceeding initiated as an extraordinary right of the defendant before this court.

The main reasons for this underdevelopment relate to the absence of a specific legal framework and collective redress mechanism in the WB countries' legal systems.[65] While Western Balkan NCAs have found in several cases the restrictive agreement or abuse of dominant position in different sectors, no claim for damages has been put forward. Another reason relates to the lack of competition culture among undertakings or consumers to claim compensation for infringement of competition rules.

9 Concluding Remarks

In this chapter, we present a comparative analysis of the main features of competition law systems in the Western Balkans, based on the national chapters compiled in this volume. Our brief historical analysis reveals that the introduction of competition law systems in these jurisdictions emerged within the framework of the EU rapprochement process. The impetus for enacting competition legislation was predominantly external, driven by these countries' aspirations to eventually join the EU. Over the years, considerable effort in the Western Balkans has been devoted to establishing coherent competition law frameworks in alignment with the EU acquis. However, the numerous rounds of legislative alignment arguably diverted attention from the actual enforcement of the law.

Our examination of the WB NCA budgets and staff numbers reveals insightful trends. In terms of NCA budgets relative to population, Montenegro and Serbia stand out as outliers with the largest overall budgets. However, when analysing budgets relative to staff members, Serbia emerges as the most advantageous, boasting over EUR 90,000 per staff member—three times more than B&H and nine times more than Kosovo. In terms of NCA staff dynamics over the period 2012–2022, certain WB countries, namely Albania, Montenegro, Serbia, have seen an increase in staff numbers, unlike B&H and North Macedonia, where no such increase was observed.

---

[63] Decision TS-79/18 of 23.9.2019, Basic Civil Court, Skopje.

[64] Decision TSZ-387/20 of 01.4.2020, Court of Appeal, Skopje.

[65] Bogdani and Canco (2021), Skara (2021), Skara (2022), pp. 268–271; Koevski (2022), p. 69.

Limited human resources and expertise delay enforcement efforts in many WB countries, particularly in Kosovo. In addition, in some other countries like B&H, internal political complexities related to state structure and mandatory participation of representatives of constituent peoples adversely affect the functioning of the NCA.

The use of inspection powers varies significantly across jurisdictions, with Albania conducting a disproportionately higher number of dawn raids compared to other jurisdictions.

Regarding the application of EU law by NCAs and national courts, our findings indicate that in all WB jurisdictions, the SAAs provide a stable legal basis for relying on the EU acquis when implementing competition rules. In practice, the NCAs and national courts occasionally reference EU law sources—primarily CJEU case law or the Commission's soft law—mainly to interpret national competition law.

Turning our attention to national peculiarities, it is evident that, despite the harmonization process with the EU competition law acquis, all WB countries have retained certain national features, which can be categorized in two groups. The first group of divergences arises from the historical reliance on market regulation by state authorities and an initially limited understanding of the functionalities of competition law in a market economy. This includes issues such as the initial positioning of NCAs as non-independent bodies, the application of competition law to actions by public authorities, and some legislative drafting inconsistencies. Most WB countries have eliminated these divergencies through legislative amendments or complete overhauls of their competition law enforcement systems. The second group of national peculiarities relates to deeply rooted legal traditions in the WB countries' legal systems, particularly the separation of powers between administrative and judicial branches and the organisation of investigative and sanctioning proceedings. Adhering to these traditions arguably results in sub-optimal enforcement.

With our analysis of the NCA enforcement data (2012–2022), we provide original insights that shed light on the main enforcement trends and key challenges. The number of merger cases, primarily resolved in Phase 1, steadily increased in most WB jurisdictions, except B&H (no data for Kosovo). Enforcement against restrictive agreements remained relatively stable in most jurisdictions, with Albania adopting the highest total number of decisions during this period. In Serbia, half of the decisions on restrictive agreements involved cartels, the highest ratio in the WB region. The number of abuse of dominant position decisions varied across WB jurisdictions, with Albania and B&H adopting the most decisions. However, in absolute terms, Serbia imposed the highest total amount of fines (EUR 16.2 million), followed by North Macedonia (EUR 15.9 million). In Serbia and Albania, fines mostly related to antitrust infringements, whereas in B&H, most fines were for failure to notify a concentration. In Serbia, consistent levels of fines for antitrust infringements were observed annually, particularly during the 2018–2022 period.

Regarding judicial review, it is observed that none of the WB jurisdictions have established or designated specialised court exclusively for competition cases. The absence of specialisation, coupled with generally insufficient knowledge about competition law specifics and overall modest enforcement records of NCAs, has led to inconsistent judicial review practices marked by incoherent reasoning (or lack thereof) and a reluctance of courts to engage in substantive assessments of anticompetitive practices.

Lastly, private enforcement remains both under-regulated and under-developed in WB jurisdictions. North Macedonia and Serbia were the only countries that have reported cases on private enforcement of competition rules in the national chapters contained in this volume.[66]

In this chapter, we examined the efforts of WB countries to prepare for effective functioning as future EU Member States in the realm of competition law. We analyzed national-level quantitative data on NCA budgets, staff, and competition law enforcement to compare Western Balkan jurisdictions, offering a fresh contribution to the existing literature. We hope our findings will inspire further research into the evolving landscape of competition law enforcement in WB countries.

Table of Cases

Albania

Judgment of 24 July 2009, Albanian Constitutional Court, V-24/09, [2009] OJ 119
Judgment of 24 July 2009, Albanian Constitutional Court, V-24/09, [2009] OJ 119
Judgment of 21 March 2014, Albanian Constitutional Court, V-14/14, [2014] OJ 50
Judgment of 27 July 2016, Albanian Constitutional Court, V-56/16, [2016] OJ 152

Bosnia and Herzegovina

Judgment of Constitutional Court of B&H, U 68/02
Court of Bosnia and Herzegovina, *Federal Ministry of Health v. Competition Council of B&H*, S1 3 U 035154 22 Uvp, 23.04.2022.

European Court of Human Rights

Judgment of 22 December 2009, *Sejdić and Finci v. Bosnia and Herzegovina*, Applications Nos. 27796/06 and 34836/06

[66] Also see Marković-Bajalović (2024).

European Union

Judgment of 5 May 1982, *Schul*, C-15/81, ECLI:EU:C:1982:135
Judgment of 19 May 1993, *Paul CORBEAU*, C-320/91, ECLI:EU:C:1993:198
Judgment of 19 January 1994, *SAT Fluggesellschaft mbH v Eurocontrol*, C-364/92, ECLI:EU:C:1994:7
Judgment of 18 March 1997, *Cali v. Servizi ecologici porto di Genova SpA*, C-343/95, ECLI:EU:C:1997:160
Judgment of 29 April 2004, *IMS Health.*, C-418/01 [2004] ECLI:EU:C:2004:257

North Macedonia

Decision TS-79/18 of 23.9.2019, Basic Civil Court, Skopje
Decision TSZ-387/20 of 01.4.2020, Court of Appeal, Skopje

Table of Legislation

Albania

Law 9121/2003 for Competition Protection [2003] OJ 71 as last amended by Law 10 317/2010 For some additions and changes in the law no 9121 date 28. 07. 2003 for Competition Protection [2010] OJ 135
Law 97/2013 On audio and audio-visual media services in the Republic of Albania [2013] OJ 37/1497

Bosnia and Herzegovina

Law on Obligations, Official Gazette of the SFRY, No 29/1978, 39/1985, 45/1989 - decision of the Court of Justice and 57/1989, Official Gazette of the RB&H, No 2/1992, 13/1993 and 13/1994 and Official Gazette of FB&H, No 29/2003 and 42/2011
Law on Obligations, Official Gazette of the SFRY, No. 29/1978, 39/1985, 45/1989 - decision of the Supreme Court of Justice and 57/1989 and Official Gazette of the RS, No. 17/1993, 3/1996, 37/2001, 39/2003 and 74/2004
Law on Competition, Official Gazette of B&H, No 48/05, 76/07, 80/09

European Union

Stabilisation and Association Agreement between the European Communities and their Member States, of the one part, and the former Yugoslav Republic of Macedonia, of the other part [2004] OJ 84/13

Stabilisation and Association Agreement between the European Communities and their Member States, of the one part, and the Republic of Albania, of the other part – Protocols – Declaration [2009] OJ L 107/166

Stabilisation and Association Agreement between the European Communities and their Member States, of the one part, and the Republic of Montenegro, of the other part [2010] OJ L 108/3

Stabilisation and Association Agreement between the European Communities and their Member States of the one part, and the Republic of Serbia, of the other part [2013] OJ L 278/16

Stabilisation and Association Agreement between the European Communities and their Member States, of the one part, and B&H, of the other part [2015] OJ L 164/2

Stabilisation and Association Agreement between the European Union and the European Atomic Energy Community, of the one part, and Kosovo, of the other part [2016] OJ L 71/3

Kosovo

Law 88/L-056 On Protection of Competition [2020] OJ 14/2022

Montenegro

Law on Protection of Competition [2012] Official Gazette of Montenegro No. 44/12 as amended

Serbia

Competition Act [2009] Official Gazette of the Republic of Serbia Nos 1/2009 and 95/2013.

References

Albi A (2005) EU enlargement and the constitutions of Central and Eastern Europe. Cambridge University Press, Cambridge

Albi A (2007) Selected EU judgments by CEE Constitutional Courts: Lessons on How (not) to Amend Constitutions. Croatian Yearb Eur Law Policy 3:39–58

Bačić A (2014) On the new beginning scenario for Judicial Governance in Croatia. In: Koevski G et al (eds) European Union law application by the national courts of the eu membership aspirant countries from South-East Europe. Centre for SEELS, Skopje

Balan A (2021) EU competition policy and the European integration of the countries of Central and Eastern Europe that acceded to the European Union. L'Europe/Unie / United Europe 18(2021): 42–50

Bernatt M, Botta M, Svetlicinii A (2018) The right of defence in the decentralized system of EU competition law enforcement. World Compet Law Econ Rev 41(3):309–334

Blockmans S, Lazowski A (2006) The European Union and its neighbours: questioning identity and relationships. In: Blockmans S, Lazowski A (eds) The European Union and its neighbours: a legal appraisal of the EU's policies of stabilisation, partnership and integration. TMC Asser Press, The Hague

Botta M, Svetlicinii A (2015) The right of fair trial in competition law proceedings: quo vadis the courts of the new EU Member States? In: Nihoul P, Skoczny T (eds) Procedural fairness in competition proceedings. Edward Elgar

Caka F (2014) The application of international and European Union Law by the National Courts in Albania. In: Koevski G et al (eds) European Union law application by the National Courts of the EU Membership Aspirant countries from South-East Europe. Centre for SEELS, Skopje

Čolaković M (2014) European law application by the constitutional court of BiH and the Supreme Court of the Federation of BiH. In: Koevski G et al (eds) European Union law application by the National Courts of the EU Membership Aspirant Countries from South-East Europe. Centre for SEELS, Skopje

Commission (2003) Eu-Western Balkans Summit Thessaloniki, 21 June 2003. Available at: https://ec.europa.eu/commission/presscorner/detail/en/pres_03_163. Accessed 1 June 2003.

Commission (2022) North Macedonia Report 2022. SWD(2022) 337 final

Cremona M (2003) State aid control: substance and procedure in the Europe agreements and the stabilisation and association agreements. Eur Law J 9(3):265

Cseres KJ (2008) Governance design for European Private Law: lessons from Europeanization of competition law in Central and Eastern Europe. In: Cafaggi F, Muir-Watt H (eds) Making European private law: governance design. Edward Elgar, Cheltenham and Northampton

Cseres KJ (2014) Accession to the EU's competition law regime: a law and governance approach. Yearb Antitrust Regul Stud 7(9):31–66

Džankić J, Keil S, Kmezić M (2019) Introduction: The Europeanisation of the Western Balkans. Springer International Publishing, pp 1–14

Emmert F (2004) Introducing EU competition law and policy in Central and Eastern Europe: requirements in theory and problems in practice. Fordham Int Law J 27(2):642–678

Georgievski S et al (2014) Application of the law of the European Union in the Republic of Macedonia. In: Koevski G et al (eds) European Union law application by the National Courts of the EU membership aspirant countries from South-East Europe. Centre for SEELS, Skopje

Koevski G (2022) Compensatory damages from the viewpoint of the competition law in the European Union and the Republic of North Macedonia. Revija Kopaonička škola prirodnog prava, Broj 1/2022, Godina IV, 2022

Kostić-Mandić M (2014) Implementation of international and European Union Law in Montenegro. In: Koevski G et al (eds) European Union law application by the National Courts of the EU Membership Aspirant countries from South-East Europe. Centre for SEELS, Skopje

Kühn Z (2005a) European law in the empires of mechanical Jurisprudence: the judicial application of European law in Central European Candidate Countries. Croatian Yearb Eur Law Policy 1: 55–73

Kühn Z (2005b) The application of European law in the new member states: several (early) predictions. German Law J 6:563

Lang GI, Mataija M (2014) Application of EU law by Croatian Courts and relevant constitutional provisions. In: Koevski G et al (eds) European Union law application by the National Courts of the EU Membership Aspirant countries from South-East Europe. Centre for SEELS, Skopje

Marković-Bajalović D (2024) Proving antitrust damages in civil proceedings – the compatibility of Serbian law with Directive 2014/104. February 2024. Strani pravni zivot 67(4):643–667

Meškić Z, Samardžić D (2014) The application of EU law in BiH. In: Koevski G et al (eds) European Union law application by the National Courts of the EU Membership Aspirant Countries from South-East Europe. Centre for SEELS, Skopje

Pecotić Kaufman J (2021) 'Može li u Hrvatskoj (konačno) zaživjeti sustav zaštite tržišnog natjecanja? - iskustva, izazovi i izgledi' in Jakša Barbić (ed), Pravo tržišnog natjecanja u Republici Hrvatskoj i u Europskoj uniji: okrugli stol održan 1. veljače 2021. (Hrvatska akademija znanosti i umjetnosti, 2021), pp 19–38

Pecotić Kaufman J (2022) On the development of (Not so) new competition systems – findings from an empirical study on Croatia. J Antitrust Enforcement 10(2):326–364

Pecotić Kaufman J (2023) Interpretation and competition law enforcement: authoritarian legal culture, semantic dissonance and Skewed Agencification in Post-Socialist Croatia. Rev Central East Eur Law 48(3–4)

Pecotić Kaufman J (2024) Croatia report. In: B. Rodger, O. Brook et al (eds) Judicial review of competition law enforcement in the EU Member States and the UK. Kluwer

Pecotić Kaufman J, Butorac Malnar V (2016) The Interaction between EU regulatory implants and the existing Croatian legal order in competition law. In: Kovač M, Vandenberghe AS (eds) Economic evidence in EU competition law. Intersentia

Pecotić Kaufman J, Šimić Banović R (2021) The role of (In)formal governance and culture in a national competition system: a case of a post-socialist economy'. World Compet 44(1):81–108

Skara G (2021) The transposition of the antitrust damages directive in Albania as an EU candidate country. J Eur Compet Law Pract 12(4):326

Skara G (2022) Europeanisation of private enforcement of competition law: the case of Albania. Springer

Skara G, Hajdini B (2021) Enforcement of the European Union before the Albanian Constitutional Court and the High Court. J Liberty Int Aff 7(3):229

Svetlicinii A (2009) The Macedonian Administrative Court upholds the Competition Authority's decisions establishing abusive charges on the mobile telecommunications market (T-Mobile). 17 December 2009, e-Competitions December 2009, Art. N° 30925

Svetlicinii A (2010) The Macedonian Supreme Court upholds the Competition Authority's decision finding an abuse of dominance on the electricity distribution market (Elektrostopanstvo), 6 September 2010, e-Competitions September 2010, Art. N° 33282

Svetlicinii A (2012a) Competition law enforcement in Serbia: problems and prospects. Eur Compet Law Rev 33(6):273–279

Svetlicinii A (2012b) The competition authority of Bosnia and Herzegovina prosecutes the Government of the Federation of Bosnia and Herzegovina for favoring domestic companies on the market for pharmaceuticals reimbursed under the national health insurance system. 4 October 2012, e-Competitions October 2012, Art. N° 50533

Svetlicinii A (2012c) The Competition Authority of Bosnia & Herzegovina prosecutes the regional government for public procurement infringements that resulted in restriction of competition in the transports market (Centrotrans-Eurolines). 18 April 2012, e-Competitions April 2012, Art. N ° 45896

Svetlicinii A (2012d) Abuse of Dominance in South Eastern Europe: enforcement practices of the National Competition Authorities in Bosnia & Herzegovina, Croatia, Macedonia and Serbia. Mediterranean Compet Bull 8:4–26

Svetlicinii A (2012e) The Macedonian High Administrative Court upholds the Competition Authority's infringement decision concerning an abuse of dominant position on the funeral services market (JPKD Komunalec Strumica). 9 May 2012, e-Competitions May 2012, Art. N° 49033

Svetlicinii A (2013a) Expanding the definitions of 'Undertaking' and 'Economic Activity': application of competition rules to the actions of state institutions in Bosnia and Herzegovina. Yearb Antitrust Regul Stud 6(8):11–33

Svetlicinii A (2013b) The competition authority of Bosnia & Herzegovina prosecutes healthcare administration for limiting competition in the regional market for medicines reimbursed under state health insurance system (Health Insurance Office of the Republic of Srpska). 18 April 2013, e-Competitions April 2013, Art. N° 54815

Svetlicinii A (2013c). The Bosnia and Herzegovina Court quashes the no-infringement decision of the competition authority for the failure to conduct an efficient investigation (Telekomunikacije). 10 October 2013, e-Competitions October 2013, Art. N° 64924

Svetlicinii A (2014a) The Bosnia & Herzegovina Court upholds the infringement decision of the competition authority concerning abuse of dominant positions on the market for fast money transfer services (Raiffeisen Bank). 12 March 2014, e-Competitions March 2014, Art. N° 68487

Svetlicinii A (2014b). The Bosnia and Herzegovina Court quashes the no-infringement decision of the competition authority based on the concept of 'single economic entity' (Elektrokontakt). 29 January 2014, e-Competitions January 2014, Art. N° 64923

Svetlicinii A (2015) The objectives of competition law and the effective conduct of the infringement proceedings: judgments of the Court of Bosnia and Herzegovina in BH Telecom and Telekomunikacije RS. Yearb Antitrust Regul Stud 8(11):241–248

Svetlicinii A (2018) The judicial review of the standard of proof in cartel cases: raising the bar for the Croatian competition authority. Yearb Antitrust Regul Stud 11(18):311–323

Svetlicinii A, Botta M (2015) Enforcement of competition rules in regulated industries: abuse of dominance practices in the new EU Member States, candidate countries and potential candidates. In: Drexl J, Di Porto F (eds) Competition law as regulation? Edward Elgar

Vlahek A (2024) Slovenia Report. In: Rodger B, Brook O et al (eds) Judicial review of competition law enforcement in the EU Member States and the UK. Kluwer Law International

Vukadinović DR et al (2014) Application of EU law by Serbian Courts pre-accession issues. In: Koevski G et al (eds) European Union law application by the National Courts of the EU Membership Aspirant countries from South-East Europe. Centre for SEELS, Skopje

Zyberi G, Sali S (2015) The place and application of international law in the Albanian legal system. In: Rodin S, Perišin T (eds) Judicial application of international law in Southeast Europe. Springer, Berlin

Jasminka Pecotić Kaufman is a Full Tenured Professor of Law at the University of Zagreb, Faculty of Economics and Business, Department of Business Law and a Part-Time Professor at the Robert Schuman Centre for Advanced Studies, European University Institute (EUI). Her research focuses on the challenges of enforcing competition rules in European post-socialist countries. Prof. Pecotić Kaufman's scholarly work has been published in the Journal of Antitrust Enforcement, the World Competition Law and Economics Review, the Review of Central and East European Law, and the Yearbook of Antitrust and Regulatory Studies, among other journals. She has been a Jean Monnet Fellow and a Fernand Braudel Senior Fellow at the EUI, as well as a Non-Resident Senior Research Fellow at the Institute for Consumer Antitrust Studies at Loyola University Chicago. She is a member of the Editorial Board of the Yearbook of Antitrust and

Regulatory Studies (YARS), a member of the International Advisory Board of the Institute for Consumer Antitrust Studies, and a non-governmental Advisor (NGA) to the International Competition Network. Prof. Pecotić Kaufman serves on the ASCOLA Board and co-chairs its Southeast Europe chapter. She is the President of the Croatian Competition Law and Policy Association (HDPPTN) and the founder of the Šoljan Competition Law and Policy Conference series.

Gentjan Skara is a Lecturer in EU Law and Competition Law at the Department of Law, Epoka University, Albania. Genti holds an LLB from the University of Tirana (Albania), an MA in European Studies from Epoka University (Albania) and an LLM in "South East European Law and European Integration" from the University of Graz. In 2020, Genti received a PhD from the University of Ferrara in "EU Law and National Legal Systems". A revised version of his thesis was published by Springer Nature as a monography titled "Europeanisation of Private Enforcement of Competition Law: The Case of Albania" in 2022. Additionally, Genti has been a visiting researcher at the Institute of Corporate and International Commercial Law, University of Graz (Austria), the Department of International Law, University of Ljubljana (Slovenia) and European Institute for Global Studies, University of Basel (Switzerland) and RECAS Fellow. From October 2012 until July 31, 2023, Genti was a full-time member of the Department of Law at "Bedër" University College, teaching International and EU law courses. As of 1 August 2023, Genti is a full-time lecturer of EU Law and competition law courses at Epoka University. Besides academic engagement, Genti is a National Legal expert for the "Internal Market and Competition" of EU acquis near the Ministry of European and Foreign Affairs, Republic of Albania and has provided its expertise to different organizations. His research interests relate to EU Law, competition law, the harmonization of laws, and the relations between law and technology.

Alexandr Svetlicinii is an Associate Professor at the University of Macau, Faculty of Law, where he also serves as Programme Coordinator of the Master of International Business Law in English Language. Prior to joining the University of Macau, Dr. Svetlicinii was a senior researcher at the Jean Monnet Chair of European Law at the Tallinn Law School, Tallinn University of Technology, in Estonia. Prof. Svetlicinii's work in the field of competition law has appeared in Common Market Law Review, European Law Review, Journal of Antitrust Enforcement, World Competition Law and Economics Review, Journal of European Competition Law & Practice, European Competition Law Review, Yearbook of Antitrust and Regulatory Studies, Market and Competition Law Review, among other journals. In addition to his academic work, Dr. Svetlicinii served as Co-Director of ASCOLA (Academic Society for Competition Law) South-East Europe Chapter, the Non-Governmental Advisor (NGA) to the International Competition Network (ICN) (working group Mergers). He has recently published the monograph Chinese State-Owned Enterprises and EU Merger Control (Routledge, 2021).

The manufacturer's authorised representative in the EU is Springer Nature Customer Service Centre GmbH, Europaplatz 3, 69115 Heidelberg, Germany. If you have any concerns regarding our products, please contact ProductSafety@springernature.com

Printed and bound by CPI Group (UK) Ltd, Croydon, CR0 4YY
30/09/2026
02225588-0009